Ngambika
Studies of Women in African Literature

edited by
Carole Boyce Davies & Anne Adams Graves

Africa World Press, Inc.

P.O. Box 1892
Trenton, New Jersey 08607

Africa World Press, Inc.

P.O. Box 1892
Trenton, New Jersey 08607

Copyright © 1986 Africa World Press
Second Printing 1990

All rights reserved. No part of this publication may
be reproduced, stored in a retrieval system or transmitted
in any form or by any means electronic, mechanical or
otherwise without the prior written permission of the
publisher.

Typeset by TypeHouse of Pennington

Cover design by Adjoa Jackson-Burrowes

Library of Congress Catalog Card Number: 85-71385

ISBN: 0-86543-017-9   Cloth
          0-86543-018-7   Paper

For Mariama Bâ
1929 - 1981
African woman writer,

Whose commitment and African feminism
made works such as this one necessary.

Acknowledgments

The Tshiluba phrase *Ngambika* (the 'g' is silent—pronounced Nambika) which we have used as our title was suggested by Elizabeth Mudimbe-Boyi as the equivalent of "Help me to balance/carry this load". The editors extend to her sincere acknowledgments. A number of colleagues and friends, especially the contributors, have supported this effort in a number of ways. We cannot mention them all by name but extend sincere thanks for their encouragement. Elizabeth Robinson of Africa World Press provided knowledgeable and painstaking copy-editing for which we are grateful. Her attention to detail and thoughtful suggestions contributed immensely to the realization of this work.

"Maidens, Mistresses and Matrons: Feminine Images in Selected Soyinka Works" which originally appeared in *Interdisciplinary Dimensions in African Literature* (Washington, D.C.: Three Continents Press, 1985). Reprinted with permission of Editor, Stephen Arnold and Three Continents Press.

Preface

In attempting to redress the relative inattention to women in African literary scholarship, the criticism in the present anthology is concerned with expanding and augmenting the interpretation of the whole body of African literary creativity. This objective involves both a re-reading of earlier writings, produced entirely by men, and a balanced reading of the more recent writings by women and by men. Therefore, the editorial and ideological orientation here is not just around the works of women writers (and critics), but around *African* writers whose works constitute the developing canon of African literature. (Indeed, any study devoted to women in the African novel that ignored Sembène and Ngugi simply because of their gender would be chauvinistically self-defeating.) What the critics assembled in this collection share, however, is a concern that the perspective and characterization of women heretofore relegated to the critical shadows, be brought into focus in whatever form they may manifest themselves in the works. To be sure, in a mature criticism of the developing canon the absence of a feminine perspective or the stunted characterization of women is as demanding of critical attention as is the more complete presentation of the feminine presence.

There is by now no need to defend the conscious and unapologetic commitment (indeed, urgency) that underlies the inspiration of most African writers—and most especially women writers. By the same token, the current efforts, as reflected in this collection of essays, to redress the relative omission of women in the criticism employs methodological approaches that are consciously and unapologetically devoted to the *substance*—social, political, psychological—of women's presence in the literature. This concentration, while in no way ignoring the place of questions of structure in the criticism, speaks to the primacy of the feminine as subject matter itself in the critics' view as well as in the view of many of the authors, particularly in recent years. Attention is in fact devoted to structural questions, for example by Naana Banyiwa-Horne and Elaine Savory Fido, as it bears on the content that is the focus of the discussion at hand. This collection of essays is, we feel, characterized by the range and diversity of approaches that the complexity of the subject matter of the feminine presence necessarily comprehends. The approaches employed are discussed in detail below as the basis for the ordering of the essays in the book.

The range and diversity of approaches contributed by these scholars to the analysis of the feminine in African literature signals, among other things, the fact that there is active debate in the community of scholars over the subject. Perhaps the single most productive discussion generated in the debate is the challenge to formerly promulgated roles and role categories for women in the few earlier studies published, such as those established by Kenneth Little in *The Sociology of Urban Women's Image in African Literature* (1980). The essays in the present collection, either directly or indirectly, repudiate such men-centered roles for women without, however, repudiating the fact that the women's lives obviously include men. Such re-definitions of the women's roles apply not only to the works written by women, as one would assume, or even to the most recent works by men. But, as several of these essays articulate, revised, women-centered definitions of women's roles apply to some earlier works as well, for example Sembène's, as Brenda Berrian demonstrates. Thus, in place of role-categories such as girlfriends, mistresses, and prostitutes, we can recognize prophets, decision-makers, heroines, martyrs, and challengers of the status quo. The issue in this book, then, is the opening up of the critical perspective, to look at woman in African literature standing on her own rather than in the shadow of the men with whom she shares the literary stage. If a legitimized re-definition of the feminine presence is the single new issue added by this book to African literary criticism, its contribution to the canon is made, and our efforts are justified.

The eighteen essays in this anthology must be viewed as a selection, rather than an overview or comprehensive study, of critical analyses of literature about the African woman. While the number and stature of authors and works included here are appropriately representative, the articles in this collection do not attempt to cover the waterfront of this fertile field of literary criticism. In the ethnographic, geographic, and cultural range of the literature discussed much of the diversity of the African experience is reflected. The works under study come from the several areas of the continent—East, West, Central, South, and the Maghreb—and represent Franchphone and Anglophone (though unfortunately not Luso-phone) as well as one indigenous language group; Muslim, Christian, indigenous African belief systems; urban and village settings; traditional and modern values and lifestyles; mythological, folkloric, and European literary-influenced content. Titles evoked by this literary topography are, for the most part, familiar to the Africanist: the Ghanaian Ama Ata Aidoo's short-story collection *No Sweetness Here* and her novel *Our Sister Killjoy*, for the urban and the rural, the traditional and the modern, the African in Europe; the Kenyan Ngugi wa Thiong'o's novels, *The River Between*, *A Grain of Wheat*, *Petals of Blood* and *Devil on the Cross*, for the Christianity-indigenous belief encounter, the traditional and modern lifestyles and values, the mythological and folkloric; Hausa women writing Hausa poetry who, as Muslims, attempt a balancing act between the traditional and the modern; the Senegalese novelist Mariama Bâ's *Une si longue lettre* and *Un chant écarlate* present likewise the Muslim tradition facing modernity.

The genres of short story, novel, drama, poetry, and biography are included, from works by both women and men authors, spanning the periods of colonial, independence, and post-independence writing: from Camara Laye's *L'enfant noir* (1956) of the Négritude era and Achebe's pioneering *Things Fall Apart* (1959), through Sembène's *Voltaïque* (1962), *Les Bouts de bois de Dieu* (1971), and *Xala* (1973) of the independence and early post-independence years; to Buchi Emecheta's *Double Yoke* (1983); and including the entire oeuvre of Ayi Kwei Armah, a representative selection of Soyinka's prose and drama; and Christopher Okigbo's poetry volume *Labyrinths*. The majority of the articles treat, however, prose fiction.

The differences in topical focus in the articles provide both depth and breadth of analysis of individual writers and of the works treated. The essays range in coverage from the examination of a narrowly defined issue presented in a single work, or in all the works of a single author, to a wider, sometimes evolutionary, consideration of a theme across two or several works by different writers, and even to an analysis of the comprehensive corpus of a delimited community of authors; two papers focus on the writings from specific ethnic groups. Although the crucial point of the anthology is the literature's treatment of the African woman per se, the primary attention devoted, in a few of the pieces, to the complexities of men's consciousness regarding women gives support to the underlying truth that woman's consciousness of herself—in literature as in life—cannot be considered in a vacuum.

While writers of the stature of Ngugi, Achebe, Aidoo, Sembène, Armah, and Soyinka are indeed present, as well as some who are less widely read, such as Flora Nwapa and Henri Lopès, the absence of studies on Beti, Ogot, Head, Farah, Mudimbe and others who also provide important sources for critical analyses of the African woman in literature, is recognized here by the editors as legitimizing rationale for on-going work in this area. Another, regrettably unavoidable, absence is more work by Francophone African women. Although Mariama Bâ is represented here, there are, besides Aminata Sow Fall no others who have attained any visibility as published writers. And the death, in 1981, of the Noma Prize-winning Bâ only makes the situation ironically more remarkable. However, we are beginning, happily, to see works appearing by other Francophone women, for example from Benin and from Congo. There is hope, therefore, that the ranks will increase, thus raising the volume of the literary voice of the African woman.

The organization of the papers into the three sections: "Defining 'Woman's Place': Female Portraiture in African Literature," "Towards a Critical Self-Definition of the African Woman: Writers and African Woman's Reality," and "Social and Political Themes: Women's Issues in African Literary Criticism," represents less a focus on differences in subject matter than an emphasis on common approaches to the treatment of the subject matter. Indeed, the examination of some authors and some works in several articles—as is evident in the titles—is an indication of obvious overlap of subject matter among the eighteen articles.

The first and second sections are similar to each other in that the articles in both focus on the depictions and perceptions of African women from several viewpoints. What distinguishes Part I from Part II is the relative presence or absence of the woman's own perception of herself, according to the analysis of the works studied in each paper. The studies in Part I examine the depiction of women from the male perspective or that of the general society, which is by and large dominated by the male perspective anyway. Whether the images are positive or negative, sympathetic or unsympathetic, traditional or modern, the perspective is that from which others view the woman. The articles in the second section, by contrast, present the woman's own conscious self-perception, whether as a model of the traditional African woman who knows fulfillment in her life, or as an individual questioning and challenging herself and the other people and forces that participate in the determination of the course of her life. Emphasis in Part III is on thematic analysis of literary presentation of political and social institutions in African societies as they influence women's thoughts and actions, happiness and unhappiness, life and death, or as women serving their roles in these institutions influence the condition of others' lives. Marriage in its many forms—polygamous/monogamous, interracial, intergenerational, sight-unseen arranged, divorce—is one such institution treated in this section. Other aspects of the domestic institution of family that are presented in this section include motherhood (and grandmotherhood), child custody and in-law relationships. Social practices and other institutionalized behavior based in religious and historical/mythological traditions are also examined as they affect or are affected by women. While the discussions of the institutions present them primarily in their social contexts, their significance in relation to the political structures on which the societies rest is central to the perspective of some of the essays in the section on social and political themes.

A reading of the eighteen pieces in this collection will reveal an interconnectedness that is manifested not only in the overlap among articles, as acknowledged at the outset, but also some disagreement—criticism in some articles of writers and works handled in others. Indeed, alternative ordering of the articles among the three sections is possible. We consider this not only acceptable but salutary. For feminist critical theory as applied to African literature is being developed through collections such as this, just as the canon of African literature itself is still being developed through the continued production of works such as those studied here. What is of importance now is correcting the faulty vision through which the African woman in literature has been seen. Her presence as reflected in the literature must be fully recognized and appreciated as an integral part of what Africa is going to become. Mariama Bâ draws a future picture of the African women in literature thus:

> The nostalgic songs dedicated to African mothers which express the anxieties of men concerning Mother Africa are no longer enough for us. The Black woman in African literature must be given the dimension that her role in the liberation struggles next to men has proven to be hers, the dimension which coincides with her proven contribution to the economic development of our country.*

Anne Adams Graves

---

*Cited in Hans Zell, Carol Bundy, and Virginia Coulon, eds. A New Reader's Guide to African Literature (New York: Holmes & Meier, 1983) p. 358.

Table of Contents

Introduction:
Feminist Consciousness
and African Literary
Criticism

Carole Boyce Davies

African written literature has traditionally been the preserve of male writers and critics. Today, however, accompanying an ever-growing corpus of literature by African women writers, a new generation of critics, most of them women, is impacting on this male-dominated area. The perspectives of these critics exhibit a double influence, and consequently a tension of sorts. On the one hand there is a grounding in the need to liberate African peoples from neo-colonialism and other forms of race and class oppression, coupled with a respect for certain features of traditional African cultures. On the other, there is the influence of the international woman's movement and the recognition that a feminist consciousness is necessary in examining the position of women in African societies. The tension involved in this double allegiance provides a nexus from which this criticism grows.

In examining the relative scarcity of women in African written literary tradition a few points reveal themselves. First of all, there is ample evidence of women's creativity in the production of oral literature, as there is nothing inherently male about literary creativity. According to Finnegan,

> The limitations on this general mastery of the art of storytelling arise
> from local conventions about the age and sex of the narrators. In some

1

societies, it appears, these are quite free; in others there is a definite
emphasis on one or another category as being the most suitable one for
a storyteller. In some areas it is the women, often the old women, who
tend to be the most gifted . . . Elsewhere it is the men who tend to be
the more expert . . .[1]

The available research makes it clear that there was equal billing for male
and female in the oral literary tradition and that while there was specialization
in certain genres according to gender, there was no large scale exclusion of
one group from the creative process.

As opposed to that, the first African writers to achieve prominence were
male. Reasons for this are obvious. The selection of males for formal
education was fostered by the colonial institutions which made specific
choices in educating male and female. Then too, the sex role distinctions
common to many African societies supported the notion that western
education was a barrier to a woman's role as wife and mother and an
impediment to her success in these traditional modes of acquiring status.
With few exceptions, girls were kept away from formal and especially
higher education.[2] The colonial administrations were therefore willing
accomplices because they imported a view of the world in which women
were of secondary importance. Clearly then, European colonialism, as well
as traditional attitudes of and to women, combined to exclude African
women from the educational processes which prepare one for the craft of
writing.

The criticism of African literature was subject to similar historical
realities. The earliest critics of African literature were European academicians
who communicated the Western male-oriented mode of creating and
evaluating literature. The first critical works were authored by European
and American critics in the 1950's and '60's (Janheinz Jahn, Ulli Beier,
Gerald Moore and others)[3] who, while they performed an invaluable service
in the development of a written literary tradition, maintained the Western
critical manner of approaching literary texts solely from the point of view of
male experience. This Ellman appropriately defines as "phallic criticism"[4]
as it excludes a host of woman-oriented configurations. The second school
of critics of African literature, continental Africans like writers Ezekiel
Mphalele, Eldred Jones, and Eustace Palmer[5] and Caribbean critics, like
Oscar Dathorne and John Ramsaran,[6] to a large extent maintained this
reductionism as it relates to women in the literature.

Most of the women who appear as contributors in the early anthologies
and journals are bibliographers like Margaret Amosu.[7] The few women
critics, Lilyan Kesteloot, Molly Mahood[8] and later Omolara Ogundipe-
Leslie,[9] for example, had to utilize the same critical apparata as their male
contemporaries. This meant turning a blind eye to women in African
literature. Even when the first major African women writers appeared—

Ama Ata Aidoo (1965), Flora Nwapa and Grace Ogot (1966)—the same type of alliance which was created by male critics and writers was not formed between the women critics and writers. Instead, without the benefit of a feminist focus, there was a reluctance to bring the works of African women writers under serious but sensitive critical evaluation.

Review of the Relevant Literature

Early criticism, largely written by male critics about male writers, as we have established above, viewed women as tangential to the discussion of men in the literature. A survey of African literary criticism, at this point, reveals little more than passing reference within general discussions. In cases where the main character is female, there is no evaluation of the female image and/or the writer's treatment of the female character. It must be noted that much of the early literature deals with the social and political implications of colonialism and man's struggle within, and away from, its confines. Women are usually made peripheral to all of that and function either as symbols or as instruments for the male hero's working out of his problems. Rafika Merini's title, "Women in Man's Exploration of His Country, His World" in this work, is an appropriate summation of this pattern. The standard critical approach follows this pattern to a large extent.

The first work to identify a female presence in African literature is Wilfred Cartey's *Whispers from a Continent*[10] which uses mother and child as its larger thematic and symbolic focus. It starts with "The Movement Away" from Mother Africa and works through "The Movement Back" which Négritude represents. His usage of mother as symbol for Africa, earth and nature popularized by the Négritude poets continues the mythologization of motherhood. When women are discussed, in line with the works he selects, it is only from the point of view of male experience. Cartey nonetheless, importantly, sees this symbolic mother-child relationship as central to the literature and to any discussion of African literature.

Criticism which employs the sociological approach has so far focused the most attention on women in African literature. E.M. Obiechina's *Culture, Tradition and Society and the West African Novel*,[11] because it does examine culture, gives minute space to a discussion of women as characters and provides some additional information on other minor aspects of women's lives. The first major discussion of women in the literature, however, comes from G.C.M. Mutiso in his essay "Women in African Literature".[12] In this work, he discusses a few notable women characters like Jagua Nana, Lawino, Efuru, Simi, and concludes that the most memorable women in African literature are city types with loose morals and political roles who are free from the bondage of traditional mores but for whom this freedom is a mixed blessing. Kenneth Little's *The Sociology of Urban Women's Image in African Literature*[13] is the most problematic of this group. It seems a development of the Mutiso study in that it lists the same categories of women. There is much overlap in these categories and much is left out. The major weaknesses of the Little study particularly are its overwhelming male bias along with several inaccuracies and its definition of women almost exclusively according to their relationships with men: 1) girl friends and good time girls; 2) wives; 3) free women; 4) mothers; 5) courtesans and prostitutes, and finally 6) political women and workers.

A much more important contribution is Arlette Chemain-Degrange's *Emancipation Féminine et Roman Africain*.[14] It examines female images in the works of Francophone male novelists who dominate this genre. Dividing her examination of the images of the Black woman into the pre-independence and post-independence periods, she concludes that three basic representations recur: the woman with the heart of gold, the suffering woman and the diligent, active woman working hard for change. She concludes that although women have been silent until recently, a number of male authors are able to envisage female emancipation without terror. Mongo Beti, Ferdinand Oyono, Sembène Ousmane, Henri Lopès and Ahmadou Kourouma have contributed to the promotion of women, convinced that the liberation of Africa is directly connected to the liberation of women. The Chemain-Degrange work is a fairly comprehensive study of this subject, and especially valuable since it concentrates on the Francophone African literature which often takes second place in examinations of African literature.

Anne Lippert's doctoral dissertation, "The Changing Role of Women as Viewed in the Literature of English Speaking and French Speaking West Africa"[15] does attempt some integration of the two language areas. But it is limited to West Africa unlike the Chemain-Degrange work which is continental in emphasis. Lippert's divisions are the "Traditional Role of Women in the Novel" under which she discusses the characterization of the young girl, the wife and the mother, all of whom (except some of the depictions of the wife) tend to be idealized, and "The Changing Roles of Women in the Novel", under which she delineates the prostitute, the political woman and the educated woman. A similar work is Sonia Lee's "L'Image de la femme dans le roman Francophone de l'Afrique occiden-tale."[16] This unpublished dissertation compares female characterization in the works of male and female writers, exploring the question of happiness for women.

The most impressive work to date is Lloyd Brown's *Women Writers in Black Africa*[17] in which he identifies "The Woman's Voice in African Literature" and goes on to study five major African women writers: Bessie Head, Efua Sutherland, Ama Ata Aidoo, Flora Nwapa, Buchi Emecheta. His basic position is that all of these writers have made significant contributions to their genres yet remain beyond the pale of criticism. In his introduction, he explores the idealistic images of women, symbolism of women in the literature and the question of persistent neglect. Brown makes some penetrating conclusions about the way these writers express the African women's sense of self in relation to tradition and society. Its limitations are that it deals primarily with English-speaking writers and that each of his writers has since published other major works. A more recent work in this vein is Oladele Taiwo's *Female Novelists in Modern Africa*.[18] Most attention is directed to Emecheta but, although he includes a larger cross-section of writers than does Brown, most reviewers identify several biases and inappropriate analyses.

The minor studies include Marion Kilson's "Women and African Literature"[19] which is a study of the short stories of Ama Ata Aidoo and Grace Ogot. In it she contrasts the images of women in both authors' works based on the status of women as protagonists, the racial and cultural status of women, their economic, domestic and leisure roles, and the life cycles of women. The Kilson essay, though somewhat tentative, is a valuable comparison of two African women writers. Roseann P. Bell's "The Absence of the African Woman Writer"[20] identifies several unexamined African women writers while Yinka Shoga's "Women Writers and African Literature"[21] is a brief overview of genres and writers. She posits that African women's lives as childbearers and childrearers, and the entire social situation which subordinates them, impede literary creativity. The requirements described by Virginia Woolf in "A Room of One's Own" seem to have no place in the African woman's life. Yet, she concludes "these pioneers . . . have begun a respectable and inclusive tradition for their daughters-in-art." In this connection it may be useful to examine Alice Walker's conclusions on writing as *work* as they relate to African women. In her article on Buchi Emecheta, "A Writer Because of, Not In Spite of, Her Children,"[22] she states in praise of Emecheta's creativity: "she integrates the profession of writer into the cultural concept of mother/worker that she retains from Ibo society. Just as the African mother has traditionally planted crops, pounded maize, and done her washing with her baby strapped to her back, so Adah can write a novel with her children playing in the same room." Anne Lippert's "Women Characters and African Literature"[23] is limited to Nigerian writers and is a brief look at the characterization of women. Obviously an excerpt from her dissertation discussed above, she uses similar categories as Mutiso and Little.

The landmark work *Sturdy Black Bridges*[24] which examines Black women's images in literature has representative essays and creative work from Africa, the Caribbean and Afro-America. Of importance to our discussion are the essays by Andrea Benton Rushing, Marie Linton Umeh, Karen Chapman and Sonia Lee.[25] The Rushing study remains so far the only major study of women in African poetry but it is dated in the sense that in her attempt to locate symbols and images specific to African culture, there is a tendency towards the acceptance of the glorification of motherhood and other prescribed female roles which is at the core of most African poetry. Her conclusion is, however, a plea for the voices of African women writers who are most equipped to tell of their realities. A growing number of African women writers, in both poetry and prose, are however demystifying this traditional romanticization of motherhood. For one thing, it disregards the childless woman and mythologizes the tedia involved in motherhood. Sonia Lee shows how Sembène allows his women characters greater self-awareness and in doing so links their freedom with Africa's freedom. Karen Chapman examines Aidoo's *The Dilemma of a Ghost*[26] for form, language and theme. Marie Linton Umeh's study "The African Heroine" begins the call for more heroic portrayals of African women.

Another significant contribution is Maryse Condé's "Three Female Writers in Modern Africa: Flora Nwapa, Ama Ata Aidoo and Grace Ogot".[27] In many ways it is a challenge to women writers to be more forthright in the examination of their societies and in their presentation of women characters. Recently there has been a movement away from the examination of feminine images[28] in the literature of male African writers to an increasing number of essays on individual African women writers.[29] Many of the earlier essays, such as those by Brown and Little[30] have been incorporated into the larger works by the same authors discussed above.

All of these works are of value to any study of women in African literature as they are important bases for present and future work. The criticism at this point seems to be crystallizing itself and defining its foci. In many ways, the pattern is similar to what occurred in mainstream feminist criticism which moved from the early identification of biases in male writers to an exploration of the works of women writers who have remained outside of the purview of literary criticism. The papers in this collection mark this transition.

Some Notes on African Feminism

The social and historical realities of African women's lives must be considered in any meaningful examination of women in African literature and of writings by African women writers. A number of works have examined African women from a variety of perspectives. Several statements have come from African women themselves in recent years. The only formulation of a feminist theory for African women, however, comes from Filomina Steady who, after examining the commonalities of experience and response of African women in Africa and the diaspora, defines an African feminism. In her introduction to *The Black Woman Cross-Culturally*,[31] she posits that this African brand of feminism includes female autonomy and cooperation; an emphasis on nature over culture; the centrality of children, multiple mothering and kinship; the use of ridicule in African woman's worldview. A number of traditional rights and responsibilities of women allow her to conclude that the African woman is in practice much more a feminist than her European counterpart.

> True feminism is an abnegation of male protection and a determination to be resourceful and reliant. The majority of the black women in Africa and the diaspora have developed these characteristics, though not always by choice . . . (pp. 35-36)

Steady's position is perhaps the most appropriate start for our discussion especially since she examines the socio-economic and class factors which contribute to African woman's oppression (economic exploitation and marginalization) and her responses to this oppression (self-reliance). There are a few debatable points in the Steady definition, however. Many will argue that assuming a nature over culture posture for African women denies her participation in the shaping of human culture and renders her an inert, unintelligent "vessel", not a creative person in her own right. Additionally, the discussion too quickly glosses over certain traditional inequities which continue to subordinate African women. (While acknowledging their existence, Steady devotes only a footnoted paragraph to these inequities in favor of extensive discussion of what makes black women's situation different.) Among them, lack of choice in motherhood and marriage, oppression of barren women, genital mutilation, enforced silence and a variety of other forms of oppression intrinsic to various societies which still plague African women's lives and must inevitably be at the crux of African feminist theory.

Steady's introduction, nonetheless, is still, so far, the most comprehensive detailing of the various facets of African women's experience. A closer examination of the African woman's situation vis a vis the layers of oppression that have to be torn away is offered by Molara Ogundipe-Leslie's "African Women, Culture and Another Development" which locates the condition of women in Africa within the socio-economic realities of culture and development. She makes the point (extending Mao-Tse Tung's "mountain on the back" metaphor) that African women have additional burdens bearing down on them: 1) oppression from outside (foreign intrusions, colonial domination etc.); 2) heritage of tradition (feudal, slave-based, communal, 3) her own backwardness, a product of colonization and neo-colonialism and its concomitant poverty, ignorance etc.; 4) her men, weaned on centuries of male domination who will not willingly relinquish their power and privilege; 5) her race, because the international economic order is divided along race and class lines; 6) her self. While she spends less time detailing the nature and scope of the last four "mountains" than she does on the first two, Ogundipe-Leslie makes it clear that the most important challenge to the African woman is her own self-perceptions since it is she who will have to define her own freedom:

The sixth mountain on the woman's back—herself—is the most important. Women are shackled by their own negative self-image, by centuries of the interiorization of the ideologies of patriarchy and gender hierarchy. Her own reactions to objective problems therefore are often self-defeating and self-crippling. She reacts with fear dependency complexes and attitudes to please and cajole where more self-assertive actions are needed . . . [32]

Progressive African women see the women's struggle as even more difficult than the obvious struggles for national liberation where the enemy is easily recognized. As Gwendolyn Konie describes it:

The struggle for equal rights between the sexes is going to prove even more difficult than that of de-colonization because in essence it is a struggle between husband and wife, brother and sister, father and mother. [33]

And Annabella Rodrigues who participated in the FRELIMO struggle for Mozambican liberation identifies polygamy, initiation rites and *lobolo*, or dowry, as the most difficult of traditions to eliminate and the most oppressive to women and says,

It is easier to eliminate the colonial, bourgeois influences that were imposed on us and identified with the enemy than to eliminate generations of tradition from within our own society. [34]

Inevitably, the question of national reconstruction along more egalitarian lines enters and has to be hinged to women's lives in African nations. The positions of more radically feminist organizations like C.A.M.S. Internationale (La Commission Internationale Pour l'Abolition des Mutilations Sexuelles), a Dakar-based organization which includes membership from Afro-America, the Caribbean, Africa and Europe, have to be considered here. Founded in 1979, it proposes to work toward enhancing woman's status in society through the abolition of sexual mutilation, institutionalized polygamy, obligatory motherhood, the mandatory wearing of clothing of constraint and illiteracy of women. CAMS insists that Third World Women ought not wait for a revolution initiated by men to institute certain changes in women's lives. ("Nous n'avons plus à attendre une révolution introduite et toujours menée par les hommes. Nous prenons en charge notre propre lutte sans devinir, comme toujours, la section féminine de la révolution des hommes, par les hommes.")[35]

A genuine African feminism can therefore be summarized as follows. Firstly, it recognizes a common struggle with African men for the removal of the yokes of foreign domination and European/American exploitation. It is not antagonistic to African men but it challenges them to be aware of certain salient aspects of women's subjugation which differ from the generalized oppression of all African peoples.

Secondly, an African feminist consciousness recognizes that certain inequities and limitations existed/exist in traditional societies and that colonialism reinforced them and introduced others. As such, it acknowledges its affinities with international feminism, but delineates a specific African feminism with certain specific needs and goals arising out of the concrete realities of women's lives in African societies.

Thirdly, it recognizes that African societies are ancient societies, so logically, African women must have addressed the problems of women's position in society historically. In this regard there already exist, in some societies, structures which given women equality. According to van Sertima, the colonial period and immediate pre-colonial period are not the only indices by which one evaluates traditional African society.[36] Revised historical records are indicating that African women in the pre-colonial period and in antiquity were competent rulers, warriors and participants in their societies.[37] In fact the mythology of several peoples shows women in leadership positions (See Nama's discussion on the "Daughters of Moombi"[38] in Gikuyu culture in this work for example).

Fourthly, African feminism examines African societies for institutions which are of value to women and rejects those which work to their detriment and does not simply import Western women's agendas. Thus, it respects African woman's status as mother but questions obligatory motherhood and the traditional favoring of sons. It sees utility in the positive aspects of the extended family and polygamy with respect to child care and the sharing of household responsibility, traditions which are compatible with modern working women's lives and the problems of child care but which were distorted with colonialism and continue to be distorted in the urban environment. African feminist author Buchi Emecheta was soundly attacked for daring to suggest that polygamy worked in many ways to women's benefit.[39] The CAMS colloquium examined both monogamy and polygamy, soundly criticizing the latter but not totally endorsing the former. The debate lingers as within both marital systems women may be dominated. What should be attacked is the privilege that is accorded to males in marriage in general and the concomitant loss of status that is the females'. The excesses of polygamy which most offend women include the man's prerogative to be catered to by several women, the fact that *he* usually has the *choice*, the rejection of women and the competition between them which his choices generate. Omolara Ogundipe-Leslie, in discussing the Nigerian situation says, "the woman as daughter or sister has greater status and more rights in her lineage. Married, she becomes a possession, voiceless and often rightless in her husband's family, except for what accrues to her through her children."[40] There are, however, other forms of male-female relationships which work favorably in Africa and these need adequate examination. Importantly, no system should be institutionalized and mandated, and the woman's right to choose, without censure, should be respected.

Fifthly, it respects African woman's self-reliance and the penchant to cooperative work and social organization (networking) and the fact that African women are seldom financially dependent but instead accept income-generating work as a fact of life. It rejects, however the over-burdening, exploitation and relegation to "muledom" that is often her lot.

Sixthly, an African feminist approach has to look objectively at women's situation in societies which have undergone a war of national liberation and socialist reconstruction. Urdang's[41] essay on the steps taken to equalize the sexes in Guinea Bissau is of immense value. So are the essays in *Third World. Second Sex. Women's Struggles and National Liberation.*[42] Women who have participated fully in struggles for national liberation often find that in the national reconstruction phase, a new and more sustained struggle has to be waged with and against the men along whose sides they fought.

Finally, African feminism looks at traditional and contemporary avenues of choice for women. It is important to state here that anthropologists (largely white and male) who were the first to study African women's roles took as norm outward demeanors of submissiveness and failed to extricate other modes by which African women access power. Many of these power mechanisms surface in times of crisis. New studies by African women anthropologists and sociologists are beginning to reveal more accurate findings as these women scholars are able to enter the African women's world in ways in which the male (and white) anthropologists could not.[43] Above all, African women themselves are beginning to tell their own stories.[44] All of this must contribute to the development of a true African feminist theory.

The obvious connection between African and Western feminism is that both identify gender-specific issues and recognize woman's position internationally as one of second class status and "otherness" and seek to correct that. An International Feminism[45] to which various regional perspectives are contributed seems acceptable to African women while the European/American model is not. The failure of Western feminists to deal with issues that directly affect Black women and their tendency to sensation-alize others create antagonisms[46] as does the fact that white women are often partners in the oppression of both African women and men (South Africa as the most overt example). The term "feminism" often has to be qualified when used by most African and other Third World women. The race, class and cultural allegiances that are brought to its consideration cause the most conflict. Yet, although, the concept may not enter the daily existence of the average woman, and although much of what she understands as feminism is filtered through a media that is male-dominated and male-oriented, African women recognize the inequities and, especially within the context of struggles for national liberation, are challenging entrenched male dominance.

Theoretical African feminism understands the interconnectedness of race, class and sex oppression.[47] Consequently it realizes that there are white men and women, and definitely Black men who seek to overturn the oppressive structures of their societies. Thus, it of necessity has a socialist orientation. Kenyan writer/critic Micere Mugo's position is perhaps the best summary of this interconnectedness. In a 1976 interview she stated:

> First of all, let me note that we cannot only speak of women's oppression by men. In capitalist systems, women tend to be exploited by the very nature of the society, particularly the working and peasant women, just as men are exploited. The difference is that women are hit particularly hard. Their most obvious hardship is being educationally disadvantaged. Then you have forms of abuse that cut across class lines: sexual abuse, wife-beating and the fact that men take advantage of the woman's role as child-bearer. But I won't give the impression that I foster any illusions. Sexual abuse, rape etc. do take place in socialist societies, but I believe statistics will bear me out that the degree of such abuses is less than in capitalist societies, whose conditions of maldistribution and ownership tend to breed many social problems.[48]

For this reason she projects "a system where all the oppressive institutions are dismantled—politically, socially for the sake of men and women. . . . a society which actively encourages the idea of collective responsibility." Micere Mugo's own creative work, her collaborative work with writer Ngugi wa Thiong'o and her own activism which led to her exile from Kenya demonstrates the inextricable link between an African feminist consciousness and a socialist orientation—both commited to total freedom of all people. Omolara Ogundipe-Leslie's argument as expressed in "Not Spinning on the Axis of Maleness" and "The Female Writer and Her Commitment" cited earlier (fn.9) is another articulation of this position. African men who challenge the traditional social and political dominance of patriarchy and who support women's issues are obvious partners. Among writers, Ngugi wa Thiong'o is probably the most brilliant example, seeing the woman's struggle as inextricably entertwined with the total struggle. In a 1982 interview, on his novel *Devil on the Cross* and in *Detained: A Writer's Prison Diary* Ngugi describes women as the most exploited and oppressed section of the entire working class, "exploited as workers and at home, and also by "backward elements in the culture, remnants of feudalism.' " As a result, he says, "I would create a picture of a strong, determined woman with a will to resist and to struggle against the conditions of her present being."[49]

The very fact that it is necessary to qualify feminism or limit it with the word "African" indicates implicitly the relationship between the two. In the main, therefore, African feminism is a hybrid of sorts, which seeks to combine African concerns with feminist concerns. This is the nature of the "balancing" which has to take place.

The term "womanism" defined by Alice Walker and which comes directly out of African-American and Caribbean culture is inextricably entwined in the definition of African feminism. It too is a qualification, a search for new terminology to adequately convey Black women's feminism and a recognition of the limitation of the term "feminism" for our purposes. A womanist, she says, in part, is "a black feminist, or feminist of color . . . committed to survival and wholeness of entire people, male and female . . . [but who] loves herself. Regardless."[50] Seriousness, capability, self-reliance, love of culture, love of SELF are indicated. There may be some differences in orientation but in much the same way for African feminists, the double allegiance to woman's emancipation and African liberation becomes one.

Defining an African Feminist Critical Approach

African feminist criticism is definitely engaged criticism in much the same way as progressive African literary criticism grapples with decolonization and feminist criticism with the politics of male literary dominance. This criticism therefore is both textual and contextual criticism: textual in that close reading of texts using the literary establishment's critical tools is indicated; contextual as it realizes that analyzing a text without some consideration of the world with which it has a material relationship is of little social value. So the dichotomy between textual and contextual criticism, the perennial argument about form and content, common in literary circles finds some resolution here.

Our task here is to identify critical approaches and standards and criteria which have been applied so far to the study of African literature from a feminist perspective and which can be utilized and built upon for further examination of women in/and African literature. In a larger sense, African literary criticism, in general, if it be unbiased in the future will have to come to grips with issues such as the treatment of women characters and the growing presence of African women writers.

The African feminist theoretical framework previously outlined, along with the work of feminist theorists, combine in a unique fashion in this approach. Again, the "balancing act" described above applies. African feminist critics must take what is of value from both mainstream feminist criticism and African literary criticism, keeping in mind that both are offshoots from traditional European literary criticism and in some cases its adversaries. The result then is not reduction but refinement geared specifically to deal with the concrete and literary realities of African women's lives.

It is important to underscore the fact that a substantial amount of literature exists on the development of a feminist aesthetic[51], on one hand, and a Black/African aesthetic[52] on the other. The work of Black feminist critics[53] in the United States also provides an important focus especially when examining African women writers and the question of their exclusion from the literary canon(s).

For this reason, Katherine Frank's "Feminist Criticism and the African Novel"[54], the only published work known to this writer to deal directly with this subject, loses by not understanding the critical connection between feminist criticism and African literature by not taking into consideration how African-American feminists apply feminist theory to Black literature. There, the geo-cultural differences notwithstanding, lies the link—in the explorations of Deborah Mc Dowell, Barbara Christian, Mary Helen Washington, Alice Walker, Barbara Smith and others. For example, her questions about whether "gender or race is the most significant defining characteristic of a writer" is already answered. For Black/African feminists never make that distinction. It is not a question of either/or, but one of an acceptance of BOTH and the balances and conflicts that go with that twin acceptance. Frank, moreover is guilty of some gross distortions in the way in which she interprets feminism, for example her conclusion: "Feminism, by definition, is a profoundly individualistic philosophy: it values personal growth and individual fulfilment over any larger communal needs or good" (p.45) is just the kind of conclusion that some retrograde males have made. Quite to the contrary, feminism is not individualistic but openly speaks of "sisterhood" and the need for "women" to advance in society to be on at least an equal level with men for the society's overall good. Frank also, much like Ojo-Ade in his "Female Writers, Male Critics"[55] reads feminism solely as a Western import forgetting the African-American women, like Sojourner Truth's contribution to feminism and the many African women in history whose lives and deeds can be clearly read as "feminist". Frank, nonetheless has made an important contribution to the discussion and importantly delineates the various types of feminist literary theory which can be applied. For example, she sees the need for a literary history of African women writers which would account for the "lost lives" in African literary history. Our position is that women writers are not simply seeing themselves in conflict with traditionalism but are pointing out to society where some of the inequities lie and thereby are directly involved in a struggle to reshape society.

African feminist criticism so far has engaged in a number of critical activities which can be conveniently categorized as follows: 1) Developing the canon of African women writers; 2) Examining stereotypical images of women in African literature; 3) Studying African women writers and the development of an African female aesthetic; and 4) Examining women in oral traditional literature.

1. Developing the Canon of African Women Writers.

In a sense this task is two-fold—the development of a canon of African women writers and a parallel canon of critical works with the final aim of expanding the African literary canon. To this end, it encourages women writers, yet challenges their work by providing criticism which is not punitive but challenging and which seeks to elucidate the woman writer's view of the world.[56] In this instance it is one with feminist critics in the discovering of writers considered by establishment to be minor or unimportant. It re-evaluates dismissed women writers by providing critical studies which reveal specific woman-oriented configurations. An excellent example is the case of Flora Nwapa, clearly a victim of literary politics. Cavalierly dismissed by many critics[57] as unimportant, after re-vision she is credited with recreating that oral culture that African society is noted for and making important contributions to her genre. Ernest Emenyonu's rebuttal, "Who Does Flora Nwapa Write For," which explores Nwapa's aesthetic connections with Igbo oral culture,[58] Lloyd Brown's work on Nwapa in his *Women Writers of Black Africa*, and Naana Banyiwa-Horne's essay in this collection are examples of the reassessment of this writer. Published in the same year (1966), Nwapa's *Efuru*, which has a similar plot as Elechi Amadi's *The Concubine*, has not received the same critical acceptance as Amadi's book. Yet while the former provides a resolution which is favorable to women or at least shows the protagonist grappling with the conflicts, Amadi, without any more significant creative ability than Nwapa, shows woman simply as object, unable to exert any control over her life.

2. The Examination of Female Stereotypes and Images in the Works of African Writers.

The approach here is the identification of negative and positive images. African women writers have been attacked for dwelling on the "woman as victim" image and African male writers for locking women into postures of dependence and for defining women only in terms of their association with men. Clearly the study of images of women is not a "dead-ended" enterprise nor one exhausted by Little, as Frank puts it, for Little himself has done questionable work. The study of images is an important developmental step in feminist criticism. It represents the first realization that something is wrong and is usually the first rung of consciousness for the critic. Beyond that it becomes a challenge to established male writers to recognize distortions just as it is for racist writers to recognize and correct racial caricatures. For women writers the "woman as victim" character performs a political function, directly stimulating empathetic identification in the readers and in a sense challenging them to change. Nnu Ego in Emecheta's *The Joys of Motherhood* is the best example. It is such an excellent example of the undesirable "long-suffering" character presented by a woman writer to make a statement on the depths to which women's lives can descend. A positive image, then, is one that is in tune with African historical realities and does not stereotype or limit women into postures of dependence or submergence. Instead it searches for more accurate portrayals and ones which suggest the possibility of transcendence. Writers like Ngugi wa Thiong'o and Ousmane Sembène have demonstrated this possibility in their creation of characters like Waaringa and N'Deye Touti. Flora Nwapa, Ama Ata Aidoo, Mariama Bâ, Buchi Emecheta and other women writers have worked to provide truthful assessments of women's lives, the positive and negative and to demonstrate the specific choices that women must often make. Thus African feminist critics seek to make writers conscious of unrelenting, uniformly undesirable stereotypes and other shortcomings in female portraiture. Included here also is making visible the "invisible woman", or audible, the mute, voiceless woman, the woman who exists only as tangential to man and his problems. Additionally it explores the idealization of women and motherhood in the Négritude vein—woman as supermother, symbol of Africa, earth as muse, how this supports or distorts the creation of a female mythos and how it conforms to the realities of women's lives.

3. African Women Writers and the Development of an African Female Aesthetic.

An important cornerstone of this criticism is the examination of the works of African women writers. It looks at the themes and topics which engage women writers, their language, characterization, the forms they use, images and the like. It demands new examinations into the principles of composition, thought and expression of African women writers. New studies of oral literature from this perspective are necessary, and this is discussed separately below. In the case of written literature, previous work of African-American feminist critics who are still working in this area, provide valuable examples. Mary Helen Washington, for example, in her introduction to *Black Eyed Susans*[59] provides an excellent summation of the themes which are common to African-American women's writing: Growing up Black and Female; The Intimidation of Color; The Black Woman and the Myth of the White Woman; The Black Mother-Daughter Relationship; The Disappointment of Romantic Love; Reconciliation between Black men and women. How similar are these to themes in African women's writing?

My examination of African woman's literature reveals some concerns are similar and others that are unique to African women: 1) motherhood (the presence or absence of it/its joys and pains); 2) the vagaries of living in a polygamous marriage; 3) the oppression of colonialism and white rule; 4) the struggle for economic independence; 5) the achievement of a balance between relationships with men and friendships with other women; 6) the fickleness of husbands; 6) the importance of having a support system, particularly in the urban environment; 7) the mother-daughter conflict or relationship; 8) the mother-son relationship; 9) above all, the definition of self or the development of a separate self over and beyond, but not separate from, tradition or other "man-made" restrictions. While there are similarities arising out of women's lives internationally, and while some of these themes also appear in the works of male writers, like Nuruddin Farah, the literature reveals that there are differences which point to the specific types of oppression African women face in the various cultures. For example, although we are dealing with the literature of two groups of Black women, each group has both distinct and common political and cultural realities which inform its literary concerns.

Comparative assessments of the two bodies of literature and with women's writing in other parts of the world may throw light on the uniqueness of the African woman's literary experience or its participation in an overall female aesthetic. For example, one finds the recurrence of certain forms like the epistolary form, the journal, the letter and other modes of story narration which appear here as in other women's works. Also, the inclusion within the narrative of "small talk" is often considered a weakness in women writers who have not "mastered form". But Pauline Nalova Lyonga in her recent dissertation "Uhamiri. A Feminist Approach to African Literature"[60] demonstrates a thematic and formal continuity between African women's oral and written literature. Importantly, if we are to apply the critical criteria of the literary establishment which is European and male dominated, many of these African female forms are dismissed as weaknesses. The same battle that African literary theorists had to wage to make the European/American critics realize that other African-based aesthetic criteria have to be applied to African literature, in effect has to be waged for African women writers.

4. Women In/And African Oral Literature and Comparative Studies

The examination of women in oral literature and/or of the aesthetics of oral literature created by women as compared to that created by men is another task which so far has not been sufficiently attacked. This critical inquiry is in some ways subsumed in the previous category but important enough to stand on its own. Finnegan's work raises some concerns but obviously was not geared to that endeavor, so it contains relatively little material of relevance to us. There is, however, some available material with which critics can work.[61] A few interesting studies have been done on women in the mythology and how that carries over into the written literature.[62] Several studies of the oral literature of specific groups include some discussion of women as creator/performer and as subject.[63] Several researchers (sociologists, anthropologists) have found it important to look at women's oral literature in addition to their main interests and some work is being done exclusively on African women's oral literature.[64] But there remains much more to be done. There is an overall male bias in approaching oral literary studies (as is the case in written literary studies) which assumes that the artist is always male and which consequently overlooks a large body of material or does not look for specific aesthetic features common to women when women's work is included.

All of the above cut across a number of time periods, (pre-colonial, colonial and neo-colonial contexts), political systems (socialist and capitalist states) and settings (rural and urban locales). A number of areas remain uncovered: Language, symbolic structure and how these are revealed in the works of male and female African writers is a relatively unexplored area. Additionally, in defining an African female aesthetic, it may be worthwhile to make comparisons with the art of African women and its images of women and the female characterizations of African male artists.

Any exposition of a critical approach such as this one must lay claims to incompleteness. It is a step towards a larger end rather than the end itself. This introduction represents a summary of the currents in African feminist criticism and the directions it can take. Inevitably it is derivative and its tasks in many ways are identical to the tasks of mainstream feminist theorists and African literary theorists. Obviously, it must utilize the philosophical developments of both and arrive at a necessary synthesis. The contributors in this volume are all engaged in this task, though they are not alone as several important papers emerge each year. Another collection entitled *Critical Perspectives on Women Writers from Africa*[65] edited by Brenda Berrian and Mildred Mortimer is in press. Many of the papers in this collection were presented at forums like the African Literature Association annual conferences and women's conferences which give time and space to the presentation of women's issues in literary criticism. Each of the areas outlined above must, of necessity be expanded upon and developed. A host of research possibilities reveal themselves. This is only a beginning.

NOTES

1. Ruth Finnegan, *Oral Literature in Africa*, (London, Oxford University Press, 1970), pp. 375-376. The written African literature is correctly defined as "Modern Written Literature" in recognition that Africa has a long and distinguished oral literary tradition referred to as oral literature and, more recently, "orature".

2. Ama Ata Aidoo, for example, describes her somewhat unique position coming from one of those families which saw Western formal education as important for all and especially for women, in "To Be A Woman", *Sisterhood is Global*, ed. by Robin Morgan (New York, Anchor/Doubleday, 1984), p.259.

3. See for example works like Ulli Beier ed. *Introduction to African Literature* , (London, Longman, 1967); Janheinz Jahn, *Approaches to African Literature* (Ibadan University Press, 1959); and several other books and journals which were published in the 1950's and 1960's.

4. Mary Ellman, *Thinking About Women* (New York, Harcourt Brace Jovanovich, 1968), pp. 28-54.

5. Novelist Ezekiel Mphalele has published several articles on African literature along with his book *The African Image* (London, Faber, 1962); Eldred Jones has edited a number of volumes of *African Writing Today* but is only now (Vol. 15 forthcoming) devoting space to women in African literature; Eustace Palmer, *An Introduction to the African Novel* (London, Heinemann, 1972) follows the Western critical mold exclusively. A range of perspectives exist among African critics of the late 70's and 80's however.

6. O.R. Dathorne, *African Literature in the Twentieth Century* (Heinemann, 1976) had published several other essays and monographs on African literature before this work which does contain some limited discussion of African women writers; John Ansuman Ramsaran, *New Approaches to African Literature* (Ibadan University Press, 1965).

7. Margaret Amosu is the only woman to appear in Ulli Beier's *Introduction to African Literature* cited above. Her contribution is a "Selected Bibliography of Critical Writing", pp. 265-270. She had earlier published "A Preliminary Checklist of creative African Writing in the European Languages" (University of ibadan, 1964).

8. Lilyan Lagneau-Kesteloot who is one of the few European women critics of the 60's wrote an article "Problems of the Literary Critic in Africa.", *Abbia*, 8, (1965), pp. 29-44 but does not discuss the woman as critic. Molly Mahood for some years taught at Ibadan and was a mentor of teacher/critics like Oyin Ogunba. Among her works are "Drama in Newborn States, *Presence Africaine* 60 (1966), pp.16-33.

9. Omolara Ogundipe-Leslie's work, like other African women critics writing in the late sixties and early 1970's had been geared completely to mainstream criticism. In the late 70's, however, her critical orientation became first Marxist and then Marxist/feminist. Recently, however, she published an essay, "Not Spinning on the Axis of Maleness" in *Sisterhood is Global*, pp. 498-504. This is an important step for it is the first feminist statement that has come from this critic. It is directed at an international audience and should have some bearing on future critical works by her and contribute to African feminist literary theory. A short piece "The Female Writer and Her Commitment" appeared in *The Guardian* (Lagos), December 21, 1983, p. 11. Ms. Ogundipe-Leslie has for years had to struggle almost singly in a male-dominated academic climate which Ama Ata Aidoo also describes.

10. (New York, Random House, 1969).

11. (London, Cambridge University Press, 1975).

12. *East Africa Journal,* 3:3 (March, 1971), 4-14; later included in his *Socio-*

Political Thought in African Literature (London: McMillan Press, Ltd., 1974).
13. (New Jersey, Rowman, 1980).
14. (Dakar, Les Nouvelles Editions Africaines, 1980).
15. Ph. D. dissertation for Indiana University. 1971.
16. Ph. D. Dissertation for University of Massachusetts, 1974.
17. (Connecticut, Greenwood Press, 1981).
18. (London, McMillan, 1984).
19. *Journal of African Studies* 4 (1970), 161-166.
20. *CLA Journal* 21:4 (1978), 496.
21. *Afriscope* 3:10 (October, 1973), 44-45.
22. From *In Search of Our Mother's Gardens. Womanist Prose* (San Diego, Harcourt Brace Jovanovich, 1983), pp. 66-70.
23. Her essay also appears in *Afriscope*, 3:10 (October, 1973), 45-46, 49.
24. Edited by Roseann P. Bell, Bettye J. Parker and Beverly Guy-Sheftall (New York, Anchor Press/Doubleday, 1979).
25. Andrea Benton Rushing, "Images of Black Women in Modern African Poetry: An Overview." (pp. 18-24); Marie Linton-Umeh, "The African Heroine", (pp. 393-51); Sonia Lee, "The Awakening of Self in the Heroines of Ousmane Sembene, (pp. 52-60); also Karen Chapman, "Introduction" to Ama Ata Aidoo's *Dilemma of a Ghost"*, pp. 25-38.
26. (New York, Collier, 1971). First published in London in 1965). Among African women writers, Ama Ata Aidoo has perhaps had the most critical attention. Yet the criticism is not commensurate with her output and talent when compared with that accorded male writers with similar or lesser work.
27. Condé's article is in *Presence Africaine* (2:82, 1972), 132-143.
28. For example, Kathleen Staudt, "The Characterization of Women by Soyinka and Armah," *Ba Shiru* (8:2, 1977), 63-69. Another essay "Symbolic Characterization of Women in the Plays and Prose of Wole Soyinka" by Adetokunbo Pearse appears in *Ba Shiru* 9:1&2 (1978), 39-46.
29. Many of these essays will be listed in the bibliography of criticism.
30. See fns. 13 & 16 above.
31. (Cambridge, Mass., Schenckman Publishing Company, Inc., 1981), pp. 7-41.
32. *The Journal of African Marxists* 5(February, 1984):89 pp. 35-36.
33. In *Sisterhood is Global*, p. 744.
34. In Miranda Davies, ed. *Third World—Second Sex. Women's Struggles and National Liberation* (London, Zed Books, 1983), pp. 131-132. Jane Ngwenya a political activist from Zimbabwe had much earlier made similar points in an interview "An African Woman Speaks", *Encore*, June 23, 1975, p. 48. Grace Akello, *Self Twice Removed*, a report on Ugandan women published by Change, an International Women's Research Organization in 1982 and reported in "Struggling Out of Traditional Strait-jackets", *New African*, January, 1983.
35. Le Soleil (Dakar), 29 decembre 1982. "We no longer have to wait for a revolution introduced and always led by the men. We are taking charge of our own struggle without becming, as always, the female section of the revolution of and for men." (my translation).
36. See his *They Came Before Columbus* (New York, Random House, 1976) and

Blacks in Science: Ancient and Modern (Available through African Studies Department, Rutgers University), 1983.

37. John Henrik Clarke, "African Warrior Queens" in *Black Women in Antiquity* ed. by Ivan Van Sertima (New Brunswick, Transaction Books, 1984), pp. 123-134. Caroline Ifeka-Moller, "Female Militancy and Colonial Revolt. The Woman's War of 1929, Eastern Nigeria, in *Perceiving Women* ed. Shirley Ardener (New York, John Wiley & Sons, 1975), pp. 127-157. A paper "Slavery and Women in The Pre-Colonial Kingdom of Dahomey" by Boniface Obichere (Institute of African Studies, University of ibadan, 1976) demonstrates that women participated equally in the political, social and economic life of pre-colonial Dahomey.

38. African woman writer, Charity Waciuma also has an autobiographical work entitled *Daughter of Mumbi* (Nairobi, East African Publishing House, 1969).

39. African Studies Meeting, (California) October, 1984. African women in the audience, some feminists, were appalled at Emecheta's stand on polygamy. One has to admit, however, that Emecheta, who has written several novels which show polygamy in negative light would not have come to her position casually.

40. "Not Spinning on the Axis of Maleness" in *Sisterhood is Global*, pp. 500-501.

41. Stephanie Urdang, "The Role of Women in the Revolution of Guinea-Bissau." in Steady, pp. 119-139.

42. (London, Zed Press, 1983); Essays in *Sisterhood is Global* also provide views on women in countries undergoing socialist reconstruction. Some describe it as the second struggle. Others like Jane Ngwenya, "Women and Liberation in Zimbabwe", pp. 78-83 say that suffering and fighting together erodes sexual prejudices and stereotyping. More long-term study will show if this is sustained.

43. See for example D. M. Hull's bibliography "African Women in Development: An Untapped Resource" (Moorland-Spingarn Research Center, Howard University, April, 1983) which lists a number of works by African women specifically and by women in general. Audrey Smedley, "Motherhood and Women in Patrilineal Societies" presented at the ASALH Conference, Detroit, Michigan, 1983, part of a major work being prepared on women and patriliny, holds that by assuming women have no say in the shaping of the kind of society they live in, we bring a male-oriented approach to examining African societies. African and African-American anthropologists like Bolanle Awe and Niara Sudarkasa, are providing important information on women in African societies. The essays in Steady's *The Black Woman Cross-Culturally* are additional examples.

44. African women writers are making statements on the social organization of their societies, in addition to their creative writing. A number of interviews with African women are being published.

45. *Sisterhood is Global* is subtitled "The International Women's Movement Anthology". The extent of contributions to this and other similar volumes indicates the validity of international feminism.

46. The AAWORD Statement on Genital Mutilation in *Third World-Second Sex*, pp. 217-220 is a case in point. Steady's introduction is in many ways a rebuttal to Western feminism.

47. See for example, Lillian Robinson's *Sex, Class and Culture* (Bloomington,

Indiana University Press, 1978), Angela Davis, *Women, Race and Class* (New York, Random House, 1983), Lise Vogel, *Marxism and the Oppression of Women. Toward Unitary Theory* (New Jersey, Rutgers University Press, 1983); Bonnie Thornton Dill, "Race, Class and Gender: Prospects for an All-Inclusive Sisterhood," *Feminist Studies* 9 (1983), 131-150.

48. "Dr. Micere Mugo, Kenya's outspoken Intellectual and Academic Critic, Talks to Nancy Owano," *Africa Woman* 6(September to October, 1976), pp. 14-15.

49. Profile: "Ngugi: My Novel of Blood, Sweat and Tears." *New AFrican* (August, 1982), p. 36. The works cited are published by Heinemann (London) African Writers Series Nos. 200 (1982) and 240 (1983) respectively.

50. The definition of "womanist" is a preface to her *In Search of Our Mothers Gardens: Womanist Prose*, op. cit., pp. xi-xii.

51. Among them are essays in Cheryl L. Brown and Karen Olson, *Feminist Criticism* Essays on Theory, Poetry and Prose (New Jersey, The Scarecrow Press, Inc., 1978). Cheri Register's Review essay, "Literary Criticism" in *Signs* (Winter, 1980) is a fairly comprehensive sampling of the issues and theorists of feminist criticism. Essays in Elizabeth Abel, ed., *Writing and Sexual Difference* (University of Chicago Press, 1982) and Elaine Showalter, *Feminist Criticism* (New York, Random House, 1985) are additional examples.

52. See Addison Gayle, *The Black Aesthetic* (New York, Doubleday, 1971); Carolyn Fowler's introduction to her *Black Arts and Black Aesthetics - A Bibliography* (Atlanta, First World Foundation, 1984); Zirimu and Gurr, *Black Aesthetics* (Nairobi, East African Publishing House, 1973); Wole Soyinka, *Myth, Literature and the African World* (London, Cambridge University Press, 1976); Chinweizu et al, *Towards the Decolonization of African Literature* (Washington, D.C. Howard University Press, 1983); Johnson, Cailler, Hamilton and Hill-Lubin, *Defining the African Aesthetic* (Washington, D.C. Three Continents Press, 1982).

53. Section Five of *But Some of Us Are Brave*, edited by Gloria T. Hull, Patricia Bell Scott and Barbara Smith (New York, The Feminist Press, 1982) is devoted to literature and contains Barbara Smith's "Toward a Black Feminist Criticism", pp. 157-175 which is also published separately in booklet form and distributed by The Crossing Press, 1982. Deborah McDowell, "New Directions in Black Feminist Criticism", *Black American Literature Forum* 14:4 (Winter, 1980), 153-159; Claudia Tate's *Black Women Writers at Work* (New York, Continuum, 1983), Alice Walker's essays in *In Search of Our Mothers Gardens*, Mary Helen Washington's many essays and a number of other works address this issue. Toni Cade Bambara's *The Black Woman. An Anthology* (New York, New American Library, 1970) includes essays like Francis Beale's "Double Jeopardy: To Be Black and Female" which discuss the particular situation of Black American women. Deborah Mc Dowell is preparing an extensive manuscript on feminist criticism as applied to African-American literature. Barbara Christian, *Black Feminist Criticism. Perspectives on Black Women Writers* (New York, Pergamon Press, 1985) includes Buchi Emecheta in her study.

54. Katherine Frank, "Feminist Criticism and the African Novel," *African*

Literature Today 14 (London, Heinemann, 1984), 34-48.

55. Although it has a catchy introduction and conclusion, Femi Ojo-Ade's, "Female Writers, Male Critics" does not deal with criticism but is a study of Flora Nwapa and Ama Ata Aidoo. Ojo-Ade is well recognized for an overtly belligerent, condescending-to-female-writers-and-critics language and oral style of presentation which contradicts some of the points he makes in his conclusion "Criticism, Chauvinism, Cynicism . . . Commitment". While he seems to be arguing for fairness to women here, his tone may betray his true attitude to this subject. Most Black women welcome men as fellow explorers in this field and rarely descend to the gross abuses he suggests, in his final paragraph, that are levelled against male critics. It seems instead a rehashing of some of the early stereotypical language of "women's liberation."

56. Carole Boyce Davies and Elaine Savory Fido, "African Women Writers" in *African Literature in the Twentieth Century* ed. by Oyekan Owomoyela (University of Nebraska Press, forthcoming). This chapter attempts a literary history of African women writers which approaches the works from a womanist critical perspective. Roseann P. Bell had earlier called for a "mutual" supportive and critical system sympathetic to our needs" in "The Absence of the African Woman Writer," op. cit., p. 498.

57. See Eustace Palmer's review "Elechi Amadi and Flora Nwapa" in *African Literature Today* 1-4 (1968-70), 56-58.

58. Ernest N. Emenyonu, "Who Does Flora Nwapa Write For?" *African Literature Today* 7 (London: Heinemann, 1975): 28-33.

59. (New York, Anchor/Doubleday, 1975).

60. Unpublished Ph. D. Dissertation, University of Michigan, 1985.

61. Elizabeth Gunner, "Songs of Innocence and Experience: Women as Composers and Performers of *Izibongo*, Zulu Praise Poetry," in *Research in African Literatures* 10:2 (1979), 239-267. Harold Scheub, *African Oral Narratives, Proverbs, Riddles, Poetry and Song* (Boston, G. K. Hall, 1977) is a comprehensive bibliography of African oral literature. A number of dissertations and theses and other collections contain material which is rarely used and which needs to be reviewed for women's contributions.

62. Chidi Ikonne, "Women in Igbo Folktales" presented at the 1982 (Howard) ALA conference is an example. So is Nama's paper on women in Gikuyu mythology in this work.

63. Examples are Marion Kilson, *Royal Antelope and Spider: West African Mende Tales.* (Cambridge, Mass: The Press of Langdon Associates, 1976). See also Donald Cosentino's review in *Research in African Literatures* 10 (1979): 296-307 which discusses the question of woman as performer and makes reference to his own collection and to Mama Ngembe, a highly reputed oral artist. Thirty-nine of the forty stories included in Harold Scheub's *The Xhosa "Ntsomi"* (Oxford, Clarendon Press, 1975) were told by women. See Jeff Opland's review of A. C. Jordan, *Tales From Southern Africa* (Berkeley, University of California Press, 1978) in the same issue of *RAL* pp. 307-314.

64. For example Beverly B. Mack "*Waka Daya Ba Ta Kare Nika*': One Song Will Not Finish the Grinding: Hausa Women's Oral Literature" in *Contemporary African Literature* ed. by Wylie et al. (Three Continents Press, 1983), 15-46; Enoch T. Mvula, "Tumbuka Pounding Songs in the Management of

Familial Conflicts" *Cross Rhythms* 2 ed. by Daniel Avorgbedor and Kwesi Yankah (Indiana University, Department of Folklore, The Trickster Press, 1985), 93-113. Mvula is doing some further research on African women's oral literature in East Africa.

65. (Washington, D.C. Three Continents Press, forthcoming). Brenda Berrian's *Bibliography of American Women Writers and Journalists* (Three Continents, 1985) will contribute significantly to the study of African women writers and definitely establishes that there is a substantial body of literature by African women.

PART ONE
Defining 'Woman's Place': Female Portraiture in African Literature

Part I "Defining 'Woman's Place': Female Portraiture in African Literature", looks at roles/depictions/characterizations—in short, the "place" given to women in novels, primarily, from the 1950s, which produced the earliest of the works of African literature in the European mold, to the very recent. Those images of the African woman as discussed in the papers—whether from the Négritude movement with its romanticization of women or from the more recent years in which she is depicted with greater fidelity—the images are, in the evaluations presented in the articles, less than whole, incompletely formed, images imposed on women by others, or otherwise unrealistic. All, however, are seen through the eyes of males who are the dominant figures in the literary works as well as in the lives of the women characters in those works. Whatever the depiction, whatever the sentiment that generates it, it is someone else's image of the woman, as he (they) see(s) and interact(s) with her, whether idealized, loved, pitied, or castigated. An overview of such portraiture in literature from the colonial era is the subject of Esther Smith's article. The nearly universal depiction of women is in the role of mothers, whose place in the survival of the African family in the face of colonialism is presented as critical, according to Smith. Her analysis substantiates the concept of the supremacy

25

of motherhood in the cosmology of most African peoples. Quite the contrary view of the mother's (and wife's) position is presented in Rafika Merini's paper on Driss Chraïbi's Succession Ouverte. *Merini points up the powerlessness of the wife/mother in the Moroccan Muslim society as depicted by Chraïbi, showing, for example, that women never speak for their own interests separate from those of their men. But her position as wife and mother is, of course, not the sole characterization of woman in African literature. Besides this concentration on her domestic relationships there is also attention given to woman's reaction and adaptation to the westernizing influences of colonialism. Karen Smyley-Wallace's article discusses the alienation of women in Abdoulaye Sadji's* Nini *and in Sembène's* God's Bits of Wood, Xala, *and* "Black Girl." *Smyley-Wallace shows that these women's obsession for the Europeanization of themselves, in one form or another, causes irreversible and sometimes tragic alienation.*

The unsatisfying and unrealistic self-image discussed by Smyley-Wallace is but one side of a coin whose reverse side can be described as the incomplete re-creations of historical and mythological heroines, as discussed by Carole Davies in her paper "Maidens, Mistresses, and Matrons: Feminine Images in Selected Soyinka Works." Although the contemporary versions of the heroines Soyinka creates are engaged as well as engaging, Davies sees them as confined to the state of being objects, rather than subjects. Across the dramatic and prose works she refers to for her analysis Davies is able to conclude at least that Soyinka's women characters who are modeled on heroines from Yoruba history succeed better than do those based on characters from the mythology. A qualitative distinction among women characters is also seen across the several works of another writer of equal stature, as presented in Abena Busia's "Parasites and Prophets: The Use of Women in Ayi Kwei Armah's Novels." In this article Armah's entire oeuvre of five works is studied for what Busia sees as remarkable evolution, from his first, The Beautyful Ones Are Not Yet Born *to his most recent* The Healers. *Recognizing that Armah's major women characters are in a position of having to choose between a role of "earth mother" or "public servant," Busia concludes that by his fifth novel the writer has reached a resolution between those two positions. This discussion by Busia, in its presentation of the gradual emergence of woman from a unidimensional, externally viewed character to a multi-faceted self-motivated person, can be viewed as a bridge to Part II with its decidedly feminine-centered perspective.*

A.A.G.

Images of Women in African Literature: Some Examples of Inequality in The Colonial Period

Esther Y. Smith

Studies of inequality in colonial Africa rarely focus on the status of women. Studies of women in African literature rarely focus on the colonial period, and when they do, tend to show either strong mother figures in traditional society, or rootless young women pursuing individualistic and materialistic goals in modern society. Reductionist reflections of monolithic or dualistic images of women in African literature, however, shatter to pieces with the press of data from the vast and diverse body of African literature. This study focuses on images of women in African novels which deal with the colonial period. It outlines some of the many different images of women which reflect some of the many faces of Africa and facets of inequality in the colonial period. It is a brief look at that vast and complex tableau which can only suggest productive ways of exploring images of women in African literature. It is in no way intended as an exhaustive or definitive study.

The primary data are limited to fictional sources from West and East Africa dealing with the colonial period. Limitations of genre have been imposed not only for reasons of space allotted, but in the interest of

27

consistency. A number of scholars have pointed out the relatively limited amount of drama, and the limited range of images of women in poetry from Africa, as compared to the fictional modes. Karen Chapman analyzes reasons for this lag in dramatic literature in her perceptive introduction to the Ghanaian drama, *The Dilemma of a Ghost* by Ama Ata Aidoo.[1]

> Black-African theater (and also film), still young and still forming, is a first fruit of Independence; few of its makers are yet middle-aged. More than any other literary form, theater requires for its life a physical continuity of institutions and audience, an atmospheric "place" where talent (and learning) congregates, collides, and grows old in the practice of skills; not less important, it requires a supportive community physically hooked on theatergoing. Until almost 1960, a gifted African writer had no such place to go . . .[2]

In poetic genres, Andrea Rushing points out that images of women are limited to two. Most poems reflect a vision of the strong, traditional "mother-is-gold" figure. Exceptions reflect what happens to young women cut off from their roots by the impact of colonialism, wanderlusting around in their pursuit of the big men in the big city. In her essay on "Images of Black Women in Modern African Poetry," Rushing compares this narrow focus with the broad range of images of women in modern African fiction, and offers some explanations.

> Unlike the images of African women in contemporary West African fiction, very few poetic images mirror the social change stalking Africa. One looks almost in vain for poems (like the short stories in Ama Ata Aidoo's *No Sweetness Here*), about urban women working, living alone, rejecting polygamy, deciding to have small families, agonizing over the crises of romantic love, snapping their ties to the extended family, playing critical roles in the past and present liberation struggles. On the one hand poetry, with its terse and vivid imagery, is the wrong place to go for full-scale realistic and naturalistic representations. On the other, almost all modern African poetry is written by men . . .[3]

This study will focus on images of women in novels about Africa during three stages of colonization: the first contacts with Europeans; colonial government in full control; and movements towards independence. In addition, a brief look at images of women and inequality in fiction dealing with traditional African societies and a glimpse at those about newly independent African countries will bracket the study of colonial times, providing those images of women with a perspective of historical depth.

In narrative genres of traditional oral literature from Africa, as in those from around the world, images of women show the good and the evil, the weak and the strong, the queens and heroines with magical powers, as well as the wives and mothers of more ordinary resources. The mother of the hero in *Sundiata, An Epic of Old Mali*[4] is unfailingly strong and courageous in protecting her children from danger and in fostering Sundiata's growth to heroic leadership. Sogolon is endowed with extraordinary powers which enable her to counteract the effects of her jealous co-wife's evil-doings. The machinations of Sassouma, the wicked co-mother, reflect the psychological realities of inequality in polygamous relationships.

The motif of jealousy and inequality in polygamous families is frequent in modern fiction about traditional society. Ousmane Sembène's psychological study of inequality in polygamy in "Her Three Days," is analyzed by Sonia Lee:

> The young woman, Noumbe, is the main protagonist of "Ses trois jours," a story in the collection *Voltaïque* (1962). Noumbe is the third wife of Moustaphe, who has very recently taken a fourth wife. Following the law of the Koran, the husband must treat his four wives equally in all ways and spend the same amount of time with each of them. But Sembene confronts us with reality: Husbands do not treat their wives with equal fairness, and the new wife is almost always the favorite . . .Noumbe remembers how it was to be the favorite and remembers also how she kept the husband beyond her own three days just as the new wife is doing now. She remembers how she cheated the other wives, how she tried to drain the husband of his strength so he would be "no good" to the next woman whom he was to visit. Now it is her turn, and she sees for the first time the viciousness of the competition. Noumbe realizes that she and the other wives are fighting a losing battle and that the husband is always the winner.[5]

Other aspects of inequality in traditional marriages are reflected in images of the barren woman. Pokuwaa, the central figure in *A Woman in Her Prime* by Asare Konadu,[6] is a very successful woman as a farmer, but she is in desperation over her inferior status and dismal future as childless woman. After years of rituals for the treatment of infertility, she ultimately puts a stop to the sacrifices and medicines which are poisoning her existence and finds a new peace through this rebellious act of acceptance of her state. In a tidy little ending, Pokuwaa finally gets pregnant and they all live happily ever after.

Another barren female character who finally conceives is Agom, the number one wife in *Highlife for Lizards* by Onuora Nzekwu.[7] Her new worry is that her child be a boy, so that she may enjoy higher status among her husband's people and finally earn the right to be buried there, for if she produces only female children, her body will be conveyed back to her relatives when she dies.

In contrast to these images which show women's unequal or inferior status, there are also the women of superior abilities like Adebisi, in *The Brave African Huntress*, by Amos Tutuola.[8] Marie Linton-Umeh, in her essay on "The African Heroine,"[9] shows that Adebisi uses magical powers to achieve greatness in the non-traditional role of hunter, out-doing all her brothers and freeing them from the evil beasts which she alone is able to eradicate.

These images of women in narratives dealing with traditional African society, including the jealous co-wives, the barren women, the mothers hoping for sons, and the heroines whose extraordinary abilities lift them to positions of leadership, recur repeatedly in novels about the colonial period. Images of women dealing with those aspects of inequality, in addition to those introduced by colonialist oppressors will emerge from the following analysis of novels situated in the first stages of colonialism, in the period of colonialism in full sway, and during colonialism under siege by movements for independence.

The image of the mother in *The African Child* by Camara Laye is reminiscent in a number of ways of that earlier Malinké mother, Sogolon, the mother of Sundiata: strong in her devotion to duty, and possessed of extraordinary powers in the protection of her son. Camara's highly autobiographical account of a child growing up in a peaceful town in Guinea seemingly unspoiled by the incursions of colonialism projects a strong image of the mother, given equal weight (if not strictly equal time) with the father figure. His mother is strong in her respect for tradition, in the respect she has for others and for herself, and in the great esteem in which she is held by her husband and by all. She is seen as the conserver of ancestral and Muslim traditions: teaching her children respect for family prayers, totems, medicines and rituals; sending her son and daughter to Koranic school, as well as to the government elementary school; serving meals to the men and women separately, but receiving thanks and a bow from all who had eaten. She is seen, also, as proprietor of extraordinary spiritual powers inherited from her smith family: gifts of healing; gifts of extra-sensory perception vis-à-vis her loved ones' troubles; and a special protective relationship with the crocodile, totem of her clan. She plays an important protective role: teaching her child not to play with snakes; checking on him to make sure he was well after the circumcision; chiding her husband about ruining his eyes by forging too much gold; and refusing to give permission for her son to go to Paris for his higher education. If there is any way at all in which this ideally equal partner in the home may be seen to be unequal, it is only that she is unequal to the task of preventing her son's going to France. She realizes, finally, with overflowing grief, that she has to let him go, that nothing will stem the tide of change which colonialism is bringing to their land.

Emile Snyder, in his essay on "Modern African Literature," analyzes the role of the mother on a heightened symbolic plane.[10]

> The image of the African mother is central to an understanding of Camara Laye's novel *L'Enfant Noir* . . .It is she who keeps the family traditions together because she respects them, while dispensing them. It is she who raises her son along the path of the ancestor's ways, so that even later, while a student in Paris, the son sees in the recalled image of his mother a reflection of the dignity of African life.[11]

In contrast to the central position played by the mother figure in *The African Child*, women play very minor parts in Chinua Achebe's novel about the coming of colonialism in Nigeria, with its apocalyptic title, *Things Fall Apart*.[12] The three wives of Okonkwo are merely numbered as part of his acquisitions in the end of the first chapter:

> Okonkwo was clearly cut out for great things. He was still young but he had won fame as the greatest wrestler in the nine villages. He was a wealthy farmer and had two barns full of yams, and had just married his third wife. To crown it all he had taken two titles and had shown incredible prowess in two inter-tribal wars.[13]

His wives are introduced by name, rank, and snippets of character only little by little. Ojiugo, the youngest, is beaten severely (p. 31) for forgetting her husband's dinner hour. Nwoye's mother, the first wife, tries to cover for her. She is always referred to as Nwoye's mother, which should be a term of respect, except that Okonkwo hates what he perceives as Nwoye's "weak character." Ekwefi, his second wife, is not introduced by name until later (p. 40), and much later we learn how it was that she left her first husband to come and live with Okonkwo (p. 103). There are brief glimpses of the wives preparing food for their husband, and helping each other get ready for various big events; but Ekwefi is the only wife whose character is at all developed.

Ekwefi receives more than her equal share of attention from Okonkwo, partly because of her irresistible love for the wrestling hero, but also because of her "changeling" child, her daughter, Ezinma, cherished as the child who finally decided to stay, after Ekwefi had lost ten children, most of them in infancy. Ezinma is a neverending source of delight to Okonkwo for her intelligence, understanding and spunk, and he never ceases wishing under his breath that she had been born a boy.

References by Okonkwo, as well as by other men in the village, to the inferiority of women recur with sufficient regularity to act as a leit-motif, setting the tone for images of inequality perceived through the insecure defensiveness of Okonkwo. Early in the novel, for example, we see Okonkwo worried about supporting his father's household, as well as his own:

> His mother and sisters worked hard enough, but they grew women's crops, like coco-yams, beans and cassava. Yam, the king of crops, was a man's crop.[14]

Later on in the novel, he curses his own weakness with the worst insult he can think of:

> "When did you become a shivering old woman," Okonkwo asked himself, "you, who are known in all the nine villages for your valor in war? How can a man who has killed five men in battle fall to pieces because he has added a boy to their number? Okonkwo, you have become a woman indeed."[15]

In yet another scene, Okonkwo discusses cultural differences stranger than fiction with a neighbor:

> "The world is large," said Okonkwo. "I have even heard that in some tribes a man's children belong to his wife and her family."

> "That cannot be," said Machi. "You might as well say that the woman lies on top of the man when they are making children."[16]

Near the end of the novel, in a supreme irony, Okonkwo names one of his children "Mother is Supreme," based on an Igbo aphorism. The fact that this was done merely out of politeness to his mother's kinsmen, where he had been exiled, was revealed two years later when he named his next child "Nwofia," "Begotten in the Wilderness."[17]

These images of women during the early stages of colonialism, whether functioning in a secondary role in the novel as in *Things Fall Apart*, or playing a major role as in *The African Child*, all function similarly in their society as conservers of tradition. Through good times and adversity, women struggle to protect their children from dangers perceived in the coming of colonialism.

In contrast, the images of women in the following examples of novels about colonialism at its height reflect a new strategy for dealing with the aliens and their culture: the politics of so-called accommodation. No longer able to protect themselves and their children from the dangers of colonialism, Africans practice the politics of survival with a new approach. By cooperating to a certain extent with the colonial oppressors, they acquire sufficient knowledge of alien ways to survive their destructiveness.

The image of the Most Royal Lady in *Ambiguous Adventure* by Cheikh Hamidou Kane[18] reflects the strategy of a powerful Fulani aristocrat of what is today Senegal in dealing with the incursion of French civilization:

> "I have done something which is not pleasing to us and which is not in accordance with our customs. I have asked the women to come to this meeting today. We Diallobé hate that, and rightly, for we think that the women should remain at home. But more and more we shall have to do things which we hate doing, and which do not accord with our customs. It is to exhort you to do one of those things that I have asked you to come to this meeting today.
>
> "I come here to say this to you: I, Most Royal Lady, do not like the foreign school. I detest it. My opinion, nevertheless, is that we should send our children there."[19]

The imposing "queen mother" figure then explains her strategy with powerful earth imagery symbolic of her role as the practical preserver of ancient and Islamic traditions. She compares the children to the seeds which are buried, "killed" in a sense, in the period of hibernation, in order to spring up after the rainy season as the fertile new generation.

The image of the Most Royal Lady is comparable in some ways to that of the mother of *The African Child*. Tall, strong, and dignified in her bearing, she is equally committed to the ancient and to the Islamic traditions of her people.

> The Most Royal Lady, who could well have been six feet tall, had lost none of her impressive bearing, in spite of her age.
>
> The little white gauze veil clung to the oval of a face full of contours . . . it was like a living page from the history of the Diallobé country. Everything that the country treasured of epic tradition could be read there. All the features were in long lines, on the axis of a slightly aquiline nose. The mouth was large and strong, without expression. An extraordinarily luminous gaze bestowed a kind of imperious lustre upon this face. All the rest disappeared under the gauze, which, more than a coiffure would have done, took on here a distinct significance. Islam restrained the formidable turbulence of those features, in the same way that the little veil hemmed them in.[20]

The Most Royal Lady, however, is more than equal to the tasks she undertakes as preserver of traditions. As older sister of the chief of the Diallobé, is was she who had pacified the peoples of the North by her firmness. "The chief of the Diallobé was by nature more inclined to be peaceable. Where he preferred to appeal to understanding, his sister would cut through on the path of authority. 'My brother is not a prince,' she was in the habit of saying, 'he is a sage.'"[21] The most powerful example of this image of strength, however, is her victory over rulers and people alike, in persuading them of the practical necessity of cooperating with the colonial government: seeking self-preservation through calculated self-destruction, by sending their children to the colonialist schools.

Unlike the Most Royal Lady, the female characters in *Houseboy* by Ferdinand Oyono[22] play secondary roles in the novel as well as in their society. They are comparable in some ways to the non-aristocratic, female folk in *Things Fall Apart*. They in no wise attempt to interact with their men on any plane of equality, but rather deal with them from a seemingly supportive stance, in the background of the main action. Behind the scenes, however, the women in *Houseboy* play the politics of collaboration, secretly undermining the power of the colonial oppressors.

The image of women in Oyono's sardonic novel about colonialism at its most brutal heights reflects the politics of intimacy at its most devastating depths. Similar strategies of sexual politics are employed by the African women who are wise and very practical, and by the European women who are silly, vapid, and blindly prejudiced. The degree of their comparative success seems to reflect the quality of their strength of character.

Kalisia, the beautiful, self-sufficient young African woman drifts into the employ of the Commandant with the same earthy, bright insouciance with which she has moved from man to man, black and white, loving and leaving them with a carelessness that bespeaks a viable strategy of survival. Hers is in no way the image of a hapless, helpless creature shunted from man to man in the psychology of dependency. Her actions and reactions rather reflect the feisty image of the successful entrepreneur, very much in control of all her undertakings, and of her choice of clientele.

Sophie, the African mistress of the agricultural engineer, employs a similar strategy of survival, but at times suffers from lack of control over the humiliations she sustains at the hands of the colonials. Hurting physically as well as emotionally one day as she was being jounced all over the back of a truck, Sophie breaks down to Toundi, the young protagonist of *Houseboy*:

> A violent swerve nearly flung us over the side. "Christ," cried Sophie. 'What have they got that I haven't got?' She turned towards me. Two big tears were rolling down her cheeks. I laid my arm on hers. She wiped her eyes with her cloth.
> 'What lovely manners they've got, these whites . . .even if it's only among themselves . . .my arse is just as delicate as the arses of the ladies they have up there in the driver's cabin. . . . '[23]

Another day, Sophie is furious with herself for missing a chance to pick the engineer's pocket for the keys to his strongbox. She explains to Toundi that she's "sick and tired of hearing 'Sophie, don't come today. I've got a European coming to see me at the house', 'Sophie, you can come, the

European has gone', 'Sophie, when you see me with a white lady don't look at me, don't greet me' and all the rest."[24] She continues to wait for her big chance, however, and finally leaves the engineer with nothing in his cashbox and even less understanding of how this could have happened.

Like the African women, the wives of the colonial administrators also control their men by playing up the dependency role, flattering their insatiable and fragile egos with ostensible supportiveness. Behind the scenes, they are vicious in their betrayals of their men, of each other, and of the Africans they victimize as scapegoats. Their petty politics of manipulation through collaboration reflect the narrow minds and shallow souls of the oppressors. The colonial women are playing the same game, but for much smaller stakes than the African women who put their lives on the line in the politics of survival.

These images of women in novels about the hey-day of colonialism in Africa, whether reflecting those dealing from a position of strength as in *Ambiguous Adventure*, or from a secondary position as in *Houseboy*, all demonstrate the same strategies of survival characteristic of oppressed people. They collaborate and accommodate and seemingly accept the power of the colonizers, while studying the situation and biding their time, until the time comes for more direct action.

It is in the novels dealing with the final stages of colonialism in Africa, under siege by movements for independence, that images of women reflect a new, active response to inequality. In *God's Bits of Wood* by Ousmane Sembène,[25] the march of the women in support of the railway strike on the Dakar-Niger line from October, 1948 to March, 1949 is described by A. Adu Boahen in the "Introduction" as a critical point in the colonial period: "the point of the beginnings of mass African nationalist movements and political parties."[26]

The images of women in this dramatic fictionalized account of that historical event reflect a broad spectrum of ages, classes, ethnic groups, occupations and degrees of political awareness. There are many of them, of which ten are composed with a judicious and dramatically effective choice of detail by the master of African cinema of commitment, Ousmane Sembène.

The first we meet are a young schoolgirl, Ad'jibid'ji, and her old grandmother, Niakoro, representing the future generation and the passing generation of African women. The grandmother expresses her malaise about the fastpaced events which have left her far behind. She scolds the child about running messages to and from the meetings of the strikers, as well as about running off to the colonial school.

> "Why are you always poking your nose in the affairs of men? They are preparing a strike, and that's not a thing for you . . .
> "What use is the white man's language to a woman? To be a good mother you have no need of that . . .I have never heard of a white man

who had learned to speak Bambara, or any other language of this
country. But you rootless people think only of learning his, while our
language dies . . .In my time we learned only some verses of the
Koran for our prayers."[27]
    . . .It was this that disturbed and haunted her. In her time the young
people undertook nothing without the advice of their elders, but now,
alone, they were deciding on a strike . . .and she had seen one. A
terrible strike . . .it had taken a husband and a son from her, but no one
even came to seek her advice. Were the ways of the old time gone
forever?[28]

In contrast to the old Niakoro, sitting alone in the courtyard reflecting on
how changing times had changed her people, we see Ramatoulaye, the
capable bustling organizer of her district. "Her responsibilities had become
very great, because the house of which she was the eldest was large: there
were no less than twenty of 'God's bits of wood.'"[29] This expression was the
traditional method, used by the strikers and their supporters, to count heads
without drawing the attention of any unfriendly spirits who might happen to
be listening for names.
    Others who joined the march included Mame Sofi, wife of the guard at
union headquarters, who cooperated with her co-wife Bineta in organizing
activities. There was N'Deye Touti, the committed young student whose
love for strike leader Bakayoko would have led her to abandon her
principles and become his second wife, had his stronger stance against
polygamy not prevailed. We see a very young girl, Anta, the "little
watcher" standing sentinel before the unsuspecting eyes of the enemy while
her mother, Houdia M'Baye hustles food for neighbors involved in the
strike. The most developed and consequently most powerful character is
Penda. This radical young woman was chosen to lead the women's march
because of her self-reliance and objective distance from her neighbors, as
evidenced by incidents of sexual liberation which had everybody talking.
As we see her grow from strength to strength, we trace as well the
development of her seemingly passive but calm and effective counterpart,
Maïmouna, the blind market woman. An established figure in the community,
her compassion for one of the strikers leads her to another type of sexual
liberation, and motherhood of illegitimate twins, Maïmouna's calm commitment to the march, in spite of hunger, cold, pain, exhaustion and the
sacrifice of one of her children to the trampling horde of marchers,
combined with Penda's active, militant command, and ultimate sacrifice of
her own life to the soldiers' bullets, rally the thousands of women from every
walk of life, and every village and language along the march from Thiès to
Dakar. In the face of the staggering odds facing this act of revolt against
colonial opression, the differences of languages, the distance to be covered,
the poverty and the sheer starvation, the participants supported and rallied

one another to renewed commitment to their common cause.

> Someone would say, "Let's go to see so-and-so. Perhaps she still has
> a little millett." But most of the time so-and-so could only answer 'No, I
> have nothing more. Wait, and I'll come with you." Then, carrying a
> baby against a flaccid breast, she would join the procession . . .
> And the men began to understand that if the times were bringing
> forth a new breed of men, they were also bringing forth a new breed of
> women.[30]

A similar change in the images of women reflecting the changing times, as
colonialism reached its last bloody throes in Africa, can be seen in roles of
the women characters in *A Grain of Wheat* by Ngugi wa Thiong'o.[31]

Instead of a single dramatic event like the march of the women in Senegal,
in Kenya we see the bloody and protracted struggles of the "Mau-Mau"
freedom fighters, and the complex levels of awareness and involvement on
the part of the women. The two poles of that broad spectrum of involvement
are represented by the characters of Wambui and Mumbi.

Wambui becomes a leader of women's revolutionary activities, participating fully in the risks and decisions of the movement. It is she who is chosen
by General R(ussia) to be the judge of Mugo the traitor in the dramatic but
painfully anticlimactic aftermath of the fight for freedom. It is therefore she
who feels most acutely the grey muddied emotions facing all the women and
men who have survived the days of bold action in the cause of right, to face
the years of painful healing of a society torn assunder by accommodation to
and revolution against colonial opression.

> Wambui sat on and watched the drizzle and the grey mist for a few
> minutes. Darkness was creeping into the hut. Wambui was lost in a
> solid consciousness of a terrible anti-climax to her activities in the
> fight for freedom. Perhaps we should not have tried [Mugo], she
> muttered. Then she shook herself, trying to bring her thoughts to the
> present. I must light the fire. First I must sweep the room. How dirt can
> so quickly collect in a clean hut! But she did not rise to do anything.[32]

Her counterpart, Mumbi, represents the collaborators, those whose lives
were more liveable as long as the oppressor was in control, and who now
face the painful process of reintegration into a community which was
always hostile, but which is now free of fear of the oppressor/protector.
Mumbi is the wife of Gikonyo, one of the freedom fighters now released
from detention camp and convalescing in the hospital. It will take hime time
to learn of the extenuating circumstances which led his wife to accept food
from Karanja, and to become the mother of Karanja's child—Karanja, his
old friend—Karanja, the collaborator.

For her part, Mumbi will also need time to open herself up to her husband, to try to bridge the chasm wreaked by the effects of colonialism. As she speaks to him, he hears a message behind her words, and sees behind her face the image of a changing Mumbi.

> 'No, Gikonyo. People try to rub out things, but they cannot. Things are not so easy. What has passed between us is too much to be passed over in a sentence. We need to talk, to open our hearts to one another, examine them, and then together plan the future we want. But now, I must go, for the child is ill.
>
> 'Will you—will you come tomorrow? he asked, unable to hide his anxiety and fear. He knew, at once, that in future he would reckon with her feelings, her thoughts, her desires—a new Mumbi.[33]

In the changing images of women in African novels about the colonial period, from the mother protecting her children and her culture against the first incursions of alien ways, to those who sought more practical approaches to preservation through accommodation with colonialism in full sway, to those who found themselves changed by the roles they played in the nationalist struggles against colonialism, reflections of African women's responses to inequality mirror the progressive movements characteristic of the psychology of oppression.

In order to lend a perspective of historical depth to images of women in novels dealing with colonial times, it would be productive to take a look at those in novels about Africa since independence. Many of these depict women in traditional supportive roles, but with a new dimension of political significance. The women in *A Man of the People*[34] by Chinua Achebe resemble the wives, mothers and lovers in novels about traditional and colonial times, but with one important difference. Their relationships with "Chief the Honourable Micah A. Nanga, M.P." all have political ramifications. His wife is as unhappy as any other might be about her husband's relationships with other women, but when his political career is threatened by those who wanted to break up his pending marriage to Edna, the beautiful young second-wife-to-be, Mrs. Nanga betrayed them. Elsie, the girlfriend of the narrator Odili, is seduced by the old man's power and prestige, and even the village women playing traditional roles as dancers and singers of praise songs are now mobilized for the political campaign.

> Five or six dancing groups were performing at different points in the compound. The popular 'Ego Women's Party' wore a new uniform of expensive accra cloth. In spite of the din you could still hear as clear as a bird the high-powered voice of their soloist, whom they admiringly nicknamed 'Grammar-Phone'. . . .

She was now praising Micah's handsomeness, which she likened to the perfect, sculpted beauty of a carved eagle, and his popularity which would be the envy of the proverbial traveller-to-distant-places who must not cultivate enmity on his route.[35]

The note of warning here might well have been heeded by the narrator. As a traveller-to-be, he needed to beware of incurring the enmity of so popular a man of the people. Whatever Chief Nanga's limitations regarding fiscal responsibility, morals, and service to his constituency, he knew how to win friends and influence his people.

In addition to the images of women playing traditional roles, those of women with their own careers also take on a new political significance. One of the most frequent examples is that of the market women whose importance goes far beyond that of the traditional small trader using the egg money for extra household expenses. In *The Ashanti Doll*[36] by Francis Bebey, the central characters are Ghanaian market women shown after giving their vast resources and powerful organization to elect "the Doctor" as Prime Minister. They are disgruntled by his neglect of their interests in policy decisions affecting commerce.

"You have to take my place here, child of my heart, that's essential. I thought you had understood that long ago. You know, to be a market woman is important. She is a person who has a real part to play in the life of the country. She is the backbone of the country, child of my heart."

"Yes, she makes up the country and then lets herself be governed by idiots more cunning than herself. Why isn't there a market woman in an important position in our country?"

"But, Edna, you can't be both at the market and in an office at the same time!"

"Especially if you can neither read nor write, nor do any of the things that people generally do in offices."

"That may be a good reason. But that doesn't prevent the market women being active in every sphere in the country and their union being the most important. My child, face facts: could the Doctor, for example, ever have come to power without the agreement, without the active support of the market women?"

"Mom, that's true. However, you must admit that, since he's been in power, the Doctor hasn't done much to show the market women that he's grateful for the campaign they waged on his behalf. I would even say that quite the reverse is true, if I think of your own grievances, and that the life of the market women has hardly improved since the Doctor formed his government."

"Because he included in his government only members of his family or men of his party. That's politics, child of my heart, what can you do about it?"[37]

What Mom decided to do about it was to organize a demonstration by the market women in support of a member of their union. Mrs. Amiofi's commercial license had been illegally revoked for political reasons. Because of her association with a leading member of the opposition party, when he was arrested her permit was revoked without any justification whatsoever.

The influence of the market women's union in the eventual erosion of support for the Doctor (Nkrumah) and his removal from office are referred to but not depicted in this novel dealing with early years of independence.

> In these circumstances, it must be recognized that questions like the Amiofi affair demonstrated clearly to the Doctor that his team and his Party were less imbued with the same idea of democracy, and therefore gradually sharpened his authoritarian tendencies, leading to crises which were to culminate, later, in the historic outcome which is familiar to the reader.
>
> But let us return to the days when an injustice done to a market woman still profoundly troubled the Prime Minister.[38]

In addition to the expanded political role of market women, another changing image of women with political ramifications is that of the "good-time" girls. Beyond the traditional roles of village beer-makers and single women, the introduction of prostitution is shown as a legacy of colonialism in post-independence Africa.

For example, in *Ripples in the Pool* by Rebeka Njau,[39] Selina represents the debilitating aftermath of colonialism on some independent young women pursuing an education or career, sidetracked by the easy money and good times offered by foreigners in the big city. Similarly, in *Petals of Blood* by Ngugi wa Thiong'o,[40] the political ramifications of Wanja's slide into prostitution are presented in heavy ideological terms:

> "KCO and Imperialism stand for the rich against the poor. They take from the poor and that's why they hate to see the poor organize and you are helping them. . .Whatever you are, you have chosen sides . . .we must struggle for a world . . .in which the wealth of our land shall belong to us all, in which we shall all be workers for one another's happiness and well-being."
>
> She had chosen. This she could not now hide from herself. . .In doing so she had murdered her own life and now she took her final burial in property and degradation as a glorious achievement. She

tried to look at this coolly, without this time shifting the blame onto others.

She could not now return to a previous state of innocence. But she could do something about her present circumstances.[41]

Wanja sees suddenly that she does have other options. She chooses to turn her back on a lucrative trade, and to take a strong stand against the perpetrators of economic oppression in her town.

Also noteworthy in this period of renewal of images of women in African literature is the entry of African women writers into the publishing market. In Ama Ata Aidoo's short stories *No Sweetness Here*,[42] modern Ghanaian women in the village and in the city lead complex lives in which many seemingly picayune details take on a political significance. In the lead story entitled significantly "Everything Counts," the wig assumes a symbolic importance representing the temptation of facile materialism and imitation of Western mores:

> 'But what has wearing wigs got to do with revolution?' 'A lot sister,' they would say. 'How?' she would ask, struggling not to understand. 'Because it means that we have no confidence in ourselves.[43]

Aidoo's works depict the delicate balance in daily decision-making by women in Africa as elsewhere today. The complex images of women in this collection reflect conflicting objectives juggled by women pursuing what they find of value in traditional and modern roles.

In comparison with these images of women in novels from East and West Africa, it is instructive to see the politicization of women's roles in novels by South African writers in exile. Examples from South Africa were omitted from this study of novels about colonial times vis-à-vis traditional and post-independence societies. The struggle for liberation has yet to see African peoples there in control of their destiny.

Yet, images of women in traditional supportive roles, as well as independent entrepreneurs and urban free women also carry important political overtones in novels about southern African peoples still in colonial bondage. A glimpse of several novels by South African authors reveals images similar to those from post-independence African nations. In *A Wreath for Udomo*[44] by Peter Abrahams, for example, we see again the powerful market women at work in support of an aspiring politician. Selina the market woman plays a major role in the rise and fall of Udomo's regime in the early years of independence.

Similarly, political ramifications complicate the entrepreneurship of loose women in South African fiction. For example, in "Life,"[45] a short story by Bessie Head, the central character is a woman named Life who returns to Botswana from Johannesburg and causes considerable social upheaval in her quiet village by opening a house of prostitution. Even her beer-making women friends were taken aback because no one had ever thought of sex for sale, and the novelty of it turns the village upside down until Life's untimely death. In contrast, in *Mine Boy*[46] by Peter Abrahams, women like Leah who make illegal beer in Johannesburg also play a strong supportive role in tending the wounds of bodies and souls of victims of apartheid.

Even marriage becomes a political act in *Maru*[47] by Bessie Head. The wedding of Margaret Cadmore (a Masarwa, or Bushman) to Maru (the chief of the ruling Batswana of the village) opens a new perspective of freedom for the enslaved people of her ethnic group.

> When people of the Masarwa tribe heard about Maru's marriage to one of their own, a door silently opened on the small, dark airless room in which their souls had been shut for a long time. The wind of freedom, which was blowing throughout the world for all people, turned and flowed into the room.
>
> People like the Batswana, who did not know that the wind of freedom had also reached people of the Masarwa tribe, were in for an unpleasant surprise because it would be no longer possible to treat Masarwa people in an inhuman way without getting killed yourself.[48]

This complex collage of images of women in African fiction reflects complex realities, but if an image is worth a thousand words, the tableau of a thousand women in the vast panorama of African literature projects a powerful picture. Beyond the inequalities seen in novels about traditional, colonial or post-independence societies, these images communicate a strength of purpose of women more than equal to the tasks they set themselves, vis-à-vis families, friends, careers, communities and nation.

NOTES

1. Christina Ama Ata Aidoo, *The Dilemma of a Ghost* (New York: Collier, 1965).
2. Karen Chapman, Introduction to *The Dilemma of a Ghost*, by Christina Ama Ata Aidoo (New York: Collier, 1965), pp. 7-8.
3. Andrea B. Rushing, "Images of Black Women in Modern African Poetry: An Overview" in *Sturdy Black Bridges: Visisions of Black Women in Literature*, edited by Roseann P. Bell, Bettye J. Parker, and Beverly Guy-Sheftall (Garden City, NY: Anchor, 1979), pp. 18-24.
4. D. T. Niane, ed., Sundiata: *An Epic of Old Mali* (London: Longman, 1965).
5. Sonia Lee, "The Awakening of the Self in the Heroines of Ousmane Sembène," in *Sturdy Black Bridges*, Bell *et al*, eds., pp. 54-55.

6. S. Asare Konadu, *A Woman in Her Prime* (London: Heinemann, 1967).
7. Onuora Nzekwu, *Highlife for Lizards* (London: Hutchinson, 1965).
8. Amos Tutuola, *The Brave African Huntress* (London: Faber and Faber, 1958).
9. Marie Linton-Umeh, "The African Heroine," in *Sturdy Black Bridges*, Bell *et al.*, pp. 42-44.
10. Emile Snyder, "Modern Africa in Literature," in *Africa* edited by Phyllis M. Martin and Patrick O'Meara (Bloomington, Indiana: Indiana University Press, 1977), pp. 331-347.
11. Ibid., p. 334.
12. Chinua Achebe, *Things Fall Apart* (Greenwich, Conn: Fawcett Crest, 1959).
13. Ibid., pp. 11-12.
14. Ibid., p. 25.
15. Ibid., pp. 62-63.
16. Ibid., p. 71.
17. Ibid., p. 151.
18. Cheikh Hamidou Kane, *Ambiguous Adventure* (New York: Collier, 1969), copyright 1963 by Walker and Co., first published in French as *L'aventure ambiguë* in Paris by René Julliard in 1962.
19. Ibid., p. 41.
20. Ibid., p. 19.
21. Ibid.
22. Ferdinand Oyono, *Houseboy* (London: Heinemann, 1966), African Writers Series, John Reed, translator; first published in French as *Une Vie de Boy* in Paris by Editions Julliard, in 1960.
23. Ibid., p. 45.
24. Ibid., p. 31.
25. Ousmane Sembène, *God's Bits of Wood* (Garden City, New York: Anchor, 1970), translated by Francis Price, originally published in French as *Les Bouts de bois de Dieu*.
26. Ibid., p. 13.
27. Ibid., p. 37.
28. Ibid., p. 34.
29. Ibid., p. 84.
30. Ibid., p. 76.
31. James Ngugi, *A Grain of Wheat* (London: Heinemann, 1967).
32. Ibid., pp. 275-76.
33. Ibid., p. 280.
34. Chinua Achebe, *A Man of the People* (Garden City, NY: Doubleday Anchor Books, 1967).
35. Ibid., p. 1.
36. Francis Bebey, *The Ashanti Doll* (London: Heinemann, 1978).
37. Ibid., p. 20.
38. Ibid., p. 134.
39. Rebeka Njau, *Ripples in the Pool* (London: Heinemann, 1975).
40. Ngugi wa Thiong'o, *Petals of Blood* (London: Heinemann, 1977).
41. Ibid., pp. 327-328.
42. Ama Ata Aidoo, *No Sweetness Here* (Garden City, NY: Doubleday, 1971).

43. Ibid., p. 2.
44. Peter Abrahams, *A Wreath for Udomo* (New York: Alfred A. Knopf, 1956).
45. Bessie Head, "Life" in *The Collector of Treasures* (London: Heinemann, 1977), pp. 37-46.
46. Peter Abrahams, *Mine Boy* (New York: Macmillan, 1970).
47. Bessie Head, *Maru* (New York: McCall Publishing Company, 1971).
48. Ibid., p. 126-127.

Women in a Man's Exploration of His Country, His World: Chraïbi's Succession Ouverte

Rafika Merini

While it has been said that the works of North African writer, Driss Chraïbi are preoccupied with women[1], it is my thesis that that is so only in a limited way. While accepting the statement that women play a major role in his fiction, I would argue that women do not have the author's full, dedicated attention, but are often limited to being communication channels for his deviated cult of the mother and his own angst. The mother figure and/or the cult of the mother is definitely a central issue in the North African psyche, and is certainly evidenced in Chraïbi's semi-autobiographical work *Succession Ouverte* as well as in *Le Passé Simple* and *La Civilisation, ma Mère! . . .* [2] where it is a recurrent theme. However, I would argue that Chraïbi's literature keeps tugging at this concern without eludicating it. A. Bouhdibi characterizes the cult of the mother as "une des clés maîtresses pour la compréhension de la personnalité de base des sociétés arabo-musulmanes" ["one of the key factors in the understanding of the basic personality of Arabo-Muslim societies"][3].* I will be more concerned, however, with how the author uses this theme with a different ultimate result in mind than simply understanding Arab cultures. In *La civilisation, ma Mère! . . .*, both mother and son evolve from a restricted world to one where

*Translations are the author's.

45

their fantasies are given full expression; the mother's troubles strangely parallel the son's, and the hero frees himself at the same time that he frees his mother. Would it then be appropriate to speak of an Oedipal complex "mal resolu" with J. Déjeux?[4] That is not a possibility which I propose to explore here, although it could be one of the major obstacles in the coverage of the female condition by male authors. That theory would also explain the focus on the mother as a facade, an excuse for focusing on one's self. My assumption is that women are not usually portrayed to objectively represent themselves, rather, they are used to convey what the author needs to say about himself and his malaise.

Underdevelopment (comprising the search for identity) constitutes the second and most important unifying theme of *Succession Ouverte*. This theme forms a looking glass through which a whole society is analyzed: the "Seigneur" (the father/patriarch) is the live illustration of it. He represents a once powerful society which crumbled and left behind poverty, lethargy, pharisaism, and corruption. The mother, who remains as nameless as she is powerless, is the woman whose odyssey the writer will manipulate to metaphorically convey his own feelings of helplessness, frustration and despair sprung from a common background.

The son in revolt talks through his mother, by a strange procuration. In a skilled twist, their destinies are joined in the author's mind. It is this confusion which detracts from the socio-literary value of *Succession Ouverte*. Both the mother and the son suffer under the same yoke. They both have had to, and still will have to (in spite of his death) bend to the wishes of the "Seigneur," their lord and master who presides on top of their culture, its weight crushing them. Driss, stricken by this realization acknowledges: "il a fallu qu'il meure pour que je réalise soudain que j'étais un être vivant". ["It was necessary that he die for me to come to the sudden realization that I was a living being."] (Pt. II, Ch. xi; p. 182). The nearly unbearable malaise engendered by the situation is pervasive. But the author would be more convincing if he did not put the general disarray in masculine terms as a rule. The mother passively complies. Ignoring herself and her feelings the way society ignores her, she merely becomes the mirror of her son's agony. Her pain is compounded by the fact that there is no escape for her aggravations and affliction. As for similarities, we see them both clinging to the same pain-inducing roots, their fate hanging from a thin weathered thread. The mother's persistent good will only leads to acute feelings of uselessness, lack of importance and influence.

From an exclusively literary standpoint, there is nothing wrong with this. It makes the novel more complex and fascinating, especially when one knows what a crucial part Chraïbi's own mother played in his past and the large place she still claims in his private world. It is when the socio-critical values inherent in this kind of literature are introduced that one is forced to take the author to task. Chraïbi is a feminist. He is one of a handful of male

North African authors dealing with women's status. His contribution is unique. His influence—although I concede that his number of North African readers might be quite small at the present time—is great among those who do read his works. They themselves are often highly placed and have influence (or sheer power) over others. That is why, although I greatly enjoy and appreciate Chraïbi's work, as a feminist and a socio-literary critic I must raise a few questions, hoping that I can contribute something of value to it.

The climax mentioned at the beginning finds the mother portrayed by the author as being utterly unable to directly express her feelings. We guess what they might be through what her son feels looking at her after a sixteen year separation and his father's death.[5] The extreme hardening in the hero— Chraïbi's lack of disinterestedness notwithstanding—amounts to a very dramatic and effective description of what any Moroccan woman would inspire in a loving son at her husband's death when the latter had always treated her like a child. She has spent her life in a children's (her children's) world, cut-off from everything else, voiceless and vacant (except when pregnant; which happens to her more than a half-dozen times). From what we already know about Moroccan women in general, Ferdi's mother is genuine. Why not let her speak for herself at this, the most revealing and intense moment of the book? The author's main concern must then be construed to be his own feelings transmitted through the male hero's character.[6] This is only another instance of women given second place. Again, they are made to be the means and not the end.

We are told that for years, she was "espiègle et vive au dépit de n'importe quelle souffrance," ["mischievous and spirited whatever pain and suffering she was going through"] (Pt. I, Ch. iii; p. 68) but we cannot believe it. It just does not fit in with all we know about her. After all, *Succession Ouverte* is not *La Civilisation, ma Mère!* . . . where fantasy and wishful thinking are the avowed rule. Once more, reality has been shirked.

When we read ". . . . je savais que quelque chose était mort en elle," ["I knew that something inside her was dead"] it strikes us as such an understatement and stereotypical way of expediting the action that the author's whole description seems preposterous (Pt. I, Ch. iii; p. 72). We see through the author's underhanded trick when he adds a few pages later: "J'évitais soigneusement ses yeux" ["I carefully avoided her eyes"] (Pt. I, Ch. iii; p. 77). There is no need for further clarification. In my eyes, it seems that Driss is primarily engrossed by his own lingering dependence on the "Seigneur". His brother Nagib is not only speaking for himself when he posits: "Il était notre maître mai de fer, mais aussi notre nourricier et notre dignité" ["He was Master with the iron grip, but also our provider and the source of our dignity"] (Pt. II, Ch. v; p. 109). Driss and his brothers have been caught in the same trap as their mother. Do they have a future of their own or will they forever be living in the past? Nagib's embittered questioning restates the ultimate question: when will Moroccans shake off the yoke of the past? This question is an anguished one since its answer seems to be: never. It is reflected in the mother's eyes that Driss refuses to look at, while inwardly staring at them. They contain ". . . une intense angoisse . . . " ["an intense anxiety . . . "] (Pt. I, Ch. iii; p. 67). In a face drained of all life, they hurt and shame him not only because of what she has been through as a woman, but also because of the shackled and decaying culture behind them. Driss is still a part of her (as she is a part of him), and a part of his culture, inescapably.

Nagib, who bought all of his society's values, revered and loved the old man so much that he pictures everyone including his family as undeserving pests who helped cause the fall of his father, for him a kind of Hercules, a superior being and protector to whom life itself, as well as other beings, should have deferred.[7] Driss shares these feelings somehow until the sick "Seigneur" comes back. He is "inside" the tape recorder, not weakened at all, not disarmed in the least, still carrying his final instructions for his sons, their mother and all his other dependents. He now will tell them how to live out the rest of their lives. Driss thinks this whole set-up is hilarious but it is not so for anyone else, so he acquiesces. Nagib's brawn at the service of God (and the "Seigneur") will suffice indeed to convince him that the situation must be taken seriously. Meanwhile, he has been healed and freed: "Mais j'étais déchaîné, exorcisé" ["But I was freed of my chains, exorcised"] Pt. II, Ch. vi; p. 124.)

The mother best exemplifies again the ambient atmosphere of dread and muted revolt. She is "the Moroccan mother" or "ras el mehna," the root and receiver of all pain and suffering scrutinized from outside.

> "Tassée dans un coin, ma mère pleurait sans bruit et sans larmes, comme seules peuvent le faire des femmes qui ont pleuré toute leur vie redevenue petite et infantile dès qu'avait retenti la voix du Seigneur" (Pt. II, Ch. vi; p. 125).
>
> ["Crouched in a corner, my mother was crying without sobbing, without shedding tears in the way that only women who have cried all their life know how. She had become small and childlike again as soon as 'the seigneur's' voice had made itself heard."]

Her plight does not end with the death of her husband: he has arranged for her to stay dependent on him even in death, going against laws and customs in order to accomplish this. Driss Chraïbi must have been aware that he was providing the social critic with a perfect example of the discrepancy between theory and practice, showing how mores can be even more archaic than religious laws, which are themselves often used according to people's preferences and priorities.[8]

The mother placidly performs her duties at the funeral, probably not caring about anything anymore: "Elle leur répond au hasard, par mono-syllables" ["She responds to them haphazardly uttering monosyllables only."] (Pt. II, Ch. v; pp. 92-93). As for Driss, his present feelings are summed up in an often quoted passage which has led many to think it was a final admission of defeat and impotent rage in a world where he finds himself left unprovided for.

> "Jamais, jamais plus je n'irai à la recherche de cerveaux, de vérités écrites, de vérités synthétiques, d'assemblages d'idées hybrides qui n'étaient rien que des idées" ["Never again shall I go looking for brains; for written truths; for synthetic truths; for assemblies of hybrid ideas that were nothing but ideas . . . "]

The contrasted behaviors of the mother and her son converge to create a whole where she takes the passive part, reduced to simply reflecting her son's emotions. Strong impressions of malaise and confusion accumulate. The hero is too preoccupied with his own feelings to focus on those of his mother.

Madini, (another brother), asks: "Je voudrais savoir pourquoi ils deviennent des animaux" ["I would like to know why they become animals."] (Pt. I, Ch. iv; p. 85). The revolting, unacceptable answer readily springs from the Koran and seems to leave no alternatives: "That is God's will" (Pt. II, Ch. vi; p. 119). This invitation and justification of fatalism, determinism, and stagnation can of course also be applied to underdevelopment. There is then no need to blame the way women, the weak, and the poor are treated. Nagib has the last word however: "Plus on a le ventre plein et plus on est croyant" ["The fuller one's stomach, the more one believes in God."] (Pt. II, Ch. vi; p. 120). He is clearly implying that faith is only a matter of convenience and expediency.

The "Seigneur" knows that desiring freedom (as Chraïbi does for women in a highly idealistic manner) is an entirely different matter from actually acquiring it. His synthesis only seems simple: "L'aide aux pays éternellement sous-developpés" ["Assistance to the eternally under-developed countries"]. (Pt. II, Ch. vi; p. 135). This theme of underdevelopment, which is closely linked to that of the oppression of women, clearly spells lack of balance, therefore unease, malaise: a complete loss of direction as in the case of Nagib; a resentful resignation close to a desertion for Driss while at the same time spitting on his "pariah's" life, always feeling the big split in his personality. Chraïbi did progress from North Africa to more universal themes and concerns in subsequent books but he did not desert his native culture having incorporated it into his work.

La "féminitude" is given the appearance of a convenient complement to "l'arabité," an abstracted but timely vehicle for the hero's "mal de vivre" and remaining dependence. How else can the "Seigneur's" words about his wife (left helpless in the midst of her restless sons) be explained except as a substitute for the male's own sense of failure?

> "A son âge, l'émancipation, le sentiment d'une liberté souveraine ne signifieraient rien pour elle, sinon un déséquilibre" ["At her age, liberation, the feeling of a sovereign freedom within herself, meant nothing to her, except perhaps a destabilization."] (Pt. II, Ch. vi; p. 132).

The hero should be aware that the "Seigneur's" argument is the oppressor's standard weapon: giving the illusion that the status quo is permanent and that it is the only sensible way of being. These are insidious means to keep the status quo, to discourage reaction in advance, to nip it in the bud: to speak in the name of those who might want change (denying them freedom of expression) and to say that they really could not handle, or profit from, any change. The author does not make it clear that this is the ultimate form of paternalism and demagoguery combined. Indirectly the feeling for the sons' dependence is reinforced; technically speaking, Chraïbi is using the mother to emphasize it. Both the mother and her sons lack an identity upon which to base freedom and responsibility. Here, the search for identity extends into an exploration of the two cultures that have failed to provide one.

The father's criticism is to the point when he blames them for making freedom just another possession. As Madini assumes the functions of the "Seigneur" and their by-products (responsibility, dignity, power, paternalism and stagnation) he gradually will come to represent, almost in spite of himself, everything that he distrusted and disavowed in the past. His option is worse since, unlike the "Seigneur," he had a real choice. He will keep "le souvenir lancinant d'un idéal révolutionnaire, d'année en année." [the painful rememberance of a revolutionary ideal, year after year.] He will also carry the dead past with him, thus becoming one with it, "une dépouille mortelle" ["mortal remains"] (Pt. II, Ch. xi; p. 183). He will be the unwelcome symbol of a dying civilization. Tellingly enough, he is specifically put in charge of his child-mother who will not receive any money. The "Seigneur's" will regarding her takes precedence over God's laws. Hence the "Seigneur" betrays himself. He admits that, at least for her, "nous voulons espérer que nous ne sommes pas encore mort" ["we would like to think that we are not dead yet."] (Pt. II, Ch. vi; p. 132). He cannot release his hold on her even when only his spirit remains.

What this amounts to is protracted dependence for the mother since it is in his father's name that her son will take care of her. She will be the only one who will not acquire more freedom as a result of the "lord's" death. She represents the predicament that a family (the nucleus of a whole society) finds itself in when it refuses to look forward to the future and takes refuge in the past instead.

The chapter "Ma Mère" would by itself furnish ample material for a study of the everyday reality of Moroccan women.[9] Characteristically, when the mother is finally allowed a monologue, she makes an uninterrupted speech, a plea for understanding. The only answer she gets is a desperate request on the part of her son that she stop her long litany. He too has no answer to the dilemma turned sour.

When the mother says: "J'ai trop de bile dans le ventre," ["I have too much bile in my belly"] we are reminded that bile (choler) used to be considered the reason for anger, irritability and bitterness in the Middle Ages (Pt. II, Ch. ix; p. 166). Her physical and mental health must be seen as a result of a life of abuse and indifference. Two other imaginary cardinal humors (blood and phlegm) were respectively attributed by the author to Driss (for his restrained passion followed by violent outbursts) and to the "Seigneur" for his calm and composure.

Chraïbi coins a perfect appellation for Driss' character: "la violence de la sensibilité . . . ;; ["The violence of sensitivity"] (Pt. II, Ch. iii; p. 33). He means that Driss' callousness comes from sensitivity.

The mother's principal complaint is a habitual one. She invokes the isolation, silence, and ignorance that surround her and sap her strength.

> "Et j'étais là, moi, à perpétuité, entre un homme qui ne disait pas un mot et des démons qui ne me disaient rien, jamais" ["There I was, perpetually caught between a man who did not say a word to me, and demons who never ever told me anything."] (Pt. II, Ch. ix; p. 167).

Chraïbi could be credited with objective and efficient reporting at this point, if he had made the mother specify that she strongly resented the shroud of silence around her since it was a permanent situation, mostly engineered by her closest relatives.

From the otherwise realistic account, we are left with a painful reminder: the Seigneur knew his sons well (and how they would act) yet he still chose to entrust his wife to them. In doing so, he is denying her all feeling and humanity. Chraïbi seems to support such conduct when he makes her say apologetically that she grew to actually like her prison. She outlives her husband but she can only be a "vestige" of the dying past in the patriarch's own words (Pt. II, C. vi; p. 133). When his illness made him leave, her husband didn't even tell her his destination or if he would return. He removed himself from his family for his last five years, and became a recluse while awaiting death. The old woman explains that childbearing was the only thing that comforted her and gave her a sense of identity and fulfillment since her children could at least understand her for a few years. They then became precocious little "men" in a society that demands it of boys (Pt. II,

Ch. ix; p. 169). She begs Driss to understand that she is trying hard to figure out the world with her limited means of knowledge.[10] The echoes of the son's own fears of lack of creativity and of loneliness and loss are loudest where they tell of their mutual suffering.

> "Je voulais bien qu'on me protège, qu'on me colonise, me civilise, me donne un brevet d'existence, mais ça?" ["I went along willingly, seeking the protection, colonization, civilization, mere acknowledgement of my presence on earth that were promised me but what was I left with in the end?"] (Pt. I, Ch. ii; p. 34).

They also represent the national feeling towards colonization at the start of the French infiltration into Morocco.

The chapter "Ma Mère" remains a sincere attempt—and a most compelling one—to portray a woman trying to express herself and to make a case for herself. Chraïbi could not ignore any further the crucial difference between the son's mental prison and the mother's, whose entrapment is grounded in reality. Chraïbi luckily lets her say in plain words that she has been living in a real prison:

> "Une prison, petite ou grande, est toujours une prison" ["A jail, whether it is large or small is still a jail."] (Pt. II, Ch. ix; p. 171).

This lifts her torture above that of her son and temporarily makes her stand for herself, apart from her son's malaise. The urgency of that malaise renders him temporarily unable to bear the unveiled, unobstructed pain that finally overflows and spills from his mother's innermost self.

The father ultimately had to put an end to his life: the cancer in his body took residence within his mind and brought down the seemingly unimpeachable fortress he was. Driss, although thus far he has received no part of the inheritance, is in charge of solving the puzzle that his father concocted. The astute father knew his son would be present, and the feelings that he would harbor.[11] In the same manner that he had found a way to directly reach his successors through the grave, the Seigneur will now guide Driss in his dispirited wanderings. Driss' continuing dialogue with the old man might breathe some new life into him. He is worn out by the adversities and contradictions of his ethnic background and his aspirations, and simply yearns to returns to his "tribe" suggesting the way the body of a dead soldier would be returned to be buried in his native land. Driss' own admission of defeat leads him to exclaim in a passage mentioned before in this chapter that truth belongs inside the voice of religion, Islam, "en dépit de l'immense héritage d'incrédulité que j'avais reçu de l'Occident" ["Despite the immense incredulity I had inherited from the West"] (Pt. I, Ch. iv; p. 81).

One is tempted to interpret this brief confession of faith as a mere coincidence. Such an effusive and hasty decision and feverish outpouring coming at the time when the hero is weakened by his grief over his father's death is not convincing. Driss is at the burial site during a soothing, merciful chant promising forgiveness and oblivion; the temptation is great therefore to see the entire nagging puzzle as but one of this life's petty preoccupations. The end of all evil is what appeals most to this abused audience. Driss is well aware of that fact. His denial of all idealism outside of religion is thus tainted: no other ideology wins him over, and like a prisoner subjected to torture, he gives in under duress.

His mother took no part in this event (although D. Chraïbi mentions that "hommes, femmes et enfants" were in attendance) at the funeral (Pt. I, Ch. iv; p. 81). As a woman relative, tradition forbids her to attend burials. She does not even appear to provide the background and complement of her son's lack of peace of mind. Once again, she is completely excluded. She cannot share in public functions. This observation leads to the next question: is there ever a true connection between a man and a woman in this book, or are their mental and physical beings forever separate and unequal?

It must be acknowledged, in Chraïbi's defense, that one woman is portrayed relatively favorably in such a situation of communion. It is Safia, Jaad's wife, the shack dweller who goes so far as to speak up for her husband—but not for herself. The female image she projects is typically one of complete self-denial and sacrifice for her husband's sake.[12] Such love by a Moroccan woman for a man is not only unusual and significant in its unabashed avowal, it is downright rash and adventurous. She says she loves him "plus que mes yeux" ["more than my own eyes"] and "plus que mes enfants" [more than my own children] breaking with a long-established tradition for women to see future security and salvation in their children, not in their husbands (Pt. II, Ch. viii; p. 161).[13]

The merging of Jaad and Safia in the destitute lifestyle he opted to share with her is not free of unconscious double standards. His trials take precedence and justify her seven unwanted pregnancies.[14] This hint by the author aiming at the lack of availability of contraceptive information and methods, shows that he does not condone a state of affairs which is unfortunately the norm. No mention is made of the woman's sexuality and her physical appearance is dispatched in three or four sentences (Pt. II, Ch. iii; p. 160). A lively but distancing use of dialogue sets in.

The description of "l'étrangère" [the female stranger] had been more erotic and tantalizing: "une longue chevelure couleur de bronze soulevée et tordue par le vent..." ["long heavy locks of hair the color of bronze, picked up and twisted by the wind"] (Pt. II, Ch. ii; p. 46). At first, the author had led us to think that she might be "frigid" (thus casting the all-powerful male curse upon her) but he finally lets her "passionate" feelings show through. J. Déjeux did not seem to have fully realized how much truth there is to his statement that "les problèmes sexuels sont passés sous silence . . . " ["sexual problems are brushed aside . . . "] (Pt. I, Ch. i; p. 19). He precludes its application to those authors of "la contestation," however. Even Khair-Eddine who is one of them manifests very little positive interest for women; hence one cannot easily generalize in this area.[15]

"L'étrangère" is seen as being shameless but sexier. She has more freedom of action. Indeed, she can free the Arab male of his own inhibition and sexual superiority complexes. She is often older and "knows better." She has usually not grown accustomed to throwing opprobrium on her own sex such as routinely qualifying any bad event as being "like the day she was born a girl," a female expression. She has not, brainwashed by her society, idolized the male sex in practice and in theory. Many Arab women, although they might know what an orgasm is, have never had the courage to claim and enjoy one in male-female intercourse.[16] They sometimes openly resort to other women in exclusively female circles.

Chraïbi only whets our appetite with his feminist thirst for justice. He seduces us instead with his consummate literary art. One small example is his handling of the wind blowing the hair of 'l'étrangère': "Elle essayait de la maîtriser, mais ses mains tremblaient et le vent était plus fort que n'importe quel sentiment humain" ["She tried to control it but her hands were trembling, and the wind was stronger than any human feeling"] (Pt. I, Ch. ii; p. 46). His desire for change has yet to produce a novel able to withstand clearheaded criticism that the heroine would make a poor role model for readers, for a better society.[17]

Many conservative North African writers think that the time is not right for women's liberation in their countries. Their reasoning is that if there are no grounds to build a man's life on, how can there be any for a woman's? They argue that women need to keep sacrificing themselves to the cause of progress and wait for a better tomorrow. That is unfortunately the overall message one gets from *Succession Ouverte. La Civilisation, ma mère! . . .* differs in this respect showing the author's heightened consciousness.

However, in *Succession Ouverte* no attempt is made to seriously discuss "une vie de femme" ["a woman's life"] although descriptions of women contributed largely to establishing the atmosphere of uneasiness and dread, and the hero's malaise.

Driss' mother had looked radiant at the time of her husband's funeral. Watching her and her female counterparts, Driss had felt compelled to attest that: "S'il y avait un mort dans cette demeure, il était mort depuis longtemps" ["If there was indeed a dead person in this dwelling, he was long since dead"] (Pt. I, Ch. iii; pp. 73-74). Another question which occurred to me at this point was whether the dead man's disappearance heralded that of the culture the characters had known and been distressed by. It was left unanswered by the author. The mother never progressed from a childish sense of relief to asserting herself. The pace had been set early for female representation in the novel when Driss dispatched romantic involvements with French women in this manner: "J'ai connu nombre de femmes et ça s'est toujours limité là." ["I have intimately known a great number of women, and it never went beyond that."] He makes things worse by adding that he was only a "sauvage" [savage] un "étalon" [stud] for them, and they never meant anything to him as a result: he is conveniently laying all the blame on them (Pt. I, Ch. ii; p. 36).

There was also the first experience Driss had on landing, one that made the persona ask: "Mais où était donc l'humain?" ["But where was the human element hiding?"] The foreign woman (the typical "étrangère," whose physical appearance alone is depicted at first) with a cold invisible laughter has a chest "tendue par la vie qu'elle s'acharnait à tuer en elle à tout moment" ["made more compact by the life within that she was rabidly bent on suppressing at all times"] (Pt. I, Ch. ii; p. 32). Not only is this woman described without her participation to compound the effect, she is in addition, made to reflect Driss' feelings and not her own.

A first journey to a foreign country such as Morocco for her, as the bride of one of its nationals, ought to have plentifully excused the rigidity and apprehension on her face. As for her husband, the old "malaise" is written on his face since he is another person Driss can closely identify with. As it turns out the "educated" man will slight and neglect his poor old primitive father who came to take him home on his donkey, preferring to tell his new wife that the party concerned is only a "domestique" (Pt. I, Ch. ii; p. 50). Suspecting the truth, she makes an attempt at gaining control of the heart-breaking events around her. Her efforts are doomed however. She is the outsider unable to reach out to others. This episode is further altered to artfully suggest that Driss' self-assigned mission might fail also. The foreign woman eventually manages to let her true personality come out. She becomes a refreshing, thinking and feeling person, human if perhaps not quite a man's equal: "elle n'avait plus rien d'une phobo-obsessionnelle" ["She had now shed all remains of her obsessional phobia"] (Pt. I, Ch. ii; p. 50). After the clash, the two cultures temporarily seem to merge in a show of common humanity.

Unfortunately, East and West did not meet for the female characters of the book who in reverse to what Driss had been undergoing, were saturated with the older, more stagnant culture which always denied them an identity. Inside their traditional background, revolt itself does not mean anything. All they can feel, numbed as they are by their early training for submissiveness (as in the extreme case of Jaad's wife) is impotent rage, the rage of those who have been discarded from life, but do not want to lose their minds (Pt. II, Ch. viii; p. 160). Misery-laden women are definitely not allowed into respectable families, hence Safia's raging efforts can at best be channeled into a fervent desire to help her husband. He was rejected for having dared to marry outside and below his social class.

This revolves back to my main objection to Chraïbi's work. Women's plight is often indirectly and sometimes ambiguously stated and takes the form of one man's search for his own liberation in the reader's mind, as well as in the author's mind, even as he is dealing with a topic as close to his heart as the Moroccan mother, his mother.

Chraïbi did not seem to have any bright alternatives to offer the three female characters in the book. They stand powerless and disoriented when confronted with life. The French woman is not of course informed of the critical situation at hand. She might however be better off to learn on her own and wage her own fight. The mother and Safia, Jaad's wife, must lower themselves to the ground and beg, the first still hoping for a chance to assist her distant dying husband, and the second to be granted forgiveness, acceptance and help for her sick and exhausted but proud spouse (Pt. II, Ch. viii; p. 162). This work betrays on the whole, a traditionally moderate to conservative, belittling treatment of women. *La Civilisation, ma mère!* ... gives Chraïbi a more legitimate claim to being a feminist writer as it illustrates better, but on whimsical terms, his growing support for women's liberation.

Except on a brief occasion in the chapter "Ma Mère," women never speak for themselves or for their own interests separate from those of their men, at least not in the course of *Succession Ouverte*. They never accede to an identity of their own. Further, the interaction between East and West is made to seem certain to fail where women are concerned.[18] I believe this is a bad omen since that interaction will be the decisive factor as to whether or not women will succeed in emancipating themselves in literature as well as in reality and become more able to help a country experiencing a dire need of improvement. More optimistic books are needed, if only to show women more favorable choices at work.[19]

NOTES

1. M. A. Alaoui attests: "Driss Chraibi et Rachid Boujedra, deux écrivains maghrebins, deux générations différentes, mais une preoccupation commune: la femme. Le héros, au sens litteraire de La Civilisation, ma Mère!... est précisément la mère." [Driss Chraibi and Rachid Boujedra are North African writers from two different generations but who have a common preoccupation: woman. The hero in *La Civilisation, ma Mère!*... is precisely the mother." *Afrique Littéraire et Artistique*, No. 34, 1974, p. 34.
2. Driss Chraibi, *Le Passé Simple*, Paris: Editions Denoël, 1954.
   _____, *La Civilisation, ma Mère...*, Paris, Denoël, 1954.
   _____, *Succession Ouverte*, Paris, Denoël, 1962.
3. Bouhdiba, *La Sexualite en Islam*, p. 66.

4. In one of his articles on the literature of the Maghreb, the mother is likened to a "caverne" inside a vicious circle in the authors' minds (Déjeux, La Littérature Maghrébine," pp. 17-19). J. F. A. Clément prefers to see this phenomenon as a "polygonisation" to use his own neologism (J. F. A. Clément, "Panorama de la Littérature Marocaine," *Esprit*, No. 34, 1974, p. 1059). I assume, for lack of further clarification and available information, and basing myself on J. Déjeux' explanation of *Le Polygone Etoilé* that J.F.A. Clément refers to "polygonisation" as the expression of personal and national alientation and fixation on the past. Déjeux' interpretation is needless to say, the one which resembles most the theory behind this work (Déjeux, *Littérature Maghrébine*, p. 217.)

5. "Son visage n'avait pas une seule ride. Elle le levait vers moi et, s'il m'avait été donné de voir à cet instant-là une scène de torture, je l'eusse supporteé sans faiblir, probablement" (Pt. I, Ch. iii; p. 68.)
   ["There wasn't a single line on her face which she raised towards me. Had I suddenly been exposed, at that instant, to a scene of torture, I would have probably withstood it without blinking."]

6. Even Chraïbi's childhood paralleled his mother's life. If one can judge from *Le Passé Simple*, his family life was empty and entirely dominated by his father: "Les affamés et moi nous nous ressemblons: nous sommes fonction, eux de treizes siècles d'Islam, moi du Seigneur, cristallisation de l'Islam"
   ["The hungry and I are alike: while they are descended from thirteen years of Islam, I am descended from 'the seigneur' (lord) who is a crystallization of Islam."] (Chraïbi, *Le Passè*, p. 12). J. F. A. Clément sees this "tendre haine" hovering over family relationships in Morocco and permeating everyone's consciousness" (Clément, p. 1059).

7. "Ils l'ont vidé de son sang et tué" (Pt. II, Ch. v; p. 106). [They emptied him of his life-sustaining blood"]

8. See A. Tillion's description of the practice called "Habous": "Afin de 'violer légalement la loi' dès qu'il achetait un terrain, le père de famille de Petite Kabylie ou de l'Aurès s'empressait de faire établir un acte par le qadi, stipulant qu'il avait choisi Dieu comme Héritier Final; toutefois en attendant que le 'Grand Héritier' prenne posssession de son bien, la jouissance en devait être exclusivement réservée à sa descendance masculine" Tillion, p. 177).
   ["As soon as he had bought a parcel of land, in order to 'legally violate the law', the father of a farming family in La Petite Kabilye or in L'Aurès hastened to have a testament drawn up by a justice of the peace stipulating that he had elected God as his Final Heir; however, until the 'Great Heir' had taken possession of His inheritance, the enjoyment and use of the land had to be exclusively reserved for his male progeny."]
   In other words: ". . . les paysans maghrébins—tous musulmans dévôts cela va sans dire,—ont opté pour les grandes flammes de l'enfer plutôt que de sacrifier l'appropriation de leur terre par leur lignée" (Tillion, p. 173).
   ["North African peasants—all devout Muslims of course—have opted for hell's inferno rather than sacrifice the appropriation of the land by their male lineage."

9. Mothers do share, theoretically, in the prestige of "la soeur-cousine" ["the sister/cousin"] mentioned by J. Déjeux (Déjeux, *Littérature Maghrébine*, p.

228). They too represent "la pureté inviolable du groupe" ["the inviolate purity of the group"] as J. Déjeux said of his sisters (Déjeux, "La Littérature Maghrébine," p. 34). However, during the independence war, the alleged "unassailability" and "veneration" granted to women were exposed. These false claims conceal harsh confinement and desertion. Evasion, mental illness, and suicide (rebellion and exile being available to only a few) are seen as being the only outlets available. A modern alternative (in an Arab context) is, increasingly, prostitution. *Harrouda* skillfully suggests this. M. N'Aït Attik had discovered its comparative advantages as early as the 1930s (M. N'Aït Attik, p. 15). J. F. A. Clément notes that it is mostly among women—and in their midst, peasant women—especially in land promotion areas that suicide rates are the highest. Economic progress does not go hand in hand with better conditions for women. The reverse is happening. In the cities, women are phased out and deprived of their traditional livelihood in favor of a few better trained men. He adds: "Au Maroc, le suicide semble surtout choisi par les femmes mais celles-ci ne font guère de littérature. Autant en Français qu'en Arabe, elles restent les grandes muettes" ["In Morocco, suicide seems to be an option that is taken mostly by women but Moroccan women do not express themselves through literature. In French as well as in Arabic, they remain mute."] (Clément, p. 1066).

In the countryside, where emigration has drained the available manpower, V. Maher tells us that "Agricultural tasks have been redistributed in such a way as to increase the workload of women" but that "it is commercial exchange, the value of commodities and their desirability—and the possibility of undertaking paid work in order to buy them that women must not discover" (L. Beck and N. Keddie, eds., *Women in the Muslim World*, England: Harvard University Press, 1978, p. 110). The same debilitating lifestyle is still dictated to the majority of Moroccan women, according to her. The dilemma resides in having to choose between subjection and physical ease or, a degree of independence marred by poverty and exploitation. Various forms of rebellion are more and more widespread: "high divorce rate, casual prostitution, intrigue, solidarity among women, ritual ridicule, ecstatic religion's validating nonsexual roles. . ." (Beck and Keddie, eds., pp. 121-122).

If in reality their outlook is bleak, in fiction, on the whole, it appears even somber. E. Accad, for instance is of the opinion that the main solution to women's problems in fiction is "victimization" when the books are written by men; and, more rarely for lack of more female authors, "la fuite, l'existentialisme dans le sens saganien du terme et l'engagement politique. . . " ["escape, existentialism in the context of Françoise Sagan's novels, and political engagement and action"] when they are written by women (Evelyne Accad, "La Longue Marche," *Présence Francophone*, No. 12, 1976, p. 4). Full feminist awareness remains to be acquired.

10. She is groping in the dark, half-aware that in her society as V. Maher said:
   Women must be kept from "understanding" their relation to the world, or realizing their real capacities or opportunities. The emphasis on trammeled perception of which the Tassaout woman. . .complains—"I have always been kept blindfolded, blinded"—is a recurrent theme. (Beck and Keddie, eds., p. 118'

It is not surprising that continuous years of childbearing, raising and domestic activities from age 16 (to the exclusion of any other occupation) amounted to total annihilation of many mental capacities.

11. "Au bout de seize ans, je n'avais pas encore trouvé un seul petit lopin de terre où enterrer mon arbre mort depuis longtemps" ["After sixteen years, I still had not found a single plot of ground where to bury my long-dead tree."] (Pt. II, Ch. xi; p. 180).

12. In his book *La Sexualité en Islam*, A. Bouhdiba, who sees through the lack of love in Arabo-Muslim societies where divorce is too common and too easy to obtain, makes a good analysis of the possessive mother. Having been denied any inherent value, women, frustrated and stripped of significant inheritance rights on their own, have to have as many children as possible for comfort and security. In a related article he explains that children constitute "un véritable système d'assurance vieillesse, d'assurance maladie, une garantie contre le destin . . . " ["a veritable insurance system against aging and illness, and a guarantee against the blows of destiny. . ."] However, the destiny their society—and their men—impose on them is not so easily deflected: the security acquired is a negative and illusory one. It is only through "total" emancipation that women can better their lives (Bouhdiba, "Le Royaume," p. 68).

13. From a literary standpoint, female inhibition can be evidenced in the complete lack of romans-poèmes by women. Those require the free flow of consciousness that women, risking violent censure and retribution, cannot afford. The exception, Mririda N'Aït Attik can be seen as a feminist "avant la lettre" expressing as early as 1946 the poetic inspiration of a free woman refusing to live by men's rules. Therefore, women seldom write, especially in Morocco. As can be guessed, they share equally the problem of censorship with men. The authors who dare touch taboo topics are either "unknown" in their countries of origin or read by a small number of people. They often attack the new nationalism and regression to traditional values that they blame for their country's backwardness. In *Le Passé Simple* Chraïbi threw into full view the dark corners of everyday life and caused much embarrassement. Here is one sarcastic quote he made of the Koran, concerning those "créatures de Dieu que le Koran a parquées" ["creatures of God that the Koran had fenced in. . ."]:
   "Baisez-les et les rebaisez; par le vagin, c'est plus utile; ensuite ignorez les jusqu'à la jouissance prochaine" ["Copulate with them a few times; inside their vagina since that is more useful. Then ignore them until your next pleasure-seeking."] (Chraïbi, *Le Passé*, pp. 40-41).
   Chraïbi was made to disown this book which he now regrets having done (see Déjeux, *Littérature*, pp. 280-281).

14. In North African literature however, even Assia Djebar the author who champions "le couple," has seriously asked herself if she were not too far ahead of her times (Déjeux, *Littérature*, p. 255).

15. See his novel *Agadir* (Mohamed Khair Eddine, *Agadir*, Paris: Editions du Seuil, 1967, pp. 119-120). Jean Déjeux notices that in his work as can be expected from the author's background: "la femme est dégradée et inféririsée..." ["woman is degraded and given an inferior status"] (Déjeux, *Littérature*, p. 415). Of Arabo-Muslim cultures, A. Bouhdiba writes: "on limite l'amour au

ludique et on ravale l'épouse au rang de femme-objet, dont l'unique fonction est la satisfaction du plaisir sexuel du mari" ["Love is limited to lust and the wife is relegated to the low ranking of a sex-object whose sole function is to insure the husband's sexual enjoyment."] (Bouhdiba, "Le Royaume," p. 66.).

There is no need therefore, to speak of any sexual problems since simple coital ejaculation is all that the husband owes to his wife. Even that right is limited by polygamy for instance. Taking into account their preordained relationship, one must admit that that is all he learns how to give her. The rest is entirely left to the woman alone who has no sexual education whatsoever and many socially induced inhibitions filling that function. Some of these inhibitions are derived from knowing that for her lover, embracing her means embracing evil and irreligion.

16. E. Accad transposes that into mores in fiction when she asserts that: "Nowhere is sex seen as an act of enjoyment, an act fulfilling in itself, a rapport of mutuality of feeling, a sharing and giving. It is a role-playing in a contractual sense, and it is the many evils of the contractual sex that the novels emphasize" (Beck and Keddie, p. 626). E. Accad lists a few related examples in fiction: "inevitably tragic endings to adulterous love affairs, the isolation of women from society. . .the fear old women have of being parasites because they can no longer procreate; the sadness with which the birth of girls is greeted. . .the punishment of sexual dishonor by death; the general acceptance of such practices as polygamy, prostitution, slavery, and arranged marriages. . .and the enforced seclusion and veiling of women, all of which demonstrate the refusal of society to grant women the right to seek sexual fulfillment" (Beck and Keddie, pp. 617-618).

Other examples of equal importance in novels as well as in real life need to be added to the endless catalog:—the hatred between the parents, and between them and their children, which make the family live in an atmosphere of "tendre haine" to quote again an ingenious apposition of Chraïbi's;
—the prevention of the formation of normal affectionate brother-sister relationships due to the brother's role as the sister's guardian even if he is much younger;
—the constant fear where a woman lives that she might find herself repudiated and without support and have to either return to her reluctant family or become a "huriya" (or "prostitutée");
—the exploitation of school-age girls from the countryside as twenty-four-hour-a-day maids and drudges in urban households.
—the all-inclusive suspicion which leaves no room for any kind of trust or real friendship between anyone for fear that one's "honor" will be besmirched in any of the hundred possible ways related to women;
—the early marrying off of daughters by possessive and dejected mothers hoping to saddle them down with children and a husband in close proximity, to help relieve their loneliness.

17. Female circumcision is a related area that no North African author has mentioned to my knowledge (with the exception of the highly dedicated novelist Nawal el Saadawi who is Egyptian). Perhaps things will change now that articles have appeared focusing on this tragic and demeaning custom of the Third World (Claire Brisset, "Excisées, jusqu'à quand?" *Le Monde*, 3 Apr.

1980, Sec. 1, p. 1, col. 2); and *Ms. Magazine*'s March issue covering Nawal el
Saadawi's own retelling of her childhood clitoridectomy by Robin Morgan and
Gloria Steinem, "The International Crime," (*Ms.*, March 1980, pp. 65-69).
[*Editors' Note*: See Evelyen Accad's *L'Excisée* (Paris, L'Harmattan, 1982) and
Tobe Levin's paper in this collection for further discussion of female genital
mutilation.]

18. "Toute entreprise humaine vaut qu'on la commence. Et commencer, c'est faire
     la moitié du chemin" [Any human enterprise, deserves an attempt, a beginning
     which is half the amount of work it requires"] (Pt. II, Ch. vi, p. 131). The key
     word is "bilan," appraisal. The idea of "faire un bilan," taking inventory is one
     common denominator of many of Chraïbi's works. This theme betrays, in my
     opinion, an obsession with production, le "rendement," which is more
     indicative of the western influence in the author's psychological make-up. He
     keeps making his characters ask what the tangible results are of the struggle
     waged but there is no satisfactory response. Comparatively, when the mother
     leaves at the end of *La Civilisation ma Mère!*...she does not merely do so
     "pour constater" as M. A. Alaoui contends but in order to appraise and
     ascertain what has been done and what can be done in the future (Alaoui, p.
     38). In that respect D. Chraïbi is very positive and shows that he is abreast of
     realities. The characters must accomplish something, in our social context, to
     make the reader care, and D. Chraïbi knows that.

19. As J. F. A. Clément has said, we need a work from a North African writer who
     will not opt for expediency: "Il n'y a aucune oeuvre de longue haleine, bien
     travaillée" ["There is no well crafted, long-term, all-encompassing work"]
     (Clément, p. 1068).

Women and Alienation: Analysis of the Works of Two Francophone African Novelists

Karen Smyley Wallace

Currently, there is a burgeoning emphasis on the Black female Francophone writer and her portrayal of the female character in the novel. African female novelists Mariama Bâ (*Une Si Longue Lettre*, 1980, *Un Chant Ecarlate*, 1984); Aminata Sow Fall (*Le Revenant*, 1976, *La Grève des Battu*, 1979, *L'Appel des Arènes*, 1982) and Nafissatou Diallo (*De Tilène Au Plateau: Une Enfance Dakaroise*, 1975) are among those noted for their accurate and penetrating portrayals of the woman. It is undeniable that the contributions of these African female novelists have been crucial in the meaningful evolution and revelation of the Black female character, particularly with regard to themes involving her search for identity.

Detailed examination of the powerful new presence of this Black female perspective is being carried out by this writer. But, it is nevertheless significant to reflect upon the image of the woman, as she was initially presented by male Francophone novelists. From this vantage point, one may better analyze the patterns of development and their success or failure in the characterizations of the Black female in Francophone African literature.

The inclusion of the female character within the scope of Francophone African literature, is certainly not a novel idea, for she has always occupied a position of some merit. Although poetry has provided a useful mode of expression for the depiction of the Black woman, (see David Diop's "A Une Danseuse Noire," *Coups de Pilon* (1957) and Léopold Senghor's "Femme Noire," *Chants d'Ombre* (1956), it was the novel which encouraged the broadest investigation of the female image. From the appearance of what is known as the first Francophone Black novel, (René Maran's *Batouala*, 1928) to the late 1950s, male Francophone novelists projected the images of the woman in her traditional setting, where the matters of home and family were her singular concern. Some of the more well-known examples are the depiction of the mother in Camara Laye's *L'Enfant Noir* (1953); the grandmother, wife, and other village women in Ousmane Sembène's *Les Bouts de Bois de Dieu* (1960); the mother and the old woman in Aboulaye Sadji's *Maïmouna* (1958); or Ousmane Socé's heroine in *Karim: Roman Sénégalais* (1948). Characterized as the symbol of the earth mother, the dutiful and obedient wife, or the nubile love goddess, the female character was often portrayed as a one dimensional figure, lacking any great literary palpability. The most characteristic and noteworthy feature of these earlier works, however, was the consistent representation of the African woman as a symbol of strength.

While the larger body of African literature has focused primarily upon the male protagonist and his conflict with western assimilation (see Ferdinand Oyono's *Le Vieux Nègre et la Médaille*, 1956; Bernard Dadié's *Un Nègre à Paris*, 1959; Cheikh Hamidou Kane's *L'Adventure Ambiguë*, 1961), the female character has consistently occupied a significant role in the works of Senegalese novelists Aboulaye Sadji and Ousmane Sembène. Sadji (1910-1960), a lesser known literary figure, whose style was greatly imitative of the late nineteenth century novel, is noted for two major works which highlight the impact of acculturation upon the African woman: *Nini: Mulâtresse de Sénégal*, 1947 and *Maïmouna*, 1958. (He also wrote a short fictional piece entitled *Tounka: une nouvelle*, 1946). Despite minor stylistic limitations, the heroines in Sadji's works have become classic in African literature. Due to his artful portrayals of African women frought with cultural ambivalence, he is acknowledged for having made a singular contribution to earlier colonial Francophone African literature, and has been acclaimed an "excellent portraitist of the Senegalese woman."[1]

Ousmane Sembène, a contemporary Senegalese novelist and filmmaker, is noted for his finely chiseled portraits of females as real, palpable individuals.[2] By creating women figures who do not merely represent shadows of the male figure, nor echoes of the male voice, Sembène's works reflect the complexities of a changing Africa. He departs measurably from the rather static images carved by Sadji, and renders the female character a dynamic being, who must constantly struggle to redefine her perception of self in the developing African continent and in the world.[3]

In their respective works, yet, often contrasting literary styles, Sadji and Sembène attempt to delve beyond the superficial portraits of the woman as mere exotic accompaniment to the male, in order to reveal her own psychic universe. Although in different degrees, both writers have spoken out against the effects of Western assimilation upon African culture, by focusing upon the woman and her reaction to this phenomenon. While Sadji paints a Senegal of 1947, and Sembene, one of 1960, the long range effects of colonization and cultural ambivalence are nevertheless startlingly visible in the female characters of both authors.

Thus, through their vast and colorful tableaux of women figures (market women, wives, mothers, daughters, political leaders, prostitutes, teachers, secretaries, etc.) Sadji and Sembène illustrate the tormenting world of the double self, anxiety and alienation. Although the notion of duality is expressed differently by each character, they are all linked by two factors: their intense struggle for survival in the colonial world, and the disintegration of their sense of "africanité." Thus, this article will provide a comparative analysis of each author's works, and of their compelling female characters, who have embarked upon a labyrinthine search for self.

Ironically, it was the colonial system, itself, which provided the impetus for the development of more intricate and subtle literary treatment of the Black female persona. From the period of the late 1950s and into the early years of independence from colonial rule, Francophone literature witnessed the emergence of a new and problematic female character. The goal of these new characters was "to redefine the position of the African individual in a changing and developing society."[4] Forced to struggle with social, political, philosophical or sentimental problems, the Black female character often found herself cut off from her past, and trapped within the confines of a system of alienation. In her work, *L'Angoisse chez les romanciers africains*, Monique Battestini comments upon this phenomenon of alienation and its impact upon African literature:

> In this rapidly developing universe, a new concern emerged: that of no longer being oneself. The West had overturned traditional Africa, and the African had sought in Negritude, a refuge, a triumph, and finally a new anxiety. This sense of uprooting, which resulted from the influx of foreign values, was experienced by all of the writers: thus, from this came the birth of a new generation of "dual souls."[5]

In the novel, *Nini: Mulâtresse du Sénégal*, Sadji created the unforgettable female character, Nini. As the embodiment of "things French" and "things Black," she remains an intriguing example of the alienated being. Nini's character may be analyzed from two perspectives. As an individual, her story reveals the psychological discord of one woman's search for racial identity.

On a larger plane, she becomes a part of a collective drama and the prototype of a people whose very existence is determined by the conflicting duality of an African soul trapped within a white skin:

> Nini is the eternal portrait of the mulatto female, whether she is from Senegal, the Caribbean or the Americas. It is the portrait of the physically and morally hybrid being, who . . .constantly seeks to elevate herself above a level of humanity she considers inferior, but to which destiny has inexorably linked her.[6]

Nini is both a product and a victim of the French colonial system in Senegal. Since the island of Saint Louis (original capital of Senegal and the setting for the story) was one of the most thriving centers for trade and banking in West Africa, it offers a clear picture of French assimilative policies in microcosm. In the early days of settlement, during the first half of the seventeenth century, close contact between Europeans and Africans in commerce was inevitable. As there were few, if any, French women among the first arrivals, "French companies often encouraged marriage with local African women."[7] These women became known as "*signaras;*" an adaptation of the Portuguese term *sinhora* (a title of respect, like *madame*, accorded a married woman). Although sanctioned by the government, these marriages were not legally binding so these women were technically concubines. History records, however, that some of the French settlers gave their names, some property, or a European education to the children of these unions. Having received privileges and benefits unknown to their darker skinned brothers, the "assimilés" became the first class of Africans eager to assimilate with France. Yet, the irony of their world was one of refuge behind the ivory tower of their "almost whiteness."

The story of Mademoiselle Virginia de Maerle is essentially simple. Nini, 22, unmarried, lives with her two older relatives, Tante Hortense and Grand'mère Hélène. Employed as a "perfectly stupid little secretary,"[8] at the Department of Rivers, she spends the majority of her time in pursuit of white men. Her list of previous suitors is long, although unsuccessful. Currently, her interest is focused upon a certain Monsieur Martineau, a middle management functionary, recently arrived from France. Nini's happiness, as well as the good name of her family, depends upon the ensnarement of the unsuspecting Frenchman. In her eyes, she has had the misfortune of becoming the love interest of an African co-worker, who, although far superior to her in education and in character, is nonetheless, representative of the Blackness she so loathes. The African is duly rejected; the Frenchman, actively pursued; Nini is seduced and abandoned; her ultimate escape is sought in France, in the arms of new white men.

As Nini gazes into the looking glass, the reflections she beholds provide either a false image of self and reality, or no image whatsoever. This symbolic mirror, as Nini's life itself, reflects a world of illusion and fantasy. These are poignantly brought to life by the dream-like atmosphere into which Sadji draws his readers. The descriptive passages artfully capture the old de Maerle house, with its southern French architecture, common to Saint Louis. The dilapidated exterior and faded, cluttered interior are the only remaining souvenirs of the family, and of a glory that is decidedly past.

The two old ladies, both "signaras" in their time, live in a faded world of memories. Having failed at the illusory search for whiteness, they have resigned themselves to the more comforting world of religion. Nini's search for white identity is a natural consequence of that "dream deferred." Sadji has created a demi-world of soft lights, playful shadows, half-closed venetian blinds, through which the symbol of the brilliant African sun is never allowed to penetrate.

The softly muted tones of the fading world of the old mulatto ladies is sharply contrasted with Nini's own agressive behavior. No matter how fixedly she stares into her looking glass, she is unable to see what she so desperately craves: the image of "a real white lady." Instead, she uses her skill and artistry to mold a reality more to her liking. Structuring her own behavior to accommodate her perception of whiteness, Nini embraces a world of controlled artificiality. She rises early, becomes exceedingly punctual, quickens her pace, sharpens her gestures, and raises the level and tone of her voice. Using language to further widen the gap between herself and "the Niggers," Nini exemplifies the impact of colonial bilingualism, as described by Fanon: "To speak a language is to take on a world, a culture...The colonized person is elevated above his jungle status in proportion to his adoption of the mother country's cultural standards. He becomes whiter as he renounces his blackness."[9] The adoption of the colonized language as a means of cultural acceptance, has also been poignantly captured by the poet Léon Damas, in the biting lines:

> Be quiet
> Did I not tell you to speak French
> French from France
> French of the Frenchman
> French French[10]

The robot-like gestures and the structured language, however, do little to camouflage traces of Nini's African past. It is not the reflection in the mirror that lies; rather it is Nini who refuses to see evidence of her African blood. What little she does see, she attempts to mask, in the same way as she uses face powder to cover her full lips and flattened nose and in the same way as she tightly disciplines the sway of somewhat generous hips. Despite these attempts, the African heritage Nini has long despised and tried to escape, is readily discernible. We see it in the depth of her passions and sensual nature, for it is she who encourages the erotic adventures with her white admirers. We sense it as she sways invitingly to the sound of the "rumbas and beguines" on the dance floor. We see it in her belief in the forces of traditional African magic. Although outwardly rebuking the use of fetishes and *gris-gris* (charms or amulets), Nini obediently swallows the magic love potion, prescribed by the old African marabout. It is only when the effects are negative that self-hatred motivates her to declare her hatred of "things black."

The irony of Sadji's story is bitter, for Nini is rejected by the Frenchman, Martineau, who returns to France and eventually marries "a real white lady." What is startlingly clear is that for him, Nini is after all, only several shades lighter of "café au lait": ". . .a Negress is a Negress. There's no way she could ever become white." (*Nini*, p. 303) Martineau's brutal departure provides the ultimate crack in Nini's distorted looking glass. Having rejected all avenues leading to her African heritage, and compelled by the twisted self-images from within, Nini's only means to escape lies in departure from the island: a consequence depicting the Stendhalien "search for happiness." The alienated Nini has condemned herself to an endless pursuit of whiteness.

Sadji's novel is neither a defense, an apology, nor a polemical discussion of the role of the mulatto female: "one can neither condemn nor blame these beings. I believe it is more charitable . . . to show them, as in a mirror, the reality of who they really are." (*Nini*, p. 315) As a prisoner of his time, and of his islamic beliefs in fatalism, Sadji could not envisage a rebellious mulatto character (as in Simone Schwarz-Bart's *La Mulâtresse Solitude*). While Sadji's novel provides a vivid portrayal of this particular tormented soul, it reveals aspects of the broader drama of racial and cultural alienation known to other Blacks. In this respect, Nini has achieved the dimension of a classic, although alienated, persona.

Ousmane Sembène has also produced several works in which the dominant motif is the alienation of the African woman. While none share the burden of the double heredity of French and African parentage, as had Nini, their sense of anxiety is nonetheless pronounced. For each, there is an intense emotional and psychological desire for assimilation into European-like society. N'Deye Touti, from the classic nevel, *God's Bits of Wood (Les Bouts de Bois de Dieu)*, provides a fine example of this inner conflict. This 1960 work tells the story of the Senegalese struggle for unionization along the Dakar-Niger railroad line, and for ultimate independence from French rule.

N'Deye, a young Wolof girl, lives in a humble compound outside of Dakar. One might say that she lives among the people, yet, not of them, for she has succeeded in creating an imaginary shield that protects her from what she views as an undesirable life. N'Deye's sense of duality is not caused by her desire to whiten herself or her race; rather to whiten her style of living. The torment she experiences, however, is as profound as that of her counterpart, Nini. The first step in the process of assimilation is to feel shame for one's own heritage. Nini had successfully removed herself from any close contact with her African roots, while N'Deye still lives among them. We note an intense sense of ambivalence, as she contemplates her childhood surroundings with shame, and withdraws more and more into a world peopled by school books and fantasies. Her very demeanor reveals a sense of superiority over those around her: what the author describes as "a great distance from those who were a part of her daily world."[11] The contrast is particularly notable in those passages which refer to *their* lack of civilization and to *her* acculturation.

Sembène, as Sadji, uses the image of the dream and imagination to portray N'Deye's existence. Amidst her daily activities, fantasies provide a temporary escape from what she refers to as "a living graveyard." The author has not created an insensitive character, so much as he has produced a woman who is prey to the same pangs of envy as are all colonized people. The fact that N'Deye wishes to avoid the issues of the railroad strike and seeks refuge in "the European sector, where the houses are bordered by gardens, and not the metal and wooden huts that are enclosed behind a wall of bamboo," (*GBW*, p. 107) does not make her a shallow individual. According to Fanon's observations in *The Wretched of the Earth*, she is merely paying one of the prices of the assimilative process. "The gaze of the colonized person upon the villa of the colonizer is a look of envy."[12]

Although the authors' styles differ, several factors unite Nini and N'Deye, as alienated beings. Both women conveniently ignore the opinions of the European, in their regard. Both must be shocked into the reality of their double existence. Having accepted all forms of ridicule on the part of white men, Nini had acquired the facility to soon forget the pain of their rejection and to proceed to newer prey. N'Deye, expressly created by Sembène to reveal African reality to Africans, must also suffer the pangs of humiliation. Having closely patterned her life after European standards, she is devasted upon overhearing two gendarmes crudely discuss her body, her people, her human worth: ". . .Say! Have one of your guards find her and offer two kilos of rice. Right now, they'll sleep with you for less than that!" (*GBW*, p. 186) The impact of this incident was considerable. It, along with the encouragement of Bakayoko, the leader of the strike, propels N'Deye into a type of self-redefinition. In this way, Sembene provides the once-alienated character with an opportunity for emotional and political growth through self-realization.

In many respects, Oumi N'Doye, the second wife of El Hadji, in the 1974 novel *Xala*, has achieved the material success so longed for by N'Deye Touti. As the wife of a prominent businessman, she benefits from her husband's high standing in the community. Oumi lives in a European sector of Dakar; she has her own villa; her children attend private schools in a chauffeured car; and there is even talk of buying a new Fiat for her daughter, Mariem. Oumi's is a world of prestige and acquisition.

Through her portrait, the author reveals the transition of Senegal from the days of colonialism to those of independence. As the story is set in the 1970s, one is able to see the long range effects of Western influence. Oumi speaks casually of such things as "black wig;" "Evian water:" "discotheques;" "Afro-American soul music." She prides herself on her knowledge of the latest European styles and is an avid reader of photo-magazines. She listens to radio broadcasts in French, refers to her husband in the third person, as "Monsieur," and bases her culinary skills upon ideas gleaned exclusively from French magazines.

Although unaware of the socio-political influences of neo-colonialism upon her world and her thinking, Oumi represents still another form of the alienated female character. Depicted as shallow and artificial individuals, Oumi and her husband, El Hadji, are unfortunate victims of the temporary *xala* (Wolof, for impotence) of an African struggling with its newly won independence.

Sembène's story, "La Noire de . . . ," from the collection *Voltaïque*, focuses upon one of the most psychologically intricate of his alienated female characters. Rather than become absorbed into European culture, Diouana, a young girl from Dakar, merely wishes to taste of its novelties. Initially employed as a babysitter for a French family in one of the finer sections of Dakar, her duties are shared with three other domestics, thereby rendering work conditions favorable. Seasoned with occasional leftovers from the family table and some used clothing, Madame, has little difficulty sparking Diouana's interest in returning to France with them. To Diouana, the family represents "great white folks." She is easily seduced by the dreams which metropolitan France offers; yet, once the ocean is crossed, the initial excitement subsides and Diouana's view of France, of the French, and of herself are catapulted into a bitter and painful world of reality.

Emanating from a culture of communal living, Diouana finds it difficult to adjust to this new world of isolation. The changes in the girl's personality, which result from the sharp thrusts of racism, are depicted with dramatic impact: torment, ridicule, humiliation and embarrassment. The French children call her "Savage" and "Négresse". Madame parades her from place to place, from house to house, as if on exhibit. She is touched, fondled, teased. Her household duties multiply until she is eventually forced to serve as babysitter-maid-cook-nurse-laundress.

While the process of depersonalization is intensified and reaches its apex, Diouana withdraws slowly into herself. Her color, now objectified, becomes something exterior to herself, while she regards it with the same distant aversion as the white family; a process which Aimé Césaire describes as "thingification"[13] of the human being: "Slowly, she began to drown into the color of her skin. Suddenly she was overcome with an unshakeable terror. Her blackness. Fearfully, she sought refuge within herself."[14] Realizing that she has become a mere object, an African curio, so to speak, Diouana's sense of isolation is painfully heightened. No longer referred to by her rightful name (always mispronounced), but as "the black girl," she can no longer be Black for herself. Diouana is thus deprived of color, race, heritage and existence.

In painting Diouana's portrait, Sembène has shown the schism separating the girl from her employers; the African from the French; the colonizer from the colonized; the black from the white. Unable to either grow or survive in this stagnating situation, Diouana opts for a simple, yet final alternative. Sembène's talent as a novelist, fused with his ability as a filmmaker have produced a powerfully dramatic, yet sensitive final scene. When questioned by the inspector. Madame remarks politely, yet cooly: "I don't know why she committed suicide. She was well treated here, ate the same food and even shared a bedroom with my children." (*Noire*, p. 161).

In the works of both authors, therefore, each of these female characters faces a moment of realization in which she must reflect upon her identity. Each is presented with alternatives and consequently must make choices: for Nini the hopeless escape into the illusory world of whiteness; for N'Deye eventual self-recognition and a rekindling of African pride; for Oumi imprisonment in the unfortunate *xala* of a newly independent Africa; and for Diouana death by her own hand.

Although each author stamps the novel with his particular mark of individuality, both Sadji and Sembene have chiseled characters who highlight the painfulness associated with the emergence of a sense of duality in the African female persona, and the exorbitant cost of their alienation from self.

Greatly reflecting the early Negritude period, Aboulaye Sadji writes as a moralist; thus, his portrait of Nini is a depiction of the ill-effects of the colonial system. On the surface, Sadji's narrative seems only to describe a somewhat synthetic figure. Certainly, Sadji's work does not approach the more accurate portrayals of this dilemma, as seen from the female perspective of several well-known Francophone Caribbean female novelists. On the same topic of race and the female identity, (see Mayotte Capecia's *Je Suis Martiniquaise*, 1950; Michèle Lacrosil's *Cajou*, 1961; or Marie Chauvet's *Fonds des Nègres*, 1960). Sadji's success lies in his attempt, as an African author, to penetrate this rather lightly sketched female character, and thus, shed some necessary light upon this particular aspect of the broader and more complex drama of alienation and the African woman.

As a more biting critique and keen observer of African culture, Sembène has raised a mirror of social realism and has placed it before the eyes of the African. Through the characterizations of N'Deye, Oumi, and Diouana, he has revealed a distortion in these reflections: a distortion brought about by westernization, colonialism and neo-colonialism. These characters, by no means represent the complete protrayal of the female in Sembène's work. While he is notably perceptive in his treatment of the effects of cultural ambivalence upon the woman, his strongest characters are those who endure less inner emotional conflict than N'Deye, Oumi, or Diouana, and who emerge as politically committed women: "la femme engagée." (See, Tioumbé, in *Harmattan*; Penda, in *God's Bits of Wood*; or Rama, in *Xala*.)

Although Sadji has provided rather vivid and colorful female characterizations, he seems to focus primarily upon the woman as a victim in the developing African society of that period. While Sadji seems content to merely describe the situation which promotes anxiety in his characters, Sembène both describes it and goes on to suggest change: change, invested principally in the hands of the woman. It is the very concept of participation which most readily differentiates Sadji and Sembène's interpretation of the female character. Much of Sembene's philosophy regarding the active participation of the woman in Africa's political development, reflects his espousement of the Marxist view of the female in society.[15] By encharging the female figure with a sense of responsibility, Sembène paints his characters in optimistic tones and shows that the female, (as her male counterpart) is able to transcend the burdens of cultural alienation in order to forge newer paths for Africa, and for herself.

Within the total body of African literature, Sadji and Sembène have been among the few male novelists to focus so intensely upon the female: her life, her concerns, her conflicts, her feelings. By expanding upon some of these original views of Black women by male writers, and by articulating the feelings of the Black woman, contemporary Francophone African female novelists are adding newer insights and greater depth to these original portrayals. Nevertheless, while they are clearly providing the necessary flesh and blood, writers such as Sadji and Sembène, are to be recognized for having presented some of the initial literary framework of the African female, as a principal figure in the novel.

NOTES

1. Robert Pageard, *Littérature négro-africaine* (Paris: Le livre africain, 1966, p. 79.
2. Ousmane Sembene's literary works include: *Le Docker Noir*, 1956; *O pays, mon beau peuple*, 1957; *Les Bouts de Bois de Dieu*, 1960; *Voltaïque*, 1962; *L'Harmattan*, 1964; *Xala*, 1974.
   His major films include: *Borom Sarret*, 1963; *Niaye*, 1966; *La Noire de. . .*, 1966; *Le Mandat*, 1968; *Taw*, 1970; *Emitai*, 1971; *Xala*, 1975; *Ceddo*, 1976.

3. For further discussion of this point, see Karen Smyley, "Ousmane Sembène: Portraitist of the African Woman in the Novel," *New England Journal of Black Studies*, 1, no. 1, (June 1981), 23-27.

4. Sunday Anonzie, *Sociologie du Roman Africain: Réalisme, Structure et Détermination dans le Roman Moderne Ouest-Africain* (Paris: Tiers-Monde et Développement, 1970), p. 27.

5. Monique Battestini, *L'Angoisse chez les Romanciers Africains* (Dakar: Actes du Colloque, 1963), p. 162. Quotes have been translated by the author.

6. Aboulaye Sadij, *Nini: Mulâtresse du Sénégal* (Paris: Présence Africaine, 1947), p. 1. All subsequent references to this edition will be indicated by *Nini* and the page. All quotes have been translated by the author.

7. See Rita O'Brien, *White Society in Black Africa: The French of Senegal* (Illinois: Northwestern University Press, 1972), p. 31, for further discussion.

8. Frantz Fanon, *Black Skins, White Masks* (New York: Grove Press, Inc., 1967), p.55.

9. Ibid., p. 38.

10. Léon Damas, *Pigments et Névralgies* (Paris: Présence Africaine, 1972), p. 38. All quotes have been translated by the author.

11. Ousmane Sembène, *God's Bits of Wood* (New York: Doubleday & Co., 1962), p. 106. All subsequent references to this edition will be indicated by *GBW* and the page.

12. Frantz Fanon, *The Wretched of the Earth* (New York: Grove Press, Inc., 1963), p. 39.

13. Aimé Césaire, *Discourse on Colonialism* (New York: Monthly Review Press, 1972), p. 21.

14. Ousmane Sembène, *Voltaïque* (Paris: Présence Africaine 1962), p. 180. All subsequent references to this edition will be indicated by *Noire* and the page. All quotes have been translated by the author.

15. Sonia Lee develops this point in her article, "The Awakening of Self in the heroines of Sembène Ousmane," *Critique*, 17 (1975), 17-25.

Maidens, Mistresses and Matrons: Feminine Images in Selected Soyinka Works

Carole Boyce Davies

Literature, because it mirrors and/or recreates social, historical and economic realities, is one of the channels through which negative attitudes and stereotypes of women are perpetuated, even created. Modern African literature too, because it has adopted many of the Western patriarchal modes of thought and expression, often conveys some of these biased attitudes to which we refer. Revisionist criticism of African literature then has as one of its tasks the truthful assessment of the literary image of women. It must therefore approach already well criticized texts/authors from a critical posture which seeks to reveal and thereby correct some of these attitudes and in so doing challenge authors to project a complete picture of African social reality. Sonia Lee has already found in African literature of French expression that

> the feminine protagonist throughout the African novel presents a
> certain homogeneity of character which can be attributed to a basic
> similarity in the man's view of the woman . . . Through the role of the
> woman the writer may be re-examining man's role in his changing
> society. Consequently, the heroine often has a didactic function which
> deters her from psychological development.

Furthermore, the feminine character often plays a secondary role in the novel, frequently being placed in the fixed context of the village where she illustrates traditional life. In the changing contemporary society she seems to remain the constant factor because the social changes imposed upon traditional life by modern times are seen almost exclusively in the life drama of the male protagonist.[1]

My study of female portraiture in the Soyinka works reveals no significant departure from the above findings. In fact, a feminist reading of Soyinka reveals enough female stereotypes to suggest a definite sexist bias against women. Additionally, an examination of the characteristics of these women produces the distinct impression that the author is conjuring up the image of the same, ideal woman over and over again.

Studies which deal in any depth or detail with Soyinka's women are definitely in the minority in the canon of Soyinka criticism.[2] For the most part, discussion of women in the drama and fiction of Wole Soyinka has been peripheral to, or embraced within, more conventional literary criticism.[3] It is as if these female characters have been relegated to their "place" within this literary universe. This critical attitude, I would submit, harmonizes with the author's overwhelming treatment of women as objects of quest rather than as subjects in their own right. Soyinka's strong, Ogunnian[4] sense of the African hero has so far militated against his portrayal of women in any heroic sense.

A distinction can, however, be made between works which are set in a traditional, rural community and those in which the action takes place in an urban environment. In the traditional, rural setting, the stereotype is that of the submissive virgin, as portrayed by Sidi of *The Lion and the Jewel* (1963) and the unnamed virgin bride of Elesin in *Death and The King's Horseman* (1975). In the urban setting, the *femme fatale* or bitch-goddess dominates and here, particularly, the same woman seems to appear repeatedly. Simi of *The Interpreters* (1965) has almost identical physical features as Segi of *Kongi's Harvest* (1967), features and characteristics which are climaxed in Iriyise of *Season of Anomy* (1973). In these works which this study will limit itself to, the author creates a fantasized version of a woman, colored by a combination of Yoruba mythology and his own ideal of the feminine.

The Foolish Virgins

The most prominent physical characteristic of the Soyinka female character is exceptional beauty; a beauty which exists, however, to be possessed by the male. As early as *The Lion and the Jewel*, we find the image of the village belle with her natural, virginal, goddess-like beauty. In this play, particularly, the importance of male dominance is communicated. As the title, folkloric as it may be, connotes, the male is given the qualities of strength and prowess which the name lion suggests, while the female is endowed with the virtues of the ornament or prized *possession*.

The play can be read as a power struggle between male and female. Sidi is innocent of her beauty until she views photographs of herself in a Lagos magazine which is brought to the village by the photographer. Baroka, like the rest of the village community, becomes aware of her exceptional beauty and the fact that she is now famous while he has been symbolically relegated to a position of little importance in the magazine. Sidi says: "He shares the corner of the leaf with the lowest of the low—/With the dug-out village latrine!"[5] It becomes obvious that the *Bale*, (traditional ruler) whom Lakunle describes as a devil among women, cannot allow himself to be outstripped by a "mere woman". So Baroka immediately decides that he has to conquer this woman. Sidi has, by this time, assimilated some of Lakunle's (the village teacher) views of "modern womanhood" misguided though they are. Even before her appearance in the magazine she had exhibited an acute awareness of her self-worth, for when Lakunle tried to convince her that women had smaller brains than men she had called his thoughts "manly conceit" and when he tried to point out that women were the weaker sex, she had articulated the strength of the traditional African woman: "The weaker sex is it?/Is it the weaker breed who pounds yam/Or bends all day to plant the millet/With a child strapped to her back?" (p.5).

Clearly, Sidi becomes aware that the appearance of her photographs has kindled a power struggle between herself and Baroka. Thus when Sadiku, the Bale's senior wife who by tradition initiates the procurement of junior wives, comes with talk of marriage and the Bale's invitation to supper, Sidi, conscious of Baroka's strategy counters with,

> He seeks to have me as his property
> Where I must fade beneath his jealous hold
> Ah, Sadiku,
> The schoolman has taught me certain things
> And my images have taught me all the rest.
> Baroka merely seeks to *raise his manhood*
> Above my beauty
>   . . . .(p.21) (emphasis mine)

The denouement of this play provides a good example of Soyinka's treatment and disposal of the female character. It seems unlikely that a girl who is so aware of herself, of the positive aspects of womanhood and of the outcome of Baroka's suppers would become so gullible when confronted with his trickery. Significantly Baroka's plan involves his pretending that his manhood has failed him because with Sadiku's dance of women's triumph, Sidi's delight at being on the side of the victor: "Hurray for womankind!" (p. 33), the play has an overt feminist focus. But the extreme

opposite—masculine triumph—is the author's purpose instead. So Sidi is
made to succumb to the Bale and Sadiku to function simply as a tool in
Baroka' machinations.

As soon as Sidi enters the Baroka's chambers, with its masculine aura of
wrestling, a different passive Sidi surfaces. She is in awe of the Lion's
strength and skill in wrestling, of his use of language and eventually of his
"stamp machine".[6] True, Soyinka is obviously making a statement on
human vanity and, as others suggest, representing the symbolic merger of
tradition with youth, the triumph of measured progress over hasty Westernization, life over empty rhetoric.[7] Yet fiery Sidi, with all her potential, loses
her brilliance and slowly deflates in the estimation of the reader/viewer.
Thus ends the promising career of Sidi, relegated, one would speculate, to
pulling out the hairs of Baroka's armpits. Ogunba rightly says that at the end
of the play one is left with "the feeling that we have experienced a
distressing waste . . . Baroka regards women as commodities that must be
used, squeezed dry and then thrown into the garbage can".[8] Never simple,
Soyinka has created a situation in which the heroine has to choose between
the lesser of two evils, since neither Lakunle nor Baroka is the ideal of
African manhood. We are, of course, in the realm of comedy here, but
obviously Soyinka, in his creation of Lakunle, the caricature of a semi-
educated village teacher, was criticizing the empty, borrowed, Western
concepts and attitudes which produce a soft masculinity which is totally
undesirable in an Africa struggling with self-determination. So although
Baroka is a comic grotesque, a terrible caricature of the traditional
chieftain, his eventual triumph represents an implicit defense of the mystery
and strength of the past. Yet, in his portrayal of Sidi, the classical
stereotypical image of the foolish virgin reinforces a negative perception of
self to the female viewer/reader and, concomitantly, a condescencion in
the appraisal of women on the part of the male.

The image of the beautiful submissive virgin recurs in *Death and King's
Horseman* and although more than a decade separates these works, and the
latter is a tragedy based on an actual historical event, similar stereotyped
definitions of the maiden reappear. Here, however, the young virgin becomes
the symbol for all that detracts man from his seriousness of purpose. The
beauty/danger dichotomy is clearly present in the contradictory Eve/Virgin
Mary archetypes which inform the character. The virgin, a nameless,
voiceless votary, like the virgin Egbo takes in *The Interpreters*, is perceived
as object not subject. Her only expressions are sobs at her contribution to
Elesin's demise.

Elesin is involved in the preparation for his ritual of following the dead
Oba (king) to the spiritual region when, as the stage directions explicitly
state: "The earlier distraction, a beautiful young girl comes along the
passage through which Elesin first had his entry".[9] We discover from the
Praise Singer and Elesin's own admissions that he has a deep affection for

beautiful women and although he is challenged to maintain his sense of purpose in face of his grand task, Elesin, like Baroka, sees only the physical beauty which he is somehow obliged to possess. He describes her in words of extreme adulation: ". . .Tell me who was the goddess through whose lips I saw the ivory pebbles of Oya's river-bed. Iyaloja, who is she?" (p. 19). When he fails in his ritual suicide, Elesin tries to explain himself to the young bride who sobs near the cell in which he has been incarcerated by the British official who had intervened to stop the ritual:

> My young bride . . .
> now I feel I want to blame you
> for the mystery of the sapping of my will . . .
> Oh little mother, I have taken countless
> women in my life, but you were more than
> a desire of the flesh. I needed you
> as the abyss across which my body
> must be drawn . . .(p. 65)

Izevbaye contends that Soyinka "detests all forms of womb yearning" and what we see from Elesin is pure lust, his inability to transcend the material/physical plane.[10] Elesin's fall from grace becomes a tragedy of his own making. But another minor tragedy, a personal tragedy (though not in the Aristotelian sense) has occurred. The young bride whose life was so totally fractured by Elesin's rapaciousness is virtually ignored in the grand scheme of Elesin's demise. Her experience, like Sidi's, is the tragic loss of self-worth, which she hides in sobs. Moreover, it provides another example of the author's disposal of the female character.

Soyinka's dramatic technique had reached its height by the time of the writing of this play. Yet there are many similarities in characterization in the two plays. The older lustful man, the young maid, the young man, the "mother of brides" are the same four major actors. The peripheral characters attain more prominence here, but the main difference lies, of course, in the fact that one is a comedy, the other a tragedy. So the major characters, except the virgin bride, are more closely drawn and developed. Olunde, Elesin's son, who takes his father's place in the ritual, is the truly educated hero who is committed to the point of self-sacrifice to his people, a character which Soyinka had been developing throughout his literary career. Elesin, for his part, becomes a much more pathetic figure than Baroka.

Mothers of Brides

Before going on to a discussion of Soyinka's *femme fatale*, it is pertinent to consider his portrayal of older women, for here his characterization loses much of its subjectivity and he succeeds in creating more rounded, less stereotypical characters. Whereas in Western society middle-aged women are subject to severe depression at the loss of family, African women, as Iyaloja and Sadiku illustrate, gain, with age, additional status and power which, in some cases, equals and/or exceeds that of males.

In both plays, however, the older women bring about the capitulation of otherwise promising maidens. Sadiku of *The Lion and the Jewel* is procurer of brides for Baroka. On the surface she plays the role of the faithful senior wife but Soyinka hints that Baroka does not trust her completely. Her hidden resentment of male dominance is exhibited when she performs her wildly sexual dance of victory over Baroka's "impotence". Her ditty "Take Warning my masters/We'll scotch you in the end" becomes an anthem to the strength and endurance of women. Words like the following come from Sadiku:

> This is the world of women. At this
> moment our star sits in the centre
> of the sky. We are supreme. (p. 34)

Sadiku is talking here of sexual triumph, and if we follow her line of thought we can conclude that even though Baroka wins the minor skirmishes, the eventual victory of the battle will be the woman's, for there will eventually be one who will "scotch" the men of Baroka's type just as she "scotched" his father, Okike. Thus Sadiku's performance upsets the stereotype of the submissive wife in the polygamous household. She obviously rejects the system in which the male constantly re-enacts his dominance over the female.[11]

Sadiku's treatment in the resolution of the play is also worthy of consideration. Her triumph is cut short when she realizes that Baroka had feigned impotence, as Sidi revealed. So she mouths the resigned: "It happens to the best of us." (p. 59). But, although Sadiku has not achieved obvious triumph, every new bride that Baroka takes does indeed weaken him while it increases her status as senior wife. Ogunba has suggested that Soyinka probaly made a mistake in giving Sadiku a name which is normally a man's name.[12] One may as easily argue that her masculine name follows the general portrayal of the character as an extension of the male dominance system, for in the end Sadiku has achieved her original purpose, albeit indirectly. Again she becomes "Mother of Brides" and is in a position to bless Sidi with fertility and prosperity as she joins her household. Sadiku, from this point of view, may not be a "mere tool to be manipulated at will by the ingenious Baroka . . .";[13] her status as senior wife is assured.

This position is taken a step further in the characterization of Iyaloja in *Death and the King's Horseman.* Elesin suffers dearly, and as he descends in prominence, she ascends in stature and eventually ends the play on a note of dominance. Throughout the action, she wields tremendous power as the

"Mother of the Market", a woman who in Yoruba society is a well known social and political entity.[14] Although Iyaloja, like Sadiku, functions as the procurer of brides, in Elesin's case, she knows his desire for sexual dominance will be to his detriment. So in the end, as true earth-mother, she is in a position to castigate him for his weakness: "I wish I could pity you" (p. 68); "Oh Elesin, see what you've become" (p. 70). Indeed, she expresses much of the play's message and thus fulfills the didactic function to which Lee referred (as cited above). Iyaloja even triumphs over the colonial officer whom she constantly addresses as "Child" and, as the play closes, she charges the young bride to "forget the dead, forget even the living. Turn your mind only to the unborn" (p. 76). Sadiku had, of course, offered a similar charge to Sidi. It is important to reiterate here that in his portraiture of the mature woman, Soyinka is able to achieve greater objectivity and to capture the true position of the female elder in his society. Yet, there is no depth to the character. Instead she mouths the author's attack on the dissipation of energy on the acquisition of the material, man's inability to transcend the mundane and achieve spiritual excellence.

In this play, Sadiku's "Take warning my masters/We'll scotch you in the end" reverberates.

The Queen Bees

As early as *A Dance of the Forests* (1960) Soyinka had created Rola, who we learn had callously sent a stream of lovers to their deaths. It is here that the image of the *femme fatale* is set, and she reappears with amazing frequency in succeeding works. For the purposes of our discussion, Simi of *The Interpreters* is the first of these mysterious, quasi-mythical courtesans. Simi is a woman living and moving in the real world but she is imbued with the charcteristics of the river goddess. Simi is excessively beautiful, the "goddess of serenity" with the "skin of light pastel earth, Kano soil in the air."[15] But there is a quality of danger and hypnotism in this beauty, for she is the "Queen Bee" who destroys the drones who are nevertheless attracted to her. Because of Simi "of the slow eyelids"

> men lost hope of salvation, their homes
> and children became ghosts of past
> illusion, learning from Simi a new view
> of life, and, love immersed in a
> cannibal's reality, Simi broke men
> and friendships.   (pp. 50-51)

Soyinka does not leave Simi as the Queen Bee but juxtaposes that with another image of danger, for Simi is also the "Mammy Watta"—the mythological siren who lures men to their deaths with her alluring beauty. Egbo's relationship with Simi is a haunting one in which he seems to be

under a magic spell. Already "notorious for his fear of women" (p. 51) his
sexual desire for her is like being immersed in a flood:

> Egbo watched her while she walked
> towards him eyes ocean clams with
> her peculiar sadness . . . like a
> man drowning he was saying . . .
> only like a choice of drowning.(p. 251)

It has been pointed out that the Egbo-Simi attraction has deep roots in a
certain mystical contact which the true creekman has with a water spirit and
suggested that the mammy water figure also often functions as the African
author's muse, or the link between death as loss and the ultimate
transformation it represents.[16] Thus Egbo's "death" to Simi is only
symbolic of his own self-sacrifice and fuller acceptance of himself. Yet one
still must question the validity of the repeated use of the female character in
this way, as throughout the novel the deadliness of Simi is pervasive. As
well as the sensation of drowning, Egbo felt her impact as the "wanton strike
of a snake and welcomed the poison through his veins" (p. 53). More animal
imagery dominates the characterization as she becomes "the beast that lay
in wait to swallow him" (p. 54) and even from the plant world "the
thornbush at night". (p. 56)

Similarly, Segi of *Kongi's Harvest* is so beautiful, so alluring that she is,
like Simi, the subject of praise songs. She too has hypnotic eyes (a physical
feature which seems to fascinate the author) to which praises are sung, and
nipples as "violent as thorns". She too is the "Mammy Watta" who "frolics
by the sea at night". But this quality of danger is heightened in the
description of Segi, for there is a beauty with viciousness expressed in the
image of the *agbadu* "the coiled black glistening snake".[17]

Segi, Kongi's sometime mistress, is by far Soyinka's most dangerous
woman, but at least, in this play, her venom has a practical use. As the play
climaxes and Daodu is unable to carry through with the overthrow of
Kongi, Segi resourcefully seizes the time and valorously sends the head of
her executed father to Kongi.

As a character, Segi embodies the role of women in revolutionary
struggle. This is so because Soyinka was able to effect a balance in the
projection of Segi and to direct her quality of danger into a positive channel.
There is a tremendous amount of energy in the Segi character. Although
colored by myth, she endangers not the man she loves but the deserving
agents of oppression. This positive portrayal of Segi is effected because the
author does not limit the character to attributes of the mythical *femme
fatale* but draws on actual Yoruba history of heroic women.[18] By making
Segi a courtesan and an organizer of prostitutes and Daodu a farmer and an

organizer of farmers, in *Kongi* Soyinka toys with the notion of class struggle
and suggests a revolutionary potential for both groups. However, the author
avoids any commitment to this ideal in the resolution of the play. While
there is energy and potential, bound by the limits of actual history, the play
never moves beyond the level of protest.[19]

The depiction of Iriyise in *Season of Anomy* seems to take the positive
woman's image created in Segi several steps backwards, as the characterization moves from woman as subject to woman as object of quest. Iriyise
again has the characteristics of the goddess, the image of the exceptional
beauty that defines the Soyinka woman. She is "Celestial", "Iridiscent",
"the Cocoa Princess". But she can be moody and "bitchy" (pp. 38-39) and
one never knows if she is going to prepare breakfast for him or chase him
with a stick (p. 78). Iriyise is also the "Queen Bee" who actually lives in
what the author explicity describes as "a cell in a deep hive" (p. 58). Animal
imagery again surrounds her portrayal. "Once in a while she unleashed the
caged tigress in her at some trivial or imagined provocation . . ." (p.62)

Iriyise is mysterious too. She disappears and reappears at will without
giving plausibe explanations for her absence. Indeed her act as the Cocoa
Princess involves her disappearance into the pod and reappearance as the
new shoot. In this context, there is a definite positive quality about her as
expressed in her immersion into the life of Aiyero, a context in which
Ofeyi felt he knew little of her (p. 7). Yet this quality of Iriyise is never
developed by the author. Instead, her sexual attributes dominate as Ofeyi is
caught in a trance admiring her beauty:

> Ofeyi folded his hands behind his
> head marvelling at the apparition
> of a goddess bathed in purple
> curtain-filtered light. It seemed
> to him that the room was mysteriously
> still, that the moment was
> frozen and replete. (p. 81)

But Soyinka admits, in an apparent authorial intrusion, that "vision is
eternally of man's own creating. The woman's acceptance, her collaboration
in man's vision of life results in such periodic embodiments of earth and
ideal. Iriyise would reveal within her person a harrowing vision of the
unattainable." (p. 82) Thus Iriyise, following the lines of the Orpheus myth
disappears, and the rest of the novel involves Ofeyi's abandonment of any
involvement in the struggle all around him, a struggle which the Dentist and
the people of Aiyero are committed to, and begins his quest for Iriyise.[20]

In describing this mysterious "phantom lady" as one of the most frequent
creations of male writers, Barbara Warren says

> As the man's supreme ideal, his
> ultimate desire, an image with which
> he compares all living women, this
> "phantom lady" is a barrier between
> himself and actual experience. He
> can only waste away in a fantasy
> world if he seeks her as a real woman
> for he will never find her in the flesh. . .[21]

Thus Ofeyi blindly continues to search for Iriyise, and Tailia, whom he constantly measures against Iriyise, can never become his woman. Although she exhibits kindness and tenderness in caring for the victims of war, she is still for him wrought in the image of the nun she once wanted to become. When Ofeyi, after much searching, finally finds Iriyise, she has become merely a shell of her former self, a rag doll, for she was only a dream anyway.

In disposing of Iriyise this way, one hopes Soyinka is discarding this type of mythical creature he has a penchant for creating. Just as Ofeyi cannot find the real Iriyise, so the author will not evolve credible female characters if they are continuously shrouded in myth. The Queen Bee stereotype is not only a negative portrayal of women but stylistically it affects the quality of the work. Moreover, Soyinka is unable to make these women plausible or interesting. For it is mainly in his descriptions of these "superwomen", that one sees a shortcoming in his usually fluid style.

Several conclusions can be drawn from our analyses of Soyinka's portrayal of women. First of all, the "dearth of negative images" of women which Rushing[22] finds in modern African poetry does not hold true in the drama and fiction of Wole Soyinka. To the contrary, the author exhibits a patriarchal attitude to women which reveals itself in several stereotypes, the *femme fatale* having primacy.

Additionally, a definite ambivalence in the author's characterization of women is communicated. One constantly gets images of women that are dichotomized and contradictory. Women are beautiful/deadly, pure/sensual, submissive/assertive, wise/foolish, life/death. This ambivalent treatment of women necessarily extends itself into male-female relations. For, along with male dominance, one gets a sense of the woman as indirect victor; as prize of the quest yet simultaneously causing the destruction of the male who initiates the quest. Hence the sex-as-death theme persists in all the Soyinka works, and death is more often loss than it is transformation. Elesin, for example, dies on two levels, the obvious one in which he commits an untimely suicide, and the other in which he loses his sense of purpose in his possession of the young virgin. Ofeyi similarly loses his sense of direction in his quest for Iriyise, and implicit in the resolution of the plot is

Soyinka's condemnation of Ofeyi's avoidance of commitment, like Elesin's, to serious endeavor.[23]

According to one critic, "the more successful characters, invested with the life force and strong personality traits, tend to be women."[24] This is clearly a conclusion that the literature does not support. This study has looked at the major works and cursory examination of his most recent works reveals the same tendencies. Indeed the only other noteworthy type not discussed here is the shrew as revealed in Amope in the Jero plays and Madame Batoki in *Season of Anomy*, for example, for in *Madmen and Specialists* and *The Strong Breed*[25] the female characters are also used as symbols in the male's struggle to conquer the life-threatening forces invading his world. The point is that although there are a few female characters who are more fully realized, the outstanding Soyinka female characters fit into one of the three categories we describe. The penchant towards consistently using women primarily as symbols is at issue here. Symbolic structuring does not shield a writer from negative or limiting portrayals. Pearse for his part is very cavalier about the way in which women are disposed. For example, I disagree strongly with his arguments that Sidi is made an "ordinary woman" and hence a better person when she is successfully seduced by the Bale, or that Simi's move from her mystical aloofness to subservience enriches her and makes her a rounded character.

This is not to detract from Soyinka's substantial literary achievement but to make the point that often for male writers there is a liberty to use women for various ends and in some cases to openly relegate them to derogatory roles and descriptions. Thus, throughout Soyinka's works one finds the kernel of positive portrayal of the female image which is never fully realized. The energy of Sadiku's victory song/dance and Sidi's fire, Segi's organization of the prostitutes, the challenges of the chorus of women and the young girls in *Death and the King's Horseman*, and Iriyise's brief involvement in Aiyero provide the basis for a balanced image of women in this literature. But the author continuously abandons these potentially positive female characters or characteristics. Dehinwa, a realistic, modern African woman is never developed in *The Interpreters* for example. Instead, we find the idealization of physical attributes of women or the quest for the ideal, which limits the author's development of plausible female characters.

Legend and actual history seem to provide Soyinka with material for more positively drawn characters than does mythology. While traditional mythology becomes a viable creative force in some stages of literary development, as Soyinka's brilliant career has demonstrated, it eventually becomes a limiting factor for it circumscribes the action, themes and development of character. This is amply demonstrated in his over-use of the *La Belle Dame Sans Mercie* motif. Iyaloja, modelled on the Yoruba *Iyalode*, becomes the giant among Soyinka's female characters. Segi, also modelled on the courageous female warrior of Yoruba history, is a much more stimulating character than Simi or Iriyise. One also gets a glimpse of the real power of senior wives in Sadiku, but this again is not clearly developed.

It can be argued that the writer is merely reflecting socio-cultural realities. But we already recognize that the artist has the power to create new realities; to represent male-female relationships and the role of women as they have been in the past and might be in the future: women as neither victors nor victims but partners in struggle. Ngugi wa Thiong'o in *Petals of Blood, Devil on the Cross*, and Ousmane Sembène in *God's Bits of Wood* have already begun this process.[26] Soyinka himself has demonstrated this possibility in Segi. Skill at female portraiture is not automatic but requires sensitivity and insight in all writers, and especially in male writers. The writer must also recognize when he is creating negative images and stereotypes and seek alternative images and symbols if he is to develop positive female characters.

NOTES

1. Sonia Lee, "The Awakening of Self in the Heroines of Ousmane Sembène," in *Sturdy Black Bridges*, ed. Roseann P. Bell et al, (New York: Anchor Press/Doubleday, 1979), pp. 52-60.

2. Kathleen Staudt, "The Characterization of Women by Soyinka and Armah," *Ba Shiru* 8.2 (1977):63-69; Adetokunbo Pearse, "Symbolic Characterization of Women in the Plays and Prose of Wole Soyinka," *Ba Shiru* 9.1&2 (1978): 39-46; C. Purisch, "Soyinka's Superwomen," a paper presented at the first Ibadan Annual African Literature Conference, July, 1976, has not been available in published form. Sylvia Bryan's paper on the changing Role of Women in Soyinka will be published in the forthcoming issue of *African Literature Today* (v. 15). A few studies of women in African Literature include some discussion of women in Soyinka's works: G.C.M.M. Mutiso, "Women in African Literature," *East African Journal*, 3:No. 3 (March, 1971) 4-14; Anne Lippert, "Women Characters in African Literature," *Afriscope*, 3, No. 10 (October, 1972) 44-46, 49; Kenneth Little, *The Sociology of Urban Women's Image in African Literature* (New Jersey; Rowman, 1980).

3. Gerald Moore, *Wole Soyinka* (London: Evans, 1971); Oyin Ogunba, *The Movement of Transition* (Ibadan Univ. Press, 1975) and Eldred Durosimi Jones, *The Writings of Wole Soyinka* (London: Heinemann, 1973) make reference to women in Soyinka as part of general discussions of the author's works. James Gibbs, ed., *Critical Perspectives on Wole Soyinka* (Washington, D.C.: Three Continents Press, Inc., 1980) contains no essay on this subject.

4. See Wole Soyinka, "The Writer in a Modern African State." *Transition* 6: No. 3 (1967), 11-13 and "The Fourth Stage: Through the Mysteries of Ogun to the Origin of Yoruba Tragedy," appendixed in his *Myth, Literature and the African World* (London: Cambridge University Press, 1976). Abiodun Jeyifo,

"Soyinka Demythologized Notes on a Materialistic Reading of *A Dance of the Forests, The Road* and *Kongi's Harvest.*" Ibadan, March 1975, explores Soyinka's expropriation of Yoruba mythology.

5. Wole Soyinka, *The Lion and the Jewel* (London: OUP, 1963), p. 12. Subsequent references are to this edition and appear in the text.

6. This writer viewed a Theatre Arts production of this play at the University of Ibadan in which the "stamp machine" appeared as a giant phallus which Baroka plunged up and down into a hole at the base of the contraption. The explicit sexual reference of this scene provided considerable response from the male members of the audience which was sustained up until the final triumph over Sidi.

7. See for example discussions of *The Lion and the Jewel* by Moore, Jones and Ogunba in their works cited above.

8. Ogunba, p. 40.

9. Wole Soyinka, *Death and the King's Horseman* (London: Eyre, Methuen, Ltd., 1975), p. 18. Subsequent references are to this edition and appear in the text.

10. D. S. Izevbaye, "Mediation in Soyinka: The Case of the King's Horseman," in Gibbs, pp. 121. 124.

11. Jones, p. 30, contains a further discussion of this point. Enoch T. Mvula's "Tumbuka Pounding Songs in the Management of Familiar Conflicts," *Cross Rhythms* (2) ed. by Daniel Avorgbedor and Kwesi Yankah (Indiana University, African Folklore Publications, 1985), pp. 93-113, discusses how women use pounding songs, as Sadiku does, to comment on male-female conflicts, struggles between co-wives and to castigate their men for any failings.

12. Ogunba, p. 49.

13. Ibid.

14. Bolanle Awe, "The Iyalode in the Traditional Yoruba Political System," in *Sexual Stratification*, ed., Alice Schlegel (New York: Columbia University Press, 1977), pp. 144-159.

15. Wole Soyinka, *The Interpreters* (London: Heinemann, 1974), p. 51. Subsequent references are to this edition and appear in the text.

16. Emmanuel Obiechina, *Culture, Tradition and Society in the West African Novel* (London: Cambridge Univ. Press, 1975), p. 115; also Peter Thomas, "The Watermaid and the Dancer: Figures of the Nigerian Muse," *Literature East and West* 12: No. 1 (March, 1968), 83-93.

17. Wole Soyinka, *Kongi's Harvest* (London: OUP, 1967) pp. 32-3. Subsequent references are to this edition and appear in the text.

18. Ogunba suggests that Segi is depicted like some of the famous Yoruba or Bini women of antiquity—Moremi, Emotan, Sungbo. See *Movement of Transition*, p. 197.

19. Omafume F. Onoge contends in "The Crisis of Consciousness in Modern African Literature: A Survey," *Canadian Journal of African Studies*, 8 (1974), 387-410, that Soyinka has failed to move beyond the critical realist stage into the socialist realist stage. Soyinka's position on this issue appears in the foreword to his play *Opera Wonyosi* (Bloomington: Indiana University Press, 1981) in which he takes issue with the Nigerian New Left Critics and their prescriptions.

20. Izevbaye shows how the novel structurally follows the Orpheus myth, even to the naming of the characters, in his "Soyinka's Black Orpheus," in Gibbs, pp. 243-252.
21. *The Feminine Image in Literature* (New Jersey: Hayden Book Company, Inc., 1973), p. 8.
22. "Images of Black Women in Modern African Poetry: An Overview, " in *Sturdy Black Bridges*, pp. 18-24.
23. One reading of the novel sees The Dentist and Iriyise as *alter egos* of the hero Ofeyi; aspects of his divided self which he is trying to reintegrate.
24. Pearse, p. 39.
25. Wole Soyinka, *Three Short Plays* ("The Swamp Dwellers", "The Trials of Brother Jero", "The Strong Breed"). London, Oxford University Press, 1969; *Madmen and Specialists* (Ibadan, Oxford University Press, 1971).
26. See Marie Linton Umeh, "The African Heroine," in *Sturdy Black Bridges*, pp. 39-51 and Sonia Lee's article cited above for further discussion of this issue.

Parasites and Prophets: The Use of Women in Ayi Kwei Armah's Novels

Abena P.A. Busia

The Ghanaian writer Ayi Kwei Armah has written five novels to date. *The Beautyful Ones Are Not Yet Born* (1968), *Fragments* (1970), *Why Are We So Blest* (1972), *Two Thousand Seasons* (1973), and *The Healers* (1978). All but the third are set literally, or symbolically, in Ghana and in them Armah seems to shift between two central perceptions of women—woman as parasite, and woman as liberating prophet. Importantly, as we move through Armah's works sequentially the prophets eclipse the parasites. The major transition in this vision of women throughout the five novels is the concern of this paper.

It must first be stated that but for the qualified exception of the female figures in *Two Thousand Seasons*, women in Armah's novels never have roles independent of the novel's hero or protagonist—always a man in a male dominated society. Women are always the lovers, wives, or blood relatives of the central male characters, and have significance in the texts only in so far as they affect those characters. Furthermore, another problem shared by prophets and parasites alike, is that these women, scattered throughout Armah's texts, are frequently unsexed or choose to deny their sexuality. As we shall see, Armah never truly finds a resolution for the difficulty he has balancing the different forces of sex, love, and power, when exercised by women. Nonetheless, bearing these conflicts in mind, and taking the essentially secondary nature of their roles as given, we shall argue here that the roles played by women in Armah's novels have undergone, if not a revolution, then at least a positive reformation throughout the texts. That is, Armah's novels reveal two parallel motions concerning women, which operate in tension: on the one hand, the movement which liberates them from being predominantly symbols of opression to being symbols of liberation; and on the other, that for the most part *symbols* of womanhood, perverse or idealized, are essentially *all* they are.

Looking at the portraits of the women and the roles they play is one way of tracing the measure of resolution Armah finds in each text as he moves towards a greater understanding, or a more articulate explication, of the central problems he is exploring in all his works. For Armah, all oppression (whether social, political or cultural) is a form of disease, and the source of all division among mankind. In each of his texts the same two fundamental problems are explored—the conflict between the private and social worlds in modern Africa and the crisis of divided loyalties this creates, as well as the difficulty, for the sensitive individual, of ordering the oppression and chaos of contemporary life into a comprehensible framework which takes account of the past as well as the present.

So far as the portraits of women are concerned, in all five novels the division between parasites and prophets is stark. True to Armah's equation of things white with evil, and black with spirituality, the parasites are either Westernized African women, or, as in the case of Amy Reitsch in *Why Are We So Blest?*, both Western and white. The prophets are those women who are seen as being true to the aspirations of Black African people, true to the ancient 'way' that has long since been forgotten. In the two earliest novels, the female parasites are the mothers, wives and sisters of the heroes. That is, they are always attached to the hearth. Is is these 'loved ones', as they are called, who are portrayed as the burden on the soul of the struggling and suffering hero. They are, whether intentionally or not, seen as the oppressors. They make demands, generally material ones concerned with keeping up social appearances, which always provoke a storm of conflict in their men. Pitted against them are the liberating prophets. This conception of them springs primarily from the literal role they play in the fourth novel *Two Thousand Seasons*, the only work in which women ever initiate any action. In that novel, the voices of the prophets are female, and, at several crucial moments in the history being recounted, it is the women who save the nation, often in battle against the men. Yet, though their roles are not always so prominent, the other novels do contain women who are, in great and small ways, contending with oppression—their role being to understand their men in adverse circumstances, and, wherever possible, guard them and give them solace. They are liberating prophets in the sense that, even when powerless, they have a vision which can protect their men and at least steer them in the direction of some kind of salvation.

The stress in *The Beautyful Ones Are Not Yet Born*, Armah's first novel, is on the pervasive corrosive effect of a corrupt society whose essential decay is symbolized by Armah's much discussed imagery of filth and dung. The central problem for the hero, simply called 'the man' is to try to reconcile his vision of a whole, healthy and honest society with the need of his 'loved ones' which can only be satisfied, it seems, through compromise of those very aspirations. His relationship to his loved ones then comes to represent the fundamental illness of a society based on an unacceptable conflict between loyalty to the family and loyalty to the community at large. The representatives of the family in the first two books are strongly female characters, and in *The Beautyful Ones Are Not Yet Born* it is the wife and her mother who are seen as opposed to the service to the community that the man would like to be free to perform. They do not appreciate the sacrifice to *their* lives his refusal to be corrupt entails. They live in a world which is obsessed by the gleam of money, and the attendant glitter of prosperity, power, and success that it brings in its wake, no matter how the money is acquired. For example, the women see what they think will be a chance to share in this new and uncommon wealth by taking part in a fraudulent scheme, concerning the ownership of a fishing boat devised by the man's ignorant former classmate, Koomson, now an influential Party dignitary and 'Minister Plenipotentiary'. The women are to agree to the legal ownership of the boat on his behalf, in return for a share of the profits, for in the socialist republic in which the novel is set, a minister cannot own a profitable fishing boat operating under the rules of private capitalist enterprise. The women agree and are deceived. However, the man, while resisting this onslaught on his integrity, suffers nonetheless. His acute despair springs from his ability to understand and in some way sympathize with the needs and demands of his wife and family. His dilemma lies therefore in his sense of failure: he is the victim of their reproaches, which, when voiced, make him feel all the more guilty and responsible for the hopelessness of their situation. The family, not only the wife and mother-in-law, but the children as well, are dependent upon him, and remain a constant burden to him. They are paradoxically passive, but oppressively prominent characters. Every aspect of daily life becomes a form of criticism of the man, and even their silence in their suffering becomes a reproach to him. His situation is not improved by the fact that his wife is not averse to undermining his position by voicing her criticism. In her philosophy, life is like a series of busy roads of all descriptions, and those who go far are those who, ignoring the possibility of accidents, learn to drive fast. It matters not to her that to 'drive' means to learn to cheat the public and ride roughshod over those fellow travellers who are less capable citizens. She states in no uncertain terms that she considers her husband quite ineffectual and stupid. These unpalatable truths matter a great deal to the man, and he feels trapped. He remains trapped by his limited perception, and his feeling that it is the society, and not he, which is fundamentally wrong, remains instinctive. His spirit remains troubled and questioning, because he has no organized system of understanding. Living in his poverty, his sense of moral obligation intact, he has no faith or ideology to guide him.

In this novel the only representative of the 'prophets' is the engimatic, once beautiful and hopeful Maanan, who goes mad. She is a shadowy figure said to be beautiful in body and in spirit, who haunts the painful reminiscences of the text. She is not a prominent figure, but as a friend to the man she stands in opposition to the kind of behaviour displayed by his wife and her mother. Neither one of the troublesome 'loved ones' nor one of those who has compromised with the corrupt power structure, she represents all those Ghanaian people at the time of Independence who followed the 'leader,' were inspired by his ideals, and believed wholeheart-edly that he was indeed a redeemer come to usher in a new and glorious age. It is her hopes, and through her those peoples' hopes, which are recognized as the most betrayed.

In the book it is Maanan who tries to teach the meaning of loving and communal unity, an endeavour which is to perplex all Armah's central characters until he finds a way for them to express it in the social and political analysis which gives form to *The Healers*, the last of his novels so far. In this early work, it is best expressed in a scene by the waterside in which Maanan first teaches the man to smoke 'pot' or 'wee' as it is called. The experience is a liberating one for our frustrated hero, and he learns to see many things for the first time, including Maanan's true beauty, which becomes symbolic of the suffering of all women:

> It was as if Maanan's face was all I would ever need to look at to know that this was a woman being pushed towards destruction and there was nothing she or I could do about it. She was smiling at me, but in myself I felt accused by a silence that belonged to millions and ages of women all bearing the face and the form of Maanan, and needing no voice at all to tell me I had failed them, I and all the others who have been content to do nothing and to be nothing at all all our lives and through all the ages of their suffering. So much of the past had now been pushed into the present moment at the edge of the salt water. I would have said something to Maanan if the things to say had not been so heavy, but even then I was sure she understood, that she had understood long before I had ever seen enough to ask her forgiveness, and that she had forgiven me as much as it was possible for the suffering to forgive those who only remain to suffer with them and to

see their distress . . . Forgive me, Maanan, forgive us all if that is possible these days. (pp. 71-2)[1]

Maanan, far more a symbol than a woman, prefigures the prophetic women of *Two Thousand Seasons*. It is she who teaches the men to try to reach out, and overcome the seemingly constricting putrefying surroundings, to see, physically and spiritually, the pure salt water away from the stagnant pools. But in the end Maanan goes mad, and is last seen wandering around the beach sifting the fine sand through her fingers in search of something inexpressibly lost. In her madness, Maanan sees most clearly that the hopes of her generation have been irretrievably lost, but the man realizes neither she nor anyone else can give him the answers, for they must come from within. He finds nothing to bridge the distances between the members of the community because he has no true understanding of the reasons for the dislocation. Only Maanan knows it is possible for the breach to be healed, but the moment to reach out was lost not only historically, but spiritually. There is a recognition that something more substantial needs to be found to bring the desired peace and enlightenment. The hopeful vision which ends the novel occurs when the man, having been cleansed by the sea, sees a legend painted on a mammy wagon which gives the title to the novel, 'The Beautyful Ones Are Not Yet Born'.

As in *The Beautyful Ones Are Not Yet Born*, in *Fragments* the problem of the family being in conflict, rather than in concert with the community, remains to be resolved. We have again a similar division between those women who impose burdens, and those who wish to bring salvation. And once again it is the two women of the household who have pinned all their hopes for the future on the return of the hero, Baako, to such an extent that their expectations become a weight upon his soul. He is required to share in all their aspirations: to make the dream of a large and comfortable home come true, and to enjoy the status of being someone who, by virtue of a western education, is potentially a personage of much distinction. Their aspirations seem simple enough, but are therefore far more entrapping. They are presented as being based on an old and accepted tradition of the returning hero, the conquering son home from his travels bringing with him the fruits of his learning which produce miracles to bless the family. But there is a difference now:

Now it's taken this modern form. The voyage abroad, everything that follows; it's very much a colonial thing. But the hero idea itself is something very old. It's the myth of the extraordinary man who brings about a complete turnabout in terrible circumstances. We have the old heroes who turned defeat into victory for the whole community. But these days the community has disappeared from the story.

> Instead, there is the family, and the hero comes and turns its poverty
> into sudden wealth. And the external enemy isn't the one at whose
> expense the hero gets his victory; he's supposed to get rich, mainly at
> the expense of the community. (p. 147)[2]

The 'loved ones' are not simply corrupt, but are rather presented as
unknowingly seduced by the society in which they live. The values of this
society remain firmly materialistic and pretentious. Typically the returning
traveller not only generates a show of glory, but he must also enjoy the false
elevation this gives him in the eyes of his family and the community at large.
What matters is how ostentatious a show can be put on, no matter the
impotence it hides. As is brought out most forcefully by the attitudes of his
mother and sister, in the eyes of Baako's family, the terrible failure of his
foreign experience is dramatised by the fact that he returns home in shirt-
sleeves rather than a suit, and carrying a guitar rather than bringing a new
car, or some other status object such as a refrigerator. Neither his sister nor
his mother initially questions these values, although in the end the mother
does change. One of the burdens she had placed on the back of her son was
her hope that he would return to finish the grand house she had started to
build for herself, in his honour. Although by her standards this would seem a
reasonable expectation, she manages to understand her son and recognize
that he views the world from a different perspective. She finally takes him to
her half-built mansion to explain her dream, and apologize to him for
having expected him to fulfill it. Thus she shows a humility and a capacity
for growth which eludes her son. As the portrais of other characters
indicate, her initial expectations represent the societal norm. Once again
our hero, by regarding her as perverse, is demonstrably out of touch with the
times.

That it is the society at large, rather than the hero Baako, which is to be
regarded as centrally at fault is re-enforced by the crucial scene which
describes the name-day ceremony of his baby nephew, the child born to his
sister and her ineffectual husband. This incident is central to an understanding
of the work because it dramatizes the profound spiritual dislocation of the
family and the society of which it is a part, and for which it stands. This
traditional ceremony, to welcome the newly arrived child, and to thank the
spirits of the ancestors for ensuring his safe arrival, has become perverted.
In its new form it is a festive gathering during which the host family, in its
quest for material goods, forces the guests to vie with each other to make the
most outrageous contributions. The whole event is inauspicious; to begin
with, the baby is born premature. Then, to make matters worse, the mother
and the sister move the ceremony forward three days to the fifth day after
birth in order to capitalize on a pay day, instead of waiting until the eighth
day, the day by which traditionally the newly arrived spirit will have

decided whether he is staying, or whether he prefers to return to the world of the ancestors from which he had just arrived.

The important aspect of these changes is the failure on the part of the rest of the family to learn from Naana, the grandmother, the original value of the ceremony. It is a measure of the social breakdown that even while she lives under the same roof, neither her daughter nor her granddaughter takes the trouble to consult or even to inform her of their plans. While she worries about the meaning of such a hastily called and secular gathering, on the pretext of a spiritual occasion, her daughter's paramount concern is that the son upon whom she had such high hopes is refusing to wear a suit or tuxedo for the occasion. While Baako's protest here is based on the rejection of the new forms, Naana is the one concerned with the *spiritual* perversion of customs. On the day itself Naana is the only one disturbed that libations are not poured for the child whose celebration it is supposed to be. For her this underscores the terrible reality that her children have forgotten the ancestors themselves. They no longer look to those gone before, and they no longer even celebrate the newly arrived soul. Even Baako, in his frustration and contempt, does not speak to Naana and so fails to learn from her that he cannot change the selfishness and sham of the new ways which so anger him if he does not first understand the spiritual significance of the changes.

Baako himself is a man in conflict. Having brought a sense of panic and frustration home with him from abroad, he spends much of his time and energy in flight. Like Naana, he can see the disease in contemporary society, but unlike her, he is unable to articulate clearly the nature of the disease in terms which have relevance to the community. A writer, he returns home with high hopes of using the media as a means for community education, to agitate for change and social equality for the benefit of the country. However, the directors of the television and film industry seem, to him, far more interested in exploiting the broadcasting corporation's resources for their own private needs. Baako finds the experience of being unable to do any of the creative, constructive work he had hoped to do quite traumatic. He must acknowledge first that the society has become essentially soul destroying, and, more vitally, that the desire both to please the family, and to work for the larger social good, have become oppressively unreconcilable aims. Both these verities give rise to a conflict within him that he must try to resolve. In order to do this, he has a series of therapeutic conversations and love scenes with his lover, Juana, and all his constructive insights and revelations, both personal and social, come to him through her.

Juana, a psychiatrist introduced to him by his mother, has come to Ghana in search of her 'roots'. She is herself a women in flight, from the United States and from her native Puerto Rico. Like Naana, she too knows that the real crime of human history is the ignorance of past crimes. She had found that the burden of her youth, and had come to Ghana to find some kind of peace, only to discover there was none to be found there. However, being

stronger than Maanan, she at least manages to save herself by making a
necessary accommodation. She learns to know by what visions people led
their lives, or by what visions life led them, and for her, survival becomes a
matter of "adopting a narrower vision every time the full vision threaten[d]
danger to the visionary self." (p. 46) Like all prophets, Juana does recognize
this visionary self even if, rather than playing a leading role in the
community, it is fighting a rearguard action. She may not be able to save
society, but she does what she can to save Baako. "Like some forest woman
whose gods were in all the trees and hills and people around her, the
meaning of her life remained in her defeated attempts to purify her
environment, right down to the final, futile decision to try to salvage discrete
individuals in the general carnage." (p. 177) Like all prophets, Juana is
primarily concerned with salvation and the need to purify the environment;
for all prophets salvation, and above all the salvation of the group, is of the
utmost importance.

Because of the dislocation between the body and the spirit which occurs
in the powerful prophets of *Two Thousand Seasons*, it is notable that
Juana's role as saviour seems to take precedence over her role as mate.
Even at their first meeting, though her response to Baako's overwhelming
presence was as physical as it was spiritual, she spends much of her time
trying to forget his physical body, thinking of him instead as "a kind of
interior dome floating somewhere in her head." But they both have bodies
and he will not permit her to forget this. He controls the movements of their
friendship as he is later to control the movements of her body in love-
making. For Baako she is not only a psychiatrist, but a friend and lover, and
her strength is the source of his strength. She is a sympathetic listener for
him, because she understands his yearning to perform crative acts in union
rather than alone. In the end, after his breakdown, it is she who is preparing a
home for him to come back to after his discharge from hospital.

Juana and the grandmother Naana stand in opposition to the mother and
sister. They are the two women who understand him, and who, without his
obvious personal limitations, share his vision. Naana's observations are
fundamental to an understanding of this work. Her role in this novel is very
much that of the blind and impotent seer. She cannot see with her physical
eyes, but her spirit comprehends a great deal which she cannot or is not
permitted to communicate, except in her own private thoughts. She is the
closest to the protecting ancestral spirits, not only because of her age, but
more especially because of her understanding, her sympathy, and her
memories. Naana represents the communal memory which links the past
with the future. Her powerlessness is thus a commentary on the breakdown
of the society. She is not simply another old woman, she is the mother of the
family, and a prophet rendered helpless.

The novel opens and closes with Naana's reflections. At the start, while
awaiting the return of Baako, she establishes firmly the cycle of life—the

exits and entrances, departures and returns, of which he is a part. But the journeys are not only physical but also spiritual, and the old beliefs establish a continuity between birth and death, with the movements of earthly life in between. For Naana the perversion of customs, such as the failure to pour sincere libations at life's thresholds, augurs ill, for it represents a lack of respect for the soul. She finds this attitude spiritually and physically destructive, and sinful. In those opening reflections, she forsees that the dreams of the family were no longer justified because "woven of such heavy earth" would so crush Baako's spirit he would never 'fly' again. But she is unable to prevent the inevitable, and in her reflections which close the novel she again pin-points the symbolic meaning of these changes:

> The return of this one traveler had held out so much of good hope. But there were those left behind who had their dreams and put them on the shoulders of the traveler returned, heavy dreams and hopes filled with the mass of things here and of this time. And another spirit has already found its death in the hot embrace of people who have forgotten that fruit is not a gathered gift of the instant but seed hidden in the earth and tended and waited for and allowed to grow—so busy have they become in their reaching after new things and newer ways to consume them . . .they have smothered another human soul in all their heavy dreams of things . . . I was powerless before the knowledge that I had come upon strangers worshipping something new and powerful beyond my understanding, which made all the old wisdom small in people's minds, and twisted all things natural to the service of some newly created god . . . The baby was a sacrifice they killed, to satisfy perhaps a new god they have found much like the one that began the same long destruction of our people when the elders first— may their souls never find forgiveness on this head—split their own seed and raised half against half, part selling part to hard-eyed buyers from beyond the horizon, breaking, buying, selling, gaining, spending, till the last of our men sells the last woman to any passing white buyer and himself waits to be destroyed by this great haste to consume things we have taken no care or trouble to produce. (pp.283-4)

In this reflection Naana, contemplating the madness of Baako and the death of the new born child, waits for death. She has seen the problems extant in the society at large internalized and destroying her own family, and has been helpless. The central problems remain; the 'seer' remains fundamentally alienated from the group because an oppressed people have lost themselves in chasing after 'strange gods'. Her reverence for the role of the ancestors and the old ways should not however be regarded as a reactionary vision. Her last reflection shows her awareness that understanding the link with the past in the end leads to progress.

Why Are We So Blest? can be consdidered as a pivotal text. In this novel
the hero, dominated by his experiences with white women, reaches the nadir
of destructive experiences. His death is brought about directly as a
consequence of his sexual relationship with his white girlfriend, and in this
novel the gulf between devotion to a 'loved one' and devotion to a cause is
dramatised to the irreconcilable extreme. All relationships with women in
this text are sexual ones, and nothing good comes out of any of them. The
two most destructive relationships are with white women, and they both
prove dangerous, and finally fatal.

There are two white women of importance, and to both of them Modin,
the Ghanaian hero, is ultimately the sex object *Black* men tend to be in
relationships of imperial and cultural domination. The first is Mrs.
Jefferson, the wife of one of the wealthy 'philanthropists' who fund the
scholarship on which Modin comes to America to study. The second is
Aimee Reitsch, Modin's American girl-friend of German descent. It is with
Aimee that Modin finally travels to North Africa in search of a revolution to
purge his soul, a journey which, for her, is just another radical exercise to
find an escape from boredom. The relationship between them destroys
Modin spiritually and he loses his sense of individual identity. The journey
they jointly undertake leads only to his death in vengeance for his
association with her. Although sexually the two women play diametrically
opposed roles, they both use Modin to the same end. Mrs. Jefferson proves
as insatiable as Aimee proves frigid, but they both represent his slide to
degradation and destruction. Though the dramatization of this degradation
is explicit sexual, the relationships with these two women are to be seen as
yet another consequence of the spiritually destructive nature of the impact
with the western world, a problem addressed in all Armah's novels. The
women do not just torture him spiritually, they kill him physically as well;
and Modin, uncomprehending, participates in his own destruction. It is the
tragedy of this hero that even Naita, the woman he regards as his 'prophet',
though Black, is a thoroughly westernized Black American, and even she
most of the time is absent and cannot save him.

The relationship with Mrs Jefferson is based solely on her desire to fulfill
what is presented as a white American woman's fantasy of sleeping with a
Black man, and with Modin it is all the more rewarding as he is the genuine
article, an African man. Mrs Jefferson, in her desire to live out the
American racial fantasy of the Black man as stud initiates all the sexual
contact between them. We are subjected to explicit scenes of mutual
masturbation between them, (sitting covered in a blanket in the back seat of
the car with her husband and daughter in the front), and graphic episodes in
which she wears him out trying to make him fulfill his role as sex object.
That relationship finally ends when Mrs Jefferson, who had claimed she
could not reach an orgasm with her own husband, takes Modin out into her
garden for sex in the middle of a party, and makes so much noise reaching

her climax that her husband, to whom she had earlier confessed the affair, comes raging into the garden after them and repeatedly stabs Modin in an attempt to kill him in revenge. Mrs Jefferson is the beginning of his descent into degradation. Aimee Reitsch completes his fall.

There is nothing good about Aimee. The portrait of her is the only extended one we have of a white woman in this or any other text, and she is a frigid, voracious destroyer. She is made to carry the burden of guilt for the whole of western civilization in all its destructive energy. As with all other information in this novel, what we learn of her we learn from her own journals, from Modin's references to her in his notes, and from the observations of Solo the failed revolutionary who inherits both sources. The misnamed Aimee is revealed as a woman totally incapable of loving. Although portrayed as being completely unattractive, for some curious reason all men who know her desire her. The feeling is never reciprocated however, and she abuses sexual relationships as an ineffectual antidote for boredom. Furthermore, despite her absolute obsession with sex, she is frigidly incapable of sexual satisfaction. In the sex scenes with Modin, she is even made to indulge in the grotesque fantasy of being the wife of a distant uncle in East Africa, who has successfully seduced her 'boy' into copulating with her in the absence of her jealous husband, in order to sustain the energy required to reach her climax. The pivot of the relationship between herself and Modin is his desire to make it possible for her to have this orgasm. We are subjected to the explicit details of this odyssey, and in its progress, as Modin's initial disgust turns to tenderness, he becomes ensnared in the trap loving her is made to represent. For her, the measure of a man lies in his ability to arouse her body, and she is shown to be pathologically incapable of physical sensation. This physical numbness is paralleled by her spiritual insensitivity. She is shown to be ego-centric, narcissistic, and cruel; the incarnation of all that is aggressively individualistic and destructive about the West, as well as all that is oppressive about private relationships which do not take the larger community into account. The presentation of her is so manipulated as to preclude the generation of any sympathy for her within the limits of the discourse. She never becomes human, but remains the voraciously female entrance to Modin's private hell. The association with her ultimately leads Modin, appropriately enough, to a horrifying death by castration in the deserts of North Africa.

The representation of Naita, though slight, is most important. She is the only figure that comes close to being a means of salvation, but she offers a most ambiguous solace, and this can be taken as a measure of the desolation of the book. Unlike Juana, Naita is absent when the real trials come, and as the two women play identical roles, the depth of Modin's spiritual isolation can be seen in the difference between them.

The parallels between Juana and Naita are strong; they are both Black women of the diaspora, but whereas Juana comes 'home' in search of her roots, Modin travels to Naita in search of enlightenment in the new world. Furthermore, where Juana was fleeing that new world in search of an older salvation, Naita is herself fully aculturated into that world and attempting to become a master of that space. Both Juana and Naita act as confessor figures to their respective men, and they both become lovers whose love-making scenes we share in explicit detail, but the differences between those scenes are significant. In Armah's novels, important spiritual scenes, like the one with Maanan or the man's last walk from *The Beautyful Ones Are Not Yet Born*, or the scenes of love and friendship in *The Healers*, always take place by moving water. It is a notable contrast therefore that the love-scenes with Juana take place by the sea, whereas that with Naita takes place indoors. However, in those with Juana, Baako is always the dominant teacher, drawing the woman out and controlling her responses whereas, in the one scene between Naita and Modin, she is the one in complete control. It cannot go unnoticed that Naita, the only woman so far in complete control of her own sexuality, disappears from the scene very quickly.

Naita in this text becomes a confessional figure, and a positive force for Modin, but only after she has left. While she was with him, it was her sexuality which became for him a means of salvation. She offered him, through her body, withdrawal, peace, and release from loneliness. He desires her most when he wishes to forget completely all the circumstances that are troubling him, and she has the power and control to make him do so. Making love to her he feels as though she encompasses his universe and makes him all knowing, and under such circumstances he feels he cannot be lonely anymore. She represents a means of self-forgetting, as if resting in her all his problems could be solved.

Unlike Juana, Naita does not believe in salvation, her approach is far more earthy and pragmatic, and could be called an instinct for self-preservation. Shortly after the start of their relationship, unable to tolerate any longer the hypocrisy of the white administrators for whom she works, and even more frustrated by Modin's initial blind acceptance of their racist attitude towards him, she departs, leaving no forwarding address. Her philosophy for salvation is one of distrust and suspicion. She tries to warn Modin that no people, and in particular no white people, are worth trusting. One of her major sources of frustration is that she sees so clearly that he is being used and abused. Her knowledge of the subleties of race relations in the United States is seen as the sources of her strength. Her experience of being Black in America has taught her who are the manipulators and who the victims of the terrible social games they must play. She knows how to protect herself, and leaves, but this is no positive resolution, for she fails to teach Modin even to understand why such protection may be necessary. He does not comprehend enough to accept her wisdom for survival, until it is too late. Her social role is rendered ineffectual, and the gulf between personal knowledge and social wisdom remains.

Naita offers only a partial private solace. This factor is emphasized by the fact that after her disappearance, when he has only her memory left, Modin talks to her, and confesses to her in his journal:

> I would have come to you; I would have asked you again had you not put a limitless distance between us. *I would not have needed to ask you—I would have come to you, and these fears would have remained unknown to me.* (emphasis mine) (p. 168)[3]

It is her spirit after she has left which becomes for him a source of wisdom and salvation. Modin is not having healing conversations with a visible, tangible presence; what comfort Naita brings comes only through the memory of her. He makes his confessions to her in his journal and tries to think of what advice she would give him if she were still present. Such is the role of women seen completely as functions of the man's development, that he even writes to her about the destructive Aimee, the incarnation of all the terrible women she tried to warn him against. The most intimate scenes between himself and Aimee are presented as recorded by him in his reminiscences to Naita—as if she would want to know. In the end there is no lasting understanding between them, and no saving vision shared.

Two Thousand Seasons is a significant explication of Armah's thesis on the origins of social malaise. The title of the novel refers to the length of time,—one thousand years, each with one wet and one dry season—, covered by the prophecy narrated in the book. This is a 'monochromatic' work, with the line between black and white starkly drawn. In this novel everything white is equated with decadence and terror, and Black people essentially have virtue on their side. The two groups of white people, the Muslim, Arab, "predators" of the first invasion who swoop down southwards from the desert, and the Christian, European "destroyers" who strike northwards up from the sea, both have the same devastating effect on the Africans with whom they initially come into contact. The Africans get caught between two waves of invasion and are destroyed. *Two Thousand Seasons* is a mythical chronicle written as a record so that the people may understand the history of their continent over the last one thousand years, and, as is the function of myth, to point the way to their salvation.

The most important aspect of his thesis is an understanding of "the way". This "way" is never fully explained, because when the history begins, it is already long lost, and only a few "remembers", "seers" and "hearers" are left trying to recollect and revive a way of life almost disappeared over the many generations. According to "the way", in the beginning all Black Africans were a single united people. Their initial migrations were motivated simply by the desire to make the most of the sheer abundance of water and fertile land bounteously alloted them. Though they scattered, they remembered their original kinship, and only later forgot their essential "connectedness".

The later migrations were attempts to escape the invasion of the Arab 'predators' from the north who sought to oppress them. However, their movement south and eastwards was stopped by the European 'destroyers' at that time moving north and westwards.

Throughout *Two Thousand Seasons* we see at crucial moments that it is the women upon whom salvation depends. In this text all the liberating actions are initiated by women. Only in this novel do we see women who initiate action and who have the power to perform deeds to save the community. The two most powerful groups of women in Armah's works are found in this work. But as we have stated, the problem here is that these female figures are more often than not simply female *voices*, and, as women, are unsexed. The one exception is the first group of women who early in the history act in concert to save the community from their debauched and tyrannical Arab masters. In this case the women, in a truly disgusting episode, prey on the perverted lusts of their masters and use their sex to slaughter them. Their sexuality, divorced from any sentiment of either love or individual worth, is seen and used as a powerful political weapon. The women willingly offer themselves up to be thoroughly debased in the service of the state, for the purpose of righteous vengeance. But once successful, their matriarchy when established, fails to hold. The sexual strength which drives them and empowers them to resurrect their homeland, in the end thoroughly emasculates their own men; when, in desperation, strong sexual women take control of affairs, the men are rendered impotent.

At the other extreme, the host of prophets who guide their people out of a succession of 'Egypts' in this work seem to be simply female voices detached from their bodies and without sexuality. The only one who fleshes out into a real character is the beautiful and much desired Abena who, despite her much vaunted charm, is the most insistent on denying her individual sexuality. Abena, like the prophetic Anoa before her, spurns taking a husband. She, like all the other brave and virtuous women, performs all her deeds and channels all her desires on behalf of the group, and this exclusion of any individual sexual expression is always presented as a positive and communal act.

In *Two Thousand Seasons* the opposition is not between good women and bad women as such, but between visionary women, and those who cannot see. All the prophetic voices are female, and most of the liberators, particularly the early ones, are women. The role of women as bringers of unity and healing, always present in the earlier texts, flourishes in this novel. After the carnage of the harsh and jealous rule of men, the restoration of peace is left to women. But having restored unity, the women become overgenerous and take over all the responsibilities once shared with the men. The comfort and fertility of the life they established make the men lazy and unwary, and therefore easy prey for the first group of incoming invaders, the 'predator' Arabs, masquerading as beggars needing shelter and succor. This succor received, the strangers preyed on the readily visible weaknesses of the society and gained power.

The people are delivered from the slavery which ensues after this first invasion once again by the action of the women, on 'the night of slaughter' already alluded to. Described in all the fullness of a seemingly perverse imagination, their liberation is bought at the price of a series of gruesome and brutal sexual acts in which they use the degradation to which they have become subject, to ensnare and slaughter those who have enslaved them. Those who had been debased, become the debasers, but it is a false liberation. The people have been corrupted from within; the years of slavery have created a hierarchical social structure and a host of leeches,— indigenous "cripples" "predators" and "destroyers"—upon whom the out-siders can rely to bring about the effective destruction of the societies from within, in return for material gain and undeserved social status.

It is to this group of people in danger that the first strong prophecy comes, from Anoa, the female with two voices:

> The first, a harassed voice shrieking itself to hoarseness, uttered a terrifying catalog of deaths—deaths of the body, deaths of the spirit; deaths of single, lost ones, deaths of groups snared in some killing pursuit; deaths of nations, the threatened death of our people . . . From the same prophetic throat came a second voice. It was calmer, so calm it sounded to be talking not of matters of our life and death . . . For every shrieking horror the first voice had given sound to, this other gave calm causes, indicated effects, and never tired of iterating the hope of the issue of all disasters: the rediscovery and the following again of our way, the way. (p. 24)[4]

The actual prophecy of Anoa declares that, seduced by "the whiteness of destruction's slope", the people are willingly rushing towards the period of two thousand seasons of pain and disaster terrible to comtemplate, and that painful as the descent of one thousand seasons of bondage will be, the struggle out of bondage will be harder still until finally they regain the ancient way of life.

The people migrate southwards again, in search of freedom, and on this second migration also the women come to the rescue. Depressed by doubts and insecurities, the people despair of ever finding a new and free homeland. Agitated by just one man, they turn on their advance guard and kill them before it dawns on them that in doing so they have killed the only guides who knew the terrain. Only two women, Ningome and Noliwe, had tried to help the guards, and were beaten unconscious for their pains. On reviving they repeat the ancient prophecy of Anoa, with a vengeance, then find the wisdom and the heroic courage to walk their people out of the wilderness to their unknown 'promised land'. On arrival, responding directly to the failure of courage and the absence of any communal spirit in the face of adversity, it is the women again who remind their people that their time—two thousand seasons—has not elapsed, and that the original prophecy had spoken of an invasion of destroyers coming north from the sea, who would be abetted by their own failure to remember their true "way" and keep to the path of "reciprocity".

The concept of "reciprocity" is an important one in this work. The tribulations begin when the people forget that for everything given, something must be received in return; "the way" teaches that those who give without receiving are the victims of their recipients, and their generosity is a form of self-hatred. This is the central concept which informs the opening words of the novel; the image of springwater flowing into the desert, without hope of regeneration, is an essentially self-destructive one. "The desert takes. The desert knows no giving", so the future of that springwater is one of extinction. When the people settle in their new found lands, the men behave like the desertflowing springwater. Under the influence of the newly arrived Europeans, they forget completely all the principles of the 'way' and do not hear the voices of the female prophets who remember, and remind them of their doom. The men accept the new division of people into parasites and producers, masters and slaves.

The most important consequence of this acceptance is that women, hitherto unquestionably social equals, have a subordinate role forced upon them by the men. To the men, it seems plain that the hazardous migration having cost so many lives, the obvious plan was "to make of every female a childbearer as soon as her body showed it was ready, and for as long as her body continued to turn manseed to harvest" (p. 94). It followed naturally, childrearing and housekeeping being such arduous tasks, that the women should and would be exclusively occupied. The men therefore abrogate to themselves all other powers in the community and, schooled by Europeans, begin to establish hierarchies in states where there had previously been none. The ploy succeeds because resistance would have meant further division, so the astonished women "accepted the place of childbearing bodies, in their soul wondering why the ability to do such necessary work should bring as its reward such vindictive slavery at the hands of men" (p. 94). The subjugation of women is seen as a specifically alien form of oppression which should have been resisted. Those few women who tried to do so were either annihilated, or had their sexuality denied by being 'elevated' to the status of honorary males. However, as during the wanderings in the wilderness, so too when settled in their new land, it is women who remain at the vanguard of the forces of resistance and revolution. When the institution of kingship is still newly established it is a woman who realizes that its trappings and ceremonies are a sham to hide an inferior being and first resists its callow authority. When the Europeans first come bearing gifts and seeking friendship with their king, it is a woman who first finds her voice and speaks for the people in protest—and her words remind them of the vital need to discourage the Europeans from settling amongst them. But in the end, as the prophecy works itself out, these women are defeated by the league of treachery formed between the Europeans and their king.

As this novel is a historical saga, it is not until the closing years of the "two thousand seasons" that we have extended portraits of any of the protagonists. But the last part of the novel deals with the last two hundred seasons including the years lived through by the griot reciting the history. The most important woman in this section, whose spirit dominates the end of the story, is the woman Abena, the last in the long line of liberators. Like the other women, she sees more clearly than most people of her time, yet despite this, she has hopes for most of the human spirit. Like Anoa, Idawa, and others before her, she is physically and spiritually a beautiful person. Yet we do not actually know what she looks like. As has been mentioned, Armah's strong, prophetic women in this text are somehow always divorced from their physical bodies. Either, like Noliwe and Ningome, the pair who lead them out of the desolation in the wilderness, they remain forever *voices*, or when they are said to be beautiful, we get no true sense of their physical presence. They are all Black beauties whose dominant characteristic is grace of movement; they are all in their age the most desired; and to a woman all have better things to do than marry, in readiness for other more grand communal purposes. Only on one occasion does this desire to eschew "the need for pairing" extend itself to the men as well. The group of twenty of Abena's age group, when doing "the dance of love" which ends their initiation rites, refuse to leap into mating pairs, which is the object of the ritual. Instead they leap together as a group, and escape to the forest together in search of a better way of life. This insistence on collective action is most fully developed in Abena, to the point that she is prepared to risk the possibility of being forced into slavery with her less perceptive friends, rather than take any action which would spare her alone, but leave her friends forsaken. She realizes, as do all Armah's central characters, that individual salvation is of no consequence, without the redemption of the group. This theme becomes prominent and is the reason why they manage to escape 'the middle passage' and help each other to free themselves from slavery. In this text, the spirit of survival is a female spirit, and that of repression, is male. So it is a measure of the spiritual health of this group that in the end the women not only fight, they help lead in the fighting. This dramatizes a return to the universality of roles under the old 'way'; fighting for freedom is neither kept nor regarded as a predominantly male prerogative.

This one factor dramatizes the fact that Armah, in his later novels, is demonstrably slowly liberating himself from some of the literary conventions followed by other male writers, whether Western or African, in their

representations of women in the novel. There are basically two traditions of
oppositions governing the portrayal of women in the novel which concern us
here: women as wholesome whores or victimized or virtuous virgins, and
women as nurturing earth mothers or destructive Jezebels. Armah has
broken away from one tradition altogether—he does not subscribe to the
convention of the free-spirited harlot; there are no whores in any of his texts,
heroic or otherwise. In this he breaks away from a tradition which has
existed for several centuries in the West (represented by such well-known
characters as Defoe's Moll Flanders, and Dickens' Nancy), and which has
also been recreated in the contemporary African novel by such writers as
Ekwensi and Ngugi.

As we have noted, Armah's women are conventionally women of the
household whose role is intended to be that of supporting their men, whether
or not they succeed. And just as in its very form and scope *Two Thousand
Seasons* breaks away from the conventions of the modern realistic novel, its
liberating, powerful prophets are strong, public characters, who carry their
societies with them, rather than being carried by them. This breaks the
mould of the second convention of woman as savior or woman as destroyer
which Armah incorporated into his earlier novels, in which all the women
either fed on the life blood of the hero, or were there to try to protect him. But
this dramatic break is in a sense a reaction, not a resolution, for it still
restricts the women to a *choice* between only these two modes of being.
Furthermore, in these prophets, like Naana, who are guardians of the
collective history and prophetic memory, Armah has managed to create a
body of socially active, powerful women who willingly divorce themselves
from the expression of their sexuality in relationships with men. This is most
curious as the novel contains a very powerful argument against the
discrimination of women on the grounds of their necessary childbearing
abilities. Yet it seems that the price of power and social commitment must
be the individual sexuality of the woman concerned. The power of sex is
rarely creative, and when it is, it is either not fully expressed, or it is not
sustained; the women must be nurturing without actually being mothers—
finally, there are no creative mothers who are politically or socially
powerful in any of these texts. There is a strange inability to reconcile virtue
and any sexuality in an active, viable, and socially influential relationship.
Thus the true significance of Armah's latest novel *The Healers*, so far as the
role of women is concerned, is Armah's attempt to work towards some kind
of resolution in the conflicted representation of his nurturing women.

By the time we reach *The Healers* one side of the equation, woman as
parasite, has completely disappeared. In this novel all the women but one
are positive factors, and their positiveness is rendered in conventional
terms. They are gentle, consistent, and people of beauty rather than force;
certainly although the central Healer, the principal initiate, and the most

influential patient are all three of them male, to become a "healer" is to take on these quintessentially 'female' characteristics. Though this may be regarded as positive, what it means is that Armah's women remain on the whole one-dimensional; we never find, in the same person, a true complex of both virtues and faults. However, in spite of this, the tremendous achievement of *The Healers* is that in this novel women, represented by Ajoa and Araba Jesiwa, are at last becoming more complete—including sexually complete—private *and* public persons.

The Healers, is a historical novel set in the closing years of the ninteenth century, and recounts the history of the British imperial wars of conquest on the Gold Coast, from the point of view of the defeated Ashanti. The larger social and political concerns Armah wishes to present are woven around a domestic story of local intrigue and murder which blights the lives of a male youth, the initiate Densu, and his group of visionary medical, spiritual and social "healers" who give their name to the novel.

The pattern of women as creative beings established in *Two Thousand Seasons*, is continued in this history. Even when minor characters, women in this novel are significant because they find a kind of resolution between being women of the household and women of history, which is lacking in the earlier works. Although still associated with domesticity, they are no longer outside history, and the resolution of the home is not divorced from that of the political marketplace. Women in this novel are learning, or have learned, to occupy both private and public spaces. Their predominant function is still domestic, and they are still in the text because they are related to, or provide this service for, the important male characters. But there are important differences. In the first place even the minor characters are presented more as persons than symbols; people with joy and tears and human frailties viewed from outside the limited perceptions of the men to whom they are attached. Furthermore, like the unfamilial prophets of *Two Thousand Seasons*, they have a knowledge which addresses, in some cases quite literally, the larger arena.

In an elaboration of a theme also established in *Two Thousand Seasons*, the royal courts are in this text the center of dissension. As the catalyst for destruction, through her association with the invading British, we have Efua Kobri, the powerful queen mother who, in using her influence and the subtle force of persuasive language to protect solely her privilege and the status of her group, ensures the destruction of the kingdom she affects to save. It is important that this sole politically powerful woman is also a dominating mother who acts to keep herself and her son in power. This is the preference for the "loved ones" carried relentlessly to its logical conclusion. The queen mother, in this case the mother of the chief, is a woman with the reins of power firmly in her hands. Totally seduced by power, it is she who reminds her son it were better to be king in a violated nation than nothing in a virgin land, and sabotages the plan to defeat the British because it would have made the heroic general more powerful than her son in the united and victorious kingdom. In the royal court it is the king who is weak and hesitant and the queen who is strong and sure. Her voice, with all the authority of history, in an international political arena, rules the day. But this same voice, speaking against the domestic community, is in the end self-destructive; ultimately the individual has no potential for survival outside the group, however desperately she may try.[5] Mercifully, however, though none has as much political power as she, there are many more creative than destructive women in this novel.

Although most of the women in this novel are associated with the sacred work of the healers, Armah gives us one other woman who can serve as a remarkable contrast to the queen mother even in her own secular world. Though she is a woman of lesser political significance, and though we see her acting in a private capacity only, the portrait of the royal grandmother of the young prince Appia is a forceful one. We see Nana Esi Amanyiwa only once, in the scene in which she buries her grandson Appia, whose murder occasions the narrative which is the novel. In the scene at the graveside, in the prince's mother's room, the quiet, dignified humility with which the grandmother expresses her grief over the loss of her favorite grandchild, is contrasted dramatically with the noisy, bombastic show of mourning put on by the uncle Ababio. The old woman performs in tragic silence all the loving rituals for the burial of the dead, yielding her treasured possessions for the spirit of her child, and throwing first into the grave the customary handful of that earth which would bury his dead body. But her desire to have a speedy, yet dignified and proper burial is interrupted by the display being put on by the uncle (a performance confirmed as pure sham at the end of the novel when it is revealed that it was he himself who was responsible for having had the prince murdered):

> Ababio rushed into the burial room. He came energetic, like a hurricane . . .[his] entry was not merely stormy. It was loud.
> "Let me go with my prince!" he shouted. "I shall not let him go alone!" So saying, he rushed past the silent Esi Amanyiwa. . . .
> The grave-diggers were baffled. They had been on their way out when Ababio hurled himself into the grave. Now Ababio had moved towards the corpse and, clasping its feet, had begun an incantation to the spirit of the dead prince. Uncertain about what to do, unable to force the tearful, grovelling Ababio out yet unwilling to leave him in the grave, the grave-diggers stood undecided beside him in the hole.
> Then Nana Esi Amanyiwa's voice was heard.
> "Let him go with him", the voice said, "since that is his wish." (pp. 58-9)[6]

The power of the grandmother in this scene lies in her ability to recapture language, and quite simply to render it literal. The question of utterance is itself crucial to this novel, both with respect to its very structure, and as integral theme. The ability to speak, and to speak truly, should be a prized quality in a whole, healthy society. Nana Esi Amaniywa's words therefore expose the hollowness of Ababio's by turning a glare on the distance between his words and his meanings; therein lies their power. As we shall see, though her words are enclosed within a domestic tragedy and do not have much impact on the course of events, it is her daughter Araba Jesiwa who is the only other woman in this novel whose public words have consequences as far reaching as those of the queen mother. But by the time she speaks, she is no longer either a wife or a mother; the one woman who, with the help of the healers, finds some sort of resolution between love and power in her own private life, has, by the time her words make public impact, lost both the man and the child who blessed that resolution.

In addition to Araba Jesiwa, the group of "healers", whose search for a private and public health is the central quest of this novel, are surrounded by a number of inspired women who support and encourage them in their work, give practical aid and succor, and sustain the hope that they will eventually win through. One of the most significant of them is the healer Damfo's daughter, Ajoa, because she is herself an apprentice healer.

Ajoa is instrumental in the healing of two of the most central characters in the novel, Araba Jesiwa, the mother of the murdered prince, and Densu, the apprentice healer whose history the narrative traces. When her son is murdered, Araba Jesiwa, also left for dead by the roadside, is mercifully rescued by the healers, and sheltered in their secluded communal village. She is not only physically broken, but so spiritually distraught she loses the power of speech. She has to be carefully nursed so that her broken bones can mend, and so that her spirit and therefore her voice may be restored. Throughout all the long months that this takes, it is Ajoa who faithfully cares for her, and notices her slow return to life. It is Ajoa also who nurses Densu to recovery when this becomes necessary. Densu suffers the trauma of being falsely charged, and almost executed by burning, for the murder of the prince. He is only rescued from this ritual murder by the sacrifice of his closest friend, Anan, who dies in his attempt to secure Densu's escape. Throughout his convalescence Ajoa remains first his friend, then finally consummates this childhood friendship by becoming his lover.

The portrait of Ajoa emphasizes the fact that, even amongst an enlightened group such as the healers, the sexual division of roles remains fixed. Until the closing chapters of the novel, these strong and supportive prophets never *initiate* any action. Ajoa remains a handmaid to her father, existing solely to follow his instructions by ministering to others. Yet though her role is practical and domestic, the first sight of her is that of an ideally beautiful, mystical being:

> She was a small, fragile-looking child, but already her skin had that
> darkness that was a promise of inexhaustible depth, and her eyes were
> even then liquid, clear windows into the soul within.
> She was beautiful.
> Her eyes, those eyes, were restless, full of a nervous energy. Even
> when they came to a momentary rest, they did not rest on Densu. They
> looked far away. Still, those eyes did not reject him. It was just that
> they seemed drawn to sights far beyond the present moment. And
> Densu himself, drawn to those eyes, felt no need to resist the power in
> them, or to resent the desire that turned them away from him.
>
> It was this power of Ajoa's over his spirit, this attraction against
> which he neither needed nor wanted to struggle, that had first brought
> Densu close to Ajoa's father, Damfo. (pp. 63-6)

We are reminded of Maanan revealing the woes of womankind on her face,
only in this case the 'woman' is yet six years old, and Densu, on whom her
eyes have this power, is eight. Ajoa's knowledge is based on the instinct
which enables her to distinguish people who operate on the basis of love and
inspiration, from those who use manipulation and worldly authority. This
knowledge at a very early age, enables her to choose her humble father the
healer, over her step-father, the court physician. Years later, when Densu
starts his apprenticeship with her father, it is she who first suggests, in her
quiet unheard manner, the truth which will eventually solve the central
mystery of the young prince Appia's murder. It is this spiritual power of
Ajoa's which inspires Densu, and she becomes inextricably linked to the
search for understanding and knowledge which drives him to become a
healer.

Yet, unusually in a novel by Armah, for all this spirituality Ajoa, though
initially coy, is a young woman at ease with her sexuality, a sexuality not
entirely divorced from her soul. Like all good women, she moves with ease
and grace, yet though beautiful, unlike the prophets of *Two Thousand
Seasons*, she does not disparage her body. Furthermore, she needs neither
to be dominant, like Naita, or, like Juana, dominated, before she learns to
appreciate the wonder of love-making. The love-making scenes in this novel
are presented as a mutually joyous experience for the young couple, and it is
noteable that in each of them Armah makes Densu deliberately place her so
they lie side by side, a significant shift from the love scenes of *Fragments*
and *Why Are We So Blest?*. Ajoa has learnt the lesson it took Araba Jesiwa
the better part of her life to learn, but she is not given a role that is as
dramatically public as Jesiwa's, or even as powerful as that of her own
impressive but socially and politically circumscribed father. Outside the
personal relationships in her limited community, Ajoa is a powerless
woman. We are left with the feeling that perhaps she can blossom; the
potential is there, but not the act, and it seems a peculiar factor of Armah's

novels that, even in the case of men, creative sexuality and social or political power appear forever divorced from each other.

The character of Araba Jesiwa, the mother of the murdered prince, manifests the tensions surrounding the question of powerful, sexual women having the freedom to act wisely, in a larger social context. In keeping with the traditional male and female roles retained in this novel, Araba Jesiwa must find a resolution between being a spiritually whole woman and being a mother; and motherhood represents not simply her private but also her *public* self, as she initially perceives it. Similarly, in a story which parallels Jesiwa's, there is an Ashanti general whose central role it is to find a resolution between his private and public selves; he must learn to reconcile being a bereaved uncle with being a national warrior. He too must find that balance between the public and the private which does not threaten the spirit. Both characters dramatize the necessity for that unity between private and public sanity which has so perplexed all Armah's earlier leading figures; but whereas the *man's* story disturbs the political unity of the *state*, the woman's story is initially dramatized with respect to a private, *domestic* happiness.

The story of Araba Jesiwa is centered around her coming to terms with her sexuality. At the request of her family she had married a man solely for the purpose of consolidating dynastic political power, and then found she could not conceive. This would be a burden intolerable enough for a private woman in a traditional society, but it is unacceptable in the woman who must bear the child who will ensure the continuation of her royal line. This burden nearly destroys her life, but she overcomes it because she finally learns that no demands, even those of "loved ones", can be met if it costs your soul. With the help of the healers, she learns to identify her 'true self', and the creative aspect of her story is her recognition of the links between self-health and social health. She learns to recapture the true meaning of conception in both personal and social terms, and therefore finds happiness by returning to her soul mate, the true love of her life. When her sense of social health is no longer divorced from her own sense of sexual well-being, conception becomes truly liberating. She then conceives in love and successfully delivers the child Appia, born of love rather than convention. Yet Araba Jesiwa is a woman with social status, and the point of her story is that she must choose between a man with social status whom she does not love, and a humble carpenter whom she loves with all her soul. She chooses the carpenter, but both the husband and the child, who represent her cure, die tragically young. That is, not only is she initially punished for choosing 'society' against her true self, she is also punished for choosing her sexually creative self in contravention of societal norms: apart from its literal veracity, the murdered prince is symbolically thrust back into her womb by being buried in her room, first because she cannot be allowed a private happiness in communion with a man, and retain both her power and her virtue, and secondly because she must learn a greater lesson and pass her wisdom to another, spiritual heir.

This dilemma is partially resolved by the powerful scene at the end of the novel, orchestrated around Araba Jesiwa's first public reappearance. Jesiwa, long believed dead herself, survives the attack which took the life of her biological son. She became dumb at the loss of that one son who symbolized her access to private power and sexuality, and *also*, by virtue of her social status, to public authority. He dies because she has to be re-born into a new family where princes have no sway, in order to 'give birth' again to another son, this time her *spiritual* heir, Densu. Densu is her spiritual son by virtue of their shared conversations, his experience of her life and her sufferings, and his initiation into her cause. Speechless and paralysed for many months, she appears unexpectedly in the public courtroom, where Densu is wrongfully on trial for the murder of her dead son, to speak the words which identify Ababio as the guilty power, and bring liberty to Densu. Those words, symbolic of her restoration to health and sanity, also represent a triumph for the healers. Ultimately, Araba Jesiwa's personal decisions *do* have group consequences, and her private experiences have force as public testimony. Symbolically at least, the influence of women is finally seen beyond the hearth, in a fashion in which the private and the public are not disparate but wedded.

So far as the representation of women is concerned, the story cannot be considered complete, for we leave the women at the threshold of action. However, the triumph of *The Healers* is that it is a truly creative book when considered in the light of the history it is trying to restore, and the social and political health it attempts to bring. In that aspect it succeeds. The use of women is only a small part in the overall thesis of the text, and even this use, when seen in contrast to Armah's earlier works, as well as in a larger context, is of itself reformative. Armah himself has travelled a long journey in creating the women of *The Healers*, who, although they pay a price to perform this function, do in the end point the way towards a society in which women themselves are healthy, fully empowered beings, in reflection of a people who are at last free, whole, and joyously united.

NOTES

1. Ayi Kwei Armah, *The Beautyful Ones Are Not Yet Born*, (New York, Macmillan-Collier Books, 1974), all subsequent page references are to this edition.
2. Ayi Kwei Armah, *Fragments*, (London, Heinemann Educational Books, 1974), all subsequent page references are to this edition.

3. Ayi Kwei Armah, *Why Are We So Blest?*, (London, Heinemann Educational Books, 1974), all subsequent page references are to this edition.

4. Ayi Kwei Armah, *Two Thousand Seasons*, (Nairobi, Kenya, East African Publishing House, 1973), all subsequent page references are to this edition.

5. For a radically different interpretation of the role of the queen mother see Virginia Ola, "The Feminine Principle and the Search for Wholeness in *The Healers*", (African Literature Association Conference Papaer, University of Maryland Baltimore County, April 1984). Although I share Ms. Ola's enthusiasm for Armah's achievement, and, like her, appreciate the overall positive and transforming roles that women have come to play in these later novels, I take issue with her over specific interpretations. Most particularly in her interpretation of the role of the queen mother, I feel she ignores very crucial scenes included in the text, and yet in her praise of the grandmother Nana Esi Amanyiwa, in which I share, she attributes much to her that is not supported by the text.

6. Ayi Kwei Armah, *The Healers*, (London, Heinemann Educational Books, 1978), all subsequent page references are to this edition.

PART TWO
Towards A Critical Self-Definition of The African Woman: Writers and African Woman's Reality

The papers in Part II "Towards a Critical Self-Definition of the African Woman: Writers and African Woman's Reality" introduce her functioning as her own spokesperson and agent. These characterizations, from the pens of both male and female authors, bring women to the foreground as protagonists, character study subjects, and as actors, thinkers, writers, and commentators. In these papers we see analyzed the motivations of political activists and community leaders, university students, mothers and women without children, widows, mistresses, entrepreneurs, women in the vanguard of the changing African social order and those entrenched in the traditional order. Naana Banyiwa-Horne's paper comparing Flora Nwapa's Efuru *and Elechi Amadi's* Concubine *actually straddles this section and the preceding one, similar to Abena Busia's article on Armah located in Part I. Banyiwa-Horne finds that Amadi, like many other male writers, presents "images of African womanhood [that] tend to be from an idealized and romanticized rather than from a realistic perspective. There is little or no psychological growth in such portraitures which often reflect male fantasies of womanhood and not meaningful, in-depth, depictions." By contrast, Banyiwa-Horne says, the protagist in the work of the female writer Nwapa is the center around which everything revolves; her presence is the causal agent for all that occurs. Nwapa's* Efuru, *according to Banyiwa-Horne, shows "a determination to lead a fulfilling life. . .control her own life rather than blindly submit to tradition," a characterization that will appear again in Irene d'Almeida's discussion below of Mariama Bà's work.*

While Banyiwa-Horne's cogent and well-founded one-on-one contrast between the feminine presentations by a male and a female author reveal the male writer's handling as unrealistic and unsympathetic, his example need not be generalized to all his brother novelists. The two men writers discussed in the papers by Anne Graves and Charles Nama are outstanding examples to prove the point. If Elechi Amadi, as read by Banyiwa-Horne, shows "little or no psychological growth" no "meaningful, in-depth depicitions" of his women characters, Henri Lopès depicts women, according to Graves, who make decisions based on their consciousness of their own growth. But their self-awareness extends even beyond them as individuals, Graves points out, for a number of Lopès' women characters view the advancement or progress of their people as identical with progress for themselves as people. In this paper Graves lays out her evidence for the position, articulated earlier in the preface, calling for the re-defining of women's roles in African literature, based on women-centered, rather than man-centered criteria.

As another example, broached above, of a sensitive presentation of the feminine by a male writer we have Charles Nama's paper "Daughters of Moombi: Ngugi's Heroines and Traditional Gikuyu Aesthetics." Nama's consideration of the characters Mumbi from A Grain of Wheat, *Nyakinyua from* Petals of Blood, *and Wariinga from* Devil on the Cross *asserts that the active roles these women play as leaders and as guardians/protectors of the heritage, have a long history, being indeed part of the Gikuyu tradition, extending back to Moombi, female co-progenitor of the tribe. In demonstrating the characteristics that make each of the examined characters heroines in the Gikuyu tradition, Nama is combining two subjects of supreme importance in Ngugi's thought (as repeated in his theoretical as well as creative writing): "the concept that the unequivocal liberation of Africans lies not in Westernization but*

*in the resuscitation of traditional cultural values that have been
an intrinsic part of the people's lives from ancient times" and "the
contribution of Kenyan women in the liberation struggle." Reference
to Ngugi's work is also made by Chimalum Nwankwo in his study of
Ama Ata Aidoo's* No Sweetness Here *and* Our Sister Killjoy.
*Drawing a positive comparison between her "successful treatment
of feminist issues" and such treatment by Ngugi and Sembène,
Nwankwo bases his analysis of Aidoo's work on his theory that "the
African woman [must] accommodate that [subjective] individual
experience within the stream of history—rapidly changing cultural
and socioeconomic circumstances and consequently altered social
relations." His discussion consists of a methodical analysis of the
dilemmas that beset women in the various situations that Aidoo
draws in her short stories and novel, showing, for example, in the
title story of* No Sweetness Here *that "everything is, as usual,
wrong with women," a picture he goes on to put into the full
context of Aidoo's "controlled" presentation. One partial conclusion Nwankwo draws about the short stories is that they "successfully
reveal that no choice is a good choice for the African woman." The
significance of having a choice at all, however, is the focus of Irene
d'Almeida's piece on the novels of Mariama Bâ. For d'Almeida (who
approaches Ba's work from a different angle than does Edris
Makward in Part III), Bâ breaks new ground in presenting the
phenomenon of choice for the African woman. In the two novels
produced in the brief career of this writer d'Almeida identifies
several different types of choices, i.e. two risk-laden, costly alternatives to one situation, and choices for the individual woman that
affect other people in her life. The essayist here contends that the
African woman with education and a profession is doubly encumbered, or bears a "double yoke" that reduces, rather than increases,
her choices in life's unforeseeable but consequential situations.
The* Double Yoke *of Buchi Emecheta is discussed in Marie Linton
Umeh's article analyzing Emecheta's treatment of the educated
African woman. According to Umeh, Emecheta demonstrates not
only African society's unconscious hypocrisy toward women, but
also what she sees as a conservative fear among Nigerians of
socially corruptive consequences of education for women.
A different but related arena of intellectual activity among
women in a sector of the Nigerian populace is the writing of poetry
by Hausa women, as presented in Beverly Mack's paper. Although
Hausa women who perform* oral *poetry already have attained
some reputation, the women poets who are writing and publishing
are indeed pioneers. While consciously keeping within the prescribed bounds of the traditional society, the two poets discussed*

here, whose work is the first to be published by Hausa women, feel
that women have an important role to play in the success of their
country, and do, therefore, bring a tone of nationalism to their
verse. For Mack "...the very fact that these two women have
produced a volume of verse is the most revolutionary aspect of
their work."

A.A.G.

African Womanhood: The Contrasting Perspectives of Flora Nwapa's Efuru and Elechi Amadi's The Concubine

Naana Banyiwa-Horne

The question of African womanhood, though not given much consideration in critical evaluations of African literature until recent years, is one of
the subjects that often finds its way into the writings of both male and female
authors from the continent. Images of African womanhood abound in the
literature, with some male authors giving as much exposure to the subject as
female ones. In fact, some of the most fascinating and exotic women in
fiction have been created by male writers. Cyprian Ekwensi's Jagua Nana
is a novel by that name, and Wole Soyinka's Simi in *The Interpreters*
readily come to mind.

A close look at the various images of African womanhood provided in the
literature reveals that, to a considerable extent, depictions of African
women in the literature by African woman writers differ from the images
presented by their male counterparts. By virtue of their shared gender

experiences, women writers are inclined to depict female characters in more realistic terms, with a great deal of insight, and in meaningful interaction with their environment. Also women writers tend to create a woman's world in which women characters exist in their own right, and not as mere appendages to a male world. There are exceptions, of course,[1] but in the main, women authors explore alternate possibilities for self-actualization outside the sexual roles that are open to their women characters.

On the other hand, male depictions of female characters are often from a fiercely male perspective, reflecting male conceptions, or rather misconceptions, of female sexuality. Men writers tend to overplay the sexuality of their female characters, creating the impression that women have no identity outside their sexual roles. Their women are seen primarily in relation to male protagonists and in secondary roles. These characters usually serve to enhance the images of the male protagonists who occupy the central positions in the works. Furthermore, male images of African womanhood tend to be idealized and romanticized. There is little or no psychological growth in such portraitures which seems to suggest they are largely male fantasies of womanhood. The above does not suggest that every African male writer dabbles in stereotypes of African womanhood. There are brilliant exceptions. But generally, male depictions of African womanhood conform to the above stated observations.

These contentions are brought home forcefully when one examines two works that share a lot of superficial similarities—Flora Nwapa's *Efuru* and Elechi Amadi's *The Concubine*.[2] The term superficial is employed here to qualify the similarities between the two novels, because they are apparent mainly in the surface structure of the two works but cannot be sustained in any in-depth analysis of the themes, particularly as they reveal Nwapa's and Amadi's perspectives of African womanhood.

The titles of both novels suggest that a female character is central to each work. Nwapa's novel revolves around Efuru, whose name provides the title for the work. In Amadi's novel too, Ihuoma, a woman, plays a central role. Efuru and Ihuoma have a lot in common; they are exceptional in many respects. Moreover, both works are set in rural Igbo villages, and in both, the supernatural plays a dominant role in the lives of the women. The similarities, however, only apply to the raw materials the two authors employ in their works. Nwapa and Amadi utilize their materials in very distinct ways resulting in contrasting portrayals of their main female characters.

The following exploration of the attitudes of the two authors to the worlds they create, to their characters, and to their use of the supernatural reveals the two very different perspectives: Nwapa's *Efuru* provides a feminine perspective of African womanhood and gives a more complex treatment of the female character, while Amadi's *The Concubine* provides a perspective that is male and limiting.

In rural Ibgoland, where *Efuru* and *The Concubine* are set, close-knit family structures predominate, and everyone knows and is related to everyone else either by blood or by marriage. Each person's business is that of the entire community. No occurrence is sacrosanct. Both Amadi and Nwapa excel in creating the fabric and texture of their rural communities, bringing their characters and their worlds vividly to life for the reader. One leaves both novels with the feeling of having intimate knowledge of the fictional worlds and their inhabitants. The attitudes, beliefs, fears, loves, strengths and weaknesses of both individuals and the community at large are made apparent through the descriptions and the dialogue employed. There is very little authorial commentary in either work, though Amadi utilizes this technique a little more than Nwapa.

Nwapa depends almost exclusively on dialogue to reveal Efuru's world, and she proves very successful at it. Her novel is filled with the daily conversation mainly of women, a technique that captures most effectively the oral-aural nature of the world she unfolds. The constant banter of women reveals character as much as it paints a comprehensive, credible, social canvas against which Efuru's life can be assessed. The total world view is brought to life through dialogue. In commenting on this technique Maryse Condé observes that

> ... by making her heroine unique among her fellow-villagers and by reporting the unanimously hostile and adverse comments of the other women on every one of Efuru's decisions and actions, Flora Nwapa gives, in fact, a disturbing picture of narrow-mindedness, superstition, malevolence, and greed and fear in traditional Africa and might go contrary to what she has thought to defend. In depicting her minor characters, she conveys a very poor impression of her society. Her men are weak, dissolute and irrational. Her women, a formidable gallery of malicious gossipers.[3]

Condé, apparently disturbed by Nwapa's frankness in bringing to life her women characters with their idiosyncrasies and their entire baggage of attitudes, concludes that the result of Nwapa's technique goes contrary to her objectives. She is of the impression that Nwapa is not a conscious craftsperson. But on the contrary, what she interprets as Nwapa's weakness is one of her fortes—a conscious manipulation of dialogue in the revelation not so much of individual personality as in the creation of a tableau against which social values and attitudes can be evaluated.

The "formidable gallery of malicious gossipers" as Condé sees Nwapa's women, is definitely more than just that. They enable Nwapa to portray her world from the perspective of women. She brings out quite clearly the ways her women view the world in which they live, and their reactions not only to the other womenfolk, but to those aspects of life that touch directly on their lives as women. The thought patterns of the individual personalities as they comment on and react to Efuru are revealed. Of course, the comments of the women on Efuru's life reveal their envy, their own shortcomings, and their aspirations; but that is human nature, and Nwapa does a good job of revealing character. After all, who among the village gossips would not want to be beautiful and prosperous? Which of the married women would not bask in the attention Efuru's husband lavishes on her? Above all, which woman would not wish to be appreciated for herself rather than for her childbearing ability? Even as the women decry Efuru's beauty, her leaving her child with a maid in order to pursue her profession as a trader, or her going to the stream with her husband, their reactions reveal the restricted, limited sense of accomplishment in their own lives.

Efuru's infertility is a source of concern, yes, and the constant lamenting of her condition, more by other women than by herself, reveals the importance her society attaches to childbearing. But, at the same time, Efuru's undaunted effort to live her life as fully as possible, regardless of this shortcoming, is striking. Her misfortune does not diminish the awe in which the other women hold her, and this is equally reflected in the envious comments they pass on her. What Nwapa achieves through her setting, therefore, is a life-like recreation of the world of women in her rural Igbo community.

Elechi Amadi also employs similar tools in depicting his world and its attitudes. The world he projects, however, is a male world, and the voices heard are mainly male voices. The statements made by these voices and even by the authorial voice reflect not just a masculine attitude to women but a chauvinistic one. When friends and relatives assemble to celebrate the second burial of Ihuoma's husband, Amadi portrays his men as a dignified group while his women are bunched together as a cantankerous lot—"The old men were served. As they crunched their kola nuts slowly they talked to each other with a dignified buzz, an octave lower than the high-pitched, piping, market-chatter of the women" (p. 43).

His male characters consistently pass disparaging comments about their women. Madume dismisses his wife with the statement, "Women argue forwards and backwards" (p. 70). Wakiri confides in his friend Ekwueme, "when it comes to nagging I treat all women as children" (p. 20). Wigwe, a dignified elder, advises his son to regard his wife as "a baby needing constant correction" (p. 181). Ekwueme, the major male protagonist, sees all women as stupid and horrible and dismisses them as unworthy of him (p. 182). Even Ihuoma, who is acknowledged as being superior to other women, does not escape Ekwueme's deprecations. He perceives her as "just a simpleton with as much heart as a chicken" (p. 117). Furthermore, the exemplary behavior of Amadi's heroine is acknowledged in highly chauvinistic terms. Wigwe admits reluctantly: "True, you are only a woman but your good behaviour has placed you a little above many other women in the village" (p. 144).

What emerges from the world Amadi creates, then, is a reinforcement of stereotypical male chauvinistic impressions about African womanhood. All of his women characters are depicted as inferior and subordinate to men with even Ihuoma portrayed in subordination to the dominant male characters. The story begins, in characteristic male fashion, with a fight between two men, Emenike and Madume. Ihuoma's introduction into the story is tied to her position as Emenike's wife and as a woman on whom Madume has designs with these factors aggravating the conflict between the two men. Amadi informs the reader: "Perhaps Madume's hatred of Emenike might not have been so great if only the latter had not snatched Ihuoma from him" (p. 6).

Amadi's depiction of Ihuoma is dehumanizing. She is not portrayed as a human being with a will of her own. She is more like a piece of land, or a house, or some form of property that is there to be grabbed. Clearly, the only significance that women have in Amadi's novel is sexual. All exist in a man's world, to be used by the men as sexual vehicles. Amadi's sexism circumscribes his heroine's entire existence, and the very title of his novel, The Concubine, reveals the rigidly sexual mold in which Ihuoma is cast. Whether in the spirit world or in her life on earth, Ihuoma's relevance is thus limited by the machinations of a man: "in the spirit world she was the wife of the Sea King, the ruling spirit of the sea" (p. 253). Though reincarnated, her life on earth is still governed by her status as the wife of the Sea King. Before this information is disclosed at the end of the novel, we already know that Ihuoma is being manipulated by the author to reveal only her circumscribed role. She is always either the devoted wife and mother, the pitiable widow of highly commendable behavior, or the prospective wife to be wooed. The plot of The Concubine revolves around her successive attempts to seek fulfillment in marriage and on the attempts made by three successive men to woo and marry or bed her. After the death of her first husband, her mother continuously advises her to think of remarrying because a woman needs a man to survive. The impression one gets is that Ihuoma can have no independent life; she must always be attached to a man, as she has little or no relevance beyond her role as a sexual object.

At the same time, Amadi spares no effort in idealizing his heroine. Most of the novel concentrates on her physical and moral superiority to the other women in her world and on her relentless efforts to be an ideal wife and mother. Amadi's main preoccupation in The Concubine seems to be to portray a character who will epitomize female perfection from a sexist perspective, and he is highly successful in that respect. His heroine is all that such a man would wish a woman to be. She is endowed with the kind of physical attractiveness that makes a man proud to possess her.

> She was a pretty woman: perhaps that is why she married so early. Her three children looked more like her brothers and sisters. She was young . . . she was just about twenty-two.

> Ihuoma's complexion was that of the ant-hill. Her features were
> smoothly rounded and looking at her no one could doubt that she was
> 'enjoying her husband's wealth.' Nothing did a husband greater credit
> than the well-fed look of his wife (p. 14).

Ihuoma's attractiveness is emphasized over and over again She seems
impressed by her own beauty, gazing at herself in the mirror every little
chance she gets. Calamity, the most notorious agent of premature aging,
adds only an ameliorating quality to her beauty. It gives her a "softly
alluring, deeply enchanting... bewitching subtlety that only deep sorrow
can give... young men and even the old gazed at her... irresistibly" (p.
45). The matured Ihuoma is even more fascinating; she is "confident without
being brazen, self-respecting yet approachable, sweet but sensible" (p.
249).

Ihuoma is, above all, a model traditional wife; she shows "her great
devotion to her husband in every way she could think of" (p. 9). She is
always polite and never gives offense. She is submissive and very
understanding. In short, she has none of those qualities that make a woman
threatening to a man. She's no good at invectives and other women talk
much faster than she does. She does not talk in parables; therefore, she
cannot infringe on the male prerogative of verbal excellence. She is a
staunch upholder of her society's values, and her high sense of morality
matches her high physical endowments. She is so preoccupied with
maintaining her good name as a woman that she readily sacrifices her
happiness to her good name. For example, she declines to marry Ekwueme,
a man she is in love with, because such behavior would be considered
improper in her society. She takes it upon herself to remind him that
tradition requires him to marry a young maiden who would obey him and
give him the first fruits of her womb.

Elechi Amadi's portrayal of Ihuoma fits five of seven stereotypes
catalogued by Roseann Bell. Ihuoma is the "Earth-mother, the concubine,
the loyal doormat of a wife, the sacrificial lamb, [and] the willing
mechanism in a polygamous drama."[4]

Compare Flora Nwapa's approach to her heroine, Efuru. She is at the
center of the world Nwapa creates. There is no event or situation in the
novel that does not stem from her. The novel is Efuru's story, and her life
provides the materials for plotting it. Other characters are brought in only
as what they do and say leads to revealing or clarifying aspects of Efuru's
life. Her presence controls the action, unlike Ihuoma whose actions are
reactions to male-initiated actions. While Ihuoma becomes prominent in
Amadi's novel only when her presence is required to complete the story of
one of Amadi's male protagonists, Efuru is always present in Nwapa's
novel in her own right. And this is significant because Amadi's work
purports to deal principally with a female character.

Efuru is exceptional in many respects. She is beautiful, the daughter of one of the last survivors of a vanishing age of traditional valor and grandeur, and a highly successful businesswoman. She is prosperous; it is as though anything she touches literally transforms into riches. She is also very compassionate and unassuming, qualities that couple with her beauty to give her a striking resemblance to Ihuoma, Amadi's heroine.

However, Nwapa's Efuru is no paragon of female submissiveness. She demonstrates a marked sense of independence and a determination to lead a fulfilling life. From an early age she reveals a resolve to control her own life rather than to submit blindly to tradition. She is by no means a revolutionary because she does not completely abrogate tradition, but neither is she enslaved by it. Whenever traditional stipulations stifle her individualty, she steps out of them to adopt alternative means that best enable her to express her personality. For example, she contravenes the mores governing male-female relationships and declares herself married by moving in with her lover who is of low social status and too poor at the time to afford her dowry. But later, through her enterprising nature, she makes enough money with her husband to pay her dowry. Also when her first husband deserts her, she continues to live in his house for a considerable length of time—two years. She even goes in search of him. But after waiting long enough to avoid accusations of impropriety, she returns to her father's house, an indication that she is ready, among other things, to consider other possible suitors. She marries again, shortly after moving back to her father's house and enjoys a period of near total marital bliss with her new husband. Not only do they work together, they do everything together. She acts as his counselor, advising him on what projects are ripe for pursuit. In addition, they enjoy a closeness that is not quite usual in the rural setting within which they live. They even go to the stream together to swim and thereby attract a lot of gossip from envious women bound by unexciting lives and the values of their rural world.

Nwapa, like Amadi, highlights her heroine's physical attributes—the village gossips always comment on her beauty. Both women are exceptional in their communities. But Nwapa emphasizes Efuru's other characteristics as well, some of them not totally complimentary, and by so doing, prevents the idealization of her heroine's image. Nwapa's approach to Efuru's beauty in no way reduces the heroine to being a sex object. In fact, the manner in which her beauty is depicted often plays down its positive nature. While there is no question about Efuru's great beauty, the village gossips always juxtapose it, her wealth, and her closeness with her husband to her childlessness, thereby attempting to diminish her endowments.

Above all, Nwapa's portrayal of her heroine presents an in-depth study of womanhood. Her novel is a study of the growth of Efuru, and both her physical and psychological development are brought to light as she searches for options for self-actualization. Efuru begins by accepting the traditional sexually-oriented prescriptions for defining a woman's identity, but she moves gradually towards a new definition of a sense of self, a better option for self-definition. Initially she attempts to find fulfillment both as a wife and a mother, hence her two marriages and her striving to make them work. Also in the early years of her married life she agonizes over her childlessness and goes to some length to remedy this anomaly. She goes to see a *dibia* who assures her she will bear a child. After this assurance, she is still alarmed by her tardiness and becomes overjoyed when she finally bears a child. She feels fulfilled, at last, as a woman.

> Efuru lay there thinking of it all, "Is this happening to me or someone I know. Is that baby mine or somebody else's? Is it really true that I have had a baby, that I am a woman after all. Perhaps I am dreaming. I shall soon wake up and discover that it is not real" (p. 31).

Her sense of fulfillment is threatened when her only daughter falls ill. ' "What will I do if I lose her?" she thought. "If she dies, that will mean the end of me" ' (p. 66).

The above image is that of the growing Efuru, still struggling to come to terms with her identity. The death of her child, however and the grief it brings, does not reduce her to a non-person; neither does the failure of her two marriages. She continues with her trade and proves herself a serious and successful businesswoman. Moreover she becomes a special worshipper of the woman of the lake when she is still married to her second husband. Thus even when she was still married, her other roles played down her sexual one, pointing her in alternative directions for self-realization.

Efuru's life is in some ways wryly ironic. With all her endowments, she fails miserably to find fulfillment within the sexual modes prescribed by her society. She fails both as a wife and a mother. She ends up each time, after two brief spells of marital bliss, back in her father's home. There is no question about her possessing qualities that make men proud to be her mate. Her beauty and the prosperity she brings to her husbands, in themselves, should enamor them to her. Her strong love for her mates and her unflinching devotion to them more than compensate for those qualities such as her strong will and determination that, when unrestrained, can threaten their masculinity. Still, her first husband deserts her for a woman who is Efuru's inferior physically and morally. Her second husband maintains an enviable relationship with her for two years, then becomes inattentive and mistrusting, believing a rumor about Efuru's infidelity. Appalled by her husband's lack of faith in her, Efuru, leaves him to return to her home of birth.

Efuru's matrimonial failures, in a superficial way, recall those of Ihuoma, who loses two husbands and ends up a widow at a relatively early age. How-

ever, Efuru's life is a failure only within a very limited sexual framework, on which unfortunately her society places so much importance.
Her life is not a failure when seen through her own eyes and from a broader
perspective. That she is a remarkable human being is communicated even
more strongly than the sense of failure projected mainly through the
comments of the village gossips. Her generosity, her wealth, and her general
sense of worth to her community at large is as much a reality as her failed
marriages and childlessness. The sense of accomplishment of Nwapa's
heroine is no less strong because of her unsuccessful stint as wife and
mother, a point which sets her off from Amadi's Ihuoma, whose life
crumbles around her once she fails to lead a fulfilling sexual life.

The supernatural element plays a vital role in both novels. However,
once more, Nwapa's use of the supernatural differs markedly from the way
Amadi uses it. In Efuru's case, the supernatural becomes an extension of
her sense of self while in the case of Ihuoma, it assumes a masculine form
and hinders her development as a successful woman. In direct opposition,
Uhamiri, the woman of the lake, the supernatural element in Nwapa's
novel, is a symbolic representation of Nwapa's heroine, who is chosen as a
special worshipper of this deity. Uhamiri becomes the alter ego of the
matured Efuru who is invested with all of Uhamiri's qualities. Both of them
are rich, beautiful and worshipped by those who appreciate their worth, but
they have no children. Significantly, Uhamiri lavishes on her favorites
wealth and not children, and she is worshipped even though she does not
have children or give her worshippers children. Efuru's acceptance of her
role as a special worshipper of the woman of the lake, therefore, becomes a
symbolic representation of her acceptance of herself as a person in her own
right. The novel's end supports this contention.

> Efuru slept soundly that night. She dreamt of the woman of the lake,
> her beauty, her long hair and her riches. She had lived for ages at the
> bottom of the lake. She was as old as the lake itself. She was happy,
> she was wealthy. She was beautiful. She gave women beauty and
> wealth but she had no child. She had never experienced the joy of
> motherhood. Why then did women worship her? (p. 221).

This passage is the crux of the story of Efuru, capturing well her final
acceptance of herself, her coming to terms with her life, and her determination
to live happily and reject those traditional prescriptions of the identity of
women, which only diminish their sense of personal worth.

Maryse Condé is right in her observation that the closing lines of *Efuru*
provide the clue to the whole book, but her interpretation of it reflects her
limited understanding of Efuru's identification with the woman of the lake.
Condé's interpretation of *Efuru* is that:

No happiness can be achieved for a woman unless in childbearing.
... Efuru, for all her qualities and gifts, considers her life as valueless
since she fails to have a child. She can deliberately and willfully
decide to leave her husband and therefore live by herself, but she
cannot follow the logical consequences. She cannot find in herself
enough resources to counterbalance her sterility and never thinks of
devoting her energies to something else.[5]

Ms. Condé's statements present a gross misreading of Nwapa's heroine.
Nwapa makes it quite clear that, far from feeling that her life is valueless,
Efuru seeks new alternatives through which to realize her life. There is no
question that Efuru finds in herself enough resources to counterbalance her
sterility and devotes her energies to the pursuit of other things, symbolically
represented by her becoming a devoted worshipper of the woman of the
lake, the spiritual embodiment of her own identity.

Nwapa's use of the supernatural is not dissimilar from Amadi's in so far
as it bears directly on the life and identity of her heroine. But in this regard
too, there is a marked difference. While Nwapa's supernatural being is a
woman and functions to promote her heroine's search for identity, Amadi's
supernatural being provides another means of confining his heroine to her
sexual identity. It is a further projection of his male perspective of African
womanhood. Ihuoma's chain of unsuccessful marriages, like Efuru's, stem
from her special relationship to the supernatural. However, in her case, the
supernatural thwarts her life rather than offers her alternatives for self-actualization. Being a human reincarnation of the spirit wife of the Sea King, a
highly jealous male deity, who refuses to relinquish his hold on her, Ihuoma
can at best be only a concubine to human men, but can never marry in her
life on earth. So Ihumoa's relevance even in the spirit world is limited to a
sexual one. She is bound body and soul to the Sea King.

This study therefore supports Lloyd Brown's[6] evaluations of these two
works. The difference between Ihuoma's total sense of doom and despair at
the end of *The Concubine*, and Efuru's ability to devote herself to
something other than seeking fulfillment in the traditionally instituted
female roles illustrates a basic difference between the perception of females
from a strictly male perspective and from a female one.

While Amadi's character never becomes more than an instrument in
someone else's scheme, Nwapa's Efura transcends those proscriptions,
becoming an actor in her own, in woman's right.

NOTES

1. Buchi Emecheta is one of the exceptions. Her depiction of female characters, particularly in her early works, are limited to their sexual roles. Such titles as *The Bride Price, The Slave Girl,* and *The Joys of Motherhood* reflect the sexual emphasis she places on her characterization.

2. Elechi Amadi, *The Concubine* (London: Heinemann 1966), Flora Nwapa, *Efuru* (London: Heinemann, 1966). All references to these works are to this edition and will be referred to by page numbers only.

3. Maryse Condé, "Three Female Writers in Modern Africa: Flora Nwapa, Ama Ata Aidoo and Grace Ogot," in *Presence Africaine*, No. 82, 1972, p. 136.

4. Roseann P. Bell, "The Absence of the African Woman Writer," CLA Journal, Vol. 21, No. 4, 1978, p. 491. The other two are "The high-life floozy and the "been-to"."

5. Condé, p. 134, 136.

6. Lloyd W. Brown, *Women Writers in Black Africa* (Wesport, Conn.: Greenwood Press, 1981), p. 22.

The Work of Henri Lopès:
A Forum for African
Women's Consciousness

Anne Adams Graves

Henri Lopès is one of Congo-Brazzaville's most recognized prose writers. What has become his literary signature is a single-minded attention to—almost a pre-occupation with—the ideological parameters of the problems that affect the social, economic, and political progress of contemporary African society. His short-story collection, titled *Tribaliques*,[1] recipient, one year after its publication, of the Grand Prix Litteraire de l'Afrique Noire, includes stories such as "L'Honnête Homme," "La Fuite de la main habile," and "Monsieur le député," whose very titles imply an exposition of some of the self-acknowledged nemeses of African nations today. By effecting a tone of familial frankness Lopès engages the conscience of the members of his African family, warning, exhorting, nagging the family members to do some housecleaning.

In addition to the above-mentioned *Tribaliques*, consisting of eight short stories, published in 1971, Lopès' oeuvre includes three novels, *La nouvelle romance*, 1976, *Sans tam-tam*, 1977, and *Le pleurer-rire*, 1982. Depicting commonly found situations from all strata of contemporary African life, Lopès' works evoke such subjects as the pressures of tribal differences on individuals' lives in a now highly mobile society; the questions of management of a state's industrial resources; the means and ends of popular education; or the sociology and psychology of the changing

131

relations between men and women. In a significant portion of his work—
seven out of the ten total pieces—women and/or women-focused issues
take a central place in the narrative.

For an analysis of women's roles in African literature the model
furnished by Kenneth Little's *The Sociology of Urban Women's Image in
African Literature*[2] is of some utility, albeit limited. Arranging the
characters into six role categories, Little labels four of the six in terms of
varying levels of the women's associations with men. Those categories are
"girl-friends and good-time girls," "wives," "'free women,'" i.e. those who
"escape" the "trap" of "marriage under modern conditions" (p. 53), and
"courtesans and prostitutes." In addition to a category of "mothers"—
mostly of men characters—there is a final grouping called "'political'
women and workers," linked together apparently by virtue of their scarcity
in the literature. In drawing his conclusions Little grants that "most of the
characters are psychologically self-sufficient" and that "none of the. . .cate-
gories are mere appendages of the male sex" (p. 152). He concedes, though,
that "women have a definite place in the community as wives and sexual
partners. . .and in these terms women are, without any doubt, persons in
their own right. Political and economic affairs, however, are another matter;
and women's participation in them is usually a function of their relationship
with men". If Little finds his model to be the most functional for analyzing
the women's roles in the works of the thirty authors he takes on, that model
is not the most functional one for analyzing Hénri Lopès' women's roles.
However, some of Little's categories can serve in an analysis of our writer's
women characters, inasmuch as the situations in which they are presented
have recognizable correspondences with women's situations in other
African literature in aspects of the demographic, interpersonal, occupational
and other environmental parameters of the women's lives.

Indeed, practically every one of Lopès' female characters has a
relationship to a man, that contributes some material to the story. However,
the manner in which these characters execute their roles as wives,
girlfriends, mothers, sisters, lovers, working women, politically engaged
women, students, and teachers suggests a significant variation on a model
like Little's. Of course, there could be as many different arrangements of
such data proposed as there are individuals who care to make such a study.
Also, because of the amount of overlap or multiple membership that such
categorizations must allow for, the data become even less conclusive. But,
the Lopès technique in both the short stories and the novels draws
characterizations that present unmistakable evidence for identifying certain
other roles beyond those defined by the woman-man relationship. That
technique consists of limited action, the barest description of setting, and a
maximum of insight into characters' thoughts, reactions, motivations,
emotions. If his plots are thin, his characters are given great breadth,
Everything is conveyed through the perspective of a character, whether in

first- or third-person narrative, conversation, reportage, through indirect discourse, inner monolog, or epistolary form. (One entire novel, *Sans Tam-Tam*, is basically a series of five lengthy letters from a man fulfilled by his job as a teacher in a rural town, written to his closest friend, elucidating his refusal of a comfortable diplomatic post abroad.) In any case, owing to the limited action reflection in Lopès' works, any study of his characters must give at least equal attention to their psychological and intellectual characteristics—their consciousness—as is given to their actions or physical roles. This consciousness is given such depth of treatment through the inner monolog/conversation/epistolary form of the works, that it confers upon the characters additional roles of equal, if not greater, significance to the stories. Thus, in view of these considerations the characters examined in this study occupy multiple role categories.

The count of the female characters, covering the two novels and the five short stories in which females appear, is tallied at twenty-six. This accounts for each individual female adult (broadly construed) who appears or is introduced indirectly and receives meaningful attention, and includes also a few generalized groups of women treated as character types or collective characters. The inventory of the role categories follows here, reflecting the twenty-six characters' multiple roles, and proceeding in order from the categories denoting identification as individuals to those denoting identification in relationships with other people.

1) Working women and students. There are fourteen characters, who are either engaged in self-supporting employment or are attending some type of educational institution. In this latter sub-group we find one regular university student, one woman who at different times pursues further education, and four secondary school students. In the employed sub-group are two teachers, a seamstress, a nursemaid in an expatriate European family's household, two widows who own and operate night clubs that had been their husbands', and the prostitutes who entertain the patrons.

2)Politically engaged women and advocates of social change. There are six characters who play such roles, either through participation in formal political groups or through action or consciousness-raising on an individual, personal basis. These include two active political party workers who also do volunteer teaching in adult literacy programs; an aspiring writer; a freedom fighter in her country's war for independence; a collective character made up of the delegates at a convention of La Fédération nationale des femmes avant-gardistes; and, finally, a young betrothed woman who, during the course of a one-night stand with another man who is married, debates with him the issue of equality of sexual freedom.

3) Mothers and sisters. Of the eight characters in this category, only two, both single mothers of small children, function as parents per se. The remaining six function as emotional support and inspiration sources for other characters in their respective stories. Of the six individuals whose

lives are touched by these mothers and sisters, five are women. Thus, the role of mother and elder sister is not merely maternal here, but rather a spiritual source of strength for women. Some of the mother figures are indeed a single type: the traditional rural farmer mother whose lot, in Lopès' view, it is to till the fields while her husband sits in the sun drinking palm wine and engaging in debate with his cohorts. The sole male character whose mother is included in this category eulogizes her: "She. . .lived and died as a symbol of the country, of Africa herself. A symbol of our history, of our explication. She never knew."[3]

4) Wives, fiancèes, and girlfriends. To this group are assigned seventeen characters, all of whom are in relationships with men, based on a mutual commitment of assumed permanence, consistency, and fidelity. With seventeen of the total twenty-six women—more than two-thirds—involved in one of these committed relationships, Lopès is reflecting a situation lthat is quite normal. Even these numbers can be legitimately raised, if we include some women from other categories whose roles overlap with those in this group. For, while the two widowed entrepreneurs, who of course were once married, are numbered among the "wives" here, one single mother is also included, since she is repeatedly harrassed by family members and a traditional doctor for *refusing* to marry a certain man of the family's choice. Further, two other characters counted among these seventeen are actually one person. This is the title character in the short story "Ah, Apolline!" a university student, who, after having experienced a broken engagement dating back to her pre-university days, forms a satisfying and promising relationship with a fellow student, only to succumb finally to family and tribal pressures to return home and marry the former fiancé. But not counted in these seventeen are one or two others whose situations allow the reader to infer roles of wife, fiancée or girlfriend. One such case is that of the collective character of the women's federation convention delegates. And, finally, there are two characters, schoolgirls, who could not fit into this category by virtue of their young age.

5) Mistresses, casual lovers, and prostitutes. The seven characters in this final category have various levels of relationships or encounters with men, all of which are based on sex, and some of which involve some type of material compensation or support. Though this category encompasses women in steady associations such as three regular mistresses, two schoolgirl "pick-up" collective characters, and the prostitutes employed by the two night club owners, they account for a small number of the twenty-six women characters. Lopès does not fail to comment on the casual lovers and prostitutes. An example of such commentary is his description of one prostitute, a South African singer in one of the widows' night clubs who "entertains" the government dignitaries who frequent the club, "as her way of fighting against apartheid."[4]

Upon consideration of the last two role categories—wives/fiancées/girl-friends and mistresses/casual lovers/prostitutes—the data indicate that the majority of the characters in the seven works under discussion are indeed connected in some way with men. But this is not remarkable, nor is it unique to the work of Lopès. What does warrant more comment, however, is the fact that the great majority of the women characters who play roles as partners to men play the other roles given in this inventory, through which their consciousness of the social, political, and economic condition of their societies is projected.

Looking at the specifics of some of the works, it is immediately obvious that some characters and other elements found in the short stories, Lopès' first publication, are found in the novels in a more refined and developed form. It is as if, after creating the characters and presenting them in the confined framework of the short story, the writer had the need to let them open out in a large arena that could better accommodate their dimensions. A case in point is the young woman Mbâ, from the short story "La Fuite de la main habile," whose characteristics show up in the novel *La Nouvelle romance* primarily in its central character but shared partially with another. Mbâ, a dedicated primary school teacher and adult literacy volunteer teacher, waits faithfully for her beloved to do the welder's training in France, for which he has won a scholarship. After a few letters in the early months, his correspondence gradually drops off and then stops. Mbâ, immersed in her work, remains optimistic, until six years later she learns that he has settled down in France with his French wife and their child, earning a comfortable living in a factory. Mbâ's sustaining interests during the years of waiting are the children she teachers, their families, and the adults in the literacy class from whom she learns so much. She is also an enthusiastic participant in the local Party cell meetings. Her recollection of the difficult life of her mother and other village farm women inspires the desire to write a book on and work toward "l'émancipation de la femme Africaine"'.[5] Thus, the attention in this story is as much devoted to this depiction of Mbâ as to the lovers' story.

The personal characteristics of Mbâ outlined above are easily recognized in two prominent characters, Wali and her close friend Awa, of the novel *La Nouvelle romance*. From its title and foreword, borrowed from a novel by the French writer Louis Aragon, to its closing statement, this book speaks to "l'émancipation de la femme Africaine." Wali, the central figure, experiences much of the oppression that Lopès sees in the life of the African woman. But Wali also examines her situation and searches for viable alternatives. As the barren wife of an egotistic soccer star who manages to finagle himself a job in his government's embassy in Brussels, Wali must find a source of fulfillment and self-realization outside her marriage. Having been forced to give up her studies at the time of her marriage because her husband,

Bienvenu, believed that education took away a woman's femininity, Wali was at first occupied with caring for Bienvenu's sister's child. But later finding herself in a European capital in strange surroundings and among Europeans, who, as former colonialists, hold unconcealed prejudices against Africans, Wali feels very lonely since her husband provides no companionship for her and has long since lost sexual interest in her. Through her acquaintance with a Belgian neighbor couple Wali is introduced to and attends meetings of the communist party and is drawn to its doctrine regarding the status of women in the working class. She also enrolls in some courses in the People's University. These activities not only fill up Wali's time but also expand her consciousness of, and inform her perspective on, the developmental needs of her country.

In complement to these new acquantances and experiences, Wali maintains correspondence with her two closest friends from home, Awa and Elise. The former is a school teacher and eventually gets a scholarship to pursue the licence in Paris, the first female from her country to achieve this. Declining suggestions to study medicine or law, Awa chooses Liberal Arts to continue in her career in teaching because she believes that it is the teachers in her country who have the best opportunity to keep a vigilant eye on the direction in which the State is headed. She believes also that it is on the level of the intellect that women will achieve equality with men. Thus Awa zealously works to cultivate her own intellect, while deciding to postpone marriage. (Marriage is indeed available to the attractive Awa, as her friends Wali and Elise often tease her. Wali's husband Bienvenu says upon learning of Awa's receiving the first university scholarship awarded to a woman from their country: "Les femmes- là deviennent aussi des intellectuelles? . . . Mais elle, ça ne m'étonne pas. Ce n'est pas une femme. C'est un phénomène. Je me demande seulement comment elle fait pour être à la fois belle et intelligente?" (p. 139) ["Those women are turning into intellectuals, too?. . .But that doesn't surprise me about her. She's no woman; she's a phenomenon. I just wonder how she manages to be both beautiful and intelligent."]) Besides pursuing her own intellectual development Awa also pushes Wali to get her teaching certificate. This campaign is waged while they are still at home together before either goes to Europe as well as after they have separated and write letters to each other between Brussels and Paris.

Their other girlfriend is Elise, a seamstress and mother of a little girl, who enjoys her single life with her married lovers who give her enviable gifts. But in a conversation where the three friends analyze the situation of the married woman as compared with that of the single woman, several advantages and disadvantages are articulated for each. Elise, who at one point describes herself as "l'éternelle fiancée," also reasons that exclusivity in marriage leaves women like herself with no means of support. "Il est question de l'économie démographique!" (p. 67) ["It's a question of demographic economics!"]

That Henri Lopès the writer has a sustained commitment to using his works as a forum for the dialectics of African women's issues is evidenced by the proportion of his works that center around the status of women. Besides the novel *La Nouvelle romance* two of the *Tribaliques* stories, "Monsieur le député" and "L'Avance," are entirely concerned with women's issues, while three others, "Ancien Combattant," "Ah, Apolline," and La Fuite de la main habile" contain dominant themes involving women within stories whose focus is elsewhere. To look briefly at one of the women-focused short stories "Monsieur le député," we see an obvious conflict between theory and practice in the attitude of governments, and the men who run them, toward women. The fact that the central character here is a man, a member of parliament, in a story that features women from all five of our role categories allows the point to be made in the clearest light. Our Member of Parliament (M.P.), Ngouakou-Ngouakou addresses the convention of the Fédération nationale des femmes avant-gardistes, declaiming the immediate necessity for the effectuation of equality for women at every level of the nation's operation, including educational and employment opportunity and equalization of salaries. He closes by calling for the end of the tyranny of men over women, reminding his sisters there convened that women are the key to world peace. After receiving enthusiastic ovations he goes home, demands that his daughter get up from her mid-term math assignment to fix him a drink, turns on the TV and ogles the sexy Miriam Makeba singing and swaying, complains, when his small son brings him his slippers, that the boy is doing girl's work, and upbraids his wife, who is a little late with dinner, about having no understanding of the hardships of managing a family. After dinner he changes into casual clothers, goes out to a *rendezvous* with his mistress in the "Venez-Voir" night club, owned by an attractive widow. Later in bed with his mistress at a hotel, our MP is told by her that she is pregnant, to which he responds by suggesting that the paternity could lie with someone else. Thus Lopès sharply illustrates the discrepancy between theory and practice.

Conclusion

The presentation of the experience of the African woman is one of the qualities that makes Henri Lopès' work important in the literature of contemporary Africa. Factors such as the high frequency of women as narrators or focal characters, and topical content covering the broad spectrum of issues of the African woman's experience make the novels and short stories of this unfortunately little discussed writer a literary forum for African women's consciousness. By virtue of the quantity of attention Lopès devotes to women, the urgency for integration of women's issues into the African social process is made unequivocal. Lopès' women characters articulate their own self-consciousness. Even the fact that some of them are not able to articulate their self-consciousness is a part of their statement through the author as spokesperson. This situation is, however, representative of the contradictions surrounding women's relationships with all the other agents affecting their lives.

While the context of Lopès' creative practice is the family of African people, the context within which his works are set is quite frequently specifically Congolese but with situations drawn along broader African lines. The use of the homebased setting enables Lopès to be self-critical of Africa in general, with the attention directed at his own country. The problems, issues, contradictions which Lopès points to are presented unmistakably as African, not Congolese particularly. Thus from his own ideological stance Henri Lopès presents, in his work, the issues of social change in African society. The issues of women's status have a high place on his agenda for social change in Africa.

NOTES

1. Henri Lopès, *Tribaliques* (Yaounde: Editions CLE, 1971).
2. Kenneth Little, *The Sociology of Urban Women's Image in African Literature* (Totowa, NJ: Rowman and Littlefield, 1980).
3. Henri Lopès, *Sans Tam-Tam* (Yaounde: Editions CLE, 1977).
4. Henri Lopès, *La nouvelle romance* (Yaounde: Editions CLE, 1976).
5. Henri Lopès, "La fuite de la main habile," in *Tribaliques*, p. 5.

Daughters of Moombi;*
Ngugi's Heroines And
Traditional Gikuyu
Aesthetics

Charles A. Nama

The retrieval of the glorious, ancient age of African culture is a significant dimension of Ngugi wa Thiong'o's writings. All his works indict the importation of foreign cultures detrimental to African values. In this paper, I wish to articulate an important aspect of Ngugi's writings which has not received enough critical attention—his depiction of heroines who conform with specific conventions of traditional aesthetics, and who consequently play crucial roles as defenders of traditional cultural values.

In order to appreciate the relationship between Ngugi's heroines and his use of Gikuyu aesthetic convention it is necessary to understand the relevance of art in traditional societies. In "The Aesthetics of Old African Art," Isidore Okpweho observes:

> I have tried to identify the Old African Artist as a man with a very pressing sense of real and concrete presences, enjoying the closest intimacy with an environment that was both physical and metaphysical. By means of his dynamic sense of form he tried in all sorts of

*East African writer Charity Waciuma has an autobiographical work entitled *Daughter of Mumbi*, Nairobi: East African Publishing House, 1969.

combinations, with language and with material, to give tangible
meaning to those visible and spiritual presences who gave context to
his daily life and thought.[1]

The "physical and metaphysical" relationship implicit in many forms of
African art was also evident in traditional Gikuyu society. In this conection,
it is important to point out that, although Okpweho identifies the artist as
male, the artists and artisans in traditional Gikuyu societies were both men
and women. In *Facing Mount Kenya* Jomo Kenyatta informs us that
certain artistic activities such as pottery and basket-making were the realm
of the women. While building huts was the work of men, the women were
charged with the responsibility of beautifying it by thatching. In their songs,
the women poked fun at the artistic inadequacies of the men. As Kenyatta
records it:

> You men, you lack the most important art in building, namely
> thatching. A wall and an empty roof cannot protect you from heavy
> rain, nor from burning sun. It is our careful thatching that makes a hut
> worth living in. . .[2]

This symbolic completion of a Gikuyu homestead underscores the artistic
prowess of Gikuyu women in enhancing the "beauty" of Gikuyu art forms.
   In *Homecoming* (1972), *Writers in Politics* (1981), and *Detained*
(1981), Ngugi argues that the unequivocal liberation of Africans lies not in
Westernization but in the resuscitation of traditional cultural values that
have been an intrinsic part of the people's lives from ancient times. In
Detained, he notes the special contribution of Kenyan women in the
liberation struggle against British imperialism, remarking that:

> . . .the most remarkable of them all was Me Kitilili, the leader of the
> Giriama people's resistance to the British occupation of their country.
> She was already an old woman when she organized Giriama youth
> into a fighting force that took the British machine three years to
> subdue. Old as she was, she was very clearly the political character of
> the armed struggle. . .[3]

Like Me Kitilili, Ngugi's fictional heroines are active participants in the
liberation struggles against foreign domination; Nyakinyua in *Petals of
Blood* and Wariinga in *Devil on the Cross* are excellent examples.
   In order to appreciate their role, it is imperative to understand certain
salient aspects of Gikuyu traditional societies. The Gikuyus see life in
mythic terms and believe that each person's existence is destined and
controlled by *Ngai* the Supreme Being. Consequently, a sense of inevitability
shapes the lives, actions, and aspirations of the average Gikuyu. The

Sartrean existential notion of man being responsible for and controlling his own destiny is alien to Gikuyu metaphysics. The creation myth which Ngugi recounts in *The River Between* clearly defines the sacred, religious and political responsibilities of women in the Gikuyu view of the cosmos. He observes:

> . . .and the Creator who is called Murungu took Gikuyu *and Mumbi* from the holy mountain. He took them to the country of the ridges near Siriana. . .But he showed them all the land. . .Yes children, God showed Gikuyu and Mumbi all the land and told them. . .This land I hand over to you. O man and *woman*, its yours to rule and till in serenity sacrificing only to me, your God under my sacred tree. . .[4]
>
> (my emphasis)

This religious, functional significance of women's role in the Creation Myth is also underscored in Jomo Kenyatta's *Facing Mount Kenya*, where he traces the matrilineal families of the daughters of Mumbi until the men revolted. In most of Ngugi's works, therefore, women play a major role analogous to that played by their counterparts in traditional Gikuyu societies.

Ngugi's heroines in his earlier writings, though not as overtly political as in his more recent writings, manifest strong traditional values. Muthoni in *The River Between* is an excellent example. She is torn by inevitable circumstances between two diametrically opposed religions—one foreign, one traditional. Her plight is an instance of a pattern which recurs for his other female characters. Although her father embraces Christianity, Muthoni still upholds the initiation rites of Gikuyu women. She finally succumbs to Christianity but her ultimate objective is "to be a woman made beautiful in the manner of the tribe" (p. 44). Even on her dying bed, she does not relent; she remarks to Waiyaki, ". . . Tell Nyambura I see Jesus. And I am a woman, beautiful in the tribe. . ." (p. 53). (Editors' note: See Levin's paper in this collection for a contrasting perspective on circumcision as a female initiation rite.)

Mumbi in *A Grain of Wheat* is another heroine who embraces traditional values in Gikuyu society. Even the major characters in the novel acknowledge her singular role as they glorify her with songs which evoke the origins of the Gikuyu clan. The chorus of Gikongo's song is indicative of their admiration for her unique role:

> Gikuyu *na* Mumbi,
> Gikuyu *na* Mumbi,
> Gikuyu *na* Mumbi,
> *Nikihiu ngwatiro. . .*[5]

When Karanja, Kihika and Gitongo encounter Mumbi at Gikonyo's
workshop she is addressed in glowing terms by Karanga, "Mother of Men,
we have come make us some tea" (p. 93). These tributes to Mumbi also
illustrate her role in the world of the novel. At the height of the Emergency
which Ngugi depicts eloquently in *A Grain of Wheat*, the people are
betrayed by the enigmatic Mugo. Throughout the novel, Mugo is portrayed
as an eccentric personality who is eventually ostracized. At the crux of his
isolation and desperation he goes only to Mumbi to share his secrets and
guilt. Although their encounter is merely a temporary palliative for the
despised Mugo, it is an act of consolation for a rejected member of the
family.
Mumbi's observations about her singular role are significant:

> . . .Even when I got married, the dream did not die. I longed to make
> my husband happy, yes but I also prepared myself to stand by him
> when the time came. I could carry his sheath and as fast as he shot into
> the enemy, I would feed him with arrows. If danger came and he fell,
> he would fall into my arms and I would bring him safely to myself. . .[6]

Even the artist Gikonyo acknowledges her immense contribution to his self-
esteem. Their early encounter is deeply engraved in his memory so that
when he goes to jail, he draws upon it for emotional support. Speaking of
Mumbi he notes:

> . . .Before, I was nothing. Now I was a man. During our short period of
> married life, Mumbi made me feel it was all important. . .Every day I
> found a new Mumbi. Together we plunged into the forest. And I was
> not afraid of the darkness. . .[7]

She is eventually unfaithful to him, having an illegitimate child with his
archrival Karanja. Killam's explanation in *An Introduction to the Writings
of Ngugi* that the encounter "became the ultimate extension of her supreme
joy in hearing her husband's release and Karanja merely becomes an agent
in the process" (p. 67) seems appropriate if we consider Mumbi's
explanation after the episode and Gikongo's reluctance to come to grips
with his wife's unfaithfulness.
   Like other powerful heroines in Gikuyu history and mythology such as
Me Kitilili and Nyakinyua in *Petals of Blood*, Mumbi is an advocate of
Gikuyu culture. She is fascinated by stories about brave women in Gikuyu
culture and sees herself as a savior of her people. Although she does not
fulfill the role of the Redeemer, the emotional support she gives to Mugo and
Gikonyo in their moments of trial is an attempt to redeem the fallen though
on a smaller scale.

The two most important women in *Petals of Blood*, Wanja and Nyakinyua are good examples of strong women in Gikuyu society although on different levels. Wanja means "stranger" or "outsider". Her behavior is similar to that of Cyprian Ekwensi's Jagua Nana and true to her name, she remains an outcast in her community. Her lackluster love affair with Kimeria, her dissolute life and her acceptance of brazen Western materialism are all anathema to the traditional values of Ilmorog. However, she is one of the most prominent members of the team who undertake the epic journey to confront their nonchalant Member of Parliament, M. P. Ndcri Wa Ricra, in Nairobi.

The other major woman character in *Petals of Blood*, Nyakinyua, is the embodiment of traditional values. She celebrates Gikuyu norms and the values of the ancient age especially in her singing. Ngugi uses her as a prototype of the woman with extraordinary prowess in Gikuyu traditional society. In *Facing Mount Kenya* Jomo Kenyatta illustrates the importance of such women in Gikuyu mythology:

> ...This large group was then formed and given the ancestral collective name of *Rorere rwa Mbari ya Moombi*, namely, children or people of Moombi or Moombi's tribe. In this women continued to be the heads of their family and clans for some generations. . .[8]

Kenyatta also remarks that "there was a great medicine man known as Mogo or Moro Wa Kibiro whose national duty was to foretell future events and to advise the nation to prepare for what was in store." Ngugi assigns Nyakinyua both of these roles: mother of the clan and prophet who foretells future events. She is Wanja's grandmother and more. She is also representative of other strong women in Ngugi's novels such as Nyambura, Mwihaki and Mumbi.

In a recent interview while answering questions on the writing of *Devil on the Cross* Ngugi remarked:

> Because women are the most exploited and oppressed section of the entire working class, I would create a picture of a strong determined woman with a will to resist and struggle against conditions of her present being. Wariinga will be the fictional representation of this heroine of Kenyan history. Wariinga, heroine of toil. . .[9]

These attributes also apply to Nyakinyua in *Petals of Blood*. However, Nyakinyua's overriding role in the novel recalls the legendary period in Gikuyu history when women ruled the land. She is cast in the mold of a man, the legendary seer, Moro Wa Kibiro. That is why she expends all her energies to inculcate traditional values into the young. Even her relationships with individuals such as that with her husband have a special significance to the entire clan.

A major function of Nyakinyua's role in the novel is related to her husband's gallant defence of Ilmorog. Both of them are staunch defenders of traditional Gikuyu greatness. We are told that "Nyakinyua's husband, Njamba Nene. . .that he was so old yet pointing a gun at a white man! He redeemed Ilmorog with his blood. . ." (p. 81). In addition, she articulates the conventions and norms of her people. She fulfills the role of the "griot" and the seer. Like Sundiata's griot in *Sundiata: The Epic of Old Mali*, she is presented in epic terms. Ngugi observes:

> . . .Thus Nyakinyua talked to them, kept up their spirits with stories of the past. . .Nyakinyua was the spirit that guided and held them together. And she talked as if she had been everywhere, as if she had actually participated in the war against the Germans, as if the rhythm of the historic rise and fall of Ilmorog flowed in her veins. . .Nyakinyua, mother of men; there was sad gaiety in her voice, she was celebrating rainbow memories of gain and loss, triumph and failure, but above all suffering and knowledge in struggle. . .[10]

Very few women in African literature have been portrayed in such glowing epic proportions, as the embodiment of the struggle. Nyakinyua's role as the essence of Gikuyu existence in *Petals of Blood* is exemplified by her participation in the *Theng'eta* and the sacred ritual dance, the *Giriro*. We are told that the *Theng'eta* is the plant "only the old will talk about." Nyakinyua says that they used to brew it before the Europeans came. And they would drink it only when work was finished, and especially after the ceremony of circumcision or marriage or *itwika* and after a harvest. It was when they were drinking *Theng'eta* that poets and singers composed words for a season of Gichandi and the seer voiced his prophecy" (p. 204). Nyakinyua's association with the *Theng'eta* underscores her significance as the embodiment of traditional values. She is the only one in the novel who by virtue of her age and wisdom knows the secret recipe for the preparation of the potent drug which is invaluable to society.

Nyakinyua's special role in the novel is also expressed in her singing. As the lead singer of the *Gitiro* her singular role as the bard of the community is confirmed. Ngugi informs us that "she was good at singing and she threw erotic abuse, compliments, or straight celebratory words with ease . . . Most of the dance songs had a refrain and everybody could join the chorus. It was Njuguna and Nyakinyua who provided the dramatic tension of the opera of eros" (p. 207). In *African Art in Motion*, Robert Farris Thompson reminds us that:

> ...the chorus forms a kind of melodic handclap, testing and supporting the soloist and his ingenuity...Unsurprisingly, the leader of the dancers is, often, the leader of the song. But it is not just the aesthetic impact that is at issue here, but also the moral condition of the singer or the dancer...The chorus as in ancient Attic tragedy, is therefore, a direct expression of public sanction and opinion...[11]

To illustrate Nyakinyua's special role in the clan as sanctioned by the community and the chorus, Ngugi notes that all "listened to Nyakinyua as she sang the *Gitiro*. She was singing their recent history. She sang of two years of failing rains; of the arrival of daughters and teachers; of the exodus to the city" (p. 209). Nyakinyua's role as the principal articulator and bard of the *Gitiro* justifies the acclaim bestowed on her by the chorus and eventually all the people of Ilmorog. It also typifies her function in the novel as the embodiment of Gikuyu values in accordance with the tribe's mythology. She is the essence of Gikuyu womanhood. Later on, after the sacred dance, she continues her pervasive roles of lending moral, intellectual and physical support to the travellers. In Nyakinyua, we see Ngugi's attempts to juxtapose the sacred, the mortal and the supernatural, all beautifully depicted in a multifaceted character.

In a novel of tradition such as *Petals of Blood*, Nyakinyua's death should not be interpreted as the death of the old ways as Killam has done.[12] Instead, it should be read within the cosmic context of Gikuyu thought. It is true that the *Theng'eta* has been commercialized and adulterated but Ngugi stresses that vestiges of traditional life still thrive in the new Kenya. Nyakinyua now attains a different status in the Gikuyu hierarchy—both living and dead. This special status accorded to her is seen in the climactic moment of the novel. When a series of strikes and revolutionary actions to overthrow the system are called for, Karega invokes her assistance. He has been thrown into jail for inciting the workers and Akinyi is sent to bring him up to date on the condition of the revolution. In the closing dialogue which ensues, Ngugi observes:

> "You'll come back," she said again in a quiet affirmation of faith in eventual triumph. He looked at her, then past her to Mukami of Manguo Marshes and again back to Nyakinyua his mother, and even beyond Akinyi to the future! And he smiled through his sorrow. To-morrow . . . and he knew he was no longer alone . . . [13]

Hence, even in the forthcoming encounter Nyakinyua's prowess is invoked to continue unequivocal struggle for total liberation. Nyakinyua's death is not the end of the action; it is a transcendence into another realm of Gikuyu cosmology. Nyakinyua's death is analoguous to that of Samba Diallo in Cheikh Hamidou Kane's *L'Adventure Ambiguë*. Rather than the total destruction of traditional values, their deaths should be read as transcendence from one stage to another in the cosmic hierarchies of the respective traditional societies.

Ngugi's latest novel, *Devil on the Cross*, written in Gikuyu during the time of his detention, represents a significant milestone in his artistic development. The reasons are twofold. As he states in his earlier writings, he believes that literature must be a vehicle for the total emancipation of the masses whose dreams of *uhuru* have been betrayed by the Afro-Saxon elites. As a writer, his language or medium of expression is central to the resuscitation of African values which have been suppressed by imperialism. In *Writers in Politics*, Ngugi articulates the symbiotic relationship between literature and society and empasizes the cardinal function of language. He puts it this way:

> Kenyan national literature should mostly be produced in the languages of the various nationalities that make up modern Kenya. Kenyan national literature can only get its stamina and blood by utilizing the rich national traditions of culture and history carried by the languages of all the Kenyan nationalities. In other words, Kenyan national literature can only grow and thrive if it reaches for its roots in the rich languages, cultures and history of the Kenyan peasant masses who are the majority class in each of Kenya's several nationalities.[14]

By using artistic devices from Gikuyu lore in *Devil on the Cross* Ngugi has demonstrated his dedication to the linguistic revolution of Kenyan literature. His depiction of Wariinga as the proponent of traditional culture also enhances this concept.

As well, reflecting his concern for the suppression of women, he creates in Wariinga a very powerful heroine in *Devil on the Cross*. In *Detained: A Writer's Prison Diary*, Ngugi makes the following pertinent observations about Wariinga, language, plot, structure and characters in *Devil on the Cross*:

> ... I had resolved to use a language which did not have a modern novel, a challenge to myself, and a way of affirming my faith in the possibilities of the language of all the different Kenyan nationalities. ... But content—not language and technique—would determine the eventual form of the novel. And content? The Kenyan people's struggle against the neo-colonial form and stage of imperialism. ... [15]

Like Nyakiniyua in *Petals of Blood*, Wariinga is the embodiment of the struggle against corruption and adulteration of foreign cultures. Her fight is primarily against the neo-colonial elites which have subjugated women to secondary roles which are diametrically opposed to their revered status in traditional Gikuyu society. Wariinga's discussion with Gatuiria is illustrative: she attacks the condescending attitudes of men in the New Kenya, while Gatuiria attempts to exonerate the men by putting all the blame on foreign ideologies. Wariinga's response is poignant:

> The abilities and potential of our women are enslaved to the typewriter, the bars or the beds in those hotels we have put up in every corner of the country for the pleasure of the tourists. How insulting to our national dignity that our women have become mere flowers to decorate the beds of foreign tourists. . . . Even you, the Kenyan men, think that there is no job a woman can do other than cooking your food and massaging your bodies. . . Why have people forgotten how Kenyan women used to make guns during the Mau Mau war against the British? . . . . [16]

Devil on the Cross is dedicated "To all Kenyans struggling against the neo-colonial stage of imperialism." Wariinga is the chief architect of this struggle. The narrator of the story is the Gicaandi player who has been implored by Wariinga's mother to divulge the whole truth about the exploitation of her daughter. The narrator observes:

> . . . It was then that I heard the pleading cries of many voices; Gicaandi Player, Prophet of Justice, reveal what now lies concealed by darkness. [17]

The Gicaandi player's narration which ensues is a series of sporadic incidents which crystallize around Wariinga. She is ejected from her apartment by an unscrupulous landlord in Nairobi and fired by a lecherous employer, Boss Kihara, whose advances she had rejected. Unable to conprehend her chain of misfortunes, she concludes that her appearance is the sole cause. The narrator observes "what she hated most was her blackness, so she would disfigure her body with skin lightening creams like Ambi and Snowfire. . . " (p.11). Rescued from a suicide attempt, she decides to return to her family at Ilmorog by *matatu* (local mini-bus). In the course of this journey, she is invited to the Devil's Feast at Ilmorog, the central event of the novel. The participants at the Devil's Feast are domestic and foreign neo-colonial thieves who have stolen enormous wealth from the people. As Gatuiria and Wariinga listen to the testimonies of the exploiters, she is reminded of her own exploitation:

> She regretted having gone back to the cave for the afternoon session. The speeches, the thieves' attire, their hymns of self-praise, all these

things reminded her of the problems she had faced since she became pregnant by the rich old man from Ngorika and gave birth to a baby girl. . . . [18]

Wariinga is a victim of the educational, religious, political and social oppression by foreign and domestic exploiters. It is significant that as in the tradition of the strong Gikuyu women whom Kenyatta portrays in *Facing Mount Kenya*, Wariinga does not succumb to the stifling pressures of her oppressors. She encounters several obstacles and emerges victorious in the end. Although she is seduced by the rich old man and her original dreams of becoming an engineer are temporarily deferred, she fights gallantly and achieves her objectives in the end. Towards the end of the novel, it becomes apparent that she is unquestionably the leader of the new revolutionary movement composed of students, peasants and workers which sweeps through the country. The narrator informs us:

> . . . Wariinga was dressed the Gikuyu way. . . . Around her waist Wariinga had tied a knitted belt of white wool, the two long, loose ends of which fell the length of the cloth to her ankles. On her feet she wore leopard skin sandals. . . . She had Nyori-like earrings.[19]

Her otufit, in contrast to that of westernized Kenyans at the feast is a symbolic affirmation of Gikuyu culture. As the leader of the struggle, it is fitting that she kills the Rich Old Man, the symbol of the decadent, corrupt Kenya, even though he is her fiancé Gatuiria's father. Her active participation in the patriotic songs also underscores her dedication to Gikuyu lore. The following incantations with Gatuiria illustrate the point:

Wariinga:	Hail, the splendour of the land!
	Hail, the land ringed with deep lakes,
	Turkana to Naivasha,
	Nam-Lolwe to Mombasa!
	Hail, this necklace of blue waters!
Gatuiria:	Hail, hail, the shields of the land,
	From Kenya to the Mbiruiru mountains,
	From Kianjahi to the Nyandarua ridges,
	From Wairera to Mount Elgon!
	Hail, nature's defence to our land!
Wariinga:	And Hearken to the call of the land!
	The rivers flowing to the east,
	Ruiru, Cania, Sagana,
	Tana River, Athi River, Kerio River. . . . [20]

Ngugi's Nyakinyua in *Petals of Blood* and Wariinga in *Devil On the Cross* are two powerful heroines who possess the awesome responsibility of saving Kenya from complete foreign domination. It is significant that in attempting to retrieve the glorious age of Gikuyu greatness, Ngugi portrays his heroines in conformity with the traditional, original role assigned to them in Gikuyu mythology. Continuing the responsibilities assigned to them, such as the embodiment of traditional values, the unifying characters in their respective communities who assume epic roles and struggle for unequivocal liberation from foreign ideologies, Mumbi, Nyakinyua and Wariinga are true daughters of Moombi. Their pivotal roles in their respective communities are in conformity with their duties assigned by Murungu in the Gikuyu creation myth.

NOTES

1. Isidore Okpweho, "The Aesthetics of Old African Art," *Okike* 8 (1975), p. 10 See also Stanley Macebuh, "African Aesthetics in Traditional African Art," *Okike* 5 (1972), pp. 13-24.
2. Jomo Kenyatta, *Facing Mount Kenya* (New York: AMS Press, 1978), p. 80.
3. Ngugi Wa Thiong'o, *Detained: A Writer's Prison Diary* (London: Heinemann, 1981), p. 85.
4. James Ngugi, *The River Between* (London: Heinemann, 1965), p. 2.
5. James Ngugi, *A Grain of Wheat* (London: Heinemann, 1967), p. 41.
6. *Ibid.* p. 51.
7. *Ibid.* p. 60.
8. Kenyatta, *op. cit.*, p.6.
9. Jane Bryce, "Profile, Ngugi: My Novel of Blood, Sweat and Tears," *New African* (August, 1982), p. 36.
10. Ngugi Wa Thiong'o, *Petals of Blood* New York: E. P. Dutton, 1978), p. 123.
11. Robert Farris Thompson, *African Art in Motion* (Berkeley: University of California Press, 1974), p. 28.
12. G. D. Killam, *An Introduction to the Writings of Ngugi* (London: Heinemann, 1981), p. 117.
13. Ngugi Wa Thiong'o, *Petals of Blood*, p. 345.
14. Ngugi Wa Thiong'o, *Writers in Politics* (London: Heinemann, 1981), p. 59.
15. Ngugi Wa Thiong'o, *Detained: A Writer's Prison Diary op. cit.*, p. 8.
16. Ngugi Wa Thiong'o, *Devil on the Cross* (London: Heinemann, 1982), p. 14.
17. *Ibid.* p. 8.
18. *Ibid.* p. 182.
19. *Ibid*, p. 242.
20. *Ibid.* p. 128.

The Feminist Impulse and Social Realism in Ama Ata Aidoo's No Sweetness Here and Our Sister Killjoy

Chimalum Nwankwo

Feminism challenges, with justification, the secondary status of women in all societies. Some such challenges in African literature are suspisciously autobiographical and irredeemably subjective. Many are successful in presenting the universal dilemma of heterosexual relationships. Whether we are in the moribund traditional world of Flora Nwapa and Buchi Emecheta or wrapped in the earthy reminiscences of Charity Waciuma, certain crucial questions remain unavoidable. How does one translate individual subjective experience into legitimate questions for social redress? How does the African woman accommodate that individual experience within the stream of history—rapidly changing cultural and socioeconomic circumstances and consequently altered social relations?

If those questions are avoided, we can only read feminist literature in which suffering characters win only our empathy without our sympathy because there are no logical matrices to support the weight of feeling. It seems to me that no social issue successfully arrests attention without the

151

kind of simultaneous involvement and detachment which one finds in this
candid passage from Waciuma's *Daughter of Mumbi*:

> For myself, I have decided against polygamy but its rights and wrongs
> are still being argued furiously in our schools and colleges and
> debating clubs. There seems to have been a time in our society when
> there were many more women than men, possibly as a result of
> raidings. Under these circumstances polygamy may be socially good.
> Even today our women like to get someone to help them with the hard
> work of the farm and the house. Polygamy is clearly second nature to
> most Gikuyu men. I hate it because it hurts the position and dignity of
> women and exaggerates the selfishness of men.[1]

Here, Waciuma's indignation is subjective but historical and social
circumstances are used in such a way that individual preference or
predilection is validated.

Ama Ata Aidoo, Ghana's fine female writer perfects Waciuma's
approach in her collection of short stories *No Sweetness Here* and novel,
Our Sister Killjoy. In those works, the problems of the African woman are
expressed as integral parts of the problems of colonial and post-colonial
Africa. Aidoo's feminist concerns are not treated in isolation from Africa's
political instability, the new master complex of the so-called elite, the
atavistic problems of the rural African at the cross-roads of history, the fury
and impotence of the radical African, the lure of the Western world, and so
forth. Such problems are all neatly slotted into a cultural matrix often
evoked successfully by the writer's rich personal experience.

There are eleven stories in the *No Sweetness Here* collection. Despite the
diversity in themes, all the stories are products of an intense involvement
not just in the problem of women but the problem of the Black race as a
whole. Aidoo herself justifies her involvement in these words: "I cannot
see myself as a writer writing about lovers in Accra because, you see, there
are so many problems."[2]

Aidoo's plethora of problems is projected by various narrative voices in
shifting perspectives. What this approach accomplishes is to make us
accept the author as a detached and neutral observer advancing cases for
all the underprivileged in society instead of being a solicitor for any special
interests. Consequently we are compelled to suspend our own partisan
prejudices and look at all the problems from a fresh and correspondingly
neutral vantage point. We trust the "unseen" author and concentrate and
rely on her created mouthpieces. The limitations of space will permit a few
examples from a variety of impressively crafted situations in the short stories.

In "For Whom Things Did Not Change," the searing irony of independence
comes alive in this exchange between a new African master and his African
house servant:

'Massa, God knows I know my job.'

'Of course! As a man of the land and your wife's husband you are a man and therefore you do not cook. As a black man facing a white man, his servant, you are a black, not a man, therefore you can cook.'

'Massa, Massa. You call me woman? I swear, by God, Massa, this na tough. I no be woman. God forbid!

"Ah, Zirigu. I am only thinking something out. Ah. . . God is above, I no call you woman. Soon I go talk all for you.'

'But Massa, you no know. Don't call me woman.'

'No, I will not.'

———————

When a black man is with his wife who cooks and chores for him, he is a man. When he is with white folks for whom he cooks and chores, he is a woman. Dear Lord, what then is a black man who cooks and chores for black men?[3]

Eloquently, the colonial and neo-colonial mentality in the minds of both big and small in society is intelligently tied up with the status of women in society. A strategic and apt authorial intrusion hones up the irony. Africans accept inferior status as a result of colonialism. That acceptance is a dangerous social habit like female passivity which lingers despite independence. This affects a national beauty contest in the first story, "Everything Counts," a contest won by a long-haired mulatto. That contest and its preference points at the same problem at the root of the exchange between master and servant in "For Whom Things Did Not Change."

"In the Cutting of a Drink" male chauvinism is illustrated in the city life of a girl called Mansa. Her brother is sent from the village to the city to bring her back. Shocked by the fast-paced and sensual city life, Mansa's brother is convinced that since the women of the city were smoking and drinking, they must all be 'bad' women. His own drinking habit is taken for granted. Such myopic vision of evil also ignores the sociological impetus behind the city lifestyles led by both men and women.

Several social attitudes in "The Message" leave women at the short end of the stick. They are blamed for being fat or thin, for being unable to have normal child deliveries, or for failing to arouse traditional support during emotional emergencies.

"Certain Winds from the South" counterpoints the situation in "In the Cutting of a Drink." This time, men are attracted to the Southern cities in Ghana. Even though no dreams are fulfilled, they keep on going. Their destruction passes blamelessly. M'ma Ansa, the seeing maternal eye of the story knows why. Tradition cannot be broken:

Is his family noted for men that rot? No. Certainly not. It is us who are noted for our unlucky females. There must be something wrong with them. . . (p. 51)

In the story "No Sweetness Here" from which Aidoo's collection takes
its title, everything is, as usual, wrong with women. Circumspect traditional
narrators play down the injustices in polygamy. So are the abuses and ill-
usage which women suffer in marriage. Even women have been socialized
into accepting their inferior status happily. An age old traditional value
asserts that "a woman must sometimes be a fool" (p. 61). We are not shown
instances where men must sometimes be fools to accommodate their female
counterparts. Women are the witches nonetheless, and the tragedy is not
mitigated by mandatory maternal responsibilities and the value placed on
the accidental ability to have male issues. Death strikes the only son of a
lonely woman in "No Sweetness Here" and threatens another child of
another lonely woman in "A Gift From Somewhere" to accent the
enormity of the problems which women have to grapple with in their daily
lives.

Collectively, what these stories successfully reveal is that neither choice
is a good choice for the African woman. Neither the woman who espouses
traditional and conservative wifely values nor the woman who pursues her
social pleasures liberally find life rewarding. "Two Sisters" especially
confirms that dilemma. No matter how the characters turn out in these
stories, Aidoo always succeeds in remaining reasonably detached. When
an innocent girl is unfairly punished by her mother in "The Late Bud," we
see how this relates to the author's nonjudgmental posture. Individuals
always suffer when their worth is based on whether their behaviors fit or do
not fit conventional behavior patterns that are by no means permanent.
"The Late Bud" is therefore an indirect reference to the way women are
socialized into traditional lifestyles and expectations which ultimately
contribute to their inferior status in many societies.

The penultimate story in the collection is one of the most circumspect in
its method of addressing the underprivileged status of women. "Something
to Talk About on the Way to the Funeral" sums up one unspoken
contention, that is, whichever way we look at society women cannot escape
the vicious cycle of oppression. There are good men and good women, bad
women and bad men, but eventually the bad men appear to escape socially
unscathed. Not the women. Twice in that story women become premaritally
pregnant and twice the men neither accept responsibility nor any punishment.
The unfair assumption is that it is 'normal' for a 'bad girl' to become
pregnant in that way. Of course, the profligate male is also meant to be just
that.

"Other Versions," the final story in the collection depicts other versions
of oppression. Capitalism, racism and sexism are shown to be identical in
their *modus operandi*. The scenes shift from Africa to America but the
human drama is enacted in the same way. In Africa, man and woman,
husband and wife labor together to raise a child. The mother is shown to
have a selfless interest in the progress of the child while the father expects

material compensation. At dinner even in America, the woman is busy serving and the men eat enthusiastically.

This story suggests implicitly that any kind of power is dangerous because the wielder is without the human feeling necessary for good fellowship. The Merrows, who host Kofi, are so condescending to him that he feels, not without justification, that he is being devoured like a dinner.

The final lesson is that feeling, or intuition, a distinctive attribute of women will always triumph over that kind of power which makes men able to oppress women or the rich oppress the poor. Hence the lone woman Kofi meets in the subway ride awakens in Kofi the same kind of love he reserved for his mother.

All of Aidoo's stories share one thing in common. Even though they appear to touch many problems, their focus is the concern for women in society, but the feminist impulse is balanced in such a way that "Aidoo does not allow her criticism of this to become obsessive."[4]

Our Sister Killjoy, like Aidoo's short stories, deals with so many problems. Once again, its success depends largely on the ability of the author to lend all the problems equal spikes. In that regard Ngugi and Sembène come to mind—writers who are fully aware in their works that a campaign for social justice is meaningful only when all disadvantaged people in human society receive undiscriminating attention. It is that same principle which makes Aidoo's works feminist literature with a difference.

Our Sister Killjoy directs its opening barbs at a foe whose national origin or nature ceases to matter as soon as he/she is fully described:

> Nanabanyin Tandoh
> Who knows how to build
> people
> structures
> lives. . .[5]

We can guess immediately that the writer has no sympathy for any form of traditional structure when such structures are used for inhibiting people or artistic expression. Structurally, the work then proceeds to adopt a defiant artistic form in which prose and poetry freely blend with each other. That posture takes care of the feminist campaign for women's freedom but that is only part of the numerous problems in society, hence a quick shift to the doorsteps of the Black race.

We are brought face to face with an unfair social system within which *among other things* women are unnecessarily placed upon pedestals for sympathy which becomes irreverent because of the special attention involved. Consider, for instance, the opening vignette in *Our Sister Killjoy*. The 'heroine' is attending a send-off party or orientation session in Ghana before leaving for Europe on some form of Government sponsorship. The authorities "had pulled strings for her to obtain her passport in a week instead of three months" (p. 8). One of the men, Sammy, reflects a negative national image in his conduct at the party. Sammy "was very anxious to get her to realize one big fact. That she was unbelievably lucky to have been chosen for the trip. And that somehow, going to Europe was altogether more like a dress rehearsal for a journey to paradise" (p. 9). In Sammy, we are dealing with a situation in which an individual conceives an inferior spot for himself relative to others. We could blame or not blame Sammy depending on what we consider responsible for his diffidence and lack of self-worth. Sammy is a product of colonial intimidation and its conscious process of socialization.

In the relationship between men and women in society, identical power complexes emerge. Many women accept inferiority, many men accept mastery as the norm. Also, the distinction which Sammy makes between Africa and Europe is the same kind of distinction which enables one race to oppress the other, rich people to oppress poor people, and men to oppress women. Such relationships, no matter where they begin eventually undercut the supposedly egalitarian aspiration of all societies. This conclusion emerges easily from the end of the first part of *Our Sister Killjoy* where a reference to Sissie in German as a "black girl" (p. 12) activates a negative epiphany in which white people's skins are "the colour of pickled pig parts that used to come from foreign places" (p. 12).

Such deft linkages of feminist concerns with wider social issues opens the second section of *Our Sister Killjoy*. Here, impressions of Germany include the vision of castles superimposed on present realities indicating how long opression has been with human nature:

> And you wondered
> Looking at the river
> How many
> Virgins had
> Our sovereign Lord and Master
> Unvirgined on their nuptial nights
> For their
> Husbands in
> Red-eyed
> Teeth-gnashing
> Agony, their
> Manhoods
> Hurting. . .
> But *'all the days are not equal', said the old village wall* (p. 19)
> (my emphasis).

Of course, the major concern of the author is inequality, so there are discussions of the pitiful and peripatetic Black people from Africa to the diaspora. Their social and economic problems are fitted into the collage of oppression. A few 'Sammys' also reappear as pseudointellectuals who either dream of successful lives or pretend to live successful lives within the intimidating circumstances of Western technological society. Ironically, it is from the pediatric practice of one such medic that we find the root of sexism:

> '500 for a boy
> 400 for a girl'
> Why should it surprise
> That it costs a little more
> To make a boy?)p. 31)

Such measure of worth is universal as we find out from the discussions between Sissie and her lonely German friend, Marija.

Marija is a female prototype of Sammy in her meek acceptance of a subservient role in her society. She speaks of her only child with unconcealed delight. She "was very happy that he was a boy" (p. 51).

Throughout the rest of this second part, other sensitive issues weave in and out of feminist concerns: oppression in South Africa and Rhodesia (now Zimbabwe), cultural and socio-economic problems in Nigeria, Ghana, Upper Volta and so forth. The high point of this section is Marija's display of lesbian affection for Sissie from which the latter recoils with revulsion. Sissie's act is probably in keeping with Aidoo's. It symbolizes the gap between the European female and African female's response. Problems are not solved by running away from them, rather new ones are created as the depicted vagrant Africans in Europe and America may be aware.

Aidoo's "vision of the past and present is essentially tragic,"[6] observes Adelugba on Aidoo's short stories. That tragedy finds full expression when the writer's critical eyes show us Africans in Europe—male and female. In fact the females receive more criticism. Generally the problems of all are traced back to colonialism and its psychological aftermath. We find sarcastic references to Man in this section. There is intelligent linkage again. Man is the Christian Doctor of heart transplant fame but the feat hailed by a Nigerian psuedo-intellectual as scientific triumph is almost debunked as a product of the demonic alter ego of colonialism. Colonialism in turn is seen as Man's expression of an undying love to dehumanize his fellow man. Where Aidoo's logic appears to falter, verve is restored with poetic shots like this:

> to live in peace in man's world
> The virgin Birth
> Is not the only mystery
> One

Simply has to take
By faith. (p. 100)

However uncanny such reductionist approaches may sound, the implied relationship between Christianity, colonialism, capitalism, sexism and oppression appear to hold on well.

The three major sections of *Our Sister Killjoy* merge into each other in whorls. The concerns are the same and the examples used to support those concerns are similar as we shift from one geographical focus to the other. In the final major section, there is greater introspection because of the literary approach—a confrontational "love letter" from Sissie to an imaginary male partner. The letter suggests a way out of the morass—communication between man and woman. The same kind of self search and dialogue is endorsed for similar problems in Ngugi's *A Grain of Wheat*. Such dialogue based on a mutually comprehensible language would then form the secret springboard for the solution of *all* the spiritual and material problems bedeviling the Black world.

Aidoo has dealt with women's problems with arresting wisdom and grace. The conservative dissenter and the radical sympathiser will probably find her approach stimulating. Aidoo's forte is her tremendous *feeling* and honesty of sentiment in expressing those issues. Her works ring like the unimpugnable scold of a justly aggravated parent. "Although writers of both sexes have written about Mother" assesses McCaffrey "the woman writer naturally identifies with her female characters."[7] Aidoo's identification extends beyond "underprivileged womanhood and the arrogance of manhood"[8] to include a variety of social problems across geographical boundaries. Without doubt, like her feminist mouthpiece in her play, *Anowa*, Aidoo has learnt and heard that "in other lands a woman is nothing."[9] Despite that knowledge, "everything counts" in the way she assembles her materials in her short stories and novel, *Our Sister Killjoy*, to register a feminism reasonably in tune with social realities.

Certain problems remain apparent in spite of Aidoo's strengths. It is still difficult to avoid some degree of prejudice and presumption when dealing with issues concerning men and women especially in African societies. We still have to deal with psychological and cultural questions many of which do not appear within the scope of Aidoo's discourse. It is not enough to indicate that if human beings have values placed on their heads, 'boys' are always more 'costly' than girls. We must be willing to deal with certain root fears and desires. For instance, the predominantly African assumption that women eventually marry and leave their birth families to assist in building their husbands' families. That cultural attitude and the African love for large families still make polygamy possible in so-called modern African societies. We have to deal with the desocialization of traditional African males who still cling to the chauvinistic guns of the past despite changed and changing social relations. We must also extend our attention to certain rural circumstances where social relations remain affected by taxing agrarian occupations which restrict women to specific economic and social positions. Finally, the past is a valid reference point for understanding present reality and projecting future directions. The key to a means for resolving our problems is a reasonable degree of honesty in facing all of those problems. This is where Aidoo takes the lead among other African women in search for social justice through creative literature.

NOTES

1. Charity Waciuma. *Daughter of Mumbi* (Nairobi: East African Publishing House, 1962), p. 11

2. Dennis Duerden & Cosmo Pieterse ed. *African Writers Talking* (London: Heinemann Educational Books Ltd., 1972), p. 19.

3. Ama Ata Aidoo. *No Sweetness Here* (London: Longman Group Ltd., 1970), p. 17. All page references onward are to same text.

4. Dapo Adelugba. "Literature as Social Criticism." *Ba Shiru*, 6, 1 (1974), 16.

5. Ama Ata Aidoo. *Our Sister Killjoy* (New York: Nok Publishers International Ltd., 1979), Dedication. Further page references to same text.

6. Adelugba, p. 16.

7. Kathleen McCaffrey. "Images of the Mother in the Stories of Ama Ata Aidoo" *Africa Woman*, 23 (1979), 40.

8. Ezekiel Mphahlele's Introduction to *No Sweetness Here* (New York: Doubleday, 1972), p. x.

9. Ama Ata Aidoo. *Anowa* (London: Longman Group Ltd., 1970), p. 52.

The Concept of Choice
In Mariama Bâ's Fiction

Irène Assiba d'Almeida

One of the key concepts that emerges from Mariama Bâ's novels is that of choice. This is most striking in *Une si longue lettre* where the recurrence of words like *le choix, choisir, j'ai choisi, j'ai decide, ma decision, j'ai voulu, je ni' ai pas voulu*, [the choice, to choose, I have chosen, I have decided, my decision, I wished, I did not wish to] is in itself indicative of the importance of choice for Mariama Bâ. In *Un chant écarlate*, even though words pertaining to choice are less recurrent, crucial choices are constantly being made throughout the novel. The act of choosing is shown as being pivotal in human experience. It is indeed a powerful act which gives shape and direction to human existence.

In *Une si longue lettre* the protagonist is Ramatoulaye, a Senegalese woman who has just been widowed. In a long flash-back she recounts her story through the medium of a letter written to Aïssatou, her best friend. The letter is essentially about how Ramatoulaye manages to survive socially, economically and above all emotionally after Modu, her husband, takes a second wife. Modu's second marriage is a double slap in Ramatoulaye's face. Indeed, in contracting this marriage without telling his first wife until the very day it happens Modu betrays their thirty years of marital life and the twelve children they had together. To make matters worse, Modu chooses as a second wife Binetou, a friend and schoolmate of their own daughter.

161

Ramatoulaye chooses Aïssatou as a confidante not only because they are
friends from childhood but also because Aïssatou has gone through the
same experience. The book then deals with the isolation of married women
who refuse to accept polygamy in a society where it is sanctioned by Islam.

It is important to focus on the choices made by female characters in *Une
si longue lettre* because women are definitely at the centre of the novel.
Ramatoulaye is portrayed as a strong, dignified woman who is confronted
with a number of options throughout her life; she is therefore called upon to
make vital choices.

In a society where parents have a great influence on the choice of one's
spouse, Ramatoulaye rejects her mother's preference for Daouda Dieng, a
medical doctor who wants to marry her. Instead, her choice goes to Modu
Fall who was then a high-school student like her and who will eventually
become a lawyer. In explaining her choice Ramatoulaye gives credit to the
liberating influence of school:

> Liberée donc des tabous qui frustrent, apte à l'analyse, pourquoi
> devrais-je suivre l'index de ma mère pointée sur Daouda Dieng,
> Célibataire encore, mais trop mûr pour mes dix-huit hivernages.[1]
> [Thus, free from fustrating taboos and capable now of discernment,
> why should I follow my mother's finger pointing at Daouda Dieng,
> still a bachelor but too mature for my eighteen years.]

When she finishes school Ramatoulaye chooses a profession that she
likes. Even though she is aware that teaching is often unrewarding and
unrewarded, she chooses to become a teacher. She is dedicated to the
acquisition of knowledge for all and emphasizes the importance of
education for women in particular.

When she is told that her husband has married a second wife,
Ramatoulaye chooses to receive the news with great calm and dignity,
keeping to herself the pain and despair she feels:

> Je m'appliquais à endiguer mon remous intérieur. Surtout ne pas
> donner à mes visiteurs la satisfaction de raconter mon désarroi.
> Sourire, prendre l'évènement à la légère. (p. 58)
> [I forced myself to check my inner agitation. Above all, I must not give
> my visitors the pleasure of relating my distress. Smile, take the matter
> lightly.]

Once the news is broken to her, Ramatoulaye spends a long time thinking
about the next step to take. Now that she has a co-wife who could be her
daughter, will she leave her husband's household to express her disapproval
or will she stay? After a thorough analysis of her new situation and in a very
lucid manner, she decides to stay. Her choice is made even more difficult

because her children, her daughters in particular, cannot comprehend Ramatoulaye's choice. In the past, they had heard their mother rise up against the iniquities of polygamy. Indeed, when Mawdo, Aïssatou's husband took a second wife and wanted to justify himself and ask for understanding, Ramatoulaye was outraged:

> J'étais offusquée. Il me demandait compréhension. Mais comprendre quoi? La suprématie de l'instinct? Le droit à la trahison? La justification du désir de changement? Je ne pouvais être l'alliée des instincts polygamiques. . . (p. 62)
> [I was shocked. He was asking me for understanding. But understand what? The supremacy of 'natural' urges? The right of betrayal: Justification for the desire for change? I couldn't be the ally of polygamous urges.]

At that time, little does Ramatoulaye suspect that she also will have to go through the trauma of the numerous women who were "méprisées, reléguées ou échangées, dont on s'est séparé comme d'un boubou usé ou démodé" (p. 62). ["despised, relegated or exchanged, who were abandoned like a worn-out or out-dated boubou." (caftan worn by West African Muslim women especially)]

After Modu's death, Ramatoulaye chooses to remain single. She refuses to accept Tamsir's marriage proposal. Tamsir, who is her brother-in-law, could, according to custom, marry her, but he only wants to do so for economic reasons. Ramatoulaye, who knows this, expresses her total rejection with great indignation:

> Tu oublies que j'ai un coeur, une raison, que je ne suis pas un objet que l'on se passe de main en main. Tu ignores ce que se marier signifie pour moi: c'est un acte de foi et d'amour, un don total de soi à l'être que l'on a choisi et qui vous a choisi. (J'insistais sur le mot choisi). p. 85.
> [You forget that I have a heart, a mind, that I am not an object to be passed from hand to hand. You don't know what marriage means to me: it is an act of faith and of love, the total surrender of oneself to the person one has chosen and who has chosen you. (I emphasized the word 'chosen'.)]

In the same way, but for different reasons she turns down Daouda Dieng. She was Daouda's first love and he proposes to her again. Even though she knows that Daouda is loving and reliable, she likes him but is not in love with him. Another reason why she rejects him is that he is already married. She says: "Abandonnée hier par le fait d'une femme, je ne peux allégrement m'introduire entre toi et ta famille" (p. 100). [Abandoned yesterday because of a woman, I cannot lightly bring myself between you

and your family.] By taking this stand Ramatoulaye implies that a greater
solidarity among women is needed to alleviate the agony women go through
in polygamous situations.

As far as her relationship with her children is concerned Ramatoulaye
tries to give them a fairly liberal education. Her last choice consists in
standing by her second daughter when she discovers her to be pregnant:

> Je ne pouvais pas l'abandonner, comme le dictait l'orgueil. . . La vie
> qui frémissait en elle m'interrogeait. Elle grouillait pour s'épanouir.
> Elle vibrait pour demander protection. . . Ma décision d'aider et de
> protéger émergeait du tumulte. Elle se fortifiait au fur et à mesure que
> j'essuyais [ses] larmes, au fur et à mesure que je caressais [son] front
> brûlant. (pp. 121-2)
> [I could not abandon her, as pride would have me do. . . The life that
> fluttered in her was questioning me. It was eager to blossom. It
> vibrated, demanding protection . . . My decision to help and protect
> emerged from the tumult. It gained strength as I wiped the tears, as I
> caressed the burning brow.]

The second main character in *Une si longue lettre*, Aïssatou also had to
make significant choices. Her husband Mawdo married a second wife
because Tante Nabou, his mother, had never approved of her son's first
marriage. He, a prince, had married a goldsmith's daughter. Tante Nabou
saw this marriage as a disgrace to the family's social status and decided to
plan her son's second marriage in a thorough manner. When Mawdo gave in
to his mother's pressures Aïssatou chose to leave with her four sons, and this
she did with great dignity:

> Les princes dominent leurs sentiments pour honorer leurs devoirs.
> Les "autres" courbent leur nuque et acceptent en silence un sort qui
> les brime. . . Tu veux dissocier l'Amour tout court de l'amour
> physique. . . Si tu peux procréer sans aimer, rien que pour assouvir
> l'orgueil d'une mère déclinante, je te trouve vil. . . je me dépouille de
> ton amour, de ton nom. Vêtue du seul habit valable de la dignité, je
> poursuis ma route. (p. 50)
> [Princes master their feelings to fulfill their duties. 'Others' bend their
> heads and, in silence, accept a destiny that oppresses them. . . You
> want to draw a line between heartfelt love and physical love. . . If you
> can procreate without loving, merely to satisfy the pride of your
> declining mother, then I find you despicable . . . I am stripping myself
> of your love, your name. Clothed in my dignity, the only worthy
> garment, I go my way.]

Aïssatou then chooses to build a second life on her own. She finds that, in her society, class differences can be an obstacle to self-fulfillment. However, she knows that education is attainable by all and can serve as a levelling asset; therefore, she decides to go back to her studies. She then goes to France to train as an interpreter and eventually finds a job at the Senegalese Embassy in Washington, D.C.

What then is the significance of all these choices? In this novel Mariama Bâ affirms that "chaque femme fait de sa vie ce qu'elle souhaite" (p. 128) [Each woman makes of her life what she wishes"]. This affirmation is very reminiscent of Jean-Paul Sartre's pronouncements on choice. Indeed, in *L'être et le néant*[2] and, in more simple terms in *L'existentialisme est un humanisme*[3] Sartre posits that human beings are nothing else than what they make of themselves. They are the sum total of their choices and through the act of choosing, they create themselves. Sartre, then, views choice as essential for the creation of self. Even though Mariama Bâ does not go as far as to make choice a metaphysical concept like Sartre who thinks that human beings are condemned to choose, she does consider choice to be of vital importance, to be the ultimate affirmation of self. It is indeed through choice that Ramatoulaye and Aïssatou find the strength and courage to face problems that overburden women, to overcome what threatens to deny the self. It is also through choice that they arrive at self-realization. However, this is not achieved without pain, without conflict.

More than any other character, Ramatoulaye is the one who constantly battles with conflictual situations within and outside herself. No doubt her choices are informed by her unrelenting desire for change but they are also mediated by a strong streak of conservatism. What Ramatoulaye really wants is to be a modern woman, conscious of her rights as an individual and determined to fight for these rights. However, being a modern woman is at once seductive and threatening. Seductive because it opens up to the possibility for freedom and change, threatening because potentially, it has the power to destabilize the ground on which she stands. And so, Ramatoulaye is always torn between modernity and tradition. This *déchirement* ["tearing apart"] is characteristic of women and men of her generation as she rightly points out:

> Nous étions tous d'accord qu'il fallait bien des craquements pour asseoir la modernité dans les traditions. Ecartelés entre le passé et le présent, nous déplorions les "suintements" qui ne manqueraient pas. . . Nous dénombrions les pertes possibles. Mais nous sentions que plus rien ne serait comme avant. Nous étions pleins de nostalgie, mais résolument progressistes. (p. 32)
> [We all agreed that much dismantling was needed to introduce modernity within our traditions. Torn between the past and the

present, we deplored the 'hard sweat' that would be inevitable. We
counted the possible losses. But we knew that nothing would be as
before. We were full of nostalgia but were resolutely progressive.]

Indeed, Ramatoulaye is progressive but not radical and her choices bear
this out. For instance, she is fiercely against polygamy; yet she accepts it
implicitly by choosing to stay with Modu after he marries Binetou. In his
"La polygamie et la révolte de la femme africaine moderne", Cyril
Mokwenyé contrasts Aïssatou and Ramatoulaye's reactions to polygamy
by saying:

A travers les deux femmes nous avons deux personnages symboliques.
Aïssatou symbolise la jeune femme capricieuse et peu patiente qui
réagit trop spontanément, alors que Ramatoulaye est le symbole de la
femme qui ayant investi dans son mariage, est ouverte aux compromis.
Elle ne veut pas agir sans une réflexion profonde. Sa révolte sera une
révolte psychologique. . .[4]
[Through the two women we have two symbolic characters. Aïssatou
symbolizes the capricious, impatient young woman who reacts too
spontaneously, while Ramatoulaye is the symbol of the woman, who,
having invested in her marriage, is open to compromise. She does not
want to react without deep reflection. Her rebellion will be a
psychological one.]

The truth of the matter, however, is that Aïssatou is in no way whimsical
or overly impatient. If she wastes no time in making her decision, it is not
because she has not pondered the situation; it is because she goes *all the
way* in her protest. For her, and this is her choice, divorcing her husband is
the only acceptable solution to the problem she is confronted with.

Mokwenyé also praises Ramatoulaye for choosing to abide by the
dictates of her religion and for staging what he calls a "passive resistance",
which according to him produces positive results. He contends that by
staying in the household Ramatoulaye forces Modu into an "exil conjugal".
The point to be made here is that if Modu is ill at ease in his own home, his
exile is indeed a rosy one. After all, all he really wants is to be with his new
bride and learn how to be young again! And so, by a curious reversal of
situation, it is Modu who decides to leave the household. Thus, Ramatoulaye
ends up being on her own even though she has not had the courage to make
the necessary choice.

Another conflict that affects choice is the one which emerges from her
relationship with her children and with her daughters in particular. She
wishes to give them a liberal education; yet she has problems letting them
wear pants, seeing them smoke. She is lost in disbelief because her daughter
who is well brought up, efficient and considerate has allowed herself to get

pregnant, as if these things were mutually exclusive. She uses this incident, however, to show how unfair it is to throw pregnant girls out of school while their male counterparts are left to continue with their studies.

An area which shows the split in Ramatoulaye's behavior is that of her ideas on women issues. On the one hand, she stresses the importance of education for women and the necessity to take a more significant part in politics so as to have a say in the decision-making process. Ramatoulaye describes the plight of working women who have a double yoke to bear and she also demands recognition for the interminable work done by women who stay at home. Yet, on the other hand, she has internalized a number of stereotypes about women and women's behavior. For instance she tells Aïssatou: "Je t'envie de n'avoir mis au monde que des garcons" [I envy you for having had only boys"] (p. 127). Also, while speaking of the responsibility embedded in being a mother as well as the exaltation that motherhood provides she says: "Passionante aventure que de faire d'un bébé *un homme* sain" ["A thrilling adventure, to make a whole *man* from a baby"] (p. 71. My emphasis).

If Ramatoulaye is the persona that represents the writer's point of view, then Mariama Bâ belongs to a generation of African female novelists whose writing is characterized by a certain malaise. This malaise emerges from the dilemma women face in wanting to keep traditions while, at the same time, wanting to reject what, in society, ties women down. To find an acceptable and viable *modus vivendi* between the forces of tradition and the realities of the present is almost a *tour de force*. That is why, a writer like Flora Nwapa, for instance, sets her novels *Idu* and *Efuru* in the traditional context and deals in both novels with the importance of bearing children in African society. Indeed she takes refuge in subject matters that are safe in that they do not demand that the order of things be challenged, let alone subverted.

From Flora Nwapa's early writings to Mariama Bâ, a lot of ground has been covered. However, Mariama Bâ does not go all the way in her protest and she is aware of it. Ramatoulaye, her mouthpiece, is acutely aware that men's power on the one hand and the weight of traditions on the other coalesce to slow down women's progress:

> Je sais mouvant le terrain des acquis, difficile la survie des conquêtes: les contraintes sociales bousculent toujours et l'égoisme mâle résiste. (p.129)
> [I know that the field of our gains is unstable, the retention of conquests difficult: social constraints are ever-present, and male egoism resists.]

Given this situation, it becomes easier to understand the motives that lead Ramatoulaye to make what could be called a forward-backward motion. Indeed, when she makes two steps forward, she almost immediately makes one step backward. It then becomes clear that, in *Une si longue lettre*, choice is not perceived as a given but as a long, painful and conflictual process which ultimately has the potency to upset established rules and internalized conditioning.

Un chant écarlate deals with choice in a very different way. Here all the characters are called upon to make choices and they are all affected by each other's choices. The story revolves round two young students in philosophy who are in love and want to be married. He is Ousmane Guèye whose father is an important figure in the Muslim community and whose mother is an ordinary woman, well grounded in the African traditions. His friend, Mireille de la Vallée is a young French girl who comes from a bourgeois family. Her father is a diplomat working at the French Embassy in Dakar. All his beautiful speeches about the necessity of breaking racial barriers are put to a test that reveals his true self the day he discovers that his daughter is having an affair with a Black man. His reaction is instantaneous: he sends his daughter back to France that very day, and Mireille's mother, who is a very submissive wife, has no say in this decision. However, this separation only succeeds in strengthening Ousmane and Mireille's relationship. At the end of their studies they get married in Paris, in the Muslim tradition.

It is when they go back to Dakar that they have to deal with serious cultural clashes that cause their relationship to deteriorate to such a point that Ousmane has to seek for his emotional as well as what he calls his cultural needs outside the home. He finds them in Ouleymatou, a childhood girlfriend whom he eventually marries unbeknown to his first wife. When Mireille discovers the marriage, she is first incredulous, she is then totally broken, turns hysterical and finally becomes stark mad. She kills her son Gorgui, whom she says will never fit in any society, be it white or Black. She then attempts to kill her husband as he comes back from his second wife's house in the wee hours. Eventually, the French Embassy sends Mireille back to France where she will end up in a lunatic asylum while the reader is left to imagine what will happen to Ousmane.

All the characters in *Un chant écarlate* make important choices. Ousmane chooses to marry Mireille, and to remain faithful to his culture. He also chooses to marry a second wife even though his father who is a staunch Muslim married only one wife. However, Ousmane feels justified in his action not only because Islam allows it but also because

> Ouleymatou était devenue sa vraie moitié, celle en qui il reconnaissait son prolongement. Elle était à la fois. . . sa racine, sa souche, son élan, sa floraison. . . Les liaient. . . leurs origines: les mêmes ancêtres, les mêmes cieux. La même terre! Les mêmes traditions! La même sève des moeurs imprégnait leur âme.[5]
> [Ouleymatou had become his true other half, the one in which he recognized his extension. She was at once. . . his root, his stock, his

spirit, his blossoming. . . They shared common origins: the same
ancestors, the same heavens. The same earth! The same traditions!
The same cultural sap courses through their souls.]

Mireille, on the other hand chooses to study in Dakar so she can see
Ousmane; she also chooses to be converted to Islam without measuring the
implications of such a conversion. She also chooses to remain faithful to
her own culture. Her efforts of adaptation to Senegalese lifestyle are short-
lived and frustrated by antagonistic forces.

Mr. and Mrs. de la Vallée choose to send their daughter to France and to
reject her when they eventually learn that she married Ousmane without
their consent. In fact, it is Mr. de la Vallée who makes these choices. His
wife goes along with him even though, deep down, she does understand her
daughter.

Yaye Khady, Ousmane's mother, chooses to reject Mireille even before
she meets her, just because she is white, and she chooses to encourage and
accept Ouleymatou as her son's true wife.

Soukeyna, Ousmane's sister and the only one who makes friends with
Mireille, chooses to tell her sister-in-law that Ousmane married a second
wife. Finally, Ouleymatou chooses to seduce Ousmane and even calls in the
Griots who tell him how he went astray by marrying a Frenchwoman:

> Tu es prince Lébou.
> Une Blanche a renié sa patrie pour te suivre
> Mais mieux que la blanche,
> La fille noire te convient. (p. 180)
> [You are Prince Lebou
> A White has renounced her country to follow you
> But better than the White girl
> The Black girl is suited to you.]

After an elaborate seduction, Ouleymatou chooses to marry Ousmane.

Even though the concept of choice underlies both novels, there is an
essential difference in the way it is treated. In *Une si longue lettre* there is no
doubt that Modu, Binetou, Tante Nabou and Mawdo make choices that
affect others. However, the emphasis is clearly on the two main protagonists,
Ramatoulaye and Aïssatou. Here, choice is essentially seen as it affects the
individual lives of these two women, as it allows for growth, as it activates
the development of consciousness. In *Un chant écarlate* on the other hand
choices affect not only the individuals who make them but also the people
who are close to them.

In choosing to marry Mireille, Ousmane also chooses to sever her from
her cultural milieu and to create a cleavage between his family and him. In
choosing to remain faithful to his culture, Ousmane pays little attention to

the fact that Mireille also has a culture. He brings the discussion to a close by peremptorily saying: "En épousant un homme, on épouse aussi sa manière de vivre." ["In choosing a husband, one is also choosing a way of life."] (p. 133). In choosing to marry a second wife, Ousmane also chooses to deny Mireille his love and attention and ultimately to shatter her life. On the other hand Mireille cannot stand Ousmane's ways. She thinks that communal life is a form of parasitism and resents her mother-in-law's violation of her privacy. After a few attempts at adaptation, Mireille also chooses to remain faithful to her Western culture. By doing so she widens the gap between Ousmane and her and antagonizes Ousmane's friends and mother.

The choices made by Ousmane and Mireille's parents affect the couple. In choosing to reject their daughter, Mr. and Mrs. de la Vallée deny her a chance to turn to them in periods of crisis. In choosing to reject Mireille, Yaye Khady makes Mireille's integration into Senegalese society more arduous and sows the seeds of discord within the couple. In choosing to encourage Ouleymatou, Yaye Khady also chooses to affect Mireille's emotional balance. Djibril Guèye, Ousmane's father, makes no choice because he sees all that happens as being ordained by God. In making no choice, he still chooses to follow the course of events.

In choosing to seduce and marry Ousmane, Ouleymatou deeply affects Mireille's life. Finally Soukeyna's decision to inform Mireille of Ousmane's second marriage is made out of friendship but it is nonetheless responsible for Mireille's tragic end.

It is important to note that all the choices made in *Un chant écarlate* converge to bring about Mireille's destruction. Ironically, and even though this is only implicit in the novel, Mireille's destruction will affect all the people who have made these choices. It then becomes clear that the concept of choice in this novel is closely related to the concept of responsibility. Here again Sartre comes to mind for he feels that it is impossible to dissociate choice from responsibility:

> ...Man is responsible for what he is...When we say that man is responsible for himself, we do not mean that he is responsible only for his own individuality, but that he is responsible for all men.[6]

In *Un chant écarlate* the link between choice and responsibility is strongly made. It is responsibility toward others because choices, even if they are made by individuals, in isolation, can have an impact on other people's lives. It is also responsibility toward self for there is no doubt that Mireille and Ousmane are both weak, self-centered individuals who lack what it takes to meet each other half-way. And so, as main characters they are not only responsible for what happens to others as a result of their choices but they are also responsible for what happens to them as individuals, as a couple, as members of the larger society.

In conclusion it is possible to say that in *Une si longue lettre* Aïssatou and Ramatoulaye have made different choices in similar situations. However, what is important is that the choices have been made. For too long a time women have been denied to choose the course of their lives, even though choice is at the center of what gives significance to human existence. In this novel Mariama Bâ shows clearly that women do have a deep consciousness of the options opened to them and that they are willing to make the choices that will make their lives more wholesome, no matter what the consequences might be. There is also a strong intimation that the generation of Daba (Ramatoulaye's daughter) will go even further in their choices and will deal with that concept in a more radical way.

In *Un chant écarlate* Mariama Bâ widens the scope of the concept of choice by showing how all human beings, female and male, Black and white deal with that concept and the consequences that choice can have on the self and on the human community.

After a long silence, women like Mariama Bâ have chosen to talk. Their voices have sprung up to revive the role that women have traditionally played as story tellers. They now tell their "modern stories" through the medium of the written word. Using their female sensibility, they approach womens' issues from within, offering a female way of looking at the world. This is indeed a choice that needed to be made.

NOTES

1. Mariama Bâ. *Une si longue lettre*. Dakar, Abidjan: Les Nouvelles Editions Africaines, 1980, p. 28. All subsequent quotations from this work will be indicated by the page number within the text.
2. Jean-Paul Sartre. *L'être et le néant*. Paris: Gallimard, 1949.
3. _____. *L'existentialisme est un humanisme*. Paris: Editions Naget, 1946. Translated into english by Philip Mairet under the title of *Existentialism and Humanism*, London: Methuen & Co. Ltd., 1948.
4. Cyril Mokwenyé. "La polygamie et la révolte de la femme africaine moderne: une lecture d'*Une si longue lettre* de Mariama Bâ" in *Peuples Noirs, Peuples Africains*, no. 31, (janvier-fevrier 1983) p. 91.
5. Mariama Bâ. *Un chant écarlate*. Dakar, Abidjan: Les Nouvelles Editions Africaines, 1981, p. 183. All subsequent quotations from this work will be indicated by the page number within the text.
6. Jean-Paul Sartre. *Existentialism and Humanism*. Op. cit. p. 30.

Reintegration With The Lost Self: A Study of Buchi Emecheta's Double Yoke

Marie Linton Umeh

Double Yoke is a love story told in the blues mode. The story laments a loss; yet it sings a love song. Its theme of the perilous journey of love, is a major preoccupation in author Buchi Emecheta's dramatic work. On an equally fundamental level, *Double Yoke* describes the tragic limitations of Nigerian women in pursuit of academic excellence and the anxiety of assimilation. Similar to her earlier novels, *Double Yoke* assesses the predicament of women in Africa. By describing the sexual and cultural politics in Nigerian society, Emecheta again campaigns against female subjugation and champions her case for female emancipation. Nko, the author's intellectually oriented heroine, provides some insight into the psyche of modern African women who are encumbered by traditional African misconceptions attached to the university-educated female.

Firstly, *Double Yoke* is a love story but with tragic implications. Buchi Emecheta is at her best in describing the anxiety lovers often experience because of mutual distrust at one time or another and the inability to reconcile their difficulties. According to the author, love, if betrayed, is directly responsible for the misery that afflicts the human soul. The tale of the terrifying journey of the possibilities and failures of love is then at the dramatic center of *Double Yoke*.

This theme of romantic conflict is not entirely new in African literature. The principle characters in Chinua Achebe's *No Longer At Ease*, Chukwuemeka Ike's *Toads For Supper*, Okot p'Bitek's *Song of Lawino*, and Flora Nwapa's *One Is Enough*, similarly narrate their personal traumas over lost loves. Diverging from her theme that Igbo women are enslaved to Igbo traditions which subjugate them to certain customs, Emecheta extends her metaphor by stating that Nigerian men are similarly enslaved. Ete Kamba, a central character in the story, is described as a traditional African man who is sorely disappointed when he falls in love with Nko, a modern African girl. Because Nko gives herself to Ete Kamba who has just gained admission into the university she is faced with untold hardships. Ete Kamba's love for Nko turns to distrust. He begins to question her virginity. This develops into a kind of neurosis, forcing him to lose sleep and cease concentration on his studies. He tells Nko, "You are not a virgin are you? Were you a virgin? There was not a drop of blood. You are a prostitute, a whore and you keep putting on this air of innocence as if you were something else."[1] Their problems are magnified when Ete Kamba consults a spiritual advisor, the Reverend Professor Ikot, who dissuades him from the love affair with ulterior motives:

> Nko is from my part. She is a true Efik from Duke Town, and women from our part have always brought great honour to their families. She will be in this university in a year or two. So what do you want a graduate wife for? Why don't you get a trained teacher or a nurse or something. Let us pray my boy, so that God will give you the wisdom to learn to sew your coat according to your measurement. (p. 90).

It is not long before Ikot succeeds in seducing and impregnating Nko. Ete Kamba, unnerved by Nko's air of independence and self-assertiveness, had set the stage for this fall. He therefore expresses his grief and the pain he feels about what has happened to him to Miss Bulewao, a character in the novel apparently speaking the mind of author Emecheta.[2]

The significant tragic implication here is that Ete Kamba is not the modern African man. Despite his pursuit of western ideals, i.e., a university education and a university-educated wife, his reliance on traditional African mores stands out. His quest for a humble, chaste wife signifies one of Nigerian society's myopic perceptions of the making of the perfect African woman. Emecheta's dominant realization of women is that of a being limited by the dictates of men in a patriarchal society. Nko, with a feminist orientation, probes the root of things, questions where she is going and attempts to control her fate. Ete Kamba cannot cope with Nko's heightened sensibilities. He is unable to love and live with Nko on a plane of equality and mutual respect. Herein lies the tragedy. Although Ete Kamba wants a beautiful, educated and sophisticated wife to grace his home, his ideal seems to be the quiet, submissive, innocent female who looks after the children and the house, cooks, earns money and puts his interests before her own.[3] For the African woman, the implications are more devastating. The African woman more so than the African man, is caught in a bind. In order to be liberated and fulfilled as a woman she must renounce her African identity because of the inherent sexism of many traditional African societies. Or, if she wishes to cherish and affirm her 'Africanness' she must renounce her claims to feminine independence and self-determination. Either way she stands to lose; either way she finds herself diminished, impoverished. It is Emecheta's growing awareness of the futility of attempting to resolve this dilemma that accounts for the growing bitterness that engulfs Nko.[4] Emecheta, a sensitive artist and student of society, distinguishes between the idealization of womanhood and the realities of a woman's place in the African community. Ete Kamba's ambivalence towards Nko mirrors African society's unconscious hypocrisy towards women. It never occurs to Ete Kamba that it was Nko's innocence and purity of spirit that attracted her to him. It never occurs to him that he practically raped Nko the night she lost her virginity to him and that any resistance against his desperate advances would have been futile. He deflowers Nko, only to turn around and search for another virgin queen: someone he feels he can respect, someone his children can call mother. Ete Kamba's double standards are simply co-existent realities in his environment. The conflicting standards in Ete Kamba's perception of women is shared by his roommates. Their collective image of females is an idealized rather than a realistic portrait of the African woman's situation.[5] The African man's perception of the educated African woman often ignores some of the realities of her sex.

Emecheta in another episode, illustrates how innocent young females are often turned into prostitutes at places one would least expect: academic institutions. When approached by the Reverend Professor Ikot, Nko retorts:

> Most girls here come to read for their degrees. If they become what you think, which is 'prostitues Nigerian style', it is because people like you made them so. But with me sir, you are not going to be let off lightly. My reward is a good degree. I did not believe in bottom power until today sir. (p. 141).

One then asks, why does Nko submit to Reverend Ikot's advances? Why does she stray away from those goals she so clearly defined for herself? What is peculiar in all of Emecheta's novels up to the present time is a consistent female view that sometimes mars her art by its emphasis on the all-suffering, victimized female. However, author Emecheta generally attains a balance in that she looks at women not in the narrow advocacy of feminine rights but in a wider context of a concern for the female and by implication the species they represent. In describing some of the injustices that have been transcended, she captures the quintessential core of female discrimination in a male dominated society as it has remained among the Nigerian ethnic groups and most other patriarchal social organizations. The answer also lies here. Nko is about to fully participate in Nigerian elitist society to a level much greater than most women. Perhaps the thought of this participation places too great a psychological strain on her. She lives with the fear of disappointing her parents and community by not suceeding in earning a good degree and helping her parents to train her younger sisters and brothers. She is obsessed with succeeding. It can also be said that she has internalized a narrow and limiting role pattern which casts her as a woman into subservient behaviour. Nko's inconsistent behaviour stems from her being brought up both formally and informally to believe that this is a man's world and that she is merely a woman, a second-class citizen. Feelings of anxiety about a degree, indoctrination into acceptable female roles and Ete Kamba's ambivalent and troubled feelings towards her, pressure Nko into surrendering herself to Reverend Professor Ikot. One needs courageous determination and encouragement to stir oneself out of being programmed into passivity and psychological servitude. A related problem is the questioning and disavowal of a woman's genuine, individual merit. It is almost a common assumption that a woman's merit resides in her sexuality. This of course is a threat to the concept of female merit in institutions of higher learning. Thus Nko's reliance on stereotyped female wiles at this point is out of character. Additionally, it conflicts with Nko's inclination towards feminism, vividly portrayed in earlier parts of the novel in her struggles for equality and self-respect with Ete Kamba.

This idea which Emecheta explores introduces the elements of women's liberation and the correct role for women in Africa. The right path for them is not clear as Mrs. Nwaizu, a character in the novel, puts it: "We are still a long way from that yet. Here feminism means everything the society says is bad in women. Independence, outspokenness, immorality, all the ills you can think of. . ." (p. 104). The feminine protest in this novel is not as subtle as in Flora Nwapa's *Idu* and *Efuru* or Efua Sutherland's *Edufa*. Nko vehemently protests against female victimization which brings her psychological strains. Similarly, university women today in Nigeria find themselves at the crossroads of losing their identity in male-female relationships (marriage) or attaining self realization by earning a degree thus forfeiting family life. In any event, in the novel the basic illustration is that Emecheta attacks certain masculine preserves such as having children out of wedlock and expectations of humility in women especially in the traditional sense. Miss Bulewao asks Ete Kamba, "Are you strong enough to be a modern African man? Nko is already a modern African lady, but you are still lagging . . . oh so far, far

behind." (p. 162). Nko's characterization of a modern African lady though
is not totally impressive. Moral laxity need not be equated with the New
African woman. Ironically, Emecheta in her plot does not promote female
liberation in Africa. Instead, she strengthens the belief of conservative
Nigerians who fear that female education leads women to all sorts of
corruption.

This leads us to another issue raised in *Double Yoke*, namely, the
limitations of females in pursuit of self-realization in Nigerian society. This
subjugation of women consistently emerges as one explores Nigerian
society's history of raising women to perform the narrow, unidimensional,
traditional role of wife/mother, while at the same time encouraging the male
to expand and explore his capabilities to the fullest. Hence, society's
division of sex roles limits woman's human capacity for the pursuit of self-
realization thus destroying any attempt at fulfillment outside the family.[6] In
Double Yoke Emecheta unmasks areas of human experience so far
subsumed under the myth of the decorous stable institution of marriage as
witnessed in the social organization of Okonkwo's household in *Things
Fall Apart* and Ezeulu's most equitable household in *Arrow of God*.
Through Emecheta's characters we learn that this norm, prescribed by
traditional African society is in fact abnormal. In *Double Yoke*, the female
psyche emerges as an important quarry for concern. From multiple female
voices such as Nko's, Mrs. Nwaizu's, Miss Bulewao, and Nko's roommates,
emerge pertinent questions that put the nature of the female's well being at
the heart of traditional African social organization.

Emecheta then surpasses Flora Nwapa, another Igbo writer, with her
consistent unbiased exploration of the opressed female psyche, although
Flora Nwapa in *One Is Enough* is more decidely feminist. Emecheta points
out artistically, as have other feminist writers such as Simone de Beauvoir
and Germaine Greer, that the very structure of patriarchal social organizations creates a suppressed individual by making an existential being an
object for male subjectivity. Author Emecheta is not in a class of her own.
She shows, like Kate Millet, that patriarchy is a power structured
relationship that in most cases exploits women through a system of assigned
and devalued roles.[7] Through her characters she challenges some of the
assumptions of traditional Igbo society which frustrate the gifted woman
from the realization of herself as an entity. Through her heroine we realize
with Catherine Mackinnon that gender is a learned quality not essentially a
biological fact.[8]

A sub-theme in *Double Yoke* is the exploration of the dilemma of men
and women positioned between modernization and traditionalism in this
instance on university campuses in Nigeria. Young adults become disoriented
by conflicting standards of morality and the role of men and women in a
changing society. Ete Kamba and Nko quarrel about whether or not the

latter should attend the Reverend Elder Ikot's Revivalist meeting. They are trapped by conflicting standards in religious obligations and patriotism. Emecheta writes:

> How he [Ete Kamba] wished his girlfriend had been just a simple village girl to whom he could simply say, 'you must not go to the Revivalist meetings again, because I don't trust the head of the movement.' He could never say a thing like that to Nko. She would like to know all the reasons behind his orders. (p. 124).

At another time Ete Kamba demands Nko confess whether or not she is a virgin. He is trapped by conflicting standards in morality. What kind of woman makes the 'ideal wife'? One of his roommates rationalizes: 'Give me a fourteen-year-old village girl with uncomplicated background any time.' (p. 163).

Apart from Ete Kamba's inability to throw off the precepts of traditional African society which give certain prerogatives to men and deny them to women, author Emecheta points out that today's modern female is also torn between two worlds and unable to function properly in either. Nko is confused about the actual role the educated female should play in Nigerian society. The title of the book, *Double Yoke*, then is symbolic. According to the author, because educated Nigerian women are expected to play both the role of the submissive, gentle, docile female and the modern, sophisticated individual, there is confusion about which values to adopt: those of traditional African society or those of the west. Both African men and women are therefore in bondage. Living in two different cultures brings too much tension. Hence, they must live with a 'double yoke' for daring to walk where angels fear to tread.

There is satire too in *Double Yoke*. As well as the clash between the old and the new, there is a clash between the genuine and the false. In the character of Reverend Professor Ikot, pretentious and immoral university professors in Nigeria are attacked. Ikot, like the true trickster figure is shrewd, cunning and loquacious. Posing as a religious leader and educator, he dupes others but is rarely duped himself. His strong archetypal appeal, ability to outwit others and articulate his ideas enable him to exercise power and control over people. Even when caught in the act, he exploits the situation and emerges a winner. Note how he handles his confrontation with Ete Kamba in one of the most dramatic scenes in the book. Playing on the intelligence of his people, he fabricates a story knowing full well what the policemen want to hear. Emecheta, pointing to the exploitation of students on university campuses and the abuse of Christian teachings, protests against the corrupt, opportunistic nature of contemporary Nigerians. Rather than working towards the acquisition of souls or imparting knowledge to students, Ikot preoccupies himself with "getting a piece of the cake."

Almost risking his chances of being the next Vice-Chancellor at Unical, he shamelessly destroys the lives of both Nko and Ete Kamba.

Finally, Ete Kamba exemplifies primacy of the group ethic over individual self-interests, which is so embedded in traditional African society, by sympathizing with Nko upon hearing of her father's death. Ete Kamba begins to realize that despite their inexperience they have to resolve their problems for no other reason than because they love each other. Ete Kamba and Nko choose to grow from their blunders and bear their double burden together. Ete Kamba's deep feeling of affection for Nko, despite a certain myopia which blinds him to manifest ambiguities within himself, helps him to understand that no one knows very much about the life of another. This ignorance becomes vivid, if you love another.

This ending is not altogether convincing even in these modern times. It then becomes obvious that author Emecheta is ascribing her personal modes of thought even though they may be way ahead of her audience. Most of us are still very conservative. In the fusing of the old and the new traditional African society's intolerance of one's right to choose one's destiny rather than consider the common good seems to be strengthened. In spite of this, *Double Yoke* is quite entertaining while it explores several political and social issues common in African literature. Emecheta's simplicity of style covers her exploration of these important issues in strikingly new and provocative twists.

NOTES

1. Buchi Emecheta, *Double Yoke*. London: Ogwugwu Afor Company, 1982, p. 57 (All subsequent references to this text will be referred to by page numbers).
2. See Ezenwa-Ohaeto, "The Texture and Variation of Commitment To Protest and Violence in Recent Nigerian Fiction." Paper presented at the *Fourth Annual Conference of The Literary Society of Nigeria*, 22-25, February, 1984, University of Benin, Benin City, p. 15.
3. Kenneth Little and Anne Price, "Some Trends In Modern Marriage Among West Africans. *Africa Journal of the International African Institute*. XXXVII, October, 1967, pp. 413, 421 raise this issue in their work.
4. Katherine Frank, "African Womanhood in the Novels of Buchi Emecheta." *World Literature Written in English*. Vol. 21, No. 3, 1982, p. 478, provides interesting angles on Emecheta's works.
5. See Lloyd W. Brown, "The African Woman as Writer," *Canadian Journal of African Studies*, Vol, 9, No. 3, 1975, p. 495, for discussion of Emecheta's early work.

6. This position is validated in Chinua Achebe, "The Social Limitations of the Academic Woman to the Pursuit of Excellence." *Nigerian Journal of Education*, Vol, 2, No. 1, p. 107.
7. Simone de Beauvoir, *The Second Sex*. Translated and edited by H. M. Parshley. Harmondsworth: Penguin, 1976, p. 483.
8. Catherine Mackinnon, "Feminism, Marxism and the State: An Agenda for Theory." *SIGNS*, Spring, 1982, Vol. 7, No. 3, p. 529.

Songs from Silence: Hausa Women's Poetry

Beverly B. Mack

A significant portion of Northern Nigeria's oral and written poetry remains unknown to the world and unrecognized in its own cultural setting because it is created by women. Women's extemporaneous oral verse is not regarded as serious artistry because it is created by those who are not considered respectable; the written works remain hidden with their authors, traditional Hausa women who are secluded in their homes in urban areas. It was not always this way: female praisesingers have in earlier times been highly regarded as the guardians of social mores and historical traditions, and Nana Asma's, who lived in northern Nigeria in the nineteenth century, is still known for her contributions to the Islamic cause through her inspirational written religious verse.[1] She is remembered as an exemplary traditional Muslim woman.

The reasons that Hausa women are not now recognized as creators of oral and written poetry are based on social and religious precepts which have evolved in recent history; since the *jihad* of the early nineteenth century, local interpretation of Islam has deemed that Muslim Hausa women remain secluded in their husbands' homes. In such circumstances it is no surprise that women—who are expected to be invisible elements in Hausa society—rarely have the opportunity to flourish as popular entertainers, unless they are willing to forfeit their respectability as private secluded women. Rarely instructed in Koranic verse, or able to complete primary level secular education, Hausa women often are illiterate, and thus ill-equipped to compose written verse.

181

Despite such odds Hausa women of northern Nigeria do, however, create both oral and written literature that is reflective of their situations, attitudes, aspirations, and perspectives on their community. The creative artists discussed here are indeed exceptions in Hausa society; nevertheless their material constitutes a significant expression of the attitudes of their silent sisters—the Hausa women for whom they perform and of whom they speak. This study offers a brief survey of varieties of poetry produced by contemporary Hausa women in northern Nigeria.

Hausa Wakoki—Written and Oral Verse

Northern Nigeria has for centuries enjoyed a rich Arab/Islamic literary tradition, beginning with religious verse composed by Muslim scholars and extending to secular verse modeled on the orthodox pattern. Created in the literary form that is a legacy of Islam, these verses contain the standard opening and closing doxologies, as well as strict rhyme and meter common to Islamic religious verse. Such traditional verse was transmitted through chanting, and preserved in print by Islamic scholars. Thus Hausa literature has long been expressed in both oral and written forms.

Among the Hausa the term *waka, s. (wakoki,* p.) includes in its definition a range of compositions from the extemporaneous oral declamation to the written verse.[2] *Wakoki* may be expressed orally, for the term itself implies the concept of "song" as well as "poem." Scholars do, however, distinguish between the oral and the written *waka*, which are as diverse in style and theme as the circumstances in which they are delivered. Indeed there are situations for which one type may not be substituted for another.

The oral *waka* is appropriate to praise song for prestigious individuals, naming and wedding celebrations, spirit-possession cult ritual, pacing domestic tasks, etc. It is suited to the non-religious—the ritual, entertainment, and quotidian situation. These extemporaneously delivered *wakoki* are basic to Hausa entertainment in both private and in public settings. Although they are not preserved in print, oral *wakoki* do have form, for they follow established patterns of the genre which may be studied as readily as those of written works.[3] Repeated performances of extemporaneous, orally composed *wakoki* reveal an entertainer's own repertoire of interchangeable phrase patterns. An entertainer may be known for a particular style of phrasing, and thus may influence other entertainers who listen to his or her performance. As a genre, the oral *waka* also has been influenced by the standards of the written *waka* to the extent that the oral work often contains doxologies and repeated phrases invoking God's blessings.

The standard form of the written *waka* reflects its function, for the written verse is appropriate to religious education. Following the verse patterns of the Koran, Islamic scholars traditionally have produced religious tracts which contain opening and closing doxologies to God, and follow strict patterns of rhyme and meter. Since the 1930's these have been published in chapbook form by a northern Hausa press.[4] These *wakoki* may also appear in Hausa newspapers or be broadcast on local radio stations. In contrast to extemporaneous *wakoki*, the written works are of a private nature—they are written by individual authors who have the time to rethink and revise the work, and the subjects are usually serious, contemplative concerns. The function of the written *waka* is to inspire and instruct more than to entertain.

Oral Poetic Artistry

Despite the wealth a successful entertainer may accumulate, these Hausa creative artists have rarely enjoyed respectable social status.[5] Whether a praisesinger in a royal court, or an entertainer for celebrations around town, the *mawaka* (praisesinger or oral poet) is considered to be of a separate class with which most Hausa people do not care to be associated.

The northern Nigerian women who perform extemporaneously forfeit for their profession even more respectability than do their male counterparts because they are neither secluded nor subject to a husband's demands. Thus they do not represent the typical, traditional Hausa woman; but neither are they typical of one another. One very successful performer of bawdy songs is married to a man who farms and tends the children while his wife travels around the North taping television and radio shows and performing in public. Another entertainer is an older woman who sings at political rallies for her favorite candidate; by virtue of her age and seniority over her younger husband, she is free to be autonomous. Among the Emir of Kano's courtiers is an older, widowed woman who has for twenty years been the Emir's official *zabiya*, or female praisesinger. When her husband was alive he approved of her profession since he himself was a musician for the Emir. Yet another older woman extemporizes bawdy verse to entertain groups of secluded women at celebrations in private settings as well as mixed public audiences throughout the North. In none of these cases does the woman subordinate herself to her husband's demands, but pursues her career at the expense of her status as a respectable Hausa woman.

Typical of the bawdy verse performed by the first woman, Maimuna Coge, cited here is a song delivered to a mixed public audience of students at a university in Kano.[6] Performing extemporaneously with a chorus of women beating on upturned calabashes, the singer shapes her material to the interests of the audience. She points out that respectability and success are two distinct attributes; comparing her own profession with the higher status profession of the educated bureaucrat, she observes that both have been successful economically:

> . . .And for a long time he has held the pen; and for a long time I have been well-off[7]

The bureaucrat enjoys a high social status, and a position of affluence, the two of which are often related. But this entertainer reminds her status-conscious audience that wealth brings comforts, regardless of how it is acquired. Money earned by the prostitute buys the same comforts as a bureaucrat's money; between the well-respected bureaucrat and the prostitute there is a difference of social status only. In fact, the prostitute may be the more affluent of the two:

> I beg the forgiveness of the married women
> For I will do the movement of the European-style prostitutes
> For you know, in Funtuwa, in that city,
> There are European-style prostitutes
> Prostitutes in a European-style house,
> Drink beer and smoke cigarettes
> They wear white gowns and thrive[8]

The prostitutes *thrive*, even though their profession is not respectable. Who, the entertainer asks, can judge an individual by their income, or deny affluence to one whose profession is not "appropriate"?

For a man, respectability is related in large part to his income; for a woman, respectability has everything to do with being "proper." Implicit in this woman's song is the understanding that role-playing is central to social order, and those who deviate from the system may not enjoy the social rewards, but that does not prevent their reaping other benefits. In the ultimate irony, this entertainer is paid well for reminding her pretentious audience of the gap between their social status and her own.

A less controversial version of this genre of oral praise is performed by the Kano Emir's female praise singer, Maizargadi. She strides before the Emir shouting extemporaneously rearranged sets of epithets that warn his subjects of his proximity. Typical of her repertoire are phrases that commemorate his royal line, confirm his position of authority in Hausa culture, and express thanks for his generosity in providing gifts for her:

> Emir of Kano, Alhaji Ado Bayero, rest easy, son of Abdu,
> From today until the end of the world, thanks be to God or the
>   generosity he has shown
> Bull Elephant, ancestor of Dabo,
> Our righteous one, who is here and is well
> Greetings to the master of thousands, master of Abdu's horse,
>   Bull Elephant, ancestor of Dabo,
> I give thanks, I multiply the blessings on the Emir of Kano,
>   Alhaji Ado,
> I give thanks for his wealth, the giver of blouses . . .

> Emir of Kano, Alhaji Ado Bayero
> Grandson of Alu Mai Sango. . .[9]

This type of oral poet is closest to the griot of other cultures, the oral historian who preserves, in verse, genealogies, historical events, and meetings between a patron and other dignitaries. Although she does not enjoy royal status, she nonetheless is considered to play an important role in expressing high regard for the monarch, and reflecting such positive public opinion of him.

Yet another Hausa woman, Binta Katsina, has become known for her song advocating women's participation in the Nigerian work force. In it the entertainer encourages Nigerian women to participate in "every kind of work," thus rejecting the northern traditional injunction against women's active public roles:

> You should do every kind of work, you should know every kind of work
> You can write papers, you can pound the typewriter,
> You can fly airplanes,
> You know how to be in the office,
> You could do the government work,
> And you could be the police workers,
> You could do the customs work,
> Let's give you the chance
> Women of Nigeria
> Women of Nigeria, you know every kind of work[10]

With the exception of praise songs for royalty, oral performance by Hausa women artists represents the irreverent, the revolutionary in Hausa society. It is performed by women whose own lifestyles deviate from traditional and conservative women's roles, and represents convention only as it departs from it. Like the court jester, these women say and do what other Hausa women cannot, criticizing the status quo, and encouraging behavior that is not normally condoned. Despite their negligible social status, they play an important role in a stratified society, expressing what others dare not say.

The Written Works

In contrast to the oral poet, the writer of verse is usually respected as a scholar and is known as an author rather than as an entertainer. These are usually Hausa men, who are trained as religious scholars and writers of Islamic verse from their youth. It is rare to find a woman who is comparably trained. There are, of course, exceptions to this. Sometimes a young girl whose father is a religious scholar will learn the Koran from him. Such study

requires the rote memorization of Koranic verses—a mode of learning that
provides the educational tools for the creation of one's own verses.
Representative of this are the works of two Hausa/Fulani women in their
late forties, Hauwa Gwaram and Hajiya 'Yar Shelu. Their recently
published volume of collected verse is the first of such works by women ever
published in the North, where Hausa men's poetry has been published in
both Hausa and English for fifty years.[11] These works were chosen for
publication because they fulfill the literary expectations of Hausa male
editors; the poems are well crafted, with rhyme and meter that rival those of
traditional Arab/Islamic verse. The contents of these works is conservative,
advocating the deferential behavior expected of traditional Hausa women
and praising national heroes or political figures. These poems deviate most
expressly in their consistently secular nature; this often distinguishes
women's written *wakoki* from men's.

Several of the published works are *wakoki* that were composed for use as
teaching aids for adult education courses taught by women to other Hausa
women. These advocate methods of hygiene, child care and nutrition,
explain the aims of national census-takers or changes in public practices,
such as the transition from left to right-hand drive. Some works describe
local monuments, such as one which catalogues the animals in the Kano
zoo. Some are nationalistic or commemorative, such as the verses
eulogizing Nigerian soldiers, and recounting the events of the Biafran civil
war. Through the oral recitation of these verses the authors inform secluded
women of current events in northern Nigeria.

At the same time, though, these informative verses had to be couched in
conservative terms in order to be chosen for publication by editors who were
not sympathetic to women writers. *The Song for Modern Times* is a prime
example of the attitude that male publishers felt should be exhibited by
female writers. In it Hajiya 'Yar Shehu describes the rabble in the streets,
affirming that they bear no respect for married women, shouting at them,
grabbing them:

> If they see married women they will shout,
> Hey, Binta, Hey Hajiya—and they'll even pull at your dress.[12]

The only remedy for this is an aloofness that exhibits one's superiority—
convivial repartee is not an appropriate response. Composure is an outward
sign of the character of a proper Hausa woman; silence in such a situation is
by far the most respectable response.

In another verse the author emphasizes the low moral character of those
women who refuse the traditional woman's role—prostitutes, she warns,
are rejected even by their own children:

> See the prostitutes whose own children don't love them.
> They follow that big friend of theirs, Satan. . .[13]

Here two assumptions are reinforced: that one must love and respect one's parents and that the respect due a mother—especially in Islam—is forfeited by a prostitute. The role of domestic guardian, wife, and mother, is the role that a Hausa woman must fill.

The author elaborates on other dangers of "modern times", such as the chaos that is common in contemporary urban streets. In that setting, she notes, one finds people of questionable character:

> Then you see them, they are shouting and rushing about,
> These are Satan's advocates.[14]

The public scene, she reiterates, is no place for a proper woman. Those who hurry and shout are Satan's advocates, therefore it is not appropriate for a woman to involve herself in the threatening bustle of the urban scene lest she be caught up in modern conflicts like the following:

> If you tell them that God forbids adultery,
> And that relations with a married woman are worst of all,
>
> They'll reply to you, "Well, we must be progressive,
> It is God who has brought about these modern times."
>
> But listen to the words of our praise singer,
> When he responded to this talk about religion.
>
> He said, "As for the world, if there were no religion,
> The world itslef would not exist, much less modern times."[15]

This poem advocates devotion to one's domestic role, proper deportment whenever one must appear in public, and the desirability of keeping oneself apart from the public sphere with all its temptations and bad influences. These "modern" types she warns, are devoid of shame, fear, and respect; they are advocates of Satan—including even television programs with their cowboys and spaceships, which divert one's attention from God:

> Let us refuse to watch spaceships and cowboys
> They and shows like them are the works of Satan.[16]

In her work on the census Hauwa Gwaram moralizes in a comparable way, this time advocating active support for one's country. She insists that to omit reporting any person, however newborn an infant may be, is to do an injustice to the nation, since knowing the right population can help to improve the economic situation of the country. She emphasizes the individual's civic duty to cooperate with census officials and—most important— she insists that the census is for the benefit of Nigeria, *not* another colonial imposition.

Other verses are more informative than didactic. *The Song for Self-Sufficiency* describes the vegetable gardens that fed Nigerian families, the effort toward public hygiene, the work of expert tailors that has become known world-wide. In this work the author boasts that everyone gets along well in Nigeria, without jealousy or presumptuousness, and emphasizes the role she feels women may play in Nigeria's welfare:

> May God help us to achieve our goals,
> The women of Kano have been diligent in their work.
>
> May God help us to achieve our hearts desires
> The women of Kano persevere in their farming.
>
> I will end here, lest you say I have overdone it,
> The song on women, who will make our country successful.[17]

It is the contention of these authors that women have an important role to play in the success of their country, but in contrast to the creators of oral *wakoki*, they feel women's behavior must remain within the constraints imposed by tradition. They maintain a respectable attitude in their works; the political tone is nationalistic, the social perspective conservative.

But because women do not normally write verse, the very fact that these two women have produced a volume of verse is the most revolutionary aspect of their work. They have accomplished a great deal with this volume, not only communicating historical facts and current events to those who would not otherwise be exposed to such news, but also acting as role models for prospective women authors who might earlier have subscribed to the assumption that "women do not write poetry."

Conclusion

For Hausa women, too long presumed to be the anonymous guardians of the domestic sphere—illiterate, nonpolitical, unconcerned with public events—these oral and written poems are proof of their eagerness to know about social and political change as well as proof of their ability to participate in their society beyond the limits of the compound walls. In addition, they accomplish such participation in the public sphere without violating their religious and social mores. When their works are broadcast on local radio stations, they reach their audiences without requiring secluded women to leave their homes. Such broadcasts also mean that these works have an impact that novels cannot hope to have among the illiterate. Hausa women's poetry is no less significant than the literary works of other Nigerian women—it is only less well known because it is rarely published, and when it is, it is published in Hausa rather than in English. For the woman of northern Nigeria, however, these artists of oral and written works are more than newscasters and entertainers. Their works are representative of concerns and attitudes common among Hausa women of northern Nigeria. As artists they have forged the way for a wider variety of Hausa women's literary expression; perhaps more importantly, however, they have raised the issue of the woman's changing role in modern Nigeria.

NOTES

1. "Daughter of Usman Dan Fodio, leader of the 1804 *jihad* to promote Islam in northern Nigeria, Nana Asma'a wrote in Arabic, Fulfulde, and Hausa. One of the foremost authorities on Nana Asma'a is Jean Boyd, who lives in Sokoto, Nigeria. She has written a biography of Nana Asma'a, as well as having collected and translated Nana Asma'a's poetry.
2. These and all subsequent definitions of Hausa terms are from: R. C. Abraham, *Dictionary of the Hausa Language*, 2nd ed., London: University of London Press, 1962.
3. For an analysis of patterns in Hausa women's oral poetry see: Beverly B. Mack, *"Wakokin Mata*: Hausa Women's Oral Poetry" unpublished dissertation, University of Wisconsin-Madison, 1981.
4. The Northern Nigerian Publishing Company in Zaria, Nigeria also publishes volumes of secular poetry, educational texts, novels, etc. in Hausa and English.
5. For a full discussion of the Hausa praisesinger's social status see: M. G. Smith, "The Social Functions and Meaning of Hausa Praise Singing," *Ibadan*, 21, (October, 1965), 81-92.
6. The audience is comprised of both male and female university students as well as faculty members and their familites. This unusual circumstance of men and women sitting together in public further emphasizes the shocking nature of the risque material.
7. *Wakar Ta Yabon Kungiyar Hausa* (Praise Song for the Hausa Conference) by Maimuna Coge, 1980, 1.75. For this and all subsequent translations, this author takes responsibility. All selections cited in this study were recorded from the artists by this author in 1980 in Nigeria.
8. *Ibid*, l. 126-132.
9. *Wakar Alhaji Ado Bayero, Sarkin Kano* (Praise Song for Alhaji Ado Bayero, Emir of Kano) by Maizargadi, 1980, 1.11, 14-17, 45, 47, 61 and 62.
10. *Wakar Matan Nijeriya* (Song for the Women of Nigeria) by Binta Katsina, 1980, 1.70-79.
11. Hauwa Gwaram and Hajiya 'Yar Shehu, *Alkalami A Hannun Mata* (A Pen in the Hands of Women), Beverly B. Mack, ed. Zaria: The Northern Nigerian Publishing Company, 1983.
12. Hajiya 'Yar Shehu, *Wakar Zamani* in *Alkalami A Hannun Mata*, stanza 11. This and all subsequent citations are this author's translations of works contained in *Alkalami A Hannun Mata*, cited above.
13. *Ibid*, stanza 22.

14. *Ibid*, stanza 25.
15. *Ibid*, stanzas 26-29.
16. *Ibid*, stanza 36.
17. Hauwa Gwaram, *Wakar Mu Ci Da Kasarmu in Alkalami A Hannun Mata*, stanzas 31-33.

PART THREE
Social and Political Themes: Women's Issues in African Literary Criticism

In their treatment of African institutions the papers in Part III, "Social and Political Themes: Women's Issues in African Literary Criticism" adopt approaches that range in scope from the mythological and religious underpinnings of the institutions, to their material ramifications in daily life. In the purely fictional and the autobiographical novel, the short story, and poetry handled in these papers, the aspects of those institutions as they bear upon women—and therefore necessarily also on men—are analyzed on social scientific as well as literary criteria, bringing theories from those fields to bear on the studies, which set in relief the feminine facet of some fundamental structures in African life. The dialectics of Senegalese customs, particularly those based in Muslim tradition, as laid out by Ousmane Sembène, undergo cogent review in Brenda Berrian's paper "Through Her Prism of Social and Political Contexts: Sembène's Female Characters in Tribal Scars*." Looking at four of the short stories in the Sembène anthology (*Voltaïque*), Berrian zeroes in on the compelling arguments made by the women in challenging laws and/or practices which not only ignore any rights of women but which also do not hold up under*

191

questioning. In her selection of the four stories she treats, Berrian finds the issues of divorce, child custody, arranged marriages, and tyrannical men, as these issues are seen by the women involved. She elucidates the politically controversial nature of the women's challenges in their potential to erode some firmly entrenched pillars of Sengalese institutions that have allowed men to hold unlimited and uncontested power over women. The explosive challenge to a similarly controversial tradition is the subject of Tobe Levin's paper "Scapegoats of Culture and Cult: An Activist's View of Circumcision in Ngugi's The River Between," *As Berrian does for Sembène, Levin draws attention to Ngugi's dialectical presentation of the traditional practice of female circumcision. Using a perspective that combines elements of anthropology, psychology, theology, and comparative literature, Levin's analysis integrates Kenyatta, Freud, the Bible, and several African writers, to present the arguments and counter-arguments from the several positions represented in the narrative: the young girl who elects to undergo circumcision, her sister who does not; the Christian Church as reflected by the girls' father, the schoolteacher, and the mission hospital staff; and Gikuyu tradition as reflected by the village council opposed to the encroaching influence of Western culture. Acknowledging Ngugi's efforts to end circumcision on humanitarian grounds, Levin illustrates not only what she perceives to be the protection of a vested interest on the part of the Gikuyu men who insist on this ritual as the basis for moral and social education, but also the hypocrisy in the Christian Church's misogynous reasons against circumcision (and its basically incredible claim of virgin birth).*

The relation of sexuality to religion as well as the disorientation regarding the symbols of womanhood that has affected the Igbo man as a by-product of the conversion to Christianity, is likewise the subject of Elaine Savory Fido's paper on Christopher Okigbo's poetic work Labyrinths. *Fido's assertion that "Anxiety about the female principle is . . . a strong element in male Eastern Nigerian writers' work" forms the basis for her hypothesis that "a vital aspect of [Okigbo's] agony . . . is particular to modern post-colonial African man, and indeed to Igbo man." Grounded in the autobiographical content of the poem, this discussion offers an explication of the complexities of the poet's personal relationship with female deities vis-a-vis his own maleness, on the basis of a theory that "the feminine is closely intertwined with his idea of traditional religion, whereas the male-dominated Christian ethos is antitethetical to Igbo tradition." Another look at Igbo tradition, through the works of four other Igbo writers—here novelists—is the subject of Carole Davies' paper scrutinizing the presentation of motherhood. Davies' assessment of the differences between the presentations by women writers and by men writers reveals not only the absence of concensus on definitions of "mother" but, more significantly, divergences of view regarding the centrality of motherhood in the African woman's life, psychologically as well as physically. The comparison between male and female writers' presentations of the feminine is taken to another level in Naana Banyiwa-Horne's paper in Part II. Davies and Banyiwa-Horne both, though with different emphasis, take up the issue, in Flora Nwapa's Efuru, of the African woman who does not bear children, and the attitudes of the woman herself and of her community about this phenomenon. Motherhood is extended to the grandmother by Mildred Hill-Lubin, who discusses the continuities in grandmother depiction in different parts of the African diaspora. Basing her study on African fiction by Aidoo and Mphahlele, and African American autobiography by Maya Angelou and Frederick Douglass, Hill-Lubin sees the crucial role of the grandmother as threefold: preserver of the extended family, disseminator of family and community wisdom, and communicator of values and ideals of the family.*

That the influence exerted by the extended family can sometimes be detrimental, at least for a marriage, is the subject of Edris Makward's article "Marriage, Tradition and Women's Pursuit of Happiness in the Novels of Mariama Bâ." From his reading of Bâ's two novels Makward sees the author's position to be not a condemnation of polygamy as practiced in her country, Senegal, but as an argument in favor of the necessity in modern life for the egalitarian monogamous marriage. Of the traditional, polygamous marriage Makward finds that Bâ shows "with insistence, that the extended family's action could invariably make such relationships fizzle out in bitter failure." In viewing Bâ's novels as statements that the happiness of the whole society must be based on the happiness of the women and the men in marriages, i.e., a close association between two equals, Makward demonstrates the egalitarian, cooperative emphasis in the feminism that Bâ advocates for Senegalese society. This assessment of marriage, along with the other studies of social and political institutions in Part III, are ultimately re-assessments of the meanings these structures hold not only for the African woman but also for her family and larger community.

A.A.G.

Through Her Prism of Social and Political Contexts: Sembène's Female Characters in Tribal Scars

Brenda F. Berrian

If there is one enduring presentation in African literature it is the African mother. From the Soundiata epic to the epistolary novel, *Une si longue lettre* (1979) by the deceased Mariama Bâ, reverence for the African mother is expressed in various forms. In the past, the traditional African mother has been a Queen Mother, a trader, a soldier, an organizer of protest demonstrations, and the nurturer of future generations of children. Cognizant of the role that the mother plays in African societies is Ousmane Sembène, who prefers to set his female characters in their traditional settings as mothers and wives, in order to illustrate specific political and social points of view. Through the women, Sembène notes that in order for them to have new perceptions of themselves and to develop a more defined self-awareness, their men should no longer be the determining factor in their lives. Sembène is convinced that changes in social and political structures and attitudes in Africa are necessary if the African woman is to realize her full potential and importance in the future of her country.[1]

A self-taught man, writer, and filmmaker from Senegal, Sembène is devoted to writing about African people and their aspirations. Most importantly, he is one of the first African writers to move his female characters from a secondary role, in which they compliment their men, to a primary one in which they express their feelings, hurts, joys, and think and react to pressing situations. For instance, in four selected short stories from *Voltaïque. Nouvelles* (1962)[2] Sembène introduces his mother who demands custody of her children at a divorce hearing; the mother who defies a tyrannical king in defense of her daughter; the mother who confronts her neglectful husband with his callousness, and finally, the mother who comes to terms with her marriage to a much older man.

In the short story, "The Bilal's Fourth Wife," Sembène slips in modern ideas about marriage and divorce in a traditional village setting where he presents the couple, Suliman and Yacine. Suliman, a man past middle-age, takes great pains to present himself as a pious, devout Moslem and family man before the public whereas, in private, he berates and beats his three wives unmercifully. His appetite for women younger than his daughters has not waned, and he takes advantage of his position as the bilal of the village mosque to make lecherous remarks and to fondle them. Because of his carefully preserved public image as a humble man and a guardian of polygamy, the young victimized women dare not complain expecting that their cries of outrage would not be believed. As the story progresses, Suliman is so consumed with his lust for young women that he fails to keep the mosque clean. Sympathetic male villagers take it upon themselves to find a fourth wife for Suliman in the person of the young, Yacine N'Doye.

Yacine, a 20-year old former "tomboy," is deemed to be a good candidate for Suliman's fourth wife for she has frightened the young men in the village with her outspokenness. Presumably, an older man like Suliman will be able to tame and mold her into a submissive wife, since it is assumed that she is naive and ignorant of her rights and sexual desires as a woman. Although Yacine would have liked to raise some objections, she follows her father's wishes and marries Suliman. Later, after three years of marriage and a son, the bored Yacine takes Suliman's nephew as her lover, as Suliman's sexual drive is diminishing. Her decision to take a lover is justifiable, for, in her mind, she is in her physical prime and married to a man she does not love. However, this triangle—wife, husband, and lover— becomes the main topic of village gossip when Yacine bears a son for her lover. In an attempt to salvage his tarnished image and manhood, Suliman vents his rage and jealousy upon his three wives and demands a divorce from Yacine. To his surprise, his demand receives a rebuttal from Yacine.

In "The Bilal's Fourth Wife" Sembène, with great humor, pokes fun at Senegalese attitudes toward divorce. He attacks the practice of double moral standards, which place women at a disadvantage. Sembène uses the character of Yacine to question and to disagree with the patriarchal Moslem marriage rules drawn up by males centuries ago. In spite of the rumors and intense external pressures, Yacine reveals a tremendous self-confidence.

First, she refuses to be coerced by Suliman and her family into a divorce. Second, she is adamant about being treated on equal footing as a woman by the Cadi (special council of male elders called to review her case). Third, she questions why the woman is not free to take a lover when a man in a Moslem society can have four wives with the approval of the Koran and legal laws. These unyielding stances force the male elders to accept, with reluctance, the fact that there are two sides to every marital disagreement, and the woman's position is just as important as the man's.

As for Suliman, he has been made the laughing stock of the village by his inability to control his wife. His ego suffers a beating due to his physical limitations of not satisfying his young wife's sexual needs. What is at stake is Suliman's determination to humiliate Yacine publicly, for she has flaunted her relationship with his nephew with the birth of a child. Double standards, which govern the behavior of men and women in a Moslem polygamous marriage, are addressed again when Suliman asks for custody of his "son" and the return of the dowry.

Suliman does not regard Yacine as a human being who has feelings and rights, but as one of his possessions who is expected to boost his ego. A woman's place, he feels, is to obey her husband and to build her life around him. When his possession (Yacine) no longer brings him pleasure or bends to his needs, he must squash or beat it into submission as he has done with the other three wives. Since Yacine will not conform and retreat into the expected docility, Suliman tries to use psychological pressure and works within the traditional legal system to bring about her downfall. He becomes obsessed with the need to cause Yacine deep pain. Yacine's indiscretion must be exposed to draw attention away from his own inadequacies.

As mentioned before, through Yacine's protests and the divorce hearing, Sembène brings forth the argument that traditional Moslem marriage laws should be reevaluated and rewritten to protect the rights of women too. In support of Sembène's argument, Yacine demands that Suliman should return her virginity knowing full-well that virginity is highly prized and is linked to one's honor and esteem. With this brave announcement, she makes clear that something precious has been taken away from her—her honor and respectability.

Yacine's request to have her virginity returned is a clever tactic and approach in presenting her case in court. She knows that she was more valuable when she was chaste and that her value dropped with her affair with Suliman's nephew, making her second-hand merchandise. Suliman too cannot bear knowing that his wife has been handled by somebody else. His pride and respect have been challenged. He also fears Yacine's power over him—the power of informing the villagers of his sexual weakness.

Since Suliman cannot physically return Yacine's virginity and make her "pure as spring water" again, Yacine hopes that her request will enable the villagers to be more sympathetic toward her. The question then becomes

why should women in Moslem marriages hand over the custody of their
children to their former husbands. Fortunately, Froh-Toll, the head of the
Cadi, is wise enough to debate the custody topic and rules in favor of Yacine
with the statement:

> So by what right does Suliman demand custody of the child? There
> can always be doubt as to who is the father of a child. But never as to
> who is the mother.[3]

With this pronouncement, Froh-Toll supports women's child rearing rights,
which is an admirable step.

In Moslem societies, attitudes toward adultery are one-sided. Traditional
customs tend to endorse the fact that married men engaged in extra-marital
affairs cannot commit adultery, only women. The Senegalese society is
built upon a patriarchal system with a Moslem/Christian/Animist religious
foundation. As a consequence, the person who passes judgement on men
and women is a man; the society, in which men and women operate, is male
dominated. In the eyes of traditional Moslem law, the man's word is
accepted as being truthful and binding, but the woman's word does not have
the status and legitimacy. So while Suliman is not chastised for engaging in
a sexual act with a young woman in the village, the villagers agree that
Yacine should be punished for her affair. Yacine's actions upset the value
system, which supports the idea that women must be faithful to their
husbands. Consequently, her conscious revolt becomes a social act against
the antiquated Moslem divorce laws and ingrained value systems.

Sembène's short story, "The Mother" is another example of the
application of double moral standards n a Moslem society in Africa. This
point is presented through the personnage of the tyrannical king. The king,
who has no intentions of cultivating the love and respect of his constituents,
alienates himself and evokes the hatred and fear of his subjects to the point
that they dream about seeing him burnt alive. Meanwhile, these same
subjects are passive and obey the king's orders to murder men over fifty-
years old. Thus, the king thinks that he owes no allegiance to anyone. He
proceeds to pass a law that he will deflower every virgin before she is
married. Over the years, only a few brave mothers succeed in saving their
daughters from such a fate. When it is time for the king's daughter to marry,
he repeals the law—separate rules for the poor and rich.

For the king, women represent danger, and he wishes to destroy them. By
his actions, it appears that he harbours a deep hatred for women and cannot
resist raping them. This psychological deviant is confused, insecure, and
enjoys exerting his power through violent means. The king obviously likes
inflicting pain upon women, because they are said to be the weaker sex.

Since nobody has the courage to defy the king's orders, the people's fears
increase. It is only when the king travels that he encounters open resistance

to his overtures from a young woman he fancies. In anger he has her locked up. The young woman's mother, a woman of "certain age," fights and pushes past the six feet tall servants to gain an audience with the king. The mother verbally battles and acuses him of outlandish and unfit behavior. Further, she courageously looks the king directly in his eyes and attacks him for not showing any respect for the mothers in the kingdom. She makes the point that without the love and tenderness of his mother he would not have been born. The king responds by slapping her face.

The subjects jump to the mother's defense after the king's display of anger and guilt. The mother's words had hit their target shaming the remaining males in the kingdom for their cowardice and failure to protect their women folk. The king's rule has been divisive and had led to the distrust of one another to the detriment of the society. This exhibition of internal strength and resilience by the mother topples the king's government. One conclusion is that anyone, male or female, who abuses power will not keep it.

Clearly, the king and the mother during their confrontation had struck each other in their most vulnerable spots, he on her face, and she at his ego. Yet a reversal of roles emerges for the so-called weak, defenseless mother becomes the stronger of the two. Without his bodyguards to shield him, the king, like most bullies, is defenseless. His deliberate attempt to limit the freedom of women ultimately results in the loss of his kingdom as a consequence of the words spoken by the African mother.

There is another interesting aspect in the Mother's depiction. One could say that Sembène has succumbed to one of the biased attitudes directed toward women when he describes the mother as ugly. However, it could also be said that Sembène deliberately calls the mother ugly, because of its common use in Senegalese society for strong-willed women. In African literature the good women, who stays in her place, is always gentle, kind, and beautiful, but the woman, who possesses the courage to debate male prerogatives, is frequently labeled or pictured as a physically ugly person. Thus Sembène ends this story by singing praises in honor of mothers who rise up to protect their children.

This particular story argues that one's biological origin and sex do not alleviate one's responsibility to the collective community. Making the female character in "The Mother" bigger than life is characteristic of Sembène in both his films and literary works to convince and draw attention to the African woman's special place in contemporary African society. The men, in the story "The Mother," were paralyzed with fear and failed to challenge the maniacal orders of the king. They also did nothing to overthrow the king-dictator. It was the woman, the mother, who came to the men's rescue. By magnifying the character of the mother Sembène scolds the men for their moral impotence and reproaches them for their lack of position action to oppose the king's oppressive policies.

The mother has done what is necessary to save and protect her daughter. She is, as Lippert would say, "super human in her love.[4]" The mother may be ugly on the outside, but she is beautiful inside with her concern for her child's misfortune. She possesses spiritual qualities which allow her to look directly into the king's evil heart. This special power permits the mother to weave a hypnotic spell on the male listeners, causes them to grab the king, and renders them half-conscious of the fact that they have aided the mother in her triumph over the king.

Mores of another kind are explored in the short story, "Her Three Days," where one meet Noumbé, the third wife of Mustapha. When the story opens Noumbé is preparing for her husband's visit during her allotted three days as dictated by the Koran. Drawing upon his filmmaking skills Sembène zooms in on Noumbé to show her haggard face, her weakened body after the bearing of five children in rapid succession, her anxieties and fears of being replaced by the fourth wife, and her fight to handle a heart condition. Although Noumbé is still young, she looks older because of her full financial duties of providing for her children.

In a sympathetic voice Sembène attacks the misuse of polygamy. If a man marries more than one wife, he is to treat them equally and not differentiate between them. This is a difficult task and even the best of men find that there is always one wife that he prefers among the group. For this reason, the remaining wives do not enjoy their husbands' companionship on an equal basis. In "Her Three Days" Mustapha prefers his fourth and youngest wife. It is his fourth wife's turn to be flattered and spoiled by him, and he casts aside his other three wives.

Relying upon a technique that worked successfuly in *Les Bouts de bois de Dieu* (1960), Sembène delays Mustapha's entrance until the last pages of the short story. In this way, Mustapha is seen through Noumbé's eyes and thoughts. Hence, Mustapha is known before he actually appears in the text. Leaving Mustapha's entrance until the end of "Her Three Days" creates the necessary suspense and enables the sensitive reader to feel the internal struggles and pains that Noumbé undergoes during her long wait for Mustapha. With this combination of sympathy for Noumbé and tension it is not impossible to understand why she lashes out at Mustapha on the eve of his arrival on the third day.

During these three days of waiting Noumbé has cooked Mustapha's favorite dishes, beautified herself, dressed with extreme care, saved the meat, and borrowed money from her next-door neighbor to ensure Mustapha's comfort. When Mustapha does not show after two days and fails to send a message, Noumbé's physical pain is almost as great as her mental pain. While dosing herself with medicine to prevent a heart attack, Noumbé wonders why she and her three co-wives allow themselves to be Mustapha's playmates and wives of one man. She contemplates divorce, the hypocrisy of the co-wives in their pretense of happiness, and ponders how to escape from such an unsatisfying and demeaning relationship.

Apparently, these thoughts frighten Noumbé somewhat because they are in contradiction with her upbringing. She has been raised to be a submissive wife dependent upon her husband's whims, just as Mustapha's personality and behavior have been formed by years of indoctrination that the male is the dominant person in a male/female relationship. As his "right" and with the support of Moslem doctrines the acquisition of four wives is linked with his virility and manliness. As for Noumbé she has achieved status and esteem with her marriage and the births of her five children. Companionship, mutual respect, and sharing are not part of the bargain.

Mustapha has an exaggerated sense of his ego and masculinity. With an air of impatience he comes to see Noumbé at the end of the third day demanding that she serve him and his two male companions. No words of comfort or apologies pass across his lips. In response, Noumbè displays a sarcastic side of her personality in an attempt to preserve some shred of dignity. This small rebellious act brings on a mild heart attack, and Mustapha calmly leaves Noumbé to fend for herself while announcing his horror and disbelief that the Malian government has just passed a resolution condemning polygamy.

The collectivity of female support in the compound is demonstrated when the women rush to Noumbé's aid. It is characteristic of Sembène to show how the women come together and lend each other their strength and advice. On the first day of Noumbé's three days of waiting the women sing to share Noumbé's happiness and unconcealed joy. When Mustapha fails to show up, Aïda, the next-door neighbor, kindly helps Noumbé and offers to keep her company. For fear of hurting her feelings the women stay away from Noumbé and avoid meeting her eyes so that she can save "face." However, they all run to her defense when she collapses from the strain of asserting herself before Mustapha. In short, the women come together because they know that their turn to be the displaced wife is coming. Still, Noumbé is resolved to be a mother and resigned to joining ranks with her abandoned co-wives. She once loved Mustapha, but she now rejects him. Her sense of self-worth is linked with common sense and necessity; therefore, she will not leave Mustapha for she is entrenched in Moslem traditions.

Without a doubt, Sembène wants his readers to note that Noumbé is a victim of circumstances. At the same time, he wants his readers to know that African women are also guilty of accepting rules imposed upon them and are responsible for some of the social evils. Noumbé's physical pain ties in with her timid knowledge that she is not pleased with her marriage. She submerges the thought that she is a playmate, since it is uncharacteristic for a devoted wife to question her plight. All of her life Noumbé has been groomed to be a good wife and mother, but not at the expense of her dignity. The waiting and the slow disintegration of hope cause her to mock Mustapha, who throws around his authority. Sembène's silent suggestion is that it is up to African men and women to solve their difficulties and take the initiative to improve their lot.

By lingering over Noumbé's suffering, jealousy, loneliness, and anger Sembène pleads the case against the African male's misuse of polygamy: their failure to treat each wife equally in all ways, including their failure to provide each with adequate financial, temporal and emotional support.

Like Noumbé, Nafi in "Letters from France" has been raised in a patriarchal society where man rules over woman, and one class over another. Viewed as a second-class citizen by her society and father, she is tricked into marrying a 73-year old man, who lives in Marseilles, France. The topic of love is not entertained for marriage is based on loneliness, a wish to live in France, and an old man's desire to retain his lost youth. Nafi, the young wife, will serve Dembe, her husband, be an instrument for his pleasure, bear his children, greet his friends, and care for him in his old age. By selecting a young wife, like Suliman in "The Bilal's Fourth Wife," Demba hopes that she will be easier to control and thereby gain much from the unbalanced relationship. Unfortunately, the carefully laid plan backfires when Demba succumbs to cancer.

Alone in a damp room with four walls in Marseilles, Nafi has plenty of time to reflect upon her situation and to examine, in a proper perspective, the social and moral values that are imposed upon Senegalese women. What she sees and comes to terms with (as Yacine and Noumbé did) is that she has to bear some of the blame for her marriage. She also must admit that she was initially pleased with the possibility of living in France, and smitten with the picture of a handsome young Senegalese man. The adjustment and the astonishment occur when Nafi arrives in Marseilles to learn that the young man in the photo is actually seventy-three years old.

In isolation for the first time in her life, cut off from sunshine, gaiety, and human warmth, Nafi rebels through the medium of letters to her girl friend in Senegal. She implores her anonymous girl friend, who is her link with the happy past, to believe in her. Nafi feels that she has touched "rock bottom" with her marriage to Demba. She is furious that she has married an old, unemployed man without a pension, cannot bear for him to touch her, and even wishes to contract a mysterious disease. As the story develops, Nafi is reduced to begging for a job for her husband with a shipping company, when she learns that she is pregnant. Divorce is contemplated, but she has no independent means and no friends to turn to for aid in Marseilles. Nafi's future brightens, however, when Demba is given a short-term job on a ship, sends money to her, and asks a young dock worker, Arona, to watch over her. Closed in with a crying baby, sad to find that Demba has cancer upon his return, but miserable enough not to play the role of a grieving wife,

"Letters to France" reaches a melodramatic climax when Nafi tells Demba, on his death bed, that she is returning to Senegal.

Demba's elderly friends are greatly disappointed in Nafi for her failure to conform and exhibit some compassion for Demba. Nafi's explanation is that she is in an incompatible marriage locked in by loneliness. Her dreams to be independent and her own mistress haunt her. Nafi is not ashamed to confess to her girl friend that she had wished for Demba's death in order to be free. Nevertheless, her release does not come until the same elderly friends of Demba meet to decide her fate. Thanks to Arona's intervention she does not have to be hypocritical by mourning Demba for the required 40 days. The decision is that she will be sent back home.

With bitterness and relief, Nafi's past, present, and future have been monitored by male decisions. She is basically shy and innocent in Marseilles and finds it difficult to relate to the French and other Blacks. Nafi, who has some formal education, is a traditional young woman, who is not satisfied with her life. Although she protests loudly to her girl friend in her letters, she lacks the independence to rebel. Without recognizing it, Nafi is tied to her beliefs in the security of the clan and the extended family. There is an awareness that times are changing, but this does not lead her to disobey her father and husband. It is Demba's death that frees her from despair and makes it possible for her to return to Senegal.

Martin T. Bestman notes that: "Sembène paints the image of Africa that is convulsive, a world that questions its norms and values."[5] Indeed, Sembène does not hesitate to take to task such explosive topics as child paternity, adultery, arranged polygamous marriages, tyrannical men, divorce, child custody, and the imposition of double moral standards upon women. He identifies these issues and explores them in his fiction as a committed social critic. Sembène is committed to defending the rights of African women by insisting that they need to reclaim the economic, political, and social positions that they had held in the past. He is not afraid to expose the contradictions that control people's actions, and the collision with their menfolk that occurs when women assert themselves.

Sembène's female characters are not losers. In the four short stories each woman triumphs no matter how small the victory. By presenting such women Sembène opens up opportunities for African women to develop a more positive self-awareness and to draw upon capacities that have laid dormant within themselves. In order for Senegalese women to move forward, they must cast off outdated ideas and modes of behavior and view their plight realistically. In short, they must place themselves on the outside in order to look in. By doing so, they may begin to take steps to eliminate ignorance and mass illiteracy and improve their status in the twentieth-century. All four women—Yacine, the mother, Noumbé, and Nafi—challenge the traditional order, which condemned them to a secondary role. They, as mothers, are believable as characters. They, as mothers and women, through the prism of social and political contexts, will turn their faces to the future with hope for the future generation, their children.

NOTES

1. Martin T. Bestman, "Sembène Ousmane: Social Commitment and the Search for an African Identity," *A Celebration of Black and African Writing*, eds. Bruce King and Kolawole Ogungbesan (Oxford: Ahmadu Bello University Press and Oxford University Press, 1975), p. 142.
2. The original text was published in French entitled *Voltaïque. Nouvelles* (Paris: Nouvelles Editions Latines, 1962) by Ousmane Sembène. In this paper all quotations are from the English translation, *Tribal Scars and Other Stories* (Washington, D.C.: Inscape, 1975).
3. Sembène Ousmane, "The Bilal's Fourth Wife," *Tribal Scars and Other Stories*, p. 17.
4. Anne Lippert, "The Changing Role of Women as Viewed in the Literature of English-Speaking and French-Speaking West Africa," (Bloomington: Indiana University, Unpublished Ph. D. dissertation, 1972), p. 253.
5. Martin T. Bestman, p. 140.

Women as Scapegoats of Culture and Cult: An Activist's View of Female Circumcision in Ngugi's The River Between

Tobe Levin

I was six years old that night when I lay in my bed, warm and peaceful in that pleasurable state which lies half way between wakefulness and sleep, with the rosy dreams of childhood flitting by, like gentle fairies in quick succession. I felt something move under the blankets, something like a huge hand, cold and rough, fumbling over my body, as though looking for something. Almost simultaneously another hand, as cold and as rough and as big as the first one, was clapped over my mouth, to prevent me from screaming.

They carried me to the bathroom . . . I was frightened . . . something like an iron grasp caught hold of my hand and my arms and my thighs, so that I became unable to resist or even to move. I . . . remember the icy touch of the bathroom tiles under my naked body, and unknown voices . . . interrupted now and again by a rasping metallic sound which reminded me of the butcher when he used to sharpen his knife before slaughtering a sheep . . . My blood was frozen in my veins.[1]

205

The author of this passage, Egyptian physician and activist Nawal El
Saadawi, recalls fearing that the intruders were preparing to cut her throat,"
which was always what happened with disobedient girls like myself in the
stories that my old rural grandmother was so fond of telling me."[2] But it was
not the child's neck they were after. Instead they groped

> . . . somewhere below my belly, as though seeking something buried
> between my thighs. At that very moment I realized that my thighs had
> been pulled wide apart, and that each of my lower limbs was being
> held by steel fingers that never relinquished their pressure. . . Then
> suddenly the sharp metallic edge seemed to drop between my thighs
> and cut off a piece of flesh from my body.
> I screamed with pain despite the hand held over my mouth, for the
> pain was not just a pain, it was like a searing flame that went through
> my whole body. After a few moments, I saw a red pool of blood
> around my hips.
> I did not know what they had cut off from my body. . . I just wept, and
> called out to my mother for help. But the worst shock of all was when I
> looked around and found her standing by my side. . .
> The memory of circumcision continued to track me down like a
> nightmare.[3]

To ensure a shared understanding of the reality behind the euphemism
"female circumcision," I have begun with this quotation.[4] Circumcision of
the clitoral prepuce is indeed an anatomical possibility, given adequate
surgical instruments in a clinical setting. But such a delicate operation is
nearly impossible to perform on struggling little girls and women on the cold
floor of the bathroom or compound. Nor can it be properly carried out
during initiation rites, within a framework of 'sex education', festival and
joy. Instead, clitoridectomy and, in the Horn of Africa, labial excision and
infibulation are practiced. In the novel, *L'Excisée*, by Lebanese author
Evelyne Accad, the unmitigated horror of the latter custom is shared with
the reader as the narrator, E., a foreigner, is forced to witness the slaughter
in her home:

> Et les femmes ont saisi la première fillete. Elles la tiennent de tous les
> cotés. Elles lui soulèvent la robe et la font s'asseoir sur un tabouret qui
> surplombe un bol blanc. Elles lui écartent les jambes et exposent son
> sexe rasé. . . La sage-femme écarte les grandent lèvres et les petites
> lèvres. Elle fait jaillir le clitoris et le jette dans le bol. La fille hurle de
> douleur. Et le sang coule. Les femmes tiennent la fillette plus
> fermement. La sorcière continue son oeuvre de mutilation. Elle
> découpe les grandes lèvres, comme de grandes oreilles rouges de peur,

qui vont rejoindre le clitoris dans le bol. . . . les cris de la fillette
resemblent à ceux d'un chien qu'on égorge.[5]
[And the women siezed the first little girl and held her on all sides.
They raised her dress and made her sit on a stool that overhung a white
basin. They spread her legs apart and exposed her shaved pubic area.
The mid-wife separated the labia majora from the labia minora,
whacked off the clitoris and tossed it into the basin. The girl wailed
with pain, the blood running. The women held the girl tighter. The
sorceress continued her mutilation. She cut off the labia majora, like
large ears red with fright, that joined the clitoris in the basin. . . .The
little girl's cries sounded like those of a dog being slaughtered.]
(editor's translation)

E. is seized with compassion for the victims of what is frankly termed a
"massacre," but females are so powerless in this desert society that only
one solution seems viable: the younger, 'uncircumcised' sister of an initiate
is offered the opportunity to flee. E. herself accompanies young Nour
(meaning "light") to the seacoast where she transfers the girl to the care of
an Egyptian woman traveling to Switzerland. E., who has been threatened
with excision by the other women in her compound, chooses a different way
out. Having placed her hopes in Nour, who vows to return to "aid her
sisters,"[6] E. drowns herself. Although physically unscathed, the heroine's
knowledge of the circumcised woman's suffering seems to have irrevocably
altered her consciousness of women's oppression. Indeed, the clitoris
severed from the body is a telling symbol of female status in phallocratic
culture. For once amputation has occurred, no regeneration is possible. As
in Accad's novel, female solidarity in suffering results in the perpetuation of
that suffering, for the women present at the massacre scream and clap to
drown out the cries of the children, taking "their revenge."[7] Or, as El
Saadawi writes, she exchanged a glance with her sister after the event, a
look which "seemed to say: 'Now we know what it is. Now we know where
lies our tragedy. We were born of a special sex, the female sex. We are
destined in advance to taste of misery, and to have a part of our body torn
away by cold, unfeeling cruel hands.'"[8]
    When sympathetic human beings are exposed to these devastating facts,
they can only share the authors' hopes of exploding the cycle of horror in
which mothers become, in Mary Daly's words, the "token torturers" of
their daughters who, in turn, accept a self-denying code imposed on them by
the 'dominant' sex. As in Accad's novel, the initiates, though trembling with
anxiety and terror, struggle to maintain their composure, knowing that to
become a woman, one must accept the knife: "they will not be able to
marry if they are not cut open and resewn."[9] Other than flight, there appears
to be no alternative, for custom is tenacious where women are concerned.

When Accad's heroine E. asks her husband how he can condone his compatriot's mutilation of the women's "most delicate, most precious and most important sexual organs," reminding him that they had originally come together to his country as social revolutionaries, he snickers and replies: "It's tradition."[10] "Tradition" has become a shibboleth in the mouths of men who themselves are quite willing to accept change, provided their own privileges remain intact.

Yet "tradition" can also be invoked with pride where the customs in question are innocuous. In the international struggle to extend human rights to women, the need to distinguish between beneficent and malicious practices has become more acute than ever, for if our aim is the eradication of dangerous 'rites', western activists must learn to enter the value system of the 'circumcised' to avoid the counter-productive approach based on ignorance and indignation alone. In this regard, the Association of African Women for Research and Development (AAWORD) in Dakar, Senegal, has warned feminists against viewing African societies exclusively in terms of female oppression and insists that "solidarity can only exist alongside self-affirmation and mutual respect."[11]

One avenue to increased understanding of African traditions, providing a basis for mutual respect, is literature, for in fiction we find revealing treatment of the female circumcision theme in a number of works by African authors. For example, in *From a Crooked Rib*, Somalian novelist Nuruddin Farah demonstrates a high degree of feminist awareness in approaching the problem of infibulation,[12] criticized also by Malian writer Yambo Ouologuem in *Le Devoir de Violence*. In this ironic novel, infibulation provides the means of reconstructing virginity after the ruler has "claimed for himself the right of the first night."[13] Ouologuem ridicules male complacency and self-deception for demanding that 'purity' be feigned at such inhuman cost. Similarly, Amadou Kourouma in *Les Soleils des Indépendances*[14] renders so sympathetically the initiate's state of mind during the experience of clitoridectomy that one can hardly doubt the author's indignation. Finally, Nawal El Saadawi, in *Woman at Point Zero*, uses excision as a leit-motif of loss: the heroine, with a man she loves, cannot feel pleasure. "It was as if I could no longer recall the exact spot from which it used to arise, or as though a part of me, of my being, was gone and would never return."[15] Mutilation is permanent—an extremely serious violation of integrity which cannot be condoned.

And yet, two additional African novels deal with the theme from a perspective of compromise: Flora Nwapa's *Efuru* and Ngugi wa Thiong'o's *The River Between*.[16] Flora Nwapa is a Nigerian author and publisher whom I interviewed on the subject of female circumcision at the 1980 Frankfurt Book Fair. She felt then that the western media tended to exaggerate the extent of the problem. However, in November, 1980, I received a letter from her in which she admitted the need to revise her point of view—the practice was indeed more prevalent (and the consequences graver) than she had imagined.

Nevertheless, her fiction represents the earlier attitude, accepting female circumcision as one integral part of a vital culture. In *Efuru*, for example, "having a bath" is a euphemism for clitoridectomy, and the ritual "purification" may follow marriage but must precede the birth of a child— one baby's death is attributed directly to the mother's fear of the razor. Since Nwapa presents traditional society in a realistic mode, her portrayal of attitudes favoring genital mutilation is, on one level, entirely appropriate. In fact, she scrupulously avoids over-simplification by showing how humanly (and even humanely) concerned the midwife herself and the neighbors are for the health and comfort of the initiate, denying neither that the operation can be dangerous (the operator refuses to proceed without absolute assurance that Efuru is not pregnant), nor that certain operators arc incpt—one is named who has caused numerous casualties. Yet one disturbing aspect of the narrative lies in the defeatism of the following exchange. When asked how she is feeling, having gone to be circumcised with as much trepidation as we might feel on visiting the dentist, Efuru replies: "'It is much better now. It was dreadful the first day'," which elicits the resigned response: "'It is what every woman undergoes. So don't worry'."[17] The author seems to share this essential conservatism as she highlights the compensatory festive context in which the operation is embedded. Feted and coddled for one to three months afterwards, the former patient, her relations and neighbors are shown to relish the special situation, one given to displays of happiness, culminating in the offer of gifts in the marketplace to a woman then at the apogee of beauty. Sadly, we are given to understand the attitudes of women themselves, a type of solidarity in adversity without any significant attempt to challenge or question the *raison d'être* of a practice which causes them pain.

Ngugi's narrative takes a similarly complex approach, disconcerting at first to hard-line opponents of genital mutilation. The only fictional work I have found which elevates female circumcision to a position of central thematic importance, *The River Between* has the issue serve as battleground in the clash between conservative tribal elements and the patriarchal Christian church, a plot based on events of the nineteen twenties and thirties marked by growing nationalist sentiment in Kenya. The era witnessed the founding of two oppositional groups, the Young Kikuyu Association led by Harry Thaku, and Kenyatta's Kikuyu Central Association. (KCA), "dedicated to removing British colonialism and restoring the traditional values eroded under white rule. In the midst of this nationalist revolutionary fervour, Jomo Kenyatta, who would later become Kenya's head of state gave the definitive male view on female circumcision which would be subsequently recorded in his book *Facing Mount Kenya* (1938). Kenyatta asserted that "not a single Gikuyu worthy of the name wants to marry a non-excised woman because that operation is the basis of all moral and religious instruction,"[18] an insight which inspired his first official act as chief executive: cancelling the ban on female circumcision. Similar opposition greeted attempts by the Presbyterian Mission to eliminate the practice in the nineteen twenties. In response to the ultimatum, issued in 1929—"they must now choose the church or the KCA"[19]—many male fraternity members opted for excommunication and expulsion from the schools rather than see 'their' women freed from the knife. In fact, resistance was so strong that during the carnage taking place on both sides, some African men used English women to make their point. For instance, " . . . to show people's wrath and hate for Irigu (uncircumcised females), on 2 January, 1930, Miss Hilda Stumpf of the A.I.M. Kajabe, died in Hospital, after some men broke into her house at night and forcibly circumcised her."[20] Again in the nineteen-fifties, during the Mau Mau revolution, similar scapegoating of women occurred within the context of freedom fighting. In a strange twist, circumcision of women came to be equated with the return to traditional Kikuyu values.

Yet, this reaffirmation of the tribal heritage was not without its redeeming dimension: the Christian community's exclusion of the circumcised led to the founding of independent institutions such as the Kenya Independence Schools Association on whose leadership Ngugi bases his portrait of "The Teacher," Waiyaki, a man dedicated to following a middle road between the tribal heritage and the white man's knowledge: hence his unwavering but illusory faith in education, education against, among other things, female circumcision.

Resistance to abolition of the rite is clearly, in part, an oppositional gesture against colonialism. Although the "climax of the rivalry between the two ridges (Makuyu and Kameno, Christian and traditionalist camps) was brought on by the missionaries' ban on female circumcision,"[21] the basis for this internecine hatred is to be sought elsewhere:

> . . . and all at once Waiyaki realized what the ridges wanted. All at
> once he felt more forcefully than he had ever felt before the shame of
> the people's land being taken away, the shame of being forced to work
> on those same lands, the humiliation of paying taxes for a government
> that you knew nothing about.[22]

Ngugi places the renewed insistence on initiation rites within the context of land expropriation, the imposition of taxes and *de facto* forced labor to pay them. By highlighting this explanation he is in harmony with other influential critics of female circumcision, including Nawal El Saadawi and Stella Efua Graham. The former attributes "the lower status of women in our societies," of which genital mutilation is a symptom, "to certain economic and political forces, namely those of foreign imperialism operating mainly from the outside, and of the reactionary classes operating from the inside."[23] Confirming this analysis based on class struggle, Stella Efua Graham of Ghana, president of the London-based Women's Action Group against Excision and Infibulation, adds that:

> ... female circumcision is a very sensitive and political subject tied to complex sociocultural structures and to underdevelopment. It is directly related to the depressed political and socioeconomic position of women in these societies.[24]

Typical of many indigenous approaches to clitoridectomy,[25] El Saadawi, Graham and Ngugi understate the causal dimension accentuated by western feminists[26]—irrational male complicity in the continuance of mutilation, a complacency rooted in unconscious fears of the female and ambivalence vis-à-vis sexuality.[27] Still, whether an emphasis on sexual politics constitutes an appropriate strategy in the early stages of consciousness raising against the practice remains subject to debate.[28]

Ngugi's novel, in any case, deals with female circumcision not from a feminist, but from a humanist and progressive standpoint, leading its readers gently and ironically to understand that male insistence on female 'rites' is displaced impotence and is ultimately de-constructive. He shows, for example, how the brothers are mistaken in viewing circumcision as a still unsullied source of cultural integrity from which strength can be drawn in preparation for the battles ahead, to repossess the land. Ngugi further links this futile hope to renewal of the martial image, in turn tied to the vehement insistence on female mutilation. For without removal of the clitoris, without 'purity', it is assumed that female sexual energy would threaten the tribe with destruction, as Ngugi records:

> There was a new edge to the songs. Uncircumcised girls were the objects of cutting attacks. Everything dirty and impure was heaped on them. They were the impure things of the tribe and they would bring the wrath of the ancestral spirits on the ridges. A day would come when all these *Irigu* would be circumcised by force, to rid the land of impurities.[29]

Not the whites, but the deviant African women are to blame for the apocalypse.

Thus, in the wake of imperialism, women are assigned a new symbolic function. As critic Judith Cochrane benignly notes, they become the "guardians of the tribe," an ascribed status not necessarily of benefit to them as a group. On the contrary, excluded from the 'development' process by the importation of western-style sexism, pushed out of economic fields in which they had been sovereign, women have been systematically disempowered and abused, as illustrated by a figure from Waiyaki's nightmare, presaging the failure of his own attempts at reconciliation through marriage to an *Irigu*:

> They were all pulling her into pieces, as if she were a thing of sacrifice to the god of the river, which still flowed with life as they committed this ritual outrage on her.[30]1

It is doubtful, however, whether the 'river between' demands such sacrifice. Called *Honia*, meaning the cure or "bring-back-to-life," it separates but also potentially units the feuding hills, serving mainly as the backdrop for actors on the stage of significant events: political meetings, lovers' trysts and circumcision. The latter theme is in fact introduced on its banks, where Nyambura and Muthoni, children of the Christian convert Joshua, have come to fetch water. They discuss the rites, defying the injunction that "a daughter of God should never let a thought of circumcision come into her mind."[31] The thought, however, is clearly elicited by the river, as Nyambura notes:

> During the initiation ceremonies, boys and girls came to wet their bodies here on the morning of circumcision. It had long been discovered that very cold water numbed the skin, making it less painful during the operation. Nyambura thought of this and felt slightly guilty. She looked apprehensively at her sister, who was still drawing water. Nyambura wondered whether such thoughts ever came to Muthoni. She thought not and envied her. For Nyambura had learnt and knew that circumcision was sinful. It was a pagan rite.[32]

This passage fulfills two theoretical tasks, criticising both the critic and the rite. First, it undermines Christian teaching, for instead of opposing mutilation in order to preserve the wellspring of pleasure, the church takes the repressive puritan stance of forbidding any mention of sexuality (a position firmly rooted in misogynist tradition). Defined as "sinful" not because it destroys sexuality but recognizes it instead, the rite is dismissed, as though labeling were a sufficient deterrent.

Yet criticism of the church does not constitute approval of the custom. The passage also establishes an immediate link between the terms "circumcision," "numbness" and "pain," without attempting to revalue these states or redeem them in any way. In fact, Waiyaki ". . . thought that if he had been in (Muthoni's) position he would never have brought himself into such pain."[33] As for the male, his situation differs: first because he sees circumcision as a test of manly courage and, second, because, despite the identity in nomenclature, he is the only one actually circumcised. As we have seen, something else is done to women.

Marielouise Janssen-Jurreit, comparing female to male rites, notes the differing goals of the two interventions, the female designed mainly to produce docile wives.[34] Indeed, it is to become a wife that Muthoni undergoes the ceremony, wishing to be "made beautiful in the tribe" in order to acquire "a husband for (her) bed (and) children to play around the hearth."[35] The implication is that she must choose between chastity and mutilation, as Waiyaki's father ironically confirms:

> "Who ever heard of a girl that was not circumcised? Who would ever pay cows and goats for such a girl? Certainly it would never be his son."

The fact that it IS his son, the Teacher, who chooses to break the taboo and ally himself sexually with an Irigu accentuates the fundamental tendency of the novel—to oppose those customs which no longer fulfill a beneficent social function. Yet neither the traditionalists nor the Christians present viable alternatives for women. Indeed, the Christian model of the submissive wife, when conscientiously followed, achieves the same goal as mutilation. It is thus hypocritical to oppose circumcision in the name of the 'life-denying' creed.[37]

Miriamu represents western-style marital comportment, demonstrating a meekness so studied that the author seems compelled to contrast it with a more natural mode of being. He suggests that her Christian humility is superficial, her silence the result of instruction, not character. She has merely learned by rite "the value of Christian submission."[38] Concerned only to maintain peace in the household, her motto has become "'Obey your father'." Yet the more genuine paradigm is there, as the author notes: "Christianity was a religion learned and accepted: inside the true Kikuyu woman was sleeping."[39] For the cultural model of womanhood was not submissive but powerful, as an old Kikuyu legend shows: "Long ago women used to rule this land and its men," Chege tells Waiyaki. "They were harsh and . . . owned everything."[40] In revolt, the men took advantage of the women's pregnancies to overthrow their despotism, but traces of the (real or imagined) power relations were not erased from social memory.

Thus, it is in light of her foremothers' independence that Muthoni's controversial decision, to submit to clitoridectomy, has been judged. One is tempted to censure her, but disapproval may be softened if her gesture is seen as an act of rebellion against her father's rigid code. Eddah Gachukia, for example, goes so far as to credit her with heroism:

> Take Muthoni's unbelievable courage. . . She has great daring in deciding to do what she felt was the right thing, regardless of consequences.[41]

And Judith Cochrane agrees:

> ... (Muthoni's) act of rebellion in forsaking the home of her Christianized father in order to participate fully in the rites and ceremonies of the tribe is a personal act of courage.[42]

Certainly, this may be true, and yet Muthoni's desire to escape the stultifying lovelessness of her father's faith serves better to expose Christian sexual hypocrisy than it does to support initiation. After all, she dies as a result of circumcision, her mission a failure.

The text informs us that other girls had previously died of the operation, but Muthoni's demise differs from theirs in time and context, assuming an amplified symbolic meaning for both camps, the traditionalists blaming the victim and her father for impurity and neglect of the prescribed sacrifices that would have ensured recovery, the Christians reacting with righteous anger, finding confirmation of their belief in native barbarity. As for Muthoni, faced with two equally untenable alternatives, she expresses the hopelessness of her position in her last words to Nyambura: "'. . . I see Jesus. And I am a woman, beautiful in the tribe. . . '" Doubly alienated, her attempt to achieve wholeness through mutilation, to reconcile the tribe and Christianity, cannot bear fruit.

Christianity's failure is perhaps of greater concern to the author than the obviously reactionary stance of the Kiama. And certainly, nowhere does the western church appear more ridiculous than in the dogma of the virgin birth. Since the celebration of Christmas and the initiation season coincide, Ngugi takes the opportunity to both introduce and undermine the Christian alternative:

> (Joshua) renounced his tribe's magic, power and ritual. He turned to and felt the deep presence of the one God. Had he not given the white man power over all?
> He learned of Jesus -
>   Behold, a virgin shall conceive,
>   And bear a son . . .
> He realized the ignorance of his people.[44]

One needs little maturity to doubt the credibility of an organization condemning clitoridectomy but espousing belief in a virgin birth. In fact, concerning sexual matters, the tribe appears to be infinitely more sophisticated than the Christians. For example, the clitoris is at least acknowledged by the former (being too powerful, it is removed), while the organ has been treated by western ideology as though it didn't exist.

As a result, the Christian campaign for abolition of excision, concerned neither with female health nor with women's integrity, but rather with sexuality as sin, was seriously misguided. Furthermore, in failing to differentiate sufficiently between the mutilating aspects of initiation and the framework of festivities, it proved itself totally incapable of engaging in dialogue concerning the custom. Livingstone, for instance, once came to witness the rites but was so shocked at the partying the night before that he could not grasp the import of the following morning's events. In the evening he witnessed:

> Old and young, women and children, . . . Losing themselves in the magic motion of the dance. . . . Women, stripped to the waist, with their thin breasts flapping on their chests, went round and round the big fire, swinging their hips and contorting their bodies in all sorts of provocative ways, but always keeping the rhythm.
>
> They were free. Age and youth had become reconciled for this one night. And you could sing about anything and talk of the hidden parts of men and women without feeling that you had violated the otherwise strong social code that governed people's relationships, especially the relationship between young and old, man and woman.[45]

By failing to look below the surface of this behavior, the church cannot possibly recognize the safety-valve function of "the (illusory)chaos of locked emotions let loose," that is, sexual expression contained within prescribed limits of taboo and license. As Waiyaki points out, despite appearances, it was actually forbidden "to go with a woman on such an occasion."[46] The Christians are therefore judged incompetent to meddle with a custom whose real significance in the tribe the clerics are too "dense" to comprehend. Condemning the rite's practitioners as savages, with nothing more convincing than the celebration of a virgin birth to offer in exchange, the church is revealed as hypocritical, a judgment reinforced by the fact that Christian males are no freer from brutality than others, as the text shows. Joshua regrets having married a circumcised woman and even reproaches Miriamu for this. Yet the narrator adds:

> Not that Miriamu shared or cherished these sentiments. But she knew him. Joshua was such a staunch man of God and such a firm believer in the Old Testament, that he would never refrain from punishing a sin, even if this meant beating his wife.[47]

Christian and indigenous males alike are ultimately similar in one respect: their claim to power over the female. Both share a belief in the *femme fatale*: Like Eve, Nyambura is charged with Waiyaki's downfall: "'. . . it is the girl'," the Kiama claims. "'The girl has turned his mind the wrong way.'"[48] And the cure for such high treason? "'As we said earlier', one more (Kiama member) commented, 'all these Christians should be circumcised. By force.'"[49]

It is in light of this hostility toward women in the gynophobic *Weltanschauung* of Christian and traditional African males alike that the circumcison controversy in Ngugi's novel may be viewed. When theorizing about the conflict, the narrator himself concludes:

> Circumcision of women was not important as a physical operation. It was what it did inside a person. It could not be stopped overnight.[50]

On first reading, this seems unconscionably moderate. But what precisely is meant by "not important"? That clitoridectomy is trivial, like removing the tonsils or appendix? Or does it mean non-essential, unnecessary for effecting that transformation "inside a person" which the rite of passage is intended to accomplish; thus, "not important" to the goal of symbolizing maturity and group cohesion? The latter would seem to be the case, as the narrator goes on: "It could not be stopped overnight"—but it should be stopped! "Patience and, above all, education were needed. If the white man's religion made you abandon a custom and then did not give you something else of equal value, you became lost. An attempt at resolution of the conflict would only kill you, as it did Muthoni."[51] In fact, Muthoni's gesture illustrates this thesis: she intends to combine Christianity with custom. The isolation she would otherwise feel is suggested by her cry: "How could I be outside the tribe, when all the girls born with me at the same time have left me?"[52] Peer pressure is certainly one of the major reasons why the practice of clitoridectomy continues but, as Sigrid Peicke notes, Muthoni's act remains problematic: "We are not convinced by (her) enthusiasm in having herself initiated. Her decision has a clichéd ring to it, being too strongly charged with an untenable symbolic function."[53]

The difficulty with Ngugi's handling of the theme may be traced to his lack of feminist insight at that time (1965) into the unconscious motivation of males who support initiation for women. The text does seem to support an idealistic hope of purging the rites of their harmful dimension while maintaining the liberating, communal aspects. However, recent history shows a reverse trend. Fran Hosken's research reveals an accelerating neglect of the rite accompanied by the spread of excision performed in hospitals on girls at increasingly younger ages, for whom the amputation is totally divorced from any kind of moral, ethical or even sex-educational dimension. The death of 14 young girls resulting from this intervention in 1983 led to the passage of an edict against the operations in Kenya.[54] At the same time, law without the force of custom remains impotent, as the experiences of the Sudan and Egypt show. The practice has thus proven to be far more tenacious than a man of Ngugi's good will seems to have anticipated.

Why? Sociologist Carola Donner-Reichle sees one explanation in "gerontological African patriarchy," meaning that, where polygyny is prevalent, men fear being unable to satisfy too many non-excised women at once.[55] And psychoanalytic theory supports this view. Karen Horney's research on "the dread of women," Margaret Mead's suggestion of "womb-envy," the vast collection of vagina dentata myths—all are relevant as possible factors accounting for female excision. We even have a paper presented by Mohammed Shaalan at the 1979 U.N. Seminar in Khartoum on "Traditional Practices affecting the Health of Women" revealingly titled "Clitoris Envy: A Psychodynamic Construct Instrument in Female Circumcision." Ngugi's novel sheds little light on these aspects of initiation, though it does support the line of reasoning whereby colonialism, oppressive to both sexes, is recognized as significantly more detrimental to the welfare of women. *The River Between*, showing the connection between expropriation and repression of the indigenous male and his scapegoating of the female, reinforces the interpretation of numerous African activists engaged in fieldwork, and therein lies its relevance for the Western feminist reader.

One novel I have not yet mentioned dealing with the theme of female circumcision from both a moderate and a feminist standpoint, thus offering a constructive contrast with Ngugi, is Alice Walker's *The Color Purple*, which dramatizes an Afro-American woman's encounter with a tribe where genital mutilation takes place. In a series of letters to her sister, the missionary Nettie both evaluates Olinka tribal custom and objectively reports how she herself is evaluated. For her part, Nettie openly criticizes women's subordinate status under polygny, women's exclusion from educational opportunity, their occasional forced exile through sale "to the trader" should they refuse to marry the man chosen for them. Nettie patently applies egalitarian values to what she finds amiss in human relations. For instance, she is unable to approve of women's meekness in the presence of men, nor of the men's comandeering, supercilious attitude toward women which, she writes, "reminds me too much of Pa."[56] In fact, she retains her vision of unabridged human rights for females, including the right to self-determination and bodily inviolability.

Her hosts, however, judge her quite as harshly as she does them. She learns that they pity her for the very qualities of which she is most proud: her independence as a single woman and her professional dedication. The Olinka of both sexes regard her as a wretched creature—neither wife nor mother, she is seen as abandoned. In the opinion of Tashi's father:

> Our women are respected here—We would never let them tramp the world as American women do. There is always someone to look after the Olinka woman. A father. An uncle. A brother or nephew. Do not be offended, Sister Nettie, but our people pity women such as you who

are cast out, we know not from where, into a world unknown to you, where you must struggle all alone, for yourself.

So I am an object of pity and contempt, I thought, to men and women alike.[57]

Closing her letter, "Good-bye until the next time, Dear Celie, from a pitiful cast-out woman who may perish during the rainy season," Nettie tries to dilute her bitterness with humor. But the sting remains. Apparently, although "things are changing," views pertaining to women are not modified apace. Rather one has the impression that women's subordination is the pillar to which male tribesmen cling while everything else falls apart. Like Ngugi, Walker sees excision fulfilling this purpose. Despite the explicit "repugnance" of her American boyfriend, Tashi agrees to initiation to demonstrate that the Olinka "still have their own ways. . . even though the white man has taken everything else. Tashi didn't want to do it," Olivia remarks, "but to make her people feel better, she's resigned."[58]

Women are indeed the scapegoats of tradition. As Audrey Wipper notes, "urban African women (in western dress) are (being) used as targets of agression (sic) to symbolize the source of strains" resulting from "rapid and deep-rooted social change."[59] The returning of women to the "veil" in Northern African Islamic societies is another example. In fact, she sees in misogynistic media campaigns echoes of the European witchhunts, thus confirming Ngugi's view that increasing disempowerment of males results in intensified pressures of females. In his later works, too, Ngugi shows women suffering the devastating effects of a misguided development policy and, as Sigrid Peicke writes, "oppression becomes the central theme" in his later portrayals of women.[60] He gives us, for example, in *Petals of Blood* and *Devil on the Cross* two young heroines aware of the politics behind their disadvantages and active in the struggle to change their societies. And though both Wanja and Jacinta personally prosper, the author shows that women *as a group* have been betrayed—having fought for independence, they are denied its fruits.

Perhaps the value of Ngugi's work for feminists lies here, in his dialectic vision of women in revolt. Often in the face of crushing odds, his heroines survive. They are active, intelligent, courageous, defiant. Even Muthoni, in *The River Between*, rebels; a rebellion misdirected but of great symbolic import. For her choice is both right and wrong. It is right to defy the father's law; it is wrong to choose clitoridectomy. Her act does not allow of simplistic interpretations. Yet the activist is tempted to oversimplify. Excision is a crime, mutilation an atrocity. These 'rites' should be stopped. Yes. But how? Not merely by demanding that they cease, but also by understanding why they happen. *The River Between* takes a step in this direction, for understanding precedes change.

NOTES

1. Nawal El Saadawi, *The Hidden Face of Eve. Women in the Arab World*. Trans. Dr. Sherif Hetata (London: Zed Press, 1980), p. 7.
2. *Ibid.*
3. *Ibid.*, pp. 7-8.
4. In a letter to *Ms.* magazine, J. Knepp notes that "the term 'female circumcision' should (not) be used to mean clitoridectomy. . . The parallel mutilation of a male would be cutting off the *whole tip* of the penis, not the foreskin." *Ms.* August 1983, p. 12. Furthermore, one should be aware of the potentially devastating side and after-effects of these interventions (the more serious accompanying infibulation). These include bladder infections, tetanus and septic anemia, infrequent fatal hemorrhaging, cysts, vaginal fistula resulting in incontinence, keloid formations, infertility due to chronic pelvic infection, delay in the second stage of labor resulting from the inelasticity of scar tissue, sometimes leading to brain damage of the infant, etc.
5. Evelyne Accad, *L'Excisée* (Paris: L'Harmattan, 1982), p. 121-2.
6. *Ibid.*, 170.
7. *Ibid.*, 121.
8. Saadawi, 8.
9. Accad, 122.
10. Ibid., 140.
11. In "A Statement on Genital Mutilation," in Miranda Davies, editor, *Third World: Second Sex. Women's Struggles and National Liberation* (London: Zed Press, 1983), p. 217, AAWORD charges the western press with extreme insensitivity in the handling of this theme. A plethora of media tracts on the issue are guilty of "aggressiveness, ignorance or even contempt." Effect has been achieved through sensationalism, violating "the dignity of the very women (to be) save(d)." Finally, certain western campaigns have drawn on "the latent racism" present where "ethnocentric prejudice is so deep-rooted."
12. Nuruddin Farah, *From a Crooked Rib* (London: Heinemann, 1970).
13. Yambo Ouologuem, *Bound to Violence*. Trans. Ralph Mannheim (London: Heinemann, 1971), p. 47.
14. Amadou Kourouma, *Les Soleils des Indépendances* (Montréal: Presse de L'Université, 1968; 2nd edition Paris: Seuil, 1970).
15. Nawal El Saadawi, *Woman at Point Zero*. Trans. Dr. Sherif Hetata (London: Zed Press, 1983), p. 15.
16. As a matter of interest, influential Nigerian novelist Buchi Emecheta has also expressed moderate views on the subject, in particular expressing doubt about the efficacy of western feminist intervention (unpublished taped conversation with Sigrid Peicke, January, 1983).
17. Flora Nwapa, *Efuru* (London: Heinemann, 1966), p. 15.
18. Jomo Kenyatta cited in Benoîte Groult, *Ainsi soit-elle* (Paris: Grasset, 1975), p. 105, author's translation.
19. Carl Gustav Rosberg and John Nottingham, *The Myth of Mau Mau Nationalism in Kenya* (London: Pall Mall Press, 1966,) p. 120.

20. S. N. Ngubiah, "Ngugi's Early Writings: 'The River Between' and 'The Black Hermit'" in Chris Wanjala, editor, *Standpoints on African Literature* Nairobi: East African Literature Bureau, 1973), p. 70.
21. *Ibid.*, 66.
22. Ngugi wa Thiong'o, *The River Between* (London: Heinemann, 1965), p. 142.
23. Saadawi, *Eve*, p. 41.
24. Stella Efua Graham, "Female Sexual Mutilation," *Minority Rights Group Newsletter*, No. 15, April 1983 (London: 36 Craven Street, WC 3), p. 3.
25. A marked exception to this approach emphasizing class struggle is the view of Dr. Asma El Dareer in her book *Woman, Why Do You Weep? Circumcision and Its Consequences* (London: Zed Press, 1982). Dedicated "To All Women," her standpoint is feminist, not unlike that of Raqiya Haji Dualeh Abdalla in *Sisters in Affliction. Circumcision and Infibulation of Women in Africa* (London: Zed Press, 1982). Dealing with mutilation in the Sudan and Somalia respectively, both books are based on the authors' field research and include an account of current projects aimed at eradicating the practice.
26. Western feminists taking this approach include Mary Daly, Fran Hosken, Marielouise Janssen-Jurreit, Benoîte Groult, and Séverine Auffret.
27. For a review of 'reasons' and 'rationalizations' given for the practice, many pointing toward a psychoanalytic explanation, see Tobe Levin, "'Unspeakable Atrocities': The Psycho-sexual Etiology of Female Genital Mutilation," *The Journal of Mind and Behavior*, Autumn, 1980 (Vol. 1, No. 2), pp. 197-210.
28. For example, at a Paris meeting of European women's groups against genital mutilation, sponsored by the Commission pour l'Abolition des Mutilations Sexuelles (CAMS) on July 9 and 10, 1983, Stella Efua Graham expressed her belief that western feminist rhetoric frightens the majority of African women and that, to be effective, another tone must be used. In contrast, Awa Thiam of CAMS (with headquarters in Dakar) takes a more uncompromising view, linking clitoidectomy specifically to other forms of violence against women. Thiam goes so far as to introduce the radical lesbian alternative to dependence on men and marriage as a solution worth consideration.
29. Ngugi, 121.
30. *Ibid.*, 120.
31. *Ibid.*, 23.
32. *Ibid.*
33. *Ibid.*, 45-6.
34. Marielouise Janssen-Jurreit, *Sexismus/Über die Abtreibung der Frauenfrage* München: Carl Hanser Verlag, 1976), p. 542.
35. Ngugi, *ibid.*, 44.
36. *Ibid.*, 37-8.
37. Eddah Gachukia, *Notes on Ngugi wa Thiong'o's "The River Between"* (Nairobi: Heinemann, 1975), p. 8.
38. Ngugi, *ibid.*, 34.
39. *Ibid.*
40. *Ibid.*, 15.
41. Eddah Gachukia, "The Role of Women in Ngugi's Novels," *Busara* Vol, 3, No. 4 (1971), p. 30.

42. Judith Cochrane, "Women as the Guardians of the Tribe in Ngugi's Novels," ACLALS-Bulletin, Vol, 4, No. 5 (1977), p. 2.
43. Ngugi, *ibid.*, 53.
44. *Ibid.*, 29.
45. *Ibid.*, 41.
46. *Ibid.*, 42.
47. *Ibid.*, 129.
48. *Ibid.*, 129.
49. *Ibid.*
50. *Ibid.*, 142.
51. *Ibid.*
52. *Ibid.*, 44.
53. Sigrid Peicke, *In den Frauen liegt die Zukunft: Frauengestalten im Werk des kenianischen Schriftstellers Ngugi wa Thiong'o* (Frankfurt am Main: Nexus Verlag, 1981), p. 21-22. My translation.
54. "Kenya," *Courage* (July, 1983), p. 25.
55. Carola Donner-Reichle, *Die Last der Unterentwicklung: Frauen in Kenia* (Berlin: Dialogus Mundi, 1977), p. 41. My Translation.
56. Alice Walker, *The Color Purple* (New York: Harcourt, Brace, Jovanovich, 1982), p. 137.
57. *Ibid.*
58. *Ibid.*, 202.
59. Audrey Wipper, "African Women, Fashion, and Scapegoating," *Canadian Journal of African Studies*, VI, ii (1972), p. 329.
60. Peicke, *ibid.*, 78.

Okigbo's Labyrinths *and the Context of Igbo Attitudes to the Female Principle*

Elaine Savory Fido

Igbo culture is a complex entity, and the boundaries which define it are diffuse. Igbo people have intermarried with peoples along their borders, and the colonial intrusion and its aftermath has so changed things that it is hard even for scholars bent on determining essential facts to find them. The process of disentangling colonial influences and non-Igbo influences from the core of traditional Igbo culture is ongoing, but debates persist as to whether one element or another is old Igbo or is the product of a continually changing and adapting cultural ambience. To be sure, there are deep-seated blendings of the traditional and the modern and the Igbo have become known for their capacity to accept and absorb change (Achebe: 1958, 1964). One major area of this debate concerns Igbo attitudes to women.

Christopher Okigbo was born at Ojoto, a town near Onitsha in which a local but powerful goddess, Idoto, had her shrine.[1] Many of the riverine areas of Igboland and of Eastern Nigeria in general have goddess cults of various kinds, including the Mammy Water[2] and the sea-goddess *Owu-Miri*,[3] who is worshipped around Oguta[4] and Egbema. This prevalence of female deities is in accordance with the theory that the Igbo traditional religion was based around the female principle, centrally around the Earth Goddess Ala,[4] described by Michael Echeruo as the most likely deity to be called supreme god of the Igbos.[5] This theory is not unchallenged since Chukwu, a male deity, is often described as having become more important

223

than Ala. However, some theologians (Arazu: 1982) claim that this was only a response to Christian missionaries and Igbo Christian theologians need to find a supreme god amongst the Igbo pantheon (one is tempted to add a supreme *male* god). There is also a view that the Arochukwu people extended Chukwu's power in the service of their own aggressive expansionism.[6] Other Igbo theologians argue that "the supremacy of Chukwu has never been challenged by any divinity in the Ibgo religious pantheon" (Agwu: 4). Whatever the precise history of Chukwu and Ala may be, the fact is that female deities figure largely in the culture and literature of the Igbo people, right up to this day and even in literature written by men in the English language.

Eastern Nigeria has produced a number of significant writers, including the most well-known of all African writers at this date, Chinua Achebe. It is notable that Igbo women as a group are the most numerous and productive of African women writers. Whilst it is difficult to say for certain what factors predispose Igbo culture to encourage the development of women as creative writers, it is clear that they exist, and it is also apparent that male Igbo writers are particularly concerned with the balance of male and female values in society and write about the results of inequities in male and female principles as being dangerous to social health (Achebe: 1958, Amadi: 1969). Igbo culture is favorable to the development of relative individualism, and the variations in dialects and customs between villages reinforce an impression of social flexibility, a factor which played a part in Igbo attitudes to established colonial rule and education.[7] But beyond that circumstance which might give rise to female independence and development within cultural restraints, there are definite links made by Igbo people between strong women and specific social and cultural realities. For example, asking where the Igbo novelist Flora Nwapa was born, I was told that she comes from a place where the women are very strong (namely Oguta).

A few years after Okigbo was born, in 1932, a woman anthropologist[8] published a study of Igbo women in which she detailed their close bonding with one another and their sense of independence and identity, as well as their closeness to the female Earth Goddess, acknowledged by their men. Her comment on Igbo male attitudes to women is important:

> One hears it said that the Igbo man 'does not respect women'. He does: he even respects her in a way so original and so modern that Europeans have only just begun to think of it.
>
> (Leith-Ross: 1939, 231)

Leith-Ross' study covered both rural and urban Igbo communities and included Port Harcourt, Onitsha and the intervening area. Her findings importantly point to what amounts to a women's sub-culture amongst the Igbo, with councils which almost amount, she suggests, to the power of secret societies, belief in the fecundity of women being linked to that of the yam deity,[9] and a relation to the male world which was easy enough to permit men to say they would not mind being reincarnated as women, which could scarcely be the case in a really sexist society. Leith-Ross' position also supports the current arguments of the Bendel Igbo dramatist Zulu Sofola[10] who argues that tradition benefitted women more than the modern post-colonial situation. Furthermore, the research of the Yoruba historian J.F. Ade Ajayi[11] corroborates the idea that colonialism worsened the situation of the African woman. This is not surprising since the British colonialist period was marked in Britain itself by strong sexism.

There is some evidence that the traditional role of Igbo culture concerning gender might have been somewhat androgynous. Androgyny is defined in this sense as the capacity emotionally and intellectually to accept every human being as a mixture of male and female elements, with ideal human social relations permitting both sexes to utilize the 'other' in their nature freely and usefully.[12] Certainly there is much psychological evidence that adrogynous people are more mentally healthy than those who subject themselves to extremes of gender roles, and this may have an effect on creativity (Williams: 1979). Leith-Ross, at any rate, found that there was an androgynous flavour to Igbo culture: she describes "glimpses of some peculiar conception of sex or of a thread of bisexuality running through everything . . . or of a lack of differentiation between the sexes—or of an acceptance of the possibility of the transposition of sex." (p. 101) Chinua Achebe deals centrally with unbalanced maleness in *Things Fall Apart*, and Carole Boyce Davies argues that he seems to be saying that survival involves man in unifying male and female qualities (Davies: 1983). In one interview, Achebe said: "There is always some kind of war between the sexes, you know, but in the traditional society it was good-humored." (Evalds: 1977, 17.) This focus on male-female relations as the underpinning of society seems to characterize both female and male writers from Eastern Nigeria, such as Flora Nwapa, Buchi Emecheta, Zulu Sofola, Christopher Okigbo, Cyprian Ekwensi and Onuora Nzekwu, who are Igbo[13] and Elechi Amadi who is Ikwerre.

Yet for all the suggestions of possible advantages to women in traditional cultures, tradition was certainly not ideal, and modern influences such as British sexist colonialism further complicated gender relations. Some writers, like Amadi, have specifically written on women's issues, but only to reveal their own conflicts. Amadi's essay on the Nigerian civil war, *Sunset in Biafra*, reveals his adherence to British-style army training, not surprising since he undertook that himself. But perhaps it partly explains why, when he talks of women, he sounds very much like a Western man:

> Because man recognises instinctively that feminine powers are overwhelming, he is reluctant to concede any further powers and

> privileges to woman . . . This is the feminine sexual power which men
> fear. The women who oppose the femininst movement are mostly
> those who recognise this power . . .
>
> Amadi: 1982, 79, 80.

The same authoritarian, anti-emotional tradition which shapes soldiers in
the Western style also makes men incapable of giving up their rigid surface
controls to enjoy intimacies and equalities with women. Okigbo, whilst not
a professional soldier, was killed in the Biafran war and his poetry clearly
articulates the stress of determining identity amidst cultural crisis and
gender crisis. In his work, fear of women can also be clearly perceived.
Anxiety about the female principle is in fact a strong element in male
Eastern Nigerian writers' work, whereas in writers such as Flora Nwapa,
there is a profoundly different perception, an engagement with the reality of
trying to be female and an individual in a society which constantly tries to
mythologize about women to distance any danger they might pose.
Nwapa's *Efuru* shows a woman trying to come to terms with loss of
husband and child through her relation to a water-deity, a sort of divine role-
model who helps her to decide that childlessness is not the end of the world.
There is a great difference between using myth to make reality more
workable and endurable and using myth to create fantasies which deny the
reality. Much recent critical work by women has found the latter tendency
strong in male creative literature, and of course the anger which women
have begun to express can sometimes lead to intense hostility to men, itself a
social divisive force. Buchi Emecheta's work, influenced as it is by her
British experience, is characterised by a greater element of what one might
call Western style feminism than is true of other African women writers in
Nigeria. So it is possible to see that on both sides, male and female, there is a
mixture of dissatisfaction with present male-female relations based on the
central belief in Eastern Nigerian cultures that society is built on these
relations and that something is presently wrong. A variety of solutions
based not only on knowledge of tradition[14] but also on colonial and post-
colonial cultural influences from Britain have further polarized the sexes.

   Okigbo's poetry ought to be seen in this context, for his presentation of his
own spiritual odyssey is framed by the developing images of a female
principle which shapes and informs the adult male psyche. *Labyrinths* is a
spiritual journey to rebirth as an adult consciousness and a creative voice.
The creative artist who made the poetry was himself a collection of
contradictory elements: poet and man of action who was killed in war;
mystic with ambitions to be a financier; proud Igbo and yet lover of
European poetry; a man ambivalent about *négritude* but extremely attracted to
symbolism and committed to the rehabilitation of his race and culture after
colonialism; and Christian trained yet an adherent of older religions. The
creative process made it possible for him to find coherence in himself, and

his poetry shows the stages of integration of the disparate elements of his vision.

In his life, Okigbo had problems in his relations with women. He tried to save his marriage by making one last trip to visit his wife at Yola, a trip described in his preface to *Labyrinths* as being "in pursuit of what turned out to be an illusion". Yet women or the concept of the feminine in various forms shape the major images in his poetry. People who were close to Okigbo believe that the poems are all or almost all based on real relations with women. Yet the emotional tone of the poems is often agonized, as if when faced with the physical and emotional reality of sexual love Okigbo found great pain and self-doubt tormented him. Ideals and abstractions are, in that case, a good deal easier. Sunday Anozie[15] has written that Okigbo adored his wife and daughter. But that surely is too simple a statement. When the poetry is closely examined, there seems to be running through all of its emotional textures a tension between love and fear, desire to submit to intensities of emotional and physical love and desire to remain separate, adoration of the mother and terror of the sexual partner. Also evidenced is a need to restore the ancient mother-ruled images of traditional religious cults and so rid his culture of colonialism, countered by a need to be an adult male, independent of needs for softness and protection given by a woman. In many ways, Okigbo's twists and turns of desire are those characteristic of man in many if not all cultures, where mother-domination in early childhood creates a fear of woman's power and a desire to dominate women in order to be adult and a man (Dinnerstein: 1976). But there is a vital aspect of his agony which is particular to modern post-colonial African man, and indeed to Igbo man, with his history, it seems, of close and relatively balanced relations with the feminine. That is, while the feminine is closely intertwined with his idea of traditional religion, the male-dominated Christian ethos shaped his public idea of himself as a man in colonial and post-colonial society, and that is antithetical to Igbo tradition. In addition, British culture portrays the male poet as an effeminate man, someone less than fully developed as a masculine figure.

Okigbo's commitment to poetry coincided with his conviction that he was the reincarnation of his maternal grandfather, who was a priest of the goddess Idoto. Thus his ethnic and spiritual identity was bound up in his poetic development. His return to tradition was a return to the 'Mother' Idoto and a rejection of the male god of patriarchial Christianity. The very androgynous quality which often characterises highly developed creative writers is arguably the result of imaginative effort to transcend gender in order to create a full human canvas: Okigbo makes no attempt to depict real woman in his poetry, but instead deals with the mythic and symbolic qualities which she can hold for a male imagination. Yet his poet-protagonist's strivings for self-creation seem to point to a desire for androgyny, a sensuous and emotive union with the 'other'. Chukwuma

Azuonye links Okigbo's woman symbols with Jungian psychology (Azuonye: 1981), but resists the idea that Okigbo expresses fear of the feminine. However, the masochistic quality noted in the poetry by Sunday Anozie (Anozie: 1972) derives its force from the painful dilemma of the sensitive man—whether to submit to sensuous experience and give up control of the woman or to risk the loss of self-possession which must come in surrender to sexual experience. The fear of woman which informs Okigbo's images of the Lioness is an ambivalent one, but nevertheless there is an anxiety within it that the man will be castrated by the act of surrender.

Let us examine the spiritual quest which shapes *Labyrinths*. Critics have discussed Okigbo's use of the Idoto cult and Christianity, and occasionally note has been made of Okigbo's references to ancient Middle Eastern cultures (Izevbaye: 1973).[16] But there is a major thread of meaning in the poems which relates to Okigbo's knowledge of ancient history and which ties Idoto to the cults of an ancient Egyptian goddess, Isis,[17] who was in her various incarnations Isis, Ishtar, Inanna and finally, much reduced, the Virgin Mary, the most widespread deity in the ancient world. There are in fact three religions intertwined in the poetry: Idoto-worship and traditional Igbo worship of the femine; Christianity and the worship of Isis-Ishtar.

The very title, *Labyrinths*, is best interpreted through the ancient Cretan culture which Okigbo himself refers to in his preface. The Cretan goddess is of course connected to the legends of the Labyrinth and Nor Hall has explained it well:

> A Minoan statue of the mother goddess from Crete embodies this message in archaic form . . . With a snake in one hand and a tool (her double-edged axe) in the other, the goddess connects the chthonian realm of matter (the Mother) and the upper world of the sky-god, who calculates, measures and perceives . . .
>
> The axe came to mean many things. It is called *labrys* and is related to *labyrinth*, the underground dwelling of the goddess. In order to pass through the labyrinth it was necessary to make a full 360-degree turn, to turn completely round on oneself to go out the way one came in. In the ancient world this action was meaningful on what we would call a psychological level, as evident in the conjecture that it was the crossing sweeper *Labys* who is credited with the maxim 'know thyself'.
>
> Nor Hall: 1971, 9-10

Okigbo links the double-edged axe of Crete with the Aro culture of the Igbo people in his preface, thus connecting the ancient Middle East/North Africa together with his own ethnic traditions. The labyrinth is of course the ancient symbol of the womb, and there is a strong theme of rebirth and initiation in Okigbo's poem cycle. But that initiation takes place in the world of the Mother, opposed to which, in *Labyrinths*, is the measuring, geometric world of Kepkanly, the primary school teacher of the colonial Mission school. Earth and sky, the water goddess and the Christian sky god, are the poles of spiritual existence at the beginning of *Labyrinths*.

Okigbo's poems are obscure, symbolical, full of personal allusions and unexplained references to foreign poets and to political events or Igbo cultural traditions. Nothing is clearer than Okigbo's intention not to be fully understood, even to himself. There has been complaint about this (Chinweizu, Onuchekwa Jemie and Ihechukwu Madubuike: 1980). But perhaps it is best to accept that when a writer is deliberately obscure, out of competence rather than out of failure to be clear, there is good reason. Then, perhaps, the most appropriate way to approach Okigbo's work is as if he was writing the kind of mystical, gnomic verses which characterize ritualistic poetry in African cultures, e.g. in Ifa worship amongst the Yoruba. Okigbo's relation to spiritually tormented poets like T.S. Eliot (who also uses the symbol of a powerful and threatening woman associated with myth in his poetry) has long been recognized. If the complexity of spiritual truths felt and explored by a finely tuned intelligence is added to the complexity of Okigbo's socio-political and historical context, then it is not particularly surprising that his work is difficult.

The relation of the three religions in *Labyrinth* is difficult to disentangle for Okigbo's method of composition is associational and he does not provide explanatory links. But much of the imagery has several layers of meaning which connect religious traditions at a deep symbolic level. For example, the Igbo folktale which tells of a monkey dazzled by the armpit of a lioness until he destroys himself[18] clearly accounts for the image of the 'armpit dazzle of the lioness' in *Labyrinths*. But it is also true that one of the titles of Isis, Queen of Heaven, was Lioness of the Sacred Assembly, and that Sakmet was the lioness-headed goddess of Ancient Egypt who was symbolic of war and pestilence and who annihilated her enemies. Similarly, eggs, which are important in the worship of Igbo water-goddess[19] and which figure largely in the ritually important symbolisms of the poetry, were one of the important symbols of Isis. White light, which surrounds the Watermaid in *Labyrinths* is not only the dazzle of the Lioness, but the moonlight which has always been associated with female deities, including Isis and her various forms. Other clusters of images have this syncretic overtone, including those of water, the sea, corn and associated golden objects (the gold crop, ears of the secret, amber, golden eggs, yellow memories), Nature, snakes and birds. Most of these are strongly associated both with Igbo traditions and with Isis and goddess worship in the ancient world.

It is important to place these connections in the context of Igbo legends that the Igbo people came originally from Egypt. These legends, which are said to explain the celebrated terra-cotta skin of many Igbos as well as their

relatively small land area and their migratory tendency to resettle and
intermarry with other peoples, as well as their sense of being different from
other peoples in Nigeria, might well have been the original impetus behind
Okigbo's fascination with ancient history.

In *Labyrinths*, Okigbo interweaves Christianity complexly with Igbo
traditions. In the opening cycle of poems, the protagonist submits to Idoto
as a 'prodigal' with all the Biblical overtones of that term. He thus points to
the conflict within him which is again expressed strongly when he begs his
dead, saintly mother, Anna Okigbo, to protect him from "them fucking
angels" (p. 17). Anna is a particularly important name itself to carry
ambivalences if one remembers, as Azuonye (p. 38), that Anna was not
only Okigbo's mother's actual name but a major part of Jung's 'anima' term.
Yet again, Christianity significantly appears as the colonialist eagles who
rape Igbo culture, bringing with them their God who silences the longdrums
and causes the forest gods to be forgotten and their shrines abandoned. Yet
their violence is in the service of a religion which teaches love (and we know
from Achebe the impact of a new faith which could release some Igbos who
felt themselves persecuted by Igbo religious principles). Similarly the old
cults of Isis could involve the sacrifice of males (Stone: 132-6). So men
must have feared the power of women within that context. There is therefore
a good deal of violence in *Labyrinths*, much of it linked to female cruelties
to men via the dangerous experience of sexual attraction as well as to the
Christianizing/colonising experience. Christianity first taught toleration
and love, then suppressed women, of course, with increasing ferocity,
waging a war on the remnants of pagan cults which often reflected the place
of women in the ancient world and which seemed to give them greater power
and freedom than Christianity was willing to permit. Instead of a sexually
active ideal of women, Christianity created an ideal of virginity/chastity
and motherhood and Okigbo's poetry communicates these images together
with a great deal of ambivalence toward female beauty (linking it to power
and cruelty to men). Sunday Anozie quotes a passage from Robert de
Montesquieu which deals with the story of John the Baptist in a way very
reminiscent of Okigbo's treatement of male fear of women:

> The secret is none other than that the mystery of her being is to be
> violated by John, who catches sight of her and pays for this single
> sacrifice with his life; for this free spirited virgin will only feel pure
> again, when she is holding the head of an executed man . . .
>
> Anozie: 1972, p. 99

This passage seems to be to capture Okigbo's spirit of fear in the poems
which relate to sexual woman. But, Christianity, after all, suppressed
women so much so that such violence against men was virtually impossible
to conceive of, and the sexual strictures against women subdued their sexual

nature to the service of their god. Celibacy replaced sexuality as the spiritual centre of physical devotion to God.

The relation of sexuality to religion is crucially important in *Labyrinths*. The poet-protagonist develops from his rebirth as Idoto's returned son to a sexual awakening with the Watermaid and afterwards as agonised adult experience with the Lioness, which culminates in his 'homecoming' as the bridegroom of this powerful and destructive female presence, seen paring her fingernails amidst the carnage of dismembered limbs and blood. Even small details in the poetry bring the reader to link violence, sex and religion. In the poem to Awolowo[20] 'Lament of the Drums', the reference to Celaeno and her harpy crew, the image of the sea as raped and the waters as sultry all conjure up a disturbed female sexuality, which is either threatening or violated and thus hurt. The language of the poetry abounds with images of the fruitfulness of the goddess, of her connection with water, and with powerful and threatening nature, as in 'Distances III' where she is associated with a molten centre of earth and her labyrinths are connected with violence. The androgynous forest gods are raped. There is a strong castration theme which runs through the poetry, and which links it with the old world of self-castration associated with the cult of Cymbele, a Greek version of Isis, and Attis, who was castrated and who gave rise to the custom of self-castration by priests of Cymbele.

The origins of this connection between sexuality, religion and violence was the necessary death and rebirth of vegetation along the Nile valley as the great river ebbed and flowed. The river was Isis, the vegatation Osiris, who died and was resurrected each year. The legend went that Osiris, Isis' brother-lover was torn to pieces and Isis put his body together again, but his penis was missing. She created him whole and blew life into him and he caused her to conceive her son, the god Horus. Afterwards, the goddess' husbands and lovers were always associated with death and rebirth. But the Babylonian goddess, Ishtar, had as her consort her son, Tammuz, whose death she did not cause but rather mourned. Okigbo includes in *Labyrinths* the lament of Ishtar for Tammuz, which was identified by Dan Izevbaye as a virtual translation of an ancient Sumerian song (Izevbaye: 1973, 140). In Biblical times, Hebrew women performed a ritual lament for Tammuz, showing how ancient traditions of goddess worship had permeated even their male-oriented religious culture. It is plain that historically, men gradually resisted the self-surrender and death-rebirth myths associated with the goddess' consort. The myth of Gilgamesh, often described as the first epic, tells how Gilgamesh refuses to become the goddess' lover, saying that Ishtar has hurt too many lovers before. He goes off to become the first patriarchal hero and Enkidu is sacrificed in his stead. Okigbo weaves mention of the Gilgamesh epic[21] into 'Fragments out of the Deluge'. Christianity was the triumph of male ascendency and also the triumph of a gentle, loving god-figure in Christ himself, yet of course it has been a bloody and oppressive religion to those ground down by colonialism and slavery and forced to accept the god of those who exploited them. Okigbo's sense of conflict in relation to his Mother Idoto and to the powerful goddess images is made very clear by his references to Christian violation of Igbo culture and even by references to the drowning nuns who represent womanhood totally submissive to a god who does not save them.

Fertility, associated of course with creativity and therefore with the poet, is associated with the female deity. In the lament for Tammuz, there is mention of special concern for the loss of various kinds of fruition: 'fields of crops', 'fields of men', children in reference to 'barren wedded ones' and 'perishing children'. The sinister 'potbellied watchers' who despoil 'her' in this poem suggest a male violation of the goddess' plenty. Here Okigbo's sympathy apears to be with a hurt maternal Nature, but he seems to have ambivalence towards the feminine in many other places. When the poet-protagonist finally achieves his 'birthday of earth', there is an overtone still of fear and adoration at the same time for the goddess who has been his inspiration and his mate. It is as if the poet risks his manhood and his existence to achieve his poetic vocation through union with the Lionness. In the sensuous passage of sexual encounter with the Watermaid, the poet is a submissive and loyal subject. Even the sea is 'spent', presumably from loving her. When he washes his feet in the 'maid's pure head' at the end of *Labyrinths*, he is afraid of her variegated teeth. These tensions are charac-teristic of the poetic journey of the protagonist, in which he becomes, for example, a skeletal oblong, (the oblong is associated with both his mother Anna through the church organ panels, and with the Lionness' head), a shape created by his attraction to the female deity he follows but reduced to a skeleton. For patriarchy depends on potency, on domination of women, in fact, and the poet stands between the matriarchal world of Idoto and the patriarchal colonial one of Christian education and culture: submission to woman risks potency, yet provides fusion with the Igbo traditions which the poet desires, and also promises a delicious and masochistic pleasure of domination by another and release from the responsibility of domination.

The geometric shapes which are a linked series of images in the poems are connected to notions of ridigity and excess, hypocrisy and exploitativeness found in both religious and secular leaders and men of responsibility. The cross itself functions as a complex symbol, and a huge fiery cross links itself with geometric shapes in the poet's mind as he dreams in 'Distances' IV. Initiation ordeals, including the knife (circumcision and also the old Igbo ritual of cutting the face to prove endurance on the part of the initiate) are linked with the idea of Christian ritual. Kepkanly, who presides over the initiation of the young poet into the Catholic catechism, is the god of the schoolroom, but the world he promises is one where precise thinking and rigid attitudes (symbolised by various geometric shapes) seem to Okigbo to betray the mysteries of the spirit and put pragmatisms, and therefore moral corruptions, to the forefront. The fiery cross of 'Distances' is reminiscent of the KKK, the racist American organization which more than any other has publicized the Christian involvement with prejudice and hatred, including killing innocent people because of their colour or ethnic identification. The young poet is scarred by Christianity in the way that the old Igbo ritual scarred its initiates to prove courage on their part. In 'Distances' IV there is a surreal vision of geometric shapes in a cosmic setting, and in V Okigbo links the 'kiss' which is so much associated with Christ to the scar, and to two swords. As in the Isis myths and in Igbo religion, Christianity is a mixture of violence, sexuality and spiritual purity, a dangerous environment for the unwary.

The image of the Mother is crucial to the poems. Idoto is the deity who is symbolic mother to the young poet returning to his culture and to his spiritual base. But also Anna, the poet's earthly mother, whose funeral is the theme of the lovely poem "SILENT FACES at crossroads", in "The Passage", becomes associated by the shape of the oblong with the Lioness herself. 'Distances' V brings together the idea of form as a cosmic and religious frame for the soul with the 'panel oblong', associated with the church organ and the coffin of Anna's burial and the Lioness' head, and the sanctuary at the centre of the earth where Mother Earth will receive her children, where water runs through tunnels (with the obvious suggestion of female sexual secretions), and this looks forward to 'Distances' VI. There is a constant interweaving of symbols and thus the sexual overtones of the Lionness are interwoven with the maternal aspects of Idoto/Anna. It is interesting that Isis cults, too, had this dualism, where the female diety was both protective and nurturing and destructive and threatening to man. Similarly also Isis worship was finally destroyed (her temples sacked) and her identity subsumed into the Virgin Mary by Christianized Rome in much the same way as Idoto and the forest gods[22] were destroyed by Christian British imperialism and its local Igbo adherents. In 'Fragments Out of the Deluge' Okigbo makes reference to the Flood, which was associated with the goddess before it was Biblical (she is supposed to have sailed on the waters in a crescent moon boat and her symbols included the dove). Also in this poem, Okigbo mentions the Lionness and in a footnote explains that she had killed the hero's second self, which is a clear reference to the epic of Gilgamesh and a clear identification of the poet with Gilgamesh himself (the sacrificed Enkidu being the second self of Gilgamesh). So there is here a dualism within one poem which is repeated over and over again in *Labyrinths*: the female principle becomes the creative protective destructive cosmic centre of the universe.

Fear plays a major role in Okigbo's poetry, whether it is fear of the void or the abyss, fear of woman, fear of becoming or of dying. (Egudu: 1978, 9-13). The fear is caused by the ambivalence which a person such as the poet-protagonist must feel, for his psyche is partly shaped by colonialism and

Christianity which he regards as "fireseed", i.e. destructive to him. Of course his attitude to woman must be equally ambivalent, for she is essential to his being as well as on an ongoing threat to his potency and domination. The fear motivates the poetry in creative and constructive ways, for courage, whether creative or physical is not the absence of fear but the capacity to act despite it. *Labyrinths* was a brave thing to do, just as Okigbo's involvement with Biafra was direct and cost him his life. He was never a coward. In his last poems "Path of Thunder", he returns to the image of the ram tethered for sacrifice as presenting his own situation in the War, and in a moving and prophetic statement, indicates knowledge of likely death:

> O mother mother Earth, unbind me; let this be my last testament; let this be
> The ram's hidden wish to the sword the sword's secret player to the scabbard—
>
> —Okigbo: 1971, 72

Once again, the Mother image becomes instrumental in presenting the realities of the poet's psychic condition: he is victim again, and in need of the protection of "Earth", of becoming once more the 'prodigal', and the hints of parallels with Christ's Passion which are prevalent in *Labyrinths* seem relevant again here. The poet is one of the "stars" which come and go, as poets, prophets and leaders come, do their work and die. Okigbo's presentation of the religious vocation of poet brings him to perceive suffering and even death as a necessary offering of experience which has to be made by those who seek greater understanding and knowledge, and who seek to serve their culture in times of stress. His ambivalence about Christianity does not prevent him from seeing the isolation, self-discipline and suffering of Christ himself as a model for the fate of the poet-prophet in other conditions and times. In the syncretic world of Okigbo's poetry, however, the Christ figure is close to the male sacrificial victims of the old goddess cults, where the death and resurrection of a chosen man meant renewal of crops and life for the community, a necessary triumph for the life principle in defiance of seasonal changes. The effect of the power of the goddess in *Labyrinths* on the poet is like the relation of Isis and Osiris, so that the submission to her cruelty, her deathly aspect and her power is like a voluntary self-sacrifice in the service of greater knowledge and poetic experience. The poet becomes, as it were, the earthly servant of both Idoto and the other female deities who inhabit the poetry, and in this way becomes a kind of Christ-victim figure, serving a lone apprenticeship in preparation for his own Calvary, and being ultimately sacrificed, not, as in *Labyrinths*, in a psychic and sexual sense subsumed into the goddess' power in order to rise again, but in the final sense of his mission being completed, his star leaving the heavens, as a casualty in war.

Okigbo was self-consciously a mystic, fully accepting of the romantic ideal of the poet as seer. His own comment on the composition of his work, although perhaps misleading given the erudite texture of borrowings from European and American poets which characterizes his earlier work, suggests a reconfirmation of the spiritual core of his poetry:

> ... all I did was to create the drums and the message they deliver has nothing to do with me at all.
>
> Duerden and Pieterse: 1972, 147

It remains true that his work is essentially religious and mystical, but it should be recognised that the centre of that mysticism is the poet's complex relation with a series of female deities and with his own maleness in that context.

NOTES

1. Chukwuma Azuonye has identified a newspaper article recording the destruction of the shrine of Idoto by Christian converts at Ojoto in 1926. See Azuonye: 1981, n. 10, 47.
2. This generic name covers water deities of various sorts, including a mermaid-like creature. Cults spread all over the African diaspora, and the name is recognised in the Caribbean, South and North America and Africa. The deity is usually beautiful, seductive, powerful and can vary between malevolence and protective good nature. The relation of the nature of the cult and the social position of women in the community associated with it is an area which begs for research in the various parts of the African diaspora.
3. The word for 'sea' in Igbo varies according to dialectal differences: but may be "miri", "mini" or "mili". In Elechi Amadi's *The Concubine* 1966), there is a male stream god called "Mini Weku". Although Amadi claims the separateness of the Ikwerre, his people, from the Igbo, this has been to some extent a result of the stresses of land claims during and since the War, and in fact, their languages are close.
4. The birthplace of Flora Nwapa, the Igbo woman novelist.
5. Echeruo: 1979.
6. Aro chukwu means "sons of god". The fact that *chukwu* is *chi-ukwu* or the great *chi* means that it is odd that it has become a male entity, since *chi* is the Igbo concept of the divine essence and is not only in women as well as men but in all of nature. See Achebe: 1975, Aruzu: 1982).
7. See Isichei: 1973 for a discussion of Igbo attitudes to colonial education, and the way these changed from resistence to enthusiastic espousement.

8. Sylvia Leith-Ross' *African Women: A Study of the Ibo in Nigeria* (1939) has some crassly Eurocentric views but is on the whole an independent woman's view of women, sympathetic and original-minded.

9. The Igbo are the only people known to worship the yam as a god.

10. Sofola has written several plays on the theme of woman's role in Nigerian society and the relation of traditional to the modern. Her latest play, a television script, is on the subject of the massacre of young men in Asaba in the War, centred around a woman chief or *Omu*. (*Omu-Àkò of Isele-Oligbo*). The whole subject of women's councils and chieftaincy titles amongst the Igbo people is important and needs more research. I am grateful to my colleague Dr. Stella Ogunyemi for the information that a woman cannot become Omu until she is past the menopause since menstruating women are not allowed in the presence of men. When she assumes the title she leaves her husband's house and returns to live with her father's kin in his compound. It would be important to discover how long the taboo against menstruating women has been in operation.

11. The position of the Yoruba woman in her society is the subject of various recent studies but one most relevant to this paper is Judith Hoch-Smith's "Radical Yoruba Female Sexuality: The Witch and the Prostitute" (1978). In this she concludes that female independence amongst the Yorubas generated a vicious response on the part of men, producing witch-hunts etc. This contrasts with the findings of Leith-Ross, who observed that Igbo women had strong social roles, such as dibias, rainmakers and doctors, yet found few witches except in urban Onitsha. But the two studies certainly emphasize the ambivalence with which female power may be regarded by men.

12. See Kimbrough: 1981.

13. See Emenyonu: 1978.

14. Tradition, as exemplified in folk tale and custom, as well as historical material, reveals Igbo women possessing strength and determination, as well as organisation. For example, Chukwuma Azuonye, for whose advice on Igbo culture I am deeply indebted in the preparation of this paper, has discovered evidence that Chukwu was merely a minor trickster god in Igbo tradition, supporting the view that Ala (Ana, Ani or Ajaálá according to dialect area) was the major deity. In addition, there are epic tales of brave heroines (Azuonye: 1983) and in *Equiano's Travels*, the narrative of an Igbo slave on his culture and background, women figure importantly. Then in colonial times, the Aba Riots of Calabar and Opobo in December 1929, in which the Igbo women's stubborn resistence to colonial authority over a tax question finally provoked colonial violence killing and wounding a large number of people, proved Igbo women were a power to be reckoned with. See Leith-Ross: 1939, 23-39; Isichei: 1976, 121, 125, 151-5.

15. Anozie: 1972.

16. I am grateful to Professor Izevbaye for his comments on a draft of this paper.

17. See Witt: 1971; Stone: 1976; Hall: 1971; Frazier: 1958; Hooke: 1963; Wallis Budge: 1969; Frankfurt: 1948; Bratton: 1970; Wolkstein and Kramer: 1983.

18. I am grateful for this information to Dr. Chukwuma Azuonye.

19. Eggs and pieces of broken mirror, which also figure importantly in Okigbo's symbolism, figure in rituals associated with water goddess in the East of

Nigeria. Men who believe they have married a water spirit believe she will return to the sea or to water at will and to bring her back they must break eggs carefully in an unbroken trail back to the house. She will follow the egg-shells.

20. Chief Obafemi Awolowo was arrested for treason during the troubles in the Western Region in the period 1962-4 and was imprisoned. Okigbo's poems have definite political bias and comment embedded in them but he refused to acknowledge responsibility for this, saying that the poems had their own meaning and it was nothing to do with him.

21. See Moore: 1969, who comments on Okigbo's use of Egypt and Sumer. Izevbaye (1973) discusses the use made of Enki by Okigbo in an original line opening "Fragments out the the Deluge" section VII (see also Anozi: 1972). Enki, whose mention was cut out of the final version of the line, was the Sumerian god of wisdom and father of Inanna, the Sumerian version of Isis. He gave Inanna many powers whilst drunk and then regretted it and tried to get them back. Izevbaye offers an interpretation of the name Enki from Thomas Campbell *The Masks of God* Vol. II (Secker and Warburg London 1962) as being "The Lord *En* of the goddess Earth *ki*." It is therefore evident that Okigbo would have been attracted to Enki, although he turned from this reference in final draft.

22. Dan Izevbaye discusses the connection between Ishtar, and Irkalla, the Sumerian queen of the Underworld, to whose realm Ishtar descends in Sumerian legend and the gods of the forest in *Labyrinths* (Izevbaye: 1973). Here again there is an organic link between the female deities of the ancient world and the traditional deities of Igboland.

REFERENCES

ACHEBE, Chinua. *Arrow of God*. Heinemann London 1964; *Morning Yet On Creation Day*. Heinemann London 1975; *No Longer at Ease*. Heinemann London 1960; *Things Fall Apart*. Heinemann London 1958.

AGWU, Very Rev. Dr. A.O. Iwu. "The Supreme God in Igbo Traditional Religion: A Comment on Arazu's Thesis" 1982, published in *Uwa Ndi Igbo: Journal of Igbo Life and Culture* No. 1 April 1984.

AMADI, Elechi. *The Concubine*. Heinemann London 1966; *Ethics in Nigerian Culture*. Heinemann London 1982; *The Great Ponds*. Heinemann London 1969; *The Slave*. Heinemann London 1978; *Sunset in Biafra*. Heinemann London 1973.

ANOZIE, Sunday O. *Christopher Okigbo*. Evans London 1972.

ARAZU, Rev. Fr. Dr. Raymond C. Arazu, C.S.Sp. "The Supreme God in Igbo Traditional Religion" 1982 published in *Ùwà Ndi Igbò: Journal of Ibgo Life and Culture*. No. 1 April 1984.

AZUONYE, Chukwuma. "Okigbo and the Psychological Theories of Carl Gustav" in *Journal of African and Comparative Literature*. Vol. 1 no 1 (March 1981), 30-51; "Stability and Change in the Performance of Ohafia Igbo Singers of Tales" *Research in African Literatures* Vol. 14 no. 3 Fall 1983, 332-380.

BRATOON, F.G. *Myths and Legends of the Ancient Near-East*. Thomas Y. Crowell New York 1970.

CHINWEIZU *et al. Towards the Decolonisation of African Literature*. Vol. 1 Fourth Dimension Publishers Enugu 1980.

DAVIES, Carole Boyce. "Concepts of African Motherhood: A Comparative Assessment of Attitudes to Motherhood in Igbo Society in Selected Words by Male and Female Writers" First Draft 1983, made available by the author.

DINNERSTEIN, Dorothy. *The Mermaid and the Minotaur*. Harper New York 1976.

DUERDEN D. and PIETERSE C. *African Writers Talking*. Heinemann London 1972.

ECHERUO, Michael. "A Matter of Identity" 1979 Ahiajoku Lecture Imo Newspapers Ltd. Owerri 1979.

EMECHETA, Buchi. *The Bride Price*. Allison and Busby London 1976; *In the Ditch*. Allison and Busby London 1979; *The Joys of Motherhood*. Allison and Busby London 1979; *Second Class Citizen*. Allison and Busby London 1974; *The Slave Girl*. Allison and Busby 1977.

EMEYONU, Ernest. *The Rise of the Igbo Novel*. Oxford University Press, Ibadan 1978.

EQUIANO, Olaudah. *Equiano's Travels*. Heinemann London 1966.

EVALDS, Victoria. "An Interview with Chinua Achebe" *Studies in Black Literature*. Vol. 8 no 1 (Spring 1977).

FRAZER, Sir J.G. *The Golden Bough*. Macmillan New York 1958.

FRANKFURT, H. *Ancient Egyptian Religion*. Harper and Row New York 1948.

HALL, Nor. *The Moon and the Virgin*. Harper and Row New York 1971.

HOCH-SMITH, Judith. "Radical Yoruba Female Sexuality: The Witch and the Prostitute" in *Women in Ritual and Symbolic Roles*. ed. Hoch-Smith and Anita Spring, Plenium Press New York 1978, 245-267.

HOOKE, S.H. *Middle Eastern Mythology*. Pelican Baltimore 1953.

ISICHEI, Elizabeth. *A History of the Igbo People*. St. Martin's Press New York 1976; *The Ibo People and the Europeans*. Faber London 1973.

IZEVBAYE, Dan. "The Poetry of Christopher Okigbo" in *The Critical Evaluation of African Literature* ed. C. Heywood London 1973, 121-148.

KIMBROUGH, Robert. "Androgyny Old and New" *The Western Humanities Review* Vol. XXXV no 3 (Autumn 1981) 197-215.

LEITH-ROSS, Sylvia. *African Women: A Study of the Ibo in Nigeria*. Routledge and Kegan Paul London 1939.

MOORE, Gerald. *The Chosen Tongue*. Longmans London 1969.

NWAPA, Flora. *Efuru*. Heinemann London 1966.; *Idu*. Heinemann London 1969.

OKIGBO, Christopher. *Labyrinths*. Heinemann London 1971.

SOFOLA, Zulu. *Old Wines Are Tasty*. Ibadan U.P. Ibadan 1981; *Omu-Ako of Isele-Oligbo*. Unpublished television script; *Reveries in the Moonlight*. Unpublished playscript; *Song of a Maiden*. Unpublished playscript; *The Sweet Trap*. Oxford U.P. Ibadan 1977.

STONE, Merline. *When God Was a Woman*. Harvest New York 1976.

WALLIS BUDGE, E.A. *The Gods of the Egyptians*. Vol. 2 Dover Pub. New York 1969 (reprint from 1904).

WILLIAMS, Juanita H. *Psychology of Women*. W.W. Norton and Co. Ltd., 1979.

WITT, R.E. *Isis in the Graeco-Roman World*. Cornell University Press Ithaca New York 1971.

WOLKSTEIN, D. and KRAMER, S.N. *Inanna: Queen of Heaven and Earth Her Stories and Hymns from Sumer*. Harper and Row 1983.

Motherhood in the Works of Male and Female Igbo Writers: Achebe, Emecheta, Nwapa and Nzekwu

Carole Boyce Davies

The condition of women in African society is fraught with contradictions, tensions and oppositions, most arising out of the colonial domination of Africa, others intrinsic to the organizational structures of particular societies. A distinct African feminism therefore has already been defined by Filomina Chioma Steady in *The Black Woman Crossculturally*.[1] In her introduction, Steady delineates its features and concludes that,

> The birthplace of human life must also be the birthplace of human struggles, and feminist consciousness must in some way be related to the earliest divisions of labor according to sex on the continent. But even more significant is the fact that the forms of social organization which approach sexual equality, in addition to matrilineal societies where women are central, can be found on the African continent . . . True feminism is an abnegation of male protection and a determination to be resourceful and self-reliant. The majority of the black women in Africa and in the diaspora have developed these characteristics, though not always by choice.[2]

241

Yet the very features which make for her independence and control (for example, her economic freedoms, polygyny, motherhood), can also function for her repression and submission. A rigorous, feminist approach to African society would therefore reveal numerous examples of excesses in structures and situations which deny women equality. For example, genital mutilation, infertility as well as fertility, the lack of choice for young women, enforced silence, to cite only the most obvious, all contribute to woman's oppression.

So, the polarized discussions which claim either that African women were/are or were not/are not repressed, both fairly common in sociological and anthropological circles, neglect a host of contradictions involved in African women's reality.

Numerous stereotypes and misconceptions of African women were created during the colonial period and have been perpetuated up to the present time. According to one writer, "the personality and inner reality of African women have been hidden under . . . a heap of myths, so-called ethnological theories, rapid generalizations and patent untruths."[3]

The systematic destruction of these stereotypes and the exploration of the various facets of African womanhood is in process. First of all African male writers, on the heels of the various national movements (along with a number of African scholars) sought to present the truth of their cultures as a direct rebuttal to the distortions perpetuated by white/colonial missionaries, anthropologists and sociologists. In their writing, the image of women was in some ways and to an extent rehabilitated, but in many cases, new sexist stereotypes were created and older African ones went unchallenged. Now, African women writers are taking the process of *telling one's own story* oneself even further. One can chart a movement from a few tentative beginnings in which the woman's prescribed role was challenged from a quasi-feminist perspective or discussed from an apolitical posture to a more militant feminist position in which writers like Buchi Emecheta and Mariama Bâ question and overturn some of the more traditional attitudes to womanhood and woman's place. This paper contributes to the activity of exploring and defining African womanhood. Its concern is motherhood as portrayed by both male and female writers, but its focus is Igbo society.

I have limited my discussion to Igbo society for several reasons:

1. Igbo women have in their history a period of militancy and a documented instance of actual struggle and female assertiveness. The women's war of 1929, in Eastern Nigeria, which is described by Caroline Ifeka-Moller in "Female Militancy and Colonial Revolt,"[4] as "an African case of feminism," challenged white male domination.

2. Igbo women (like Igbo men), are proportionately the most prolific of African writers.

3. Ibgo writers, notably Chinua Achebe, were among the first writers in the post-colonial period to represent African cultural life in fiction.

4. Various studies of traditional Igbo society indicate a clearly expressed female principle in religion, politics, economics and the social sphere. Additionally there are several structures which make for female solidarity. Sylvia Leith Ross says about women's social status in Igbo society:

> ... among the women, there seems to be something—perhaps the bond of sex—that links them up over wide areas so that a woman's call to women would echo far beyond the boundaries of her own town. The fact that the men generally live in their own home town while their wives often come from other towns ... emphasizes the difference. The women are thus already members of two towns: their husbands' in which they live and their parents', which they visit. Their marketing takes them far afield, as do visits to their married daughters; but beyond these tangible factors there does seem to be an intangible communion, normally latent and without visible organization, but so profoundly felt that the slightest stir sets the whole body trembling.[5]

This Leith-Ross description is clearly borne out in the literature, especially in the works of Achebe, Elechi Amadi and Flora Nwapa.

Although a number of approaches to womanhood could be explored, my analyses center on motherhood because in many African societies *motherhood defines womanhood*. Motherhood, then, is crucial to woman's status in African society. To marry and mother a child [a son preferably], entitles a woman to more respect from her husband's kinsmen for she can now be addressed as "Mother of _____." Again, quoting Steady,

> The most important factor with regard to the woman in traditional society is her role as *mother* and the centrality of this role as a whole. Even in strictly patrilineal societies, women are important as wives and mothers since their reproductive capacity is crucial to the maintenance of the husband's lineage and it is because of women that men can have a patrilineage at all. The importance of motherhood and the evaluation of the childbearing capacity by African women is probably the most fundamental difference between the African woman and her Western counterpart in their common struggle to end discrimination against women.[6]

This preoccupation with motherhood is evident in almost all modern African fiction. At some point, almost every novel dramatizes a woman's struggle to conceive: her fear of being replaced, the consequent happiness at conception and delivery or agony at the denial of motherhood, various attempts to appease the Gods and hasten pregnancy, followed by the joys and/or pains of motherhood.

A survey of the literature written by men often reveals the mother character as the most truthfully realized character. All other women pale, in comparison, are pitied or are even treated contemptuously. Yet misconceptions about true motherhood are also evident and in fact there is often an idealization of motherhood and of suffering women who live solely for their children. This romanticizing of motherhood is furthered by its symbolic equation of mother with earth and Africa. While this is in some cases flattering and desirable, it masks the reality of motherhood. The Negritude poets, for example, luxuriated in metaphors of motherhood and land and Africa. Senghor, in his classic poem "Femme Noire" concretized this mystique of the transcendental mother. Andrea Benton Rushing sees African culture as containing several distinct images for women, including those related to motherhood, which differ from the European/American female images, but concludes, nevertheless, that almost all African poetry is written by men and that

> poems which distill the kaleidoscope of women's lives on the African continent and create images of black women with the vigor of those rooted in the religious and cultural matrix of precolonial days may not emerge until African women write the poetry . . .[7]

Preliminary surveys of African literature reveal that the novels of men, like the Negritude poetry, treat mothers more as symbols than as living, suffering individuals. This study will examine mothers and motherhood in the works of four writers: two male novelists (Achebe and Nzekwu) and two female novelists (Emecheta and Nwapa). Focusing mainly on major works, it will isolate individual author-specific portrayals and finally offer some comparisons and conclusions on the treatment of this theme.

In an important appraisal of Black American women's literature, as compared to Black men's literature, Paula Giddings says that the Black woman tended to look within while her male peers concentrated on the external forces that shaped their lives.[8] This question of differences in the literature of Black male and female writers is raised with fair frequency in the interviews by Claudia Tate, in *Black Women Writers at Work*.[9] The answer is still being sought and demands wide ranging analyses of many works.

My study does reveal some differences in the ways in which Igbo male and female writers perceive reality and supports the Giddings conclusion. The women writers deal with the conflicts of motherhood. Rather than presenting an idealized view of motherhood, they present both its joys and pains, the details of the woman's experiences of motherhood. The male writers present womanhood and motherhood but within the context of the larger societal problems. In all of the novels in this study, there is no single view of motherhood. Various types of mothers are projected. One point is clear, however, motherhood is crucial to the happiness of the woman and to her ability to control her life. From a Western perspective, this is seemingly a contradictory anti-feminist argument. But if we understand Steady's definition of African feminism and the centrality of children, it is not. Let us examine how motherhood is portrayed in the literature.

Chinua Achebe: "Mother is Supreme"

The most common name given to a child in Igbo society is Nneka— "Mother is Supreme" (p. 121). Why is this so? This is the rhetorical question which Uchendu, Okonkwo's kinsman, poses to him, and by extension to use the readers, in *Things Fall Apart* (1958).[10] Uchendu's response constitutes the novel's deliberation on the question of motherhood and femininity and nurturing as opposed to fatherhood, masculinity and aggression. This conflict becomes one of the novel's central concerns.

The question is particularly relevant to Okonkwo, who throughout his life had struggled not to be what his father was—a poor, effeminate man: a woman—in a society where masculinity is treasured. Okonkwo, a successful provider, leader of his clan, rules his compound with a heavy hand, beating wives, repressing all emotions except anger, refusing to show tenderness to his children. Because of his aggressive personality Okonkwo commits several crimes against the Earth Goddess including the accidental shooting of a man during a festival. Importantly, this accident is called a "female crime"—the equivalent of English manslaughter—as opposed to a "male crime", murder (an obvious comment on the male and female principle). It leads to Okonkwo's forced exile from his village and his having to seek refuge in his motherland. Okonkwo is depressed at this turn of events and at the fact that he has to live in Mbanta, although he is well entertained there. This is when he is chided by Uchendu, his uncle, who answers the question he had posed by saying,

> It's true that a child belongs to its father. But when a father beats his child, it seeks sympathy in its mother's hut. A man belongs to his fatherland when things are good and life is sweet. But when there is sorrow and bitterness he finds refuge in his motherland. Your mother is there to protect you. She is buried there. And that is why we say that mother is supreme (p. 122).

Further, he tells Okonkwo, "If you think you are the greatest sufferer in the world ask my daughter, Akueni, how many twins she has borne and thrown away" (p. 122). Again a deliberate distinction between male suffering and female suffering is made.

Okonkwo completes his seven-year exile and hastens to leave Mbanta. Upon return to Umuofia, he finds that the colonial government is in place, that people have lost their former dignity and have no solidarity. A series of events leads to his killing a messenger and his suicide at the novel's end.

If Okonkwo's rise and fall stands for the clan's and by extension African society's at that historical juncture, then Achebe is suggesting that for survival and transcendence and safe passage into the future one must learn to unite both male and female qualities, to fully respect both male and female and combine them into an ideal existence. If this is resisted then self-destruction follows. That this is an ideal is suggested in Ndulu and Ozoemena's (the old couple) togetherness in life and death.

> "It was always said that Ndulue and Ozeomena had one mind," said Obierika. "I remember when I was a young boy there was a song about them. He could not do anything without telling her." "I did not know that," said Okonkwo. "I thought he was a strong man in his youth." "He was indeed," said Ofoedu. (p. 62)

One must understand that Okonkwo had attained a position of leadership in the clan, but still failed to grasp the significance of uniting the male and female qualities. Okonkwo fails, additionally, because he ignores or cannot accept the wisdom of traditional respect for "Mother."

While the novel deals primarily with man's experience (and women are tangential) on the symbolic level, it clearly stresses the importance of female roles. Okonkwo's beating of his wives represents his heightened disregard for this female principle. It is well documented that in Igbo society, there is a definite female quality to religiosity. The most important Igbo deity is *Ala*, the Earth Goddess, who is characterized as a merciful mother who intercedes for her children, as the spirit of fertility who increases the productivity of the land. It is believed that women are closer to her than men and can obtain quicker hearing.[11]

In one of the most memorable scenes in African fiction, Achebe develops the significance of the priestess Chielo, whom we see, when possessed, transformed from an ordinary woman to a person of great strength and wisdom (pp. 90-7).

Achebe thus defines a separate world of women, which moves both within and beyond the purview of men. He conveys in Chielo a sense that the tragedy of Okonkwo expresses itself within the structural residues of a society which at one point had certain ideals of equality which exist now only in vestigial form.

Okonkwo's relationships with his sons and daughters also show his insensitivity. Okonkwo seeks to make his son a man, but Nwoye only puts on the veneer of manhood to please his father. Nwoye actually prefers his mother's stories to the masculine stories of wars and prowess (p. 42). The boy, who is described as having too much of his mother in him, begins to internalize those female values, and reflect on some of the excesses of his society and his own father's preoccupation with masculine achievements. In his search for an alternative, he becomes first in the family to join the Christian church.

Ironically, Okonkwo has better luck with his daughters, particularly Ezinma, although he constantly reminds her to "sit like a woman" (p. 40). Yet he repeats over and over again "she should have been a boy" (pp. 57, 58, 60, 156, 157). Again this points to Achebe's position that gender ought not to be a barrier to excellence or achievement. For Ezinma is bright and articulate, possessing all the credentials, except masculinity, for success and leadership. Another important motherhood-related structure is the mother-daughter relationship between Ekwefi and Ezinma. Ekwefi had lost many children soon after their births but, finally was able to keep Ezinma alive. Whereas Ezinma has a mother with whom she can develop closeness, Nwoye is unable to connect in the same way with his father.

Perhaps more important than the biological mother is the spiritual mother of Ezinma—Chielo. Symbolically Ezinma's journey with Chielo takes her out of Okonkwo's/society's defined role for her as a young woman and suggests larger possibilities for her life. The Chielo-Ezinma episode is one of those situations over which Okonkwo has no control (the other two are his expulsion from the clan and the colonial take-over). We see him here humbly and blindly following Chielo in the darkness. His machete, the symbol of male aggression, is of no use at all in this context.

The Chielo-Ezinma episode is an important sub-plot of the novel and actually reads like a suppressed larger story circumscribed by the exploration of Okonkwo's/man's struggle with and for his people.

In the troubled world of *Things Fall Apart*, motherhood and femininity are the unifying mitigating principles, the lessons for Okonkwo, the lessons for Africa and the world.

It is important to make a point about a second novel, *No Longer at Ease* (1960),[12] in which Achebe again deals with man's alienation and suffering but at intervals, juxtaposes that with the mother's suffering. Obi Okonkwo is Achebe's anti-hero. The women in his life are Clara, who gets pregnant with his baby but ends the pregnancy because of Obi's irresoluteness, and his mother who on the symbolic level of the book represents tradition or Africa. Again the abortion of the pregnancy comments on the abortion of the motherhood role as described above. In these two novels as well as in his subsequent two novels,[13] Achebe expresses, on literal and symbolic levels, the importance of women and motherhood. Yet his primary concern is woman's place within man's experience and man's lone struggle with larger social and political forces. While Achebe's works are obvious classics within the African literary tradition, a re-examination of his work from a feminist position reveals woman as peripheral to the larger exploration of man's experience.

Onuora Nzekwu—Motherhood as Control

Nzekwu's *Highlife for Lizards* (1965)[14] ends with a discussion of power
as it relates to men and women in Igbo society which in actuality is the
author's discourse on male/female relationships. The book deals with the
experiences of a woman, Agom, from her teenage marriage to about age
fifty. Agom has many experiences of womanhood. At first she is infertile
and as a result her husband takes a second wife without her consent. She
later becomes pregnant and successfully delivers three children. But much
more than that, she has success in trading, participates in political struggle,
takes titles and finally joins the ranks of the female elders.

Yet Agom, in her discourse in the epilogue seems to be commenting on
the folly of modern young women who use education for competing with
their husbands and claiming equality. The author has her saying,

> Instead of using her education to make herself more of an ideal wife,
> she becomes her husband's rival. She claims She is his equal (p. 191).

She continues to discuss the undesirable qualities in modern woman but her
conclusions are only a litany of stereotypes of male/female relationships.

> It is natural for man to be direct in his ways with women and she to be
> devious, him to be plain; she to be subtle; him to roam the earth as he
> pleases, she always to be home; him to be strong, she weak . . . these
> laws are not man made, and anyone who honestly believes they can be
> reversed is a freak. (pp. 191-2)

These comments seem strange coming from Agom and jar against her
reality. Agom had throughout her life struggled to attain a measure of
equality in her marriage, had taken titles, become a priestess, and even
joined the exclusive masquerade cult—the preserve of men—so that she
would be beyond the harrassment that they mete out to women in public.
Additionally she had achieved economic success and led a protest against
colonial intrusion. What is more disturbing is that the author has Agom
speaking this nonsense to a group of admiring women.

The facts of Agom's existence definitely conflict with her words in the
epilogue. It can be inferred that Agom, who had been childless in the first
years of her marriage and did not conceive until her husband had taken a
second wife, is suggesting that she is the perfect woman who has achieved
success *in all spheres*. Also, she may be mouthing certain words that would
impress men but ironically hinting at "female control" for she does in the
end smile and ask who wields the real power? The novel, at any rate, ends on
an ambivalent note. Additionally the (male) author, Nzekwu, is obviously
trying to redirect the reader from an otherwise logical conclusion for he has
in the rest of the narrative created a very positive female character. Another

point of consideration is that in Igbo society, as in many other African societies, women who have moved out of the vulnerable childbearing phase become technically "honorary men," and Agom could be playing out her new seniority role, as it relates to young women. Nzekwu, notwithstanding, communicates mixed messages on the status of women. But in the overall panorama of Agom's life, we see that having children, especially a son, marked a change in her fortunes and became an element of control.

It is instructive to make a passing comment about Nwadi, Agom's junior wife who is the stereotypical jealous wife (a character which reappears with amazing frequency in African literature), who attempts to conceive a son first, uses medicine from a traditional doctor on her husband and is eventually thrown out of the home. Nwadi's life is one of unhappiness, for she could not live with the competition among wives in her first husband's household and is thrown out of Udezue's compound in disgrace. Nwadi's demise is an interesting contrast to Agom's.

The fairytale ending of *Highlife for Lizards*, however, suggests a final peace and happiness for Agom, although Nzekwu implies that all women do not share this happiness. Whatever the ambiguities of this text, motherhood is clearly seen as crucial to that happiness and to the woman's ability to control her life.

In direct contrast to the glorified images of motherhood presented by their male counterparts, the Igbo women writers, considered here, challenge this fairytale ending of children, success and happiness. Both Emecheta and Nwapa categorically state that having children does not necessarily mean happiness or success. Instead, they present women who seek to define their lives over and beyond fecundity. In fact, one sees unhappiness, despair and death among mothers whose lives remain unfulfilled in other areas.

Flora Nwapa: The Male Woman or the Non-Mother

Flora Nwapa has written three novels, *Efuru* (1966)[15] and *Idu* (1970)[16] and *One is Enough* (1984)[17] which deal with motherhood. First of all, unlike Achebe and Nzekwu she often titles her works with the names of her heroines, indicating that she is telling strictly of the woman's experience. This is in striking contrast to the male writers who avoid names as titles altogether, even when telling essentially a woman's story as is the case of Nzekwu.

The first point to be made is that in *Efuru*, the author creates a world of women; men are shown to be intruders. Gossip, small talk, trading and selling, concern over each other's activities all have places in this women's world. In her first paragraph, Nwapa introduces her heroine simply as "the woman." It is only in subsequent paragraphs that she names Efuru.

Nwapa presents Efuru as a very assertive young woman who exercises her personal choice. She decides whom she wants to marry in defiance of the men of her family and goes to her husband without dowry . . . the first feminist statement of the book. Next she decides that she is not going to farm, contrary to her family's wishes, but will trade instead (p. 7). She refuses to stay in confinement the customary three months, but here we see she is made to submit to the cultural regulations regarding women. So she submits to the painful clitoredectomy (pp. 10-11) and is made, by her seniors, to kneel to her husband during the marriage ritual.

> Efuru was called. She was given the glass by her husband and when she was about to drink, the people shouted: "Kneel down, kneel down, *you are a woman*." Efuru quickly knelt down and drank . . .(p. 23) (Emphasis mine.)

This vacillation between independence and dependence, masculinity and feminity, characterizes Efuru's existence up until the end of the novel when she leaves her second husband. Much of her feeling of insecurity stems from her inability to conceive and be the "complete woman" her society respects. "I am still young, surely God cannot deny me the joy of motherhood," she often said to herself (p. 23). But childless "Efuru, was considered a man since she could not reproduce" (p. 23).

Efuru does eventually produce a daughter but this does not guarantee her happiness, for before the child is two, her husband leaves her for another woman. (We realize that his departure is not because of Efuru's personality but is the re-enactment of his father's desertion of his mother). Efuru's life at this point is so closely tied to her daughter's that she wails "What will I do if I lose her? If she dies, that will mean the end of me" (p. 79). The child dies but this is not the end of Efuru. She harnesses her grief and learns from the other women that woman's life is one of mastering suffering. Says one sympathizer,

> I conceived eight times. All died before they were six months old. The last one was a girl and when she did not die after six months, I killed a white fowl for my *chi*. I named her Ibiakwa—Have you come again? After a year and she did not die, I called her Nkem—My own. She was a beautiful girl . . .
>
> Then I returned from the market one day and saw that she was shivering with cold . . . In the night, she developed a convulsion and died . . .
>
> My only child died . . . The world was in darkness for me. I wept like a human being, I wept like an animal. I threatened to jump into the grave and be buried alive with my only child. but I am still alive today. I have not had another baby since then. Have a heart my daughter, you are still young. It is still morning for you . . .(pp.90-1)

Efuru recovers from her grief, makes her decision to return to her father's house. We are reminded over and over again that Efuru was a good woman. She helps the sick and acts independently until she is courted again. In her second marriage she has some happiness but the absence of children mars the relationship. Eventually the marriage ends as Efuru decides to return home again after her husband's accusations of adultery.

In the first portion of the novel a distinction is made between Efuru's handling of her husband's unfaithfulness and her mother-in-law's action in the same situation. Ossai is the long-suffering wife and mother who waits and who rears the same kind of son as her husband, both deserters of wife and mother. Ajanapu, her sister-in-law, tells her one day:

> You are the cause of your child's bad ways. You never scolded him because he was an only child. You delightfully spoilt him and failed to make him responsible . . . (p. 197)

Woman's responsibility for self is a central concern in *Efuru*. There is persistently the fear of being considered a 'male woman' (p. 129), but women seem to realize that men rarely have reins on their freedom and will oppress women if allowed. Ajanapu, for all her abrasiveness is a woman who controls her life and will not allow a younger woman to waste her life away. When Efuru is weakest, and being persecuted by her husband, Gilbert, and family, she calls on Ajanapu who comes with great haste (p. 275). Ajanapu lectures Gilbert on his betrayal of Efuru and he deals her a slap which makes her fall, but

> She got up quickly for she was a strong woman, got hold of a mortar pestle and broke it on Gilbert's head. Blood filled Gilbert's eyes (p. 276).

Before Efuru goes home to her father's compound she realizes that marriage was the beginning of her suffering (pp. 211-212), that you cannot buy happiness of children (p. 220), that living in a man's house means chores and subjugation to his whims. She wavers between helplessness and decisiveness.

In the end, Efuru finally achieves peace in her father's compound but it is a self-contained peace that is not controlled or directed by men.

> So here I am. I have ended where I began—in my father's house. The difference is that now *my father is dead.* (p. 280) (my emphasis)

There is a faint suggestion that she still considers this free and independent state to be misfortune for it suggests too much masculinity or control of one's life, a deviation from societal norms.

The novel does end on a positive note for we see Efuru realizing that her existence was not totally defined by motherhood. This confidence is given by the goddess of the lake to whom she becomes a priestess, and is the symbolic representation of the acceptance of self.[18]

> Efuru slept soundly that night. She dreamt of the woman of the lake, her beauty, her long hair and her riches. She had lived for ages at the bottom of the lake. She was as old as the lake itself. She was happy, she was wealthy. she was beautiful. She gave women beauty and wealth but she had no child. She had never experienced the joy of motherhood. Why then did the woman worship her? (p. 281)

The Woman of the Lake and Efuru's adherence to her reaffirm her belief in herself and her contributions to society and provide a societal alternative to motherhood for women "who are not so blest". Her novel *Idu* shows a woman fulfilled in a marital relationship at first without and later in spite of her children. Idu and her husband are so close that when he dies after a troubling illness, she decides that she is not going to be the wife of his brother according to tradition. Instead she wills herself to join her husband in death and does so leaving her children alive. *One is Enough* deals with themes similar to *Efuru*: the childless wife who is otherwise successful but rejected by her husband. Here, Amaka, after she has achieved her financial goals, conceives twin boys miraculously. In a sense then, the novel plays with the "immaculate conception" motif because the children's father is a man of God (a Catholic priest). Amaka disdains marriage now, hence the title, and is satisfied with her business success and her two sons. The ending of *Efuru* which deals with "the joy of motherhood" sets the theme for Emecheta's classic novel on motherhood which we will discuss next.

Buchi Emecheta: Mother as Slave

The message communicated in *Efuru* is echoed in Buchi Emecheta's *The Joys of Motherhood*.[19] The protagonist Nnu Ego, unlike Efuru had given all her life to producing and cultivating her children, had made no friends nor taken care of herself. She had followed all the traditional guidelines concerning motherhood and care of children but she realizes too late that she had all but wasted her life. As her children begin lives of their own, and she has, as yet, no grandchildren, she feels totally dislocated:

> I don't know how to be anything else but a mother. How will I talk to a woman with no children? Taking the children from me is like taking away the life I have always known, the life I am used to (p. 222).

The novel starts with Nnu Ego's agony at the loss of her four week old son. She is about to commit suicide because her life is already so tied to conception and motherhood. Emecheta ironically calls this chapter "The Mother" for we realize that Nnu Ego is no longer a mother. In fact we realize in Chapter Three that she was unable to conceive in her first marriage, that she was divorced for nursing her co-wife's child with her dry breasts. The symbolism of breasts for motherhood is evident here for when we first see Nnu Ego we feel the agony of her loss as we witness her breasts oozing milk which goes to waste for her child has died.

The story of a slave girl's death and rebirth informs the novel. Agunwa, the senior wife of Agbadi, Nnu Ego's father, had died. Her personal slave had been called to die with her but the young girl did not wish to die and begged for her life. This annoyed some of the men and she was dealt a blow and pushed into the grave. She still struggled to climb out of the hole but was given a final blow, and as she died she said to Agbadi, who had prevented any further mutilation of her:

> Thank you for this kindness, Nwokocha, the son of Agbadi. I shall come back to your household, but as a legitimate daughter. I shall come back (p. 23).

Ona, Nnu Ego's mother, had recently conceived and when the child Nnu Ego was born with a lump on her head, the *dibia* was consulted and he divined that:

> The child is the slave woman who died with your senior wife Agunwa. She promised to come back as a daughter. Now here she is. That is why this child has the fair skin of the water people and the painful lump on her head from the beating your men gave her before she fell into the grave (p. 27).

Emecheta therefore makes the slave's life and woman's life parallel and portrays Nnu Ego, the mother, as living the life of a slave, slave to her children, slave to tradition.

Ona, Nnu Ego's mother, is worthy of some discussion here. Ona provides another societal alternative to marriage but it is still male defined and therefore a limited alternative. Her father and her lover Agbadi strike a bargain over ownership of her unborn child based on its sex. Nnu Ego is female so she goes to her biological father Agbadi. Unfortunately the author lets Ona die during the birth of her second child and Agbadi ignores her dying wish that her daughter's life not be circumscribed by society's regulations on marriage and female roles. Ona would have been a dynamic character had she been developed by the author.

But the author's purpose is clearly to show the tragedy of woman's existence when it remains circumscribed by motherhood alone. The only reward for Nnu Ego is a good funeral and a shrine in her name. The latter is the only distinction between the slave woman and Nnu Ego.

Yet the lesson of her life and death remain misunderstood by the rest of her community:

> Stories afterwards, however, said that Nnu Ego was a wicked woman even in death because, however many people appealed to her to make women fertile, she never did. Poor Nnu Ego, even in death she had no peace. Still many agreed that she had given all to her children. The joy of being a mother was the joy of giving all to your children, they said. (p. 224)

For the reader, however, the irony of Nnu Ego's life and death is a forceful lesson in the pains of motherhood.

Emecheta has consistently dealt with those traditional attitudes to women, including those which the woman herself accepts, which tend to enslave her. For this reason, the slave woman is a fairly common Emecheta emblem. Motherhood, therefore, is just one of the routes to woman's potential enslavement. Her other novels, *The Bride Price* (1976) and *The Slave Girl* (1977)[20] play on this "slave to tradition" theme. Her two painful autobiographical novels *In The Ditch* (1972) and *Second Class Citizen* (1975)[21] deal with the personal race, class and sex oppression which came out of her experiences in Nigeria and London as girl-child and woman.

Conclusion

The novels in this study project no single view of motherhood. Various types of mothers are presented. Invariably the image of motherhood fits into the writer's larger political view and his/her purpose for writing. So for Achebe, perhaps the best representative of the African male writer, it is man's experience, colonial domination and the struggles of Afreican man, personal and political, within the traditional and contemporary situation. Motherhood is then a symbolic representation of tradition and Africa, within a larger frame.

In Nzekwu's work, largely a male interpretation of a woman's experience, we have a writer's commitment to the revelation of specific social and cultural information and the woman's place and possibilities within Igbo society. But we have an idealization of motherhood, the inability of the male writer to present the details of woman's experience. The writer's truthfulness gives us a positive female image in Agom but several stereotypical presentations of other women. His decision to include an epilogue which comments on male-female relationships and Agom's successes collides violently with the reality of Agom's life and her transcendence.

African women writers provide the other half of African people's story. They present reality from the woman's point of view and create distinct female worlds. They present the "great unwritten" stories of African literature. Importantly motherhood is not idealized but many of its pains detailed. Children are not the final and only happiness for their mothers but are elements in the acquisition of success in life as Nwapa demonstrates in all her works. But all women and men do not have children and they may not bring the happiness or success that is supposedly assured by their presence in the society. Alternative routes to success may be chosen by women. Indeed, African women have never been limited totally to childbearing but have consistently attained excellence in other spheres. This is why Nnu Ego's life is such a tragedy.

In the works of Nwapa, there is the conscious movement of women against restrictions of sex. In Emecheta, the true African feminist is revealed in the consciousness of political oppression of colonialism, Western domination and societal domination of a sexist nature. Women seek to liberate themselves from these various types of oppression and to exercise individual choice and are as Lloyd Brown suggests engaged in,

> striving to achieve a fulfilling sense of themselves, as distinctice human personalities while remaining loyal to all the encompassing community around them.[22]

African women writers in detailing the submerged realities of African women's lives are participating in the struggle to achieve the correct balance.

NOTES

1. Filomina Chioma Steady, *The Black Woman Crossculturally*, (Cambridge, Mass.: Schenkman, 1981), pp. 7-36.
2. Ibid., p. 35.
3. Maryse Condé, "Three Female Writers in Modern Africa: Flora Nwapa, Ama Ata Aidoo and Grace Ogot," *Presence Africaine* 82(2nd quarter, 1972), p. 132.
4. Caroline Ifeka-Moller, "Female Militancy and Colonial Revolt", in *Perceiving Women* ed. by Shirley Ardener (New York: John Wiley and Sons, Ltd., 1975), p. 127.
5. Sylvia Leith-Ross, *African Women* (New York: Praeger, 1965), pp. 21-22.
6. Steady, p. 29.
7. Andrea Benton Rushing, "Images of Black Women in Modern African Poetry: An Overview" in *Sturdy Black Bridges*, ed. by Bell, et al (New York: Anchor Press, 1979), p. 24.
8. Paula Giddings, "A Special Vision, A Common Goal," *Encore* (June 23, 1975), pp. 44, 46, 48.
9. Claudia Tate, *Black Women Writers at Work*, (New York: Continuum, 1983).
10. Chinua Achebe, *Things Fall Apart*, (London: Heinemann [African Writers Series], 1958).
11. Victor Uchendu, *The Igbo-Speaking People of South East Nigeria* (New York: Holt, Rinehart and Winston, 1965), p. 87.

12. Chinua Achebe, *No Longer at Ease*, (London, Heinemann [African Writer Series], 1960). Philip Rogers, "Achebe's 'Heart of Whiteness,'" *Research in African Literatures* 14:2 (Summer, 1983),pp. 165-183, explores Obi's growing alienation from his people and includes a discussion of the mother's place within Obi's distancing of himself from tradition.

13. Chinua Achebe, *Arrow of God* (London: Heinemann, 1960), AWS 16 and *A Man of the People* (London: Heinemann, 1970), AWS 31. Another writer, Elechi Amadi, is omitted from this study but his work is amply covered in this edition.

14. Onuora Nzekwu, *Highlife for Lizards*, (London: Hutchinson & Co., Ltd., 1965).

15. Flora Nwapa, *Efuru*, (London: Heinemann, 1966), AWS 26.

16. Flora Nwapa, *Idu*, (London: Heinemann, 1970), AWS 86.

17. Flora Nwapa, *One is Enough*, (Enugu, Nigeria: Tana Press, 1984).

18. See Lloyd Brown's incisive discussion of this point and several other important ones in his *Women Writers in Black Africa* (Westport, Conn.: Greenwood Press, 1981).

19. Buchi Emecheta, *The Joys of Motherhood*, (New York: George Braziller, 1979).

20. Buchi Emecheta, *The Bride Price* (New York, George Braziller, 1976); *The Slave Girl* (New York, George Braziller, 1977).

21. Buchi Emecheta, *In the Ditch* (London: Allison and Bushy, 1972); *Second Class Citizen* (New York: George Braziller, 1975).

22. Brown, pp. 182-3.

The Grandmother in African and African-American Literature: A Survivor of the African Extended Family

Mildred A. Hill-Lubin

The Black family in America has been the subject of considerable discussion. Earlier sociologists and theorists such as E. Franklin Frazier and Daniel Moynihan followed the traditional line of scholarship and argued that the distinguishing features represent weaknesses.[1] A new group of scholars led by Andrew Billingsley, Robert Hill, Demitri Shimkin, and Herbert Gutman, point out that many of these irregular features in the Black family may be termed strengths.[2] Furthermore, they assert that despite the upheaval and damage created as a result of slavery, Blacks in America have preserved many of the qualities associated with a strong family and community life which characterized the existence of their forebears in traditional Africa. One such strength has been the Black grandmother, who has been a significant force in the stability and the continuity of the Black family and the community. Her function, role, and importance can be traced to the revered status, position, and responsibilities which elders hold in West African society. The Black grandmother in America, then, represents the most tenacious survival of the African extended family.

257

In African-American literature, she re-appears as a central character in numerous novels, autobiographies, short stories, plays and poems; but unfortunately, as in real life, she has not received the scholarly and critical attention that she deserves. In like manner, though the grandmother has been important in most African societies,[3] she has not found a prominent place in the creative works of the major African writers. Surely, one reason for this omission is that the field has been dominated by male authors and their leading characters have been men. The grandmother does, however, occupy a noteworthy position in the imaginative works of some Ghanaian and South African writers. With more female voices entering the arena and more males willing to acknowledge and remember the contributions and the fundamental role women have played in Black societies and in history, I anticipate more images of the grandmother to be revealed.[4] Certainly, as teachers and critics become more aware of the need to clarify and define issues and to establish the fact that the hero need not always be a male, our critical and scholarly activities will inevitably lead us to this courageous, heroic, and giving figure.

Using examples from both African literature in English and African-American literature of the United States, this paper will explore the image of the Black grandmother. Through this comparative study, we shall be able to observe that, whether in Africa or in America, in traditional or colonial society, during and after slavery, post independence, she has been a pivotal figure in Black life and literature.

While the literature does not provide us with the grandmother of traditional Africa, we are able to reconstruct her image. With the assistance of materials from ethnographers, social historians, anthropologists, and folklorists and by looking at the Black grandmother as she has been depicted in other periods, we observe that both the African and the Black American grandmother stem from a common cultural background. As women who possess a common African heritage and who have participated in kindred subjugating experiences, we note that they, in turn, have responded in parallel fashion when confronted with foreign situations. To illustrate, this discussion will focus on four works, two by African-American authors and two by Africans. For the Black experience in the United States, we refer to the autobiographies of Frederick Douglass, *My Bondage and My Freedom* and Maya Angelou's *I Know Why the Caged Bird Sings*. For the African analogies, we turn to the excellent book of short stories by the Ghanaian author, Ama Ata Aidoo and the heart-warming autobiography, *Down Second Avenue* by the South African, Ezekiel Mphahlele. In these works, the grandmother functions in three major capacities: one, as the preserver of the African extended family; second, as the repository and distributor of family history, wisdom, and Black lore; and third, as the retainer and communicator of values and ideals which support and enhance her personhood, her family, and her community.

Of the many patterns undergirding the traditional African family and its American extension, one was the importance of the grandparents. In the motherland grandparents were honored because it was believed that they were the closest to the ancestors, and the ancestors were important because they could assume revered status. It was from the grandparents that children learned their family history, family wisdom, community lore, and traditional values. Among certain groups, the grandparents named their newborn grandchildren. With others, such as the Ashanti, grandmothers, both maternal and paternal, tremendously influenced the growth and development of their offspring. When Blacks were brought to the United States, they brought with them this ancient and honorable tradition of family. While slavery caused tremendous disruptions in these patterns of family life, it did not eliminate all of them. In some instances, it inadvertently reinforced many of these patterns, because it prevented the complete assimilation of Blacks into the new world cultures, and it also created situations which fostered many of the traditional customs and beliefs of Africa.

One of the earliest examples in literature of a household where the grandmother is a major force in the preservation of the family is in the narrative account *My Bondage and My Freedom* by Frederick Douglass. Here the author credits his grandmother with providing him with a positive self- concept and for creating a family for him. As a slave and the child of his master, Douglass was deprived of a normal family life. At an early age, he was separated from his mother, but he writes, "Living here, with my dear old grandmother and grandfather, it was a long time before I knew myself to be a slave."[5] These grandparents not only provided a home for Douglass, but for the children of all of their five daughters." The mothers had been sent elsewhere to work. While the author acknowledges that both of his grandparents shared in this endeavor, he relates most vividly throughout the autobiography that his grandmother was a central influence in his growth and development. As we will see later, he was most proud of her independence, resourcefulness, and skills.

In the literature which mirrors every period of Black life in the United States, we find examples of the grandmother who has assumed the role of heading an extended family. Most often her household includes some of her unmarried children, a married child and spouse, grandchildren and frequently non-related members whom she has taken in. In many of the works, especially those set in the early or middle twentieth century, the grandmother is a widow. Although the grandfather is dead, his presence is still a part of the family. He is kept alive through the stories of the grandmother, who usually describes him as having been a good man, a rigid disciplinarian who worked hard, loved his family and struggled to provide a decent home and livelihood for his family. Now that he is no longer alive, the grandmother is committed to keeping the home together and to making

sure members will survive. Realizing that most often her financial resources
are too meager to give extra money to her children and grandchildren, she
permits them to return to the family dwelling where they all live together and
pool their resources. In this manner, they are assured of the necessities of
life or if not, they are able to support each other in their suffering and hard
times. Langston Hughes' single novel, *Not Without Laughter* and Lorraine
Hansberry's play, *A Raisin in the Sun* serve as two examples with such a
figure and family. Maya Angelou's *I Know Why the Caged Bird Sings*
offers a marvelous illustration; for in this magnificent autobiography, we
have two grandmothers, one living in rural Arkansas and the other in urban
St. Louis. In both instances, we have strong, independent, skillful women
who are able to manage their families and to insure their survival in a
segregated and hostile society. Both grandmothers take their grandchildren
into their homes. In reflecting on her and her brother's return to her
grandmother in Arkansas, Ms. Angelou writes: "Years later I discovered
that the United States had been crossed thousands of times by frightened
Black children traveling alone to their newly affluent parents in Northern
cities or back to grandmothers in Southern towns when the urban North
reneged on its economic promises."[6] As in this work, many Black children
were sent or taken to their grandmothers while their parents remained in the
North to work and to improve their situation. In many such homes, the
grandmother fulfilled the role of the parents for a limited time and remained
a major factor in the growing up process of the children. In other cases, the
grandchildren were given to the grandmother when they were babies, and
the older woman reared them to adulthood. Sometimes the mother lives in
the home but works on a job that takes her away from the home. There are
other pieces which reveal that during the summer, grandmothers received
their grandchildren to help out the family so that the parents would not have
to worry about child care or bear this expense while the children were out of
school. By having them in the summer, it also meant that parents would not
have to be concerned about their children's safety and well-being on the city
streets. In works which describe urban life as in Langston Hughes and Roy
De Carava's *The Sweet Flypaper of Life*, many of these grandmothers take
their grandchildren in because they believe they will be able to save them
from the streets. In all cases, the primary concern of these grandmothers as
heads of their extended families has been to preserve their families at all
costs.

Turning to African literature, we find literary models in parallel
situations. Ama Ata Aidoo's *No Sweetness Here* contains short stories set
in the period after independence. As in the Black American works, we
witness a similar kind of uprootedness and devastation in the African family
as a result of colonization. The roles of the male have become confused. In
the pre-colonial family, women were most often associated with the
preparation of food; but in colonial Africa, many Black males were trained

to cook for their masters. To accept this change in family roles, it was agreed that African men could cook European foods, but African women would still be in charge of the African "chop" foods. With independence, problems erupted over this issue. "For Whom Things Did Not Change," one of the short stories in this volume details the trouble. The white master is replaced by a Black as "Big Man." He desires African foods, but the African cook does not know how to handle the situation when he is asked by his new master to prepare the indigenous dishes.[7] Other stories demonstrate the devastating impact of colonialism on the African families. They explore situations where the males had to leave their families to find work or as one of the characters reveals, be involved in "other people's wars." Consequently, women and specifically grandmothers, are forced to assume the role of heads of the extended family. "Certain Winds from the South" provides an example of a grandmother who is determined to preserve her family. This tale, as many of Aidoo's works, projects a sense of continuity and a feeling of repetitiveness; for it describes two generations, in which the life of the younger family appears to be a repeat of the experiences of the older family. Upon learning that her son-in-law is leaving on the night of her grandson's birth to go South to find work, the grandmother M'ma Asana recalls her own life. She relates that a few days after her daughter was born, her husband too had come to tell her that he was going South to join the army to help "the Anglis-people" fight their war against the Germans. Although the husband had promised that he would return and take her South with him, he never did. As we eavesdrop on the grandmother's revelation to her daughter, both about her son-in-law's plans to leave and her husband's going, we recognize that the grandmother is hurt and feels unlucky; nevertheless, we are impressed with her strength and determination. As she describes how she managed to survive and provide for her daughter, we know that she will keep her larger family going. The story ends on a positive, determined note: "I am going to market now. . .Today even if it takes all the money, I hope to get us some smoked fish, the biggest I can find, to make us a real sauce. . ." (p. 67).

M'ma Asana is not the only grandmother in this collection who is concerned with the well-being and care of her grandchild and with the perpetuation and survival of her family. In the story "The Message," we have a grandmother, Esi Amfoa, who has already buried all of her children, including her son who went "to sodja in the great war overseas." She has recently been informed that "her only pot," the one daughter of her son has been "opened up" in order to have her baby removed. Having never heard of a caesarean section, the grandmother is convinced that the big doctors up at Cape Coast have killed her granddaughter and will now use the body for instruction. We follow her as she boards the bus, anxious and heavy with sorrow, because she believes she has lost all. We also enjoy the communal spirit, the rivalry and jostling she takes on her trip. Finally, she arrives at the hospital and we are told, "The old woman somersaulted into the room and lay groaning, not screaming by the bed. For was not her last pot broken?" (p. 55). But to her surprise, she hears the voice of young, Esi Amfoa, her name-sake. She looks up to discover that her "only pot" had refused to break. Her family remains alive.

Ezekiel Mphahlele's classic, *Down Second Avenue*, as Maya Angelou's *I Know Why the Caged Bird Sings*, portrays a Black youth growing up in a segregated society. This autobiography offers a picture of life in apartheid South Africa while Angelou describes life in the American South. Both works show grandmothers who serve as heads of their extended families and in both books, the grandchildren live with their paternal and maternal grandmothers. But, in each case, one grandmother plays a much more significant role in the life and development of the narrator. Similar to Angelou's work, *Down Second Avenue*, opens with the grandchildren's being sent from the city to the country to stay with the paternal grandmother. The young Eseki recounts that his Granny of Maupaneng was not the loving, kind person as his maternal grandmother, the one he later moves in with on Second Avenue. The rural grandmother is portrayed as "big as fate, as forbidding as a mountain, stern as a mimosa tree."[8] While she is not the warm grandmother, she does take her young grandchildren into her home to help ease the burden of the troubled younger family. In addition, the Granny of the country and the mountain is described as functioning like many Black American grandmothers. She has taken other relatives and non-relatives into her home. Besides the grandchildren, an uncle and a young woman named Sarah reside in the home. Sarah has been adopted by the older woman following the death of her mother in childbirth. Thus, this South African grandmother is fulfilling another one of the functions of the traditional African extended family, that of taking care of all the kin, including, at times, members of the larger community.

In Mphahlele's autobiography, we also find evidence of the family under severe stress. The dominance of the Black male no longer exists.Most of the men have already left the village and only the middle-aged and old women, children, and old men remain. As the author writes "The land was not giving out much. The Black man could work only the strip given him by the chief. The chief had no more to give out" (p. 12). The old man complained that most of their land had been taken away by the white man.

Eseki stayed in this dreary village with the stern grandmother for over seven years. When twelve however, he and his sister and brother rejoin their parents in the city of Pretoria. But it is not long, before, in an agonizing and brutal scene, we experience the break-up of the marriage of his father and mother. Eseki and his siblings are then transferred to the home of his maternal grandmother and Aunt Dora, two women who influence his life tremendously. While his mother does not live in the home, she remains linked to the family as she works in the suburb as a domestic. She contributes to its upkeep and support. The larger household on Second Avenue, headed by the grandmother includes Aunt Dora, Aunt Dora's husband, their three children, three uncles, and four other tenants who have leased rooms from the older woman, Eseki and his sister and brother. Although the grandfather is dead, his presence still prevails. The narrator states that he never knew this grandfather, but everyone talked endearingly of him and that he must have exercised rigid discipline in his house because grandmother liked to quote some of his maxims. The grandfather is described as having been a "self-taught shoe repairer." We see that before his death he had tried to provide both a physical and spiritual foundation for his family. Now that he is gone, it is left to the grandmother to keep the family together and progressing, in spite of all the obstacles.

Serving, in E. Franklin Frazier's terms, as "the guardian of the generations," these women are the acknowledged storytellers who pass on the family history and who know who is kin to whom. Characteristic of their African ancestors, they normally possess information on childbirth and lore on medicines and herbs for healing and curing various illnesses. In America, the white and the Black communities depended upon them to keep everyone healthy. Using what can only be described as their "female" talents—good cooking skills; keen insights into human relations; creative, spiritual, and artistic capabilities; proficiency in home and people management—many of these women developed into astute businesswomen. In this way, they were able to improve the lot of their families. They then transmitted this information, lore, and skill to their children and grandchildren, just as, in many cases, it had been passed on to them earlier.

Frederick Douglass writes that his grandmother was held in high esteem, far higher than was the lot of most colored persons in the region. He describes her as being a good nurse and "a capital hand at making nets used for catching shad and herring" and was withal somewhat famous as a fisherwoman. (pp. 35-36) The grandmothers in Angelou's autobiography also demonstrate business acumen. Grandmother Henderson of Stamps, Arkansas runs the family grocery store and manages the rental properties of the family that many of the poor whites of the community lived on. Speaking of her success as a businesswoman, the author writes: "Her crisp meat pies and cool lemonade, when joined to her miraculous ability to be in two places at the same time assured her business success" (p. 7). The Wm. Johnson General Merchandise Store began as a mobile lunch counter with the grandmother selling lunches to the workers at the lumberyard and cotton gin. Its growth to a stand and then to the store in the heart of the Black community, permitting it to become the lay center of activities in the town, is testimony of the grandmother's knowledge and insights into business matters. Grandmother Baxter in the city was no less skillful. She had been able to gain power and pull with all of the powerful elements in the city of St. Louis. People came to her to ask favors and in return she had her own needs fulfilled. While such roles certainly added to the other tasks these women already performed, they also earned many advantages and the grandchildren almost always benefitted from the goodwill and respect these grandmothers garnered from the larger community.

In the works of the African writers, the older women are no less resourceful, talented, wise, and knowledgeable. They too are eager to share their information and history with their children and grandchildren. Aidoo, in *No Sweetness Here* provides us with the character of Auntie Araba in the short story "Something to Talk About on the Way to the Funeral." The story points out that this African grandmother has been such a force in her community that her life story is now being narrated to the readers by two women who have come to pay their respects to her at her death. They recount Auntie Araba had come from one of those families which always have some members abroad, suggesting here again that the African family is no longer that tight knit community of people all in one village; yet it still functions as a large extended family. The story is told that as a young woman, Araba had been sent to these family members in the city to learn a skill. It was here that she had learned to be a baker, but she also had run into trouble. She became pregnant; but as the narrator informs us, her life was not ruined. For when she returned home to her mother, she was graciously received by her family. It was after her son's birth, however, that Auntie Araba grew to be an expert with the dough. Possessing similar business sense as Angelou's Grandmother Henderson, Auntie Araba soon discovered that her fancy city pastries were not profitable in the small village. Therefore, she turned to baking ordinary bread and achieved tremendous success.

As we pointed out earlier, one advantage in reading the works of Aidoo and especially the stories in *No Sweetness Here* is that the writer demonstrates "the repetition of old patterns" which occur in the lives of most Black people. She accomplishes this task by usually presenting at least two generations in her stories in order to compare and contrast the lives of her characters. Consequently, we are able to see immediately the impact, contributions, and influence of the grandmother. In the story, "Someting to Talk About on the Way to the Funeral," we hear that before too long Auntie Araba has become a grandmother. Significantly, it is her son who impregnates the young woman, Mansa. Unlike Auntie Araba's family, Mansa's family, is not as supportive. Her father wants nothing to do with her. it is Auntie Araba who takes the young woman in. The storyteller relates, "People did not even know how to describe the relationship between the two. Some people said they were like mother and daughter. Others that they were like sisters" (p. 149). Finally, the baby comes. Mansa and her son continue to live with Auntie Araba because her father is not interested in sending her back to school. In addition, it has been thought, that Ato, Auntie Araba's son, would finish his education, return and marry the young woman. But as his father before him, Ato could not marry Mansa because he had impregnated another young woman from a more prestigious family. Although disappointed, Mansa has begun to grow strong like Auntie Araba. In addition, she has learned to be an excellent baker, following the instructions of the older woman. Therefore, when Ato does not marry her, she moves to the city to stay with friends whom Auntie Araba has contacted and asked to take her in. Mansa is now able to find a job where as the narrator tells us; "They bake hundreds of loaves of bread an hour with machines" (p. 154). Mansa is referred to as a "good woman," like Auntie herself. "She has all of her character." The two women narrators conclude that she will get along fine. "A good person does not rot" (p. 154). The grandson is left with the maternal grandmother and as we have seen earlier, the story will probably be repeated.

In *Down Second Avenue* the grandmother is equally hard working and resourceful. She too serves as the storyteller who relates to her grandson the history of the immediate family and the axioms of the grandfather. Eseki recounts that his grandmother never tired of telling him about Paul Kruger's day; of the hard times under Boer rule; of the way they buried Africans alive who were suspected of fighting or spying for the British; of how Boer soldiers cut off Black women's breast; how she was great at answering all the catechism questions, and of how his grandfather Titus took his family from place to place looking for a better life and who didn't think Meneer Paul was better than he. This grandmother, like Frederick Douglass' grandmother, is intent on giving her children and grandchildren a sense of history, a feeling of family, that vital concept of self-worth, even if the society around them is intent on denying them their humanity. This grandmother is the link that unites the family to its past, but also she is its source of hope. As with the other grandmothers, this South African woman expands her resources and limitations. She takes the little house and stand that the grandfather had left and divides it up in such a way that her extended family has a home, and the family is also able to receive supplementary monies by leasing rooms to tenants. Like many of the grandmothers in the Black American stories, she washes clothes for the whites of the area, but she too increases her opportunities by creating another job. The only business that most people, and especially the women, were able to carve out for themselves is that of selling beer, which according to the South African officials was illegal. Yet, these women, Grandmother and Aunt Dora were intent on continuing their business. And in spite of police raids and the Blacks who served as the white officials' eyes, these women persevered. Using this income, grandmother sent most of her children to boarding school or elsewhere to be educated or to learn a trade.

Describing these grandmothers as women who were resourceful and full of wisdom because they were intent on insuring that their children would have a better life moves us to the final function that most of these grandmothers performed. They did not only will their children practical and business knowledge and encourage them to get an education. Most of these women were determined to endow their families with values and ideals which would enhance their lives and provide them with the essentials for survival, growth, and development. These sterling figures transmitted these gifts through both their words and their deeds. They themselves possessed strengths that often made them appear indomitable.

Most of them benefitted from a deep, abiding, and living religious faith. Grandmama Henderson in *I Know Why the Caged Bird Sings* is depicted as a devoutly religious woman who gathered her family in prayer each morning at 4:00 A.M. to begin the day. The autobiography opens with the scene of Marguerite, the granddaughter, in the Colored Methodist Episcopal Church where her grandmother has brought her in order to recite her Easter speech. While this occasion proves frightening and embarrassing for the painfully shy, young girl, it is significant that the work begins at the church; for it is at this institution that the children are introduced to the strengths of the community, but they also become equipped with the rituals, songs, and words which will later serve them as survival tools.

Angelou writes, "Momma," the name the children had given to their Grandmother shortly after their arrival, "intended to teach Bailey and me to use the paths in life that she and her generation and all the Negroes gone before had found and found to be safe ones" (p. 46). In *Down Second Avenue*, Ezekiel Mphahlele describes his pious grandmother as one who brought her family together at night in prayer and would awaken them each morning with prayer to begin the day. In both of the autobiographies, Ezekiel and Marguerite, as youths watching their grandmothers and being socialized by them, are not as convinced as their grandmothers that religion is a viable force for Blacks in a society where the concepts of Christianity are a mockery. But neither of the older women is disturbed too much by her grandchildren's doubts and lack of faith. They remain committed and firm.

These older women, though advanced in age, have accepted the younger children back into their homes, and they remain active participants in the daily survival and management of the family. Although the grandmothers are the storytellers and they love their grandchildren, they seldom spoil them; nor do they tell them stories merely to entertain. Their stories are designed to teach them the paths to survival and progress. While in these two works, the young narrators never confront their elders, in other works we have slight confrontations; but the older women are seldom upset by the criticism of their grandchildren. Accustomed to the struggles and great vicissitudes of life, they are not easily subdued by the smaller scrimmages. Most often, these women emerge victorious and with dignity. Whether their grandchildren wish to learn of their strength, great convictions, or not, they usually are always left impressed. Maya Angelou describes such an incident. On one occasion a group of the poor white girls of the town had come to the store to try to humiliate her grandmother. They did everything possible. One of the young girls even stood on her hands and revealed that she had on no underwear. As a young Black girl, the author relates that she was so angry as her grandmother stood, prayed, and sang through it all. But in closing the episode, Angelou writes of this magnificent woman:

> She stood another whole song through and then opened the screen door to look down on me crying in rage. She looked until I looked up. Her face was a brown moon that shone on me. She was beautiful. Something had happened out there which I couldn't completely understand but I could see that she was happy (p. 32).

The author states that then her grandmother bent down and touched her as the mothers of the church lay hands on the sick and afflicted, and she quieted. Already, the young girl is beginning to recognize the power, strength, and spirit of her grandmother and to appreciate her life and teachings.

Ama Ata Aidoo gives us an example from African literature where the older woman emerges as the strong, victorious, person in a struggle with the young. In the short story, "The Message," we have the young nurse's attempt to make the older woman appear ignorant, country, and small. When the old woman comes, anxious to find "her only pot", her granddaughter who has had the operation, the nurses make fun of her. At the end, the "Draba" (driver) calls the young nurse, Jessy Treeson, "a cassava stick" and thinks about kicking her; but rationalizes that he may break his toe, if he kicked her buttocks (p. 55). It is the grandmother who is triumphant and "big" in the story rather than the young nurse who would like to think her training has made her superior to the old woman.

Throughout the literature, we have evidence of the families growing together. Although in many situations the grandchildren may not always agree with their elders, they recognize that these women have provided them with some valuable gifts. In other works, especially in the poetry of the young Black American writers of the sixties, we have the grandmothers trying to understand their grandchildren better. For example, Haki Madhubuti (Don L. Lee) has a poem entitled "Bigmomma" which portrays the relationship of the grandson with the grandmother. In the poem, the young man has come to his grandmother's home for his "weekly visit and talking to." She is aware that her grandson has changed and is now involved in the "blackness" movement and that he is now planning to be a writer. All of these changes are confusing to the grandmother, but as the poet states, she is in a "seriously funny mood." She is also eager to relate to her grandson. Therefore she weaves her conversation around his new personality "u gonta be a writer, hunh/when u gon write me some writen."[9] Later, she exclaims "now *luther*, I knows you done changed a lots but if/you think

back, we never did eat too much pork around here anyways . . . " After the
two share a smile together, the young revolutionary leaves his grandmother's modest kitchen where the *"chicago tribune"* serves as the table
cloth. But, the poet states, as the young man moves back to the streets, he
reflects on Big Momma's words. "At sixty-eight/she moves freely, is often
right. . ." (p. 32). In both sides there has been recognition and growth. The
family remains harmonious.

Linda Brown Bragg in her poem "About Beauty, Blackness, and Poetry,"
confirms that these women, through the years have been determined to
teach us that we must be beautiful, Black, and revolutionary.[10] Alice
Walker in her essay, "In Search of our Mothers' Gardens," details how
many of these women were thwarted in their efforts to be creative artists and
to write about beauty.[11] Nevertheless, they have persisted in showing
beauty. Ezekiel Mphahlele tells how valiantly his grandmother tried to
grow flowers, but the best the family was ever able to do was "set up a grape-
vine creeper which made pleasant shade for the family to do washing" (p.
25). Just as their talents and most often the flowers they planted were stifled
and could not grow, the families of these women occasionally suffered
setbacks. But these indomitable spirits struggled and were willing to make
all kinds of sacrifices to preserve and perpetuate their families. Thus, they
pass on an ancestral heritage which urges us all to be superior.

Fortunately, many of our writers have depicted these caring and resilient
grandmothers, but unfortunately the depictions have almost been ignored.
There are several reasons for this neglect; but the strongest one appears to
be that, as critics and researchers, we have lingered too long under the
influence of majority scholarship which has tended to recognize the heroes
but ignore the "sheroes," to emphasize the weaknesses in Black life rather
than its strengths, its sufferings rather than its triumphs, the destruction of
the African family rather than its survival, growth, and development. Too
often, we have overlooked female characters, perhaps in an effort to counter
the accusations that to describe strong women would help to support the
matriarchal theory which says that Black females castrate their men or the
notion that Black males are dysfunctionally weak. But we, now, as critics,
are being challenged to overcome such fears as many of our writers have
done. Certainly, the African family has suffered tremendously under the
burden of slavery and colonialism but it has also persevered. One of the
major strengths in its survival has been the grandmother, and she deserves
more of our attention and recognition. May I hasten to add that, as in real
life, all Black grandmothers in literature have not been the loving, strong,
devoted, selfless individuals. Maya Angelou, in her realistic depictions
does not totally romanticize nor idealize her grandmother figures, nor does
Ezekiel Mphahlele. Honest in her depiction, Ama Ata Aidoo in the title
story of her volume, "No Sweetness Here," portrays a grandmother who is
a vindictive and mean woman, determined to hurt her daughter-in-law (p.

84). Nevertheless, we need to look more keenly at all of these characters in fiction and above all begin to realize that these women represent heroic figures drawn from real life. By studying the works and concentrating on these female images, we can come to appreciate, affirm, celebrate as well as possibly emulate and be inspired by their many achievements and contributions.

NOTES

1. For more information on the Black family in the United States as a "destroyed" and pathological specimen of the white family, see E. Franklin Frazier's, *The Negro Family in the United States*, Chicago: The University of Chicago Press, 1939, reprinted 1968; and the Moynihan Report, offically entitled *The Negro Family: The Case for National Action*. U.S. Department of Labor, March, 1965, and reprinted in Lee Rainwater and William L. Yancy, eds., *The Moynihan Report and the Politics of the Controversy*, Cambridge, Mass. MIT Press, 1967.

2. For discussions on the Black Family in America as a continuant of the African extended family with many strengths, see Andrew Billingsley, *Black Families in White America*. Englewood Cliffs, N.J. Prentice Hall Inc. 1968; Robert Hill, *The Strength of Black Families*, New York: Emerson Hall publishers, Inc., 1972, Demitri D. Shimkin, Edithe M. Shimkin, Dennis A. Frate, editors. *The Extended Family in Black Societies.* The Hague, Paris: Mouton Publishers, 1978, and Herbert G. Gutman, *The Black Family in Slavery and Freedom, 1750-1925*, New York: Pantheon Books, 1976.

3. See the role of the grandmother in the following articles: "Marguerite Dupire, "The Position of Women in a Pastoral Society (The Fulani WoDaaBe Nomads of the Niger," in *Women of Tropical Africa*, edited by Denise Paulme, trans. by H. M. Wright (Berkeley University of California Press, 1963) 73-74; Ethel M. Albert, "Women of Burundi: A Study of Social Values," in *Women of Tropical Africa*, pp. 209-210; Elizabeth Fisher Brown, "Hehe Grandmothers"; *Journal of Royal Anthropology Institute*. XV, (1935) 83-96 quoted from "Introduction" *African Systems of Kinship and Marriage*, edited by A. R. Radcliffe-Brown and Daryl Ford (London: Oxford University Press, 1950) p. 26, 28; Hilda Kuper, "Kinship Among the Swazi," in *African Systems of Kinship and Marriage*, pp. 104-106; Meyer Fortes, "Kinship and Marriage Among the Ashanti" in *African System. . .*, pp. 263 and 276, Melville J. Herskovits. *Dahomey: An Ancient West African Kingdom* (Evanston: Northwestern University Press, 1976) p. 155.

4. As evidence of this possibility, refer to the strong and important role that Nyakinyua plays in Ngugi wa Thiong'o's last novel, *Petals of Blood*, London: Heinemann, 1977.

5. Frederick Douglass, *My Bondage and My Freedom*, (New York: Arno Press and the New York Times, 1968) p. 38. Additional references to this work will be cited in the body of the paper by page numbers.

6. Maya Angelou, *I Know Why the Caged Bird Sings* (New York: Random House, 1969) pp. 6-7. Additional references to this work will be cited in the body of the paper by page numbers.

7. Ama Ata Aidoo. *No Sweetness Here.* (London, Longman Drumbeat, 1970) p. 19. Future references to this edition will appear in the body of the paper with page numbers.

8. Ezekiel Mphahlele, *Down Second Avenue* (Garden City, New York. Anchor Books, 1971) p. 1. Future references to this work will appear in the body of the paper with page numbers.

9. Don L. Lee, "Bigmomma" in *We Walk the Way of the New World*," (Detroit: Broadside Press, 1970) p. 31. Future references will be cited by page numbers in the body of the paper.

10. Linda Brown Bragg, "Poem About Beauty, Blackness, Poetry (and how to be all three)" in *A Love Song to Black Men* (Detroit: Broadside Press, 1974) p.17.

11. Alice Walker, "In Search of Our Mothers' Gardens: The Creativity of Black Women in the South," *Ms*. (May 1974) pp. 64-70, 105.

Marriage, Tradition and Woman's Pursuit of Happiness in the Novels of Mariama Bâ

Edris Makward

Fatna Air Sabbah—a pseudonym for a well-known Algerian female writer—opens her recent stunning essay *La Femme Dans L'inconscient Musulman—Désir et Pouvoir*[1] with a vivid reminder of the famous and still highly respected XIth century Persian philosopher and theologian, Al Ghazzali's warning against what he considered as the most serious imperfection in a would-be-bride, that is, *vadaka* or talkativeness, a woman's legendary propensity to talk too much.

Fatna Ait Sabbah then exposes the premise of her essay in the form of a compelling series of questions:

> Pourquoi donc le silence et l'immobilité, c'est-à-dire les signes et la manifestation de l'inertie, sont-ils les critères de la beauté chez la femme musulmane? Qu'est-ce que la beauté a à voir avec le droit à l'expression? Pourquoi, selon les canons de la beauté en Islam, une femme qui ne s'exprime pas doit exciter le désir chez l'homme?. . . .[2]
>
> [Why is it that silence and immobility, that is, the signs and manifestations of inertia, are the criteria for the beauty of the Muslim

271

woman? What has beauty to do with the right to self-expression? Why is a woman who does not express herself, supposed to arouse desire in men, according to the Muslim canons of beauty?. . .]

These questions raised by Fatna Ait Sabbah indeed have relevance in the world of the late Mariama Bâ, the author of the celebrated *Une Si Longue Lettre*[3] [*So Long A Letter*]. For although the literary, cultural and theological corpus on which the Algerian author's study is based is, above all, Middle Eastern—Arab and Persian in particular—there is no denying that this corpus has had a very strong influence on many Islamized "Sub-Saharan" African societies over several centuries. And Sénégal is undoubtedly among these countries, considering its age-old contacts with North African and Middle Eastern Islam.[4]

Marima Bâ's discourse, however, while never questioning the fundamental precepts of Islam, stemmed deliberately and convincingly from a dynamic conception of society, a strong belief in social and political change and progress. At first glance, each of her two novels seems to center around one specific topic: the evils of polygamy in *Une Si Longue Lettre* and the failure of a racially mixed marriage in *Un Chant Ecarlate*[5] [*A Scarlet Song*], her second novel, published posthumously. However it is my contention that despite their apparently different foci, there is one underlying theme that runs through both novels, and that is the theme of personal happiness.

Une Si Longue Lettre is the story of two western-educated African women, Aïssatou and Ramatoulaye (Rama). They are both very actively involved in the process of social change that has been taking place in their country for two or three generations. The time framework is the effervescent and immediate era of independence and post-independence in Sénégal. Both women are happily married to dynamic conscientious, loving and understanding African husbands, and their marriages are indeed modern marriages in the sense that they originated from their own free choices and were not prearranged by their parents. Both women are confronted with the second marriages of their husbands as a *fait accompli*, but while Aïssatou rejects vehemently the polygamous situation and leaves her husband Mawdo, a doctor, for a successful professional career as an interpreter in New York, Ramatoulaye, the narrator, stays with her husband Modou with the hope that he will at least follow the traditional Islamic rule and practice of equal attention and sharing of the husband in a polygamous household. But in fact Ramatoulaye and her children will be deserted by Modou in favor of the new wife, Binetou. When Modou dies suddenly of a heart attack, Ramatoulaye will reject all the polygamous suitors who wish to take Modou's place. For, as she puts it in the closing paragraph of her "long letter" to her friend Aissatou:

Je t'avertis déjà, je ne renonce pas à refaire ma vie. Malgré tout—déceptions et humiliations—l'espérance m'habite. C'est de l'humus sale et nauséabond que jaillit la plante verte et je sens pointer en moi, des bourgeons neufs.[6]

[I warn you already. I have not given up wanting to refashion my life. Despite everything—disappointments and humiliations—hope still lives on within me. It is from the dirty and nauseating humus that the green plant sprouts into life, and I can feel new buds springing up in me.]

Un Chant Ecarlate relates the story of an initially beautiful love affair between two young students—the Sénégalese Ousmane and the French Mireille—who end up marrying in France after completing separately their studies, he, in Dakar, and she, in France where her intransigent father had sent her by force when he found out about their relationship. Although Ousmane does not neglect any of his duties towards his parents, his mother Yaye Khady is not satisfied with her son's marriage with a foreigner, for Mireille does not—and cannot possibly—fulfill towards her, all the functions of a true daughter-in-law in accordance with traditional Wolof expectations. Mireille has not been culturally prepared by her own husband. Ousmane will then fall back on a childhood flame and former neighbor Ouleymatou, in the name of "authenticity," and he will marry her as a second wife. This "triangle," unlike the polygamous situation experienced by Aïssatou and Ramatoulaye in Mariama Bâ's first novel, will end tragically with Mireille, the French heroine, losing her mind and killing her son—the symbol of her failed mixed marriage.

From these two summaries, one could be tempted to conclude that Mariama Bâ's novels were nothing but pleas against polygamy. But that would be definitely superficial. Mariama Bâ's central preoccupation in these novels was more the pursuit of happiness than an outright attack on polygamy. And when Rama praises her friend Aïssatou and calls her "pionnière hardie d'une nouvelle vie" [daring pioneer of a new life], she was indeed expressing her admiration for her friend's courage in continuing her search for true happiness without any compromise with polygamy or any other binding traditions. However, although she did not embark on an outright diatribe against polygamy, Mariama Bâ was convinced that happiness—and not just women's happiness, but men's as well, a whole society's happiness—must be based on a monogamous marriage. And in the modern context, for her, monogamous marriage meant a close association between two equals, and the sharing of pains, joys, hopes, disappointments and successes. The foundation stone of this happiness is without doubt in the couple, a concept, an ideal that is clearly new in Africa. Rama expresses this conviction in a revealing passage of her letter to her friend Aïssatou who chose courageously to leave her husband Mawdo when he decided to "please his mother" by marrying a young cousin, a member of his caste:

> Je suis de celles qui ne peuvent se réaliser et s'épanouir que dans le couple. Je n'ai jamais conçu le bonheur hors du couple, tout en te comprenant, tout en respectant le choix des femmes libres.[7]
> [I am one of those who can realize themselves fully and bloom only when they form part of a couple. Even though I understand your stand, even though I respect the choice of liberated women, I have never conceived of happiness outside marriage.]

In rejecting her brother-in-law Tamsir's offer to replace his brother in accordance with Sénégalese Muslim traditions, Rama reasserts her desire to adhere to all the implications of the ideal of the couple:

> Tu oublies que j'ai un coeur, une raison, que je ne suis pas un objet que l'on se passe de main en main. Tu ignores ce que se marier signifie pour moi: c'est un acte de foi et d'amour, un don total de soi à l'être que l'on a choisi et qui vous a choisi. (J'insistais sur le mot choisi.)[8]
> [You forget that I have a heart, a mind, that I am not an object to be passed from hand to hand. You don't know what marriage means to me: it is an act of faith and love, the total surrender of oneself to the person one has chosen and who has chosen you. (I emphasized the word 'chosen'.)]

In emphasizing the idea of choice, Rama is clearly expressing her disapproval of the traditional "arranged" marriage where the parents or other relatives—the family—make the choice for the bride and groom.

Hence the clash with tradition is obvious, for marriage with its function for procreation is definitely a central institution in traditional African society. It is therefore not a matter under the primary responsibility of the individuals concerned, that is, the bride and groom, but for the community, the family, to decide.

Mariama Bâ did not attack tradition and custom blatantly, but she expressed her disapproval of certain glaring abuses of tradition which impede progress. While she demonstrated an unflinching faith in the freedom of choice and the personal nature of marriage and romantic love, she also expressed her belief in the gain that the community in the modern context—the nation—would reap from the success and the attainment of happiness by individual couples. For her, family success depended on the harmony of the founding couple, and in turn, it was the grouping of all these successful and happy families that would constitute the Nation. As in Rama's words:

C'est de l'harmonie du couple que naît la réussite familiale, comme l'accord de multiples instruments crée la symphonie agréable.

Ce sont toutes les familles, riches ou pauvres, unies ou déchirées, conscientes ou irréfléchies qui constituent la Nation. La réussite d'une nation passe donc irrémediablement par la famille.[9]

[The success of a family is born of a couple's harmony, as the harmony of multiple instruments creates a pleasant symphony.

The nation is made up of all the families, rich or poor, united or separated, aware or unaware. The success of a nation therefore depends on the family.]

One could argue that there was nothing new in this idea in the African context, for it was in the interest of the community in general that the family would initiate ties that would ultimately lead to the union in marriage of young men and women. What was new, however, was the notion that marriage was above all based on the choice and initial attraction of the two principal partners.

Mariama Bâ was not the first African writer to treat the subject. Two outstanding predecessors are the Tunisian Albert Memmi and the Sénégalese Ousmane Sembène. An even earlier precursor is René Maran with his *Un Homme Pareil Aux Autres*, published in 1947. Memmi shows in his 1955 novel, *Agar*, how enticing the western ideal of the couple can be for the young Tunisian medical student who falls in love with a blond Alsatian chemistry student. They marry and at the completion of his medical studies, travel to Tunisia where the protagonist has no doubt that they will settle and raise a family. Naturally, they are confronted with a number of cultural difficulties; the most devastating of all being the overwhelming weight of the family and the community on the young couple. Even the protagonist did not seem quite prepared for this clash of cultural world views on his "re-entry" among his own people:

Je constatais, une fois de plus, combien ils tenaient à moi et combien je leur appartenais. Pour mon père je n'étais pas seulement son fils mais un anneau de la grande chaîne. Je comprenais la responsabilité qui, d'après lui, m'incombait, et qu'il croyait me préserver d'une trahison.[10]

[Once more I was aware how much I meant to them, how closely I belonged. For my father I was not only his son, but a link in the great chain. I realized all the responsibility that he felt was mine, saw that his thought was to save me from betraying the family.]

This fear of betrayal is not just apparent in the father's mind; the son, our protagonist, is also aware of the danger and the temptation to "betray" his people and "let his French wife have her way". He is torn between two cultural worlds, and his dilemma lies in his wish to preserve both of these worlds: his adopted world, Marie's world on the one hand, and his people's world on the other. He had to admit that while he was often wary of his family's thoughtless invasion of his privacy and more often than not, tended to see their attachment to their age-old traditions and customs as offensive and backward, he could not at other times contain his genuine admiration for the profound meaning of some of his people's traditions. This paralyzing predicament is illustrated when he is choosing a name in anticipation of the birth of his first son. Tradition would want the grandson to bear his grandfather's name: Abraham, for the sake of continuity. Although the protagonist's impulsive answer to his parents is negative, he expresses later his understanding of this simple custom in compelling words:

> L'avouerai-je? Quelquefois je m'étonnais de L'espèce de grandeur de cet élan, de cette défaite du temps par la mémoire des hommes.[11]
> [And let me admit that sometimes I have wondered at the touch of greatness in this long linking, this triumph of men's memory over time.]

In spite of the somewhat apologetic tone, there is genuine admiration and profound understanding in these words. However, the conflict, the waverings persist and will eventually lead to Marie's decision to return to her native France. the significance of this failure should be seen as a sign of the deep alienation of the protagonist rather than "Memmi's unspoken conclusion that such an experiment in marriage is foredoomed to failure".[12]

It is the depth and pain of this alienation that Memmi expresses through the protagonist's thoughts in the closing chapters of the novel:

> La folie de Marie a été de croire que je serais entièrement à elle lorsqu'elle aurait tout arraché de moi, même l'odeur des pierres chaudes et du soleil. Cette femme que j'aime, qui fut le meilleur de moi-même, qui a voulu tout me donner, est devenu le symbole et la source de ma destruction. Je ne suis plus rien qu'un fantôme, mon propre ennemi et le sien. Je l'ai trahie et elle m'a détruit.
> Mais, en même temps, je ne peux plus vivre sans elle. Je n'ai plus ni pays, ni parents, ni amis; et la quitterais-je que je resterais ainsi double, en face de moi-même et juge des miens. Je supporte à peine de vivre avec elle, mais je ne supporte plus de vivre avec personne.[13]
> [It was Marie's folly to think that I would be entirely hers when she had drawn everything out of me, even the hot smell of the stones and the sun. This woman I had loved the best in myself, who wanted to give me all, had become the symbol and source of my destruction. And I was nothing now but a phantom, my own enemy and hers. I had been her betrayer, she my destroyer.

Yet at the same time I could not live without her, I was without country, relatives or friends; and if I parted from her I should be as two men, one confronting myself and one criticising my people. Though life with her was almost unbearable, life with anyone was unbearable now.]

With this novel dedicated to his wife, who is French too, Albert Memmi was not making a decidedly negative statement about the outcome of mixed marriages. Even though the novel ends with a painful failure, Memmi seemed more involved here in describing the fascination of a young African—a Tunisian Jew—with the pursuit of happiness in marriage according to western norms and the harrowing contrasts between these norms and those prevalent in the traditional North African context. In my opinion, the failure of the union between Marie and the protagonist in Memmi's novel is meant to emphasize the difficulties inherent in such marriages and the painful dilemma of cultural alienation and should not be interpreted as an expression of Memmi's verdict regarding mixed marriages.

For his part, Ousmane Sembène portrayed also a mixed couple, Oumar Faye and Isabelle in his second novel, *O Pays, Mon Beau Peuple* (1957).[14] Oumar Faye who fought in World War II in Europe on the side of the French, returns home to his native Casamance, in southern Sénégal, with his French wife, Isabelle. Unlike Memmi's protagonist in *Agar*, Oumar Faye is a strong-willed young man who has set goals for himself and knows what to do to realize them. He wants to work with his people to end their economic exploitation by the white colonials who have taken advantage of their lack of organization and their inexperience. Oumar is a pragmatist for whom the choice of what should be retained from one's traditions and what should be borrowed from European culture and technology is very clear. He is not torn between two cultures, and his wife, Isabelle, seems well prepared to back him up and help him achieve his goals. Naturally, there is at first a clash between the young couple and Oumar's family, but these initial difficulties are easily overcome, for Oumar and Isabelle agree totally in pursuing an independent course without necessarily cutting themselves off from Oumar's family and the community at large.

Thus the major issue in Sembène's novel does not originate in Oumar's own alienation or in a clash of cultures, but in the bigotry and fear of the white colonials who feel threatened by Oumar, the harbinger of a new order. These colonials will eventually succeed in eliminating him, at least, physically. Oumar dies at the hands of his enemies, but the courage and spirit of resistance that he symbolized in the eyes of his people, remain vividly present in their hearts:

Ce n'était pas la tombe qui était sa demeure, c'était le coeur de tous les hommes et de toutes les femmes. Il était présent le soir autour de feu

et le jour, dans les rizières; lorsqu'un enfant pleurait, sa mère lui
racontait l'histoire de ce jeune homme qui parlait à la terre et, sous
l'arbre à palabres, on honorait sa mémoire. Oumar n'était plus, mais
son "Beau peuple" le chantait toujours.[15]
[It was not the graveyard that was his home, it was the heart of all the
men and all the women. He was present at night around the fire and in
the daytime, in the rice-fields; when a child cried, his mother would
tell him the story of that young man who spoke to the earth and under
the shady ancestral tree, his memory was honored. Oumar was no
more, but his "Beautiful people" would sing his praises forever.]

While both Memmi and Sembène treated the couple as a central and
exalting entity, Mariama Bâ was the first African writer to stress unequivocal-
ly the strong desire of the new generation of Africans to break away from the
age-old marriage customs and adopt a decidedly more modern approach
based on free mutual choice and the equality of the two partners.

In her two novels, she pointedly showed that the extended family's action
could invariably make such relationships fizzle out in bitter failure. And
while never indulging in an outright condemnation of the traditions of her
society, she denounced the contemporary abuses of these traditions. Thus,
while playing her role as a widow during the funeral of her husband Modou,
Rama deplores the coarse attitude and the sheer materialism of her sisters-
in-law who treat her and her late husband's young second wife equally:

Nos belles-soeurs traitent avec la même égalité trente et cinq ans de
vie conjugale. Elles célèbrent, avec la même aisance et les mêmes
mots, douze et trois maternités.[16]
[Our sisters-in-law give equal consideration to thirty years and five
years of married life. With the same ease and the same words, they
celebrate twelve maternities and three.]

In *Une Si Longue Lettre*, two initially successful marriages, between
Mawdo and Aïssatou and Rama and Modou, ended in failure precipitated
by the excesses of polygamy. But while the former couple's failure is partly
due to Mawdo's mother's efforts to correct what she considered as her son's
misalliance, his marriage with a member of a lower caste, the latter is simply
caused by Modou's infatuation with a much younger woman who is, for her
part, irresistibly attracted by the material comforts that Modou can provide
for her and for her mother.

There is also the couple composed of Samba Diack and his wife
Jacqueline from Ivory Coast. The failure of this couple is due partly to the
refusal of Samba's family to accept an African from another African
country. Jacqueline is Christian and Samba Diack is Muslim. But the major

cause of this marriage's failure is Samba Diack's unfaithful and inconsiderate behavior.

Rama's two older daughters, Daba and Aïssatou, symbolize the future. Daba and her husband do indeed constitute the ideal couple and their attitudes and behavior reassure Rama in her faith in a better and more harmonious future:

> Je sens mûrir la tendresse de ce jeune couple qui est l'image du couple telle que je la rêvais. Ils s'identifient l'un à l'autre, discutent de tout pour trouver un compromis.[17]
>
> [I sense the tenderness growing between this young couple, an ideal couple, just as I have always imagined. They identify with each other, discuss everything so as to find a compromise.]

Likewise, young Aïssatou and her friend Iba seem to follow the same path with confidence and mutual esteem.

In *Un Chant Ecarlate*, the failure of the couple Ousmane/Mireille is due basically to Ousmane's nostalgic infatuation with an early flame of his adolescence, Ouleymatou. But the encouragement of his mother who benefits from Ouleymatou's triumph, is also a factor. In her description of the couple's initial happiness, Mariama Bâ uses a very convincing tone with no place for racial or even cultural considerations:

> Et le bonheur naît de rien, se nourrit de rien. On lui confère un prix énorme. Son acquisition paraît réclamer un prix fort. Et pourtant, le bonheur peut s'épanouir tout simplement dans un amphithéâtre d'Université.[18]
>
> [And happiness emerges from nothing, feeds on very little. One evaluates it at a high price. Its acquisition may appear to command a very substantial cost. And yet happiness can bloom very simply in a University lecture-room.]

Thus, while the cause for the subsequent disagreement between Ousmane and Mireille seems based only in part on racial and cultural differences, and above all, on Ousmane's own new sexual and romantic fantasies, another mixed couple's success in the novel, Pierrette and Lamine seems to indicate that these racial and cultural differences can indeed be overcome generally, but not without some amount of sacrifice and compromise from both sides.

Lamine who is said not to be "haunted by his négritude"[19] and showing "no internal anxiety" explains his position very clearly:

> On ne peut allier deux conceptions de vie différentes. Si l'on est honnête, il y a un choix à faire. Tu veux être heureux sans rien

sacrifier. Tu ne veux rien céder et tu exiges des concessions. La vie
conjugale est plutôt humaine approche et tolérance.[20]
[One cannot bring together two different conceptions of life. If one
is honest, one has to admit a choice. You want to be happy without
sacrifice. You do not want to give up anything and you demand
concessions. Married life implies above all humane approach and
tolerance.]

Albeit Mariama Bâ's second novel ends tragically with the French
heroine losing her senses and killing her child, it should not be read as an
outright condemnation of mixed marriages. For, like Memmi's *Agar*, it
exposes the question of cultural differences inherent in such marriages. But,
above all, it shows through the example of the successful and harmonious
couple, Lamine and Pierrette, that these differences can be overcome with
appropriate adjustments and compromise.

Thus Mariama Bâ upheld courageously throughout her life—in her
literary works as well as in her other involvements—her vision of an
African society where men and women would share equally in the duties as
well as in the joys and the rewards of a harmonious partnership between *one*
husband and *one* wife.

It is appropriate to conclude here with the words of another Muslim
woman who believes like Mariama Bâ that our societies are changing and
that these changes do involve both men and women in the pursuit of a
happier and a more harmonious life on this earth.

Je crois en l'être humain comme un être capable de faire et refaire son
histoire, et je crois donc qu'il est possible aux hommes et aux femmes
vivant dans les sociétés musulmanes de changer le cours de l'histoire,
de vivre mieux, d'aimer mieux. Les femmes ne sont pas condamnées
à vivre mutilées.[21]
[I believe in human beings as capable of making and remaking their
history, and I therefore, believe that it is possible for men and women
living in Muslim societies to change the course of history, *to live
better, to love better.* Women must not be condemned to live as
mutilated beings.]

NOTES

1. Editions le Sycomore, Paris, 1982, 205pp.
2. Op. cit., pp. 11-12. My translation.

3. Marima Bâ, *Une Si Longue Lettre*. Nouvelles Editions Africaines. Dakar, 1979. 131 pp. [English Trans. by Modupe Bode-Thomas, *So Long A Letter.* Heinemann.]

4. While the criteria of modesty and reserve for feminine behavior as described in the orthodox Islamic jurisprudential discourse examined by Fatna Ait Sabbah can be easily observed in most traditional African Muslim societies, I would contend that the graphic details of the Islamic erotic discourse that she quotes in her book would shock many ordinary—devout and not so devout—West African Muslims!

5. Mariama Bâ, *Un Chant Ecarlate*. Nouvelles Editions Africaines. Dakar, 1981, 251pp.

6. Op. cit., p. 131 [English trans. p. 89.]

7. Op. cit., p. 82. [English trans. p. 55-56.]

8. Op. cit., p. 85. [English trans. p. 58.]

9. Op. cit., p. 130. [English trans. p. 89.]

10. Albert Memmi, *Agar.* Corrêa, Paris, 1955, p. 119. [English trans. by Brian Rhys, *The Strangers.* Elek Books, London, 1958, p. 78]

11. Op. cit. p. 119. [English trans. p. 78.]

12. English trans., op. cit., title page.

13. Op. cit., pp. 224-225.

14. Ousmane Sembène, *O Pays, Mon Beau Peuple.* Amiot-Dumont, 243pp., 1957.

15. Op. cit., pp. 233-234. My translation.

16. Mariama Bâ, *Une Si Longue Lettre*, p. 11. [English trans. p. 4.]

17. Op. cit., p. 107. [English trans. pp. 73-74.]

18. Mariama Bâ, *Un Chant Ecarlate*, p. 28. My translation.

19. Op. cit., p. 150.

20. Op. cit., p. 151.

21. Fatna Ait Sabbah, *La Femme Dans L'inconscient Musulman.* Editions Le Sycomore, Paris, 1982, p. 15. My translation and my empahsis.

A Bibliography of Criticism and Related Works

Carole Boyce Davies

Accad, Evelyne. "Interrelationship Between Arab Nationalism and Feminist Consciousness in the North African Novels Written by Women." *Ba Shiru* 8.2 (1977): 3-12.

_____. *Veil of Shame. The Role of Women in the Contemporary Fiction of North African and the Arab World.* Sherbrooke, Quebec. Naaman, 1978.

_____. "The Theme of Sexual Oppression in the North African Novel." Lois Beck and Nikki Keddie eds. *Women in the Muslim World.* Cambridge, Mass: Harvard University Press, 1978. 617-628.

Adam, Jeanne. "Le monde féminin de 'Grande Kabylie'." *Présence Francophone. Revue Littéraire* 22 (Spring, 1981): 5-19.

Adan, Amina H. "Women and Words." *Ufahamu* 10.3 (Spring, 1981): 115-142.

Aidoo, Ama Ata. "Unwelcome Pals and Decorative Slaves. The Woman as a Writer in Modern Africa." *AFA. Journal of Creative Writing* (Imo State, Nigeria) 1 November, 1982): 34-43.

_____. "To Be A Woman". *Sisterhood is Global.* Ed. Robin Morgan. New York: Doubleday, 1984: 258-265.

Akello, Grace. *Self Twice Removed.* London: Change, 1982. Rev. by Esther Ogunmodede, "Struggling Out of Traditional Strait-Jackets." *New African* (January, 1983): 48-49.

Akoua, Solange and Ibrahime Fofana. "La femme africaine dans 'Les Bouts de Bois de Dieu'." *Eburnea* 106 (1976): 17-19.

Amaizo, E. "La femme et les changements sociaux et culturels dans l'oeuvre romanesque de Chinua Achebe." *Annales de L'Université du Bénin, Togo.* Lettres 2.2 (1975): 101-108.

Asanga, Siga. "Firebrands: Women in the Drama of J. P. Clark." Unpublished African Literature Association (ALA) paper, 1984.

Babatunde, E. D. "Ketu Myths and the Status of Women. A Structural Interpretation of Some Yoruba Myths of Origin." *Journal of the Anthropological Society of Oxford* 14.3 (1983): 301-306.

Bazin, Nancy Topping. "Feminist Perspectives in African Fiction: Bessie Head and Buchi Emecheta." Unpublished ALA paper, 1984.

Beard, Linda Susan. "Bessie Head's *A Question of Power*: The Journey Through Disintegration to Wholeness." *Colby Library Journal* 15.4 (1979): 267-274.

Bede, J. "La donna e la terra natale in *'La Terra Promessa'* di Grace Ogot." *La Letteratura Della Nuova Africa*. Eds. Lina Angioletti and Armanda Guiducci. Rome: Lerici, 1979: 117-177.

Bell, Roseann P. "The Absence of the African Woman Writer." *CLA Journal* 21.4 (1978): 491-498.

Berrian, Brenda F. "African Women As Seen in the Works of Flora Nwapa and Ama Ata Aidoo." *CLA Journal* 25.3 (1982): 331-39.

Berrian, Brenda and Mildred Mortimer. *Critical Perspectives on African Women Writers*. Washington, D.C.: Three Continents Press, (forthcoming).

Brown, Lloyd. "Ama Ata Aidoo: The Art of the Short Story and Sexual Roles in Africa. *World Literature Written in English*. 13 (1974): 172-183.

————. "The African Woman as Writer". *Canadian Journal of African Studies*. 9.3 (1975): 493-501.

————. "Creating New Worlds in Southern Africa: Bessie Head and the Question of Power." *Umoja* 3.1 (1979): 43-53.

————. *Women Writers in Black Africa*. Connecticut: Greenwood Press, 1981.

Bruner, Charlotte. "Been To or Has-Been: A Dilemma For Today's African Woman." *Ba Shiru* 8.2 (1977): 23-31.

————. "Child Africa as Depicted by Bessie Head and Ama Ata Aidoo." *Studies in the Humanities* 7.2 (1979): 5-11.

————. "Bessie Head: Restless in a Distant Land." *When the Drumbeat Changes*. Ed. Carolyn Parker and Stephen Arnold. Washington D.C.: Three Continents Press, 1980: 261-278.

————. ed. *Unwinding Threads. Writing by Women in African* London: Heinemann, 1983.

————. "A Decade for Women Writers." *African Literature Studies: The Present State L'état Présent*. Ed. by Stephen Arnold. Washington, D.C.: Three Continents Press, 1985: 217-227.

————. "First Person Feminine: A Sequel to 'Talking Sticks'. Unpublished ALA paper, 1982.

Bryce, Jane. "Profile. Ngugi: 'My Novel of Blood Sweat and Tears.'" *New African* (August, 1982): 36.

Burness, Donald. "Womanhood in the Short Stories of Ama Ata Aidoo." *Studies in Black Literature*. 4.2 (1973): 21-24.

Case, F. I. Rev. *So Long A Letter* by Mariama Bâ. *World Literature Written in English*. 21.3 (1982): 538-539.

Cham, Mbye. "The Female Condition in Africa: A Literary Exploration by Mariama Bâ." *Current Bibliography on African Affairs*. 17:1 (1984/5): 29-52.

Chapman, Karen. "'Introduction' to Ama Ata Aidoo's 'Dilemma of a Ghost'." Rpt. in *Sturdy Black Bridges*. Ed. Bell, Parker and Guy-Sheftall. New York: Anchor Press/Doubleday, 1979: 25-38.

Chemain-Degrange, Arlette. "L'image de la femme noire dans la littérature négro africaine d'expression francaise." Diss. University of Grenoble, France, 1973.

_____. *Emancipation Féminine et Roman Africain*. Dakar: Les Nouvelles Editions Africaines, 1980.

Christian, Barbara. *Black Women Novelists. The Development of a Tradition*. Westport, Conn.: Greenwood Press, 1980.

_____. *Black Feminist Criticism. Perspectives on Black Women Writers*. New York: Pergamon Press, 1985.

Cochrane, Judith. "Women as the Guardians of the Tribe in Ngugi's Novels." *ACLALS-Bulletin* 4.5 (1977): 1-11.

_____. 'Some Images of Women in East African Fiction." *ACLALS-Bulletin* 5.1 (1978): 32-41.

_____. "The Theme of Sacrifice in the Novels of Nuruddin Farah." *World Literature Written in English*. 18.1 (April, 1979): 69-77.

Condé, Maryse. "Three Female Writers in Modern Africa: Flora Nwapa, Ama Ata Aidoo, Grace Ogot." *Presence Africaine* 82 (1972): 136-139.

_____. *Paroles des Femmes*. Paris, L'Harmattan, 1979.

Cosentino, Donald J. "The Onitsha Heroine." *Ba Shiru*. 7 (Fall, 1970/Spring, 1971: 52-62.

_____. "Jagua Nana: Culture Heroine." *Ba Shiru* 8 (1971): 11-17.

_____. Rev. of *The Royal Antelope and Spider* by Marion Kilson. *Research in African Literatures* 10 (1979): 296-307.

Cutrufelli, Maria Rosa. *Women of Africa. Roots of Oppression*. Trans. Nicolas Romano. London: Zed Press, 1983.

d'Almeida, Irene Assiba. "Prostitution in African Fiction and Beyond." Unpublished Monograph, Emory University, Institute of Liberal Arts, 1984.

Dathorne, O.R. *African Literature in the Twentieth Century*. Minneapolis: University of Minnesota Press, 1974.

Davies, Carole Boyce. "Maidens, Mistresses and Matrons: Feminine Images in Selected Soyinka Works." *Interdisciplinary Dimensions of African Literature*. Ed. Anyidoho, Porter, Racine, Spleth. Washington, D.C.: Three Continents Press, 1984: 89-99.

_____. "Completing the Story: Some Unexamined South African Women Writers". Unpublished manuscript of paper presented at the 1985 ALA Conference, Northwestern University, Illinois, March, 1985.

_____. "Wrapping Oneself In Mother's Akatado Cloths: Mother-Daughter Relationships in the Works of African Women Writers." Unpublished manuscript, 1985.

_____ and Elaine Savory Fido. "African Women Writers". *A History of African Literature in the Twentieth Century*. Ed. Oyekan Owomoyela. (University of Nebraska Press, forthcoming).

Emecheta, Buchi. "'It's Me Who's Changed.' An Interview with Buchi Emecheta." *Connexions* 4 (Spring, 1982): 4.

Emeka, Abanime. "La beauté feminine chez les romanciers négro-africains. Le probleme de l'idéal blanc." *Rev. de Lit. et D'Esthétique Négro-Africaines* 3 (1981): 7-14.

Emenyonu, Ernest N. "Who Does Flora Nwapa Write For?" *African Literature Today* 7. Ed. Eldred Durosimi Jones. London, Heinemann, 1975: 28-33.

Evans, Jennifer. "Mother Africa and the Heroic Whore: Female Images in *Petals of Blood*." *Contemporary African Literature*. Ed. Wylie, Julien and Linnemann. Washington D.C.: Three Continents Press, 1983: 57-65.

Fido, Elaine Savory. "'A Guest of Honour': A Feminine View of Masculinity." *World Literature Written in English* 17:1 (1978): 30-37.

_____. "The Feminine Principle in the fiction of Elechi Amadi." Unpublished manuscript, University of the West Indies, Cave Hill, 1983.

_____. "The Changing Role of Women in Relation to African Literary Studies." Unpublished ALA paper, 1985.

_____ and Carole Boyce Davies. "African Women Writers." in *A History of African Literature in the Twentieth Century*. Ed. Oyekan Owomoyela (University of Nebraska Press, forthcoming).

Finnegan, Ruth. *Oral Literature in Africa*. Oxford: Clarendon Press, 1970.

Frank, Katherine. "The Death of A Slave Girl: African Womanhood in the Novels of Buchi Emecheta." *World Literature Written in English* 21:3 (1982): 476-496.

_____. "Feminist Criticism and the African Novel." *African Literature Today*, 14. Ed. Eldred Durosimi Jones. London: Heinemann, 1984. 34-48.

Gachukia, Eddah. "The Role of Women in Ngugi's Novels." *Busara* 3.4 (1971): 30-33.

Gérard, Albert and Laurent, Jeanine. "Sembène's Progeny: A New Trend in the Senegalese Novel." *Studies in Twentieth Century Literature*. 4.2 (1980): 133-145.

Gunner, Elizabeth. "Songs of Innocence and Experience: Women as Composers and performers of *Izibongo*, Zulu Praise Poetry." *Research in African Literatures* 10:2 (1979): 239-267.

Hall, Susan. "African Women on Film." *Africa Report* 22.1 (January-February): 15-17.

Hammonds, Evelyn. "Toward a Black Feminist Aesthetic." *Sojourner*. October, 1980: 7.

Harrow, Kenneth. "Not Such a Long Way, Baby: The Situation of the Woman Today in the Maghreb and its Thematic Representation in Literature." *Current Bibliography of African Affairs*. 9.3 (1976-77): 228-249.

Herzberger-Fofana, Pierette. "Female Literature in Francophone Africa." Unpublished ALA paper, 1985.

Hill-Lubin, Mildred. "Ama Ata Aidoo: The Story Teller as professional Performer and Psychologist." Unpublished ALA paper, 1985.

Hubbard, Louise J. "Women in Mongo Beti's '*Perpétue*'." *Annales de L'Univ. de Bénin*, Togo. Serié Lettres 4.1 (1977): 63-73.

Ifeka, Caroline. "The World of Women. '*Efuru*'." *Nigeria Magazine* 89. June, 1966: 131.

Ifeka-Moller, Caroline. "Female Militancy and Colonial Revolt. The Women's War of 1929, Eastern Nigeria." *Perceiving Women*. Ed. Shirley Ardener. New York: John Wiley and Sons, 1975: 127-156.

Ikonne, Chidi. "The Society and Woman's Quest for Selfhood in Flora Nwapa's Early Novels." *Kunapipi* 6.1 (1984): 68-72.

_____. "Women in Igbo Folktales." Unpublished ALA paper, 1982.

Kane, Mohamadou. "Le féminisme dans le roman africain de langue francaise." *Univ. de Dakar Annales de Faculté des Lettres et Sciences*. 10 (1980): 14-20.

Kapumpa, Mumba. "Theatre: A New Challenge to Our Women." *Africa Woman* 23 (1979): 52-53.

Kilson, Marion. "Women and African Literature." *Journal of African Studies* 4:2 (1970): 161-166.

_____. *Royal Antelope and Spider: West African Mende Tales*. Cambridge, Mass: The Press of Langdon Associates, 1976.

Knipp, Thomas R. "Images of Women in West African Poetry." Unpublished ALA Paper, 1984.

Kunene, Daniel P. "La Guma's Women." Unpublished ALA paper, 1985.

Lee, Sonia. "L'image de la femme dans le roman francophone de l'Afrique occidentale." Diss. University of Massachusetts, 1974. Ann Arbor: UMI, 1974. 74-15028.

_____. "The Image of the Woman in the African Folktale from the Sub-saharan Francophone Area." *Yale French Studies*. 53 (1976): 19-28.

_____. "The Awakening of Self in the Heroines of Ousmane Sembene." Bell, Parker and Guy-Sheftall: 52-60.

_____. "Le theme du bonheur chez les romancieres africaines." Unpublished ALA paper, 1982.

Lindfors, Bernth. "Nigerian Chapbook Heroines." *Journal of Popular Culture*." Winter, 1968: 441 450.

Lippert, Anne. "Women Characters and African Literature." *Afriscope* 3:10 (1973): 45, 49.

_____."The Changing Role of Women As Viewed in the Literature of English Speaking West Africa." Diss. Indiana University, 1972. Ann Arbor: UMI, 1972. 72-30425.

Little, Kenneth. "Mothers and Other Characters," *West Africa* 24 (September, 1979): 1759.

_____. *The Sociology of Urban Women's Image in African Literature*. London: Macmillan, 1980.

Lyonga, Pauline Nalova. "*Uhamiri*. A Feminist Approach to African Literature." Diss. University of Michigan, 1985.

Mack, Beverly B. "*Wakokin Mata*: Hausa Women's Oral Poetry." Diss. University of Wisconsin, 1981. Ann Arbor: UMI 82-05542.

_____. ' "*Waka Daya Ba Ta Kare Nika*'—One Song Will Not Finish the Grinding: Hausa Women's Oral Literature." *Contemporary African Literature*. Ed. Wylie, Julien and Linnemann. Washington, D.C.: Three Continents Press, 1983: 15-46.

_____. ed. *Alkalami: A Hannun Mata. A Pen in the Hand of Women*. Zaria: The Northern Nigeria Publishing Company, 1983.

_____. "Hausa Women Poets: Ghostwriters. Interviews with Hauwa Gwaram and
    Binta Katsina." *Ba Shiru* (forthcoming).
Mbughuni, L. A. Old and New Drama From East Africa. A Review of four
    Contemporary Dramatists: Rebecca Njau, Ebrahim Hussein, Peninah Muhando
    and Ngugi." *African Literature Today* 8 (London, Heinemann, 1976): 85-98.
McCaffrey, Kathleen M. "Images of Women in the Literature of Selected
    Developing Countries. Washington D.C.: Office of Women in Development,
    Agency for International Development, 1977.
_____. "Image of the Mother in the Stories of Ama Ata Aidoo." *Africa Woman* 23
    (1979): 40-1.
_____. "Images of Women in West African Literature and Film: A Struggle
    Against Dual Colonization." *International Journal of Women's Studies* 3
    (1980): 76-88.
McDowell, Deborah. "New Directions for Black Feminist Criticism." *Black
    American Literature Forum.* 14:4 (Winter, 1980): 153-159.
Melamu, M. "Prophets and Women in Nigerian Tragedy." *Pula* 1: 43-88.
Mikhail, Mona. "Senghor, Women and the African Tradition." *Rackham Literary
    Studies* (Ann Arbor, MI) 1 (1971): 63-70.
_____. *Images of Arab Women.* Washington D.C.: Three Continents Press, 1981.
Mojola, Ibiyema. "La femme dans l'oeuvre de Chinua Achebe." *Peuples Noirs,
    Peuples Africains* 16: 48-58.
Mokwenye, Cyril. "La polygamie et la revolte de la femme africaine moderne: Une
    Lecture d'*une si longue lettre* de Mariama Ba." *Peuples Noirs. Peuples
    Africains* 31: (Janvier-Fevrier, 1983): 91.
Moore, Gerald H. "Nomads and Feminists: The Novels of Nuruddin Farah." *The
    International Fiction Review.* 11.1 (Winter, 1984): 3-12.
Mortimer, Mildred. "The Feminine Image in the Algerian Novel of French
    Expression." *Ba Shiru* 8.2 (1977): 51-62.
_____. "The Evolution of Assia Djebar's Feminist Conscience." *Contemporary
    African Literature.* Ed. Wylie, Julien and Linnemann. Washington, D.C.:
    Three Continents Press, 1983: 7-14.
Mugo, Micere. Interview. "Dr. Micere Mugo, Kenya's Outspoken Intellectual and
    Academic Critic Talks to Nancy Owano." *Africa Woman* 6 (September-
    /October, 1976).
Mutiso, G-C. M. "Women in African Literature. *East Africa Journal* 3.3 (1971):
    4-14. Rpt. in his *Socio-Political Thought in African Literature.* (London:
    Macmillan, 1974): 51-72.
Mvula, Enoch T. "Tumbuka Pounding Songs in the Management of Familial
    Conflicts." *Crossrhythms.* Ed. Daniel Avorgbedor and Kwesi Yankah.
    Indiana University, African Folklore Publications, 1983: 93-113.
Nandakumar, Prema. "An Image of African Womanhood: A Study of Flora
    Nwapa's *Efuru.*" *Africa Quarterly.* 2 (1967): 136-146.
_____. "Another Image of African Womanhood: An Appreciation of Elechi
    Amadi's '*The Concubine*'." *Africa Quarterly.* 13 (1973): 38-44.
Nasser, Merun. "Achebe and His Women: A Social Science Perspective." *Africa
    Today.* 27.3: 21-28.
Ngcobo, Lauretta. "Four Women Writers in Africa Today." *South Africa
    Outlook.* 114:1355 (May, 1984): 64-69.

Nkosi, Lewis. "Women in Literature." *Africa Woman* 6 (1976): 36-7.

Nwapa, Flora. "Meeting Flora Nwapa" An Interview with Allison Perry. *West Africa* 3487 (1984): 1262.

Ojo-Ade, Femi. "Female Writers, Male Critics." *African Literature Today* 13 (London: Heinemann, 1983): 158-179.

_____. "Bessie Head's Alienated Heroine: Victim or Villain?" *Ba Shiru* 8:2 (1977): 13-21.

_____. "Still a Victim? Mariama Ba's *Une si Longue Lettre*." *African Literature Today* 12. (London: Heinemann, 1982: 71-87.

Ogot, Grace. "Interview with Grace Ogot." With Bernth Lindfors. *World Written Literature in English* 18.1 (April, 1979): 57-68.

Ogundipe-Leslie, Omolara. "The Female Writer and Her Commitment." *Guardian* (Lagos) December 21, 1983: 11.

_____. "African Women, Culture and Another Development." *The Journal of African Marxists*. 5 (February, 1984): 77-92.

_____. "Not Spinning on the Axis of Maleness." *Sisterhood is Global*. Ed. Robin Morgan. New York: Anchor Press/Doubleday. 1984: 498-504.

Ogunyemi, Chikwenye Okonjo. "Buchi Emecheta: The Shaping of a Self." *Komparatistische Hefe*, Heft 8 (1983): 65-78.

Okonkwo, Juliet I. "Nuruddin Farah and the Changing Roles of Women." *World Literature Today* 58:2 (1984): 215-221.

_____. "Adam and Eve: Igbo Marriage in the Nigerian Novel." *The Conch* 3.2 (September, 1971): 137-151.

_____. "The Talented Woman in African Literature." *Africa Quarterly* 15 (1975): 35-47.

Okonkwo, Rina. "Adelaide Casely-Hayford; Cultural Nationalist and Feminist." *Journal of History and Society of Sierra Leone* 2.2 (1978): 10, 21.

Ola, V. U. "Aspects of Development in Chinua Achebe's Treatment of Women." *Journal of English* (Sena'a University) 7: 92-119.

_____. "The Feminine Principle and the Search for Wholeness in *The Healers*." Unpublished ALA paper, 1984.

Ortova, Jamila. "Les Femmes dans l'oeuvre littéraire d'Ousmane Sembène." *Présence Africaine* 71 (1959): 69-77.

Oyesakin, Adefioye. "The Image of Women in Ifa Literary Corpus." *Nigeria Magazine* 141 (1982): 16-23.

Palmer, Eustace. "Elechi Amadi and Flora Nwapa." *African Literature Today*. 1-4 (1968-1970): 56-58.

_____. "The Feminine Point of View: Buchi Emecheta's *The Joys of Motherhood*." *African Literature Today* 13. London: Heinemann, 1983. 38-55.

Parker, Carolyn. "How to Be/Treat A Lady in Swahili Culture: An Expression of Ideal." *Ba Shiru* 8.2 (1977): 37-45.

Pearse, Adetukunbo. "Symbolic Characterization Of Women in the Plays and Prose of Wole Soyinka." *Ba Shiru* 9.1 & 2 (1978): 39-46.

Pointer, Fritz. "Laye, Lamming and Wright: Mother and Son." *African Literature Today*, 14 (London: Heinemann, 1984): 19-33.

Porter, Abioseh. "Ideology and the Image of Women: Kenyan Women in Njau and Ngugi." *Ariel: A Review of International English Literature* 12.3 (July, 1981): 61-74.

Purisch, C. "Soyinka's Superwoman." Unpublished paper, University of Ibadan
    First Annual African Literature Conference, July 1976.
Reyes, Angelita. "'Dear God. . .': Impact of Confession in *Une si longue lettre* and
    Juletane." Unpublished ALA paper, 1985.
Rushing, Andrea Benton. "Images of Black Women in Modern African Poetry: An
    Overview." Bell, Parker, Guy-Sheftall: 18-24.
_____. "Comparative Study of the Idea of Mother in Contemporary African and
    African-American Poetry." *Colby Library Quarterly* 15.4 (1979): 275-288.
_____. "Family Resemblances: A Comparative Study of Women Protagonists in
    Contemporary African-American and Anglophone African Novels." Diss.
    University of Massachusetts, 1983. Ann Arbor: UMI, 1983. DEP 8310329.
Sacks, Karen. "Women and Class Struggle in Sembene's '*God's Bits of Wood*'."
    Signs 4: 363-70.
Scheub, Harold. "Two African Women". *Revue des Langues Vivantes* 37.5
    (1971): 545-558, 664-681.
_____. *The Xhosa Ntsomi*. Oxford: Clarendon Press, 1979.
Schipper, Mineke. *Theatre and Society in Africa*. Johannesburg: Ravan Press,
    1982.
_____. "'Who Am I?' Fact and Fiction in African First Person Narrative."
    Research in African Literatures. 16.1 (Spring, 1985): 53-79.
_____. "Women and Literature in Africa." *Unheard Words*. Ed. by Mineke
    Schipper. London: Allison & Busby, 1984: 22-58.
Schmidt, Nancy. "African Women Writers of Literature for Children." *World
    Literature Written in English* 17.1 (1978): 113-15.
Senkoro, F. E. M. K. *The Prostitute in African Literature*. Tanzania: Dar Es
    Salaam University Press, 1982.
Shoga, Yinka. "Women Writers and African Literature." *Afriscope* 3.10 (1973):
    44-5.
Smith, Barbara. "Toward a Black Feminist Criticism." Trumansburg, New York:
    The Crossing Press, 1982.
Smith, Robert P. Jr. "Mongo Beti: The Novelist Looks at Independence and the
    Status of the African Woman." *CLA Journal* 19 (March, 1976): 301-311.
Smyley, Karen. "The African Woman: Interpretations of Senegalese Novelists
    Aboulaye Sadji and Ousmane Sembène." Diss. City University of New York,
    1977. Ann Arbor, UMI, 1977.
_____. "Ousmane Sembène: Portraitist of the African Woman in the Novel." *The
    New England Journal of Black Studies*. (1981): 23-29.
Smyley-Wallace, Karen. "'*Les Bouts de Bois de Dieu*' and '*Xala*': A Comparative
    Analysis of Female Roles in Sembène's Novels." *Current Bibliography on
    African Affairs*. 17.2 (1984-5): 129-136.
Sonfo, Alphamoye. "La mère dans la littérature romanesque de la Guinée, du Mali
    et du Senegal." *West African Journal of Modern Languages*. 2 (1976): 95-
    107.
Staudt, Kathleen. "The Characterization of Women in Soyinka and Armah." *Ba
    Shiru* 8:2 (1977): 63-69.
_____. "The Feminine Image in the Algerian Novel of French Expression." *Ba
    Shiru* 8.2 (1977): 51-62.

Steady, Filomina Chioma. Ed. *The Black Woman Cross-Culturally*. Cambridge, Mass.: Schenkman Publishing Company, Inc., 1981: 1-41.

Stegman, Beatrice. "The Divorce Dilemma: The New Woman in Contemporary African Novels." *Critique* 15 (1974): 81-90.

Sweetman, David. *Women Leaders in Modern Africa*. London: Heinemann, 1984.

Taiwo, Oladele. *Female Novelists in Modern Africa*. London: Macmillan/New York: St. Martins, 1984.

Tate, Claudia. *Black Women Writers at Work*. New York: Continuum, 1983.

Thiam, Awa. *La Parole aux Négresses*. Paris: Denöel/Gonthier, 1978.

Thomas, Peter. "The Watermaid and the Dancer: Figures of the Nigerian Muse." *Literature East and West*. 12:1 (March, 1968): 85-93.

Umeh, Marie, Linton. "The African Heroine." Bell, Parker and Guy-Sheftall: 39-51.

_____. "African Women in Transition in the Novels of Buchi Emecheta." *Presence Africaine* 116 (1980): 190-201.

_____. "Interview with Buchi Emecheta." *Ba Shiru* 12:2 (1981).

_____. "The Joys of Motherhood: Myth or Reality." *Colby Library Quarterly* 18.1 (March, 1982): 39-46.

Wachtel, Eleanor. "The Mother and the Whore: Image and Stereotype of African Women." *UMOJA* 1.2 (1977): 31-48.

Walker, Alice. "A Writer Because of, Not In Spite of, Her Children." *In Search of Our Mothers' Gardens. Womanist Prose*. San Diego: Harcourt Brace, Jovanovich, 1983: 66-70.

_____. "Womanist" - (A Definition), Frontispiece to *In Search of Our Mothers' Gardens*. San Diego, Harcourt Brace, Jovanovich, 1983: xi-xii.

Washington, Mary Helen. Introduction to *Black Eyed Susans*. New York: Anchor Press/Doubleday, 1975.

Willentz, Gay. "The Playwright as Activist: Community Development in Efua Sutherland's 'Foriwa'." Unpublished paper. University of Texas, Austin, 1984.

_____. "The Individual Voice in the Communal Chorus: The Search for Identity in Flora Nwapa's 'Efuru'." Unpublished ALA paper, 1985.

Zimra, Clarisse. "Circular Structures of Linguistic Alienation in Assia Djebar's Early Novels." *Research in African Literatures*." (Summer, 1980): 206-223.

_____. "Women in Contemporary Arabic Fiction." *Bulletin of Southern Association of Africanists*. 7.2-3: 30-34.

_____. "Négritude in the Feminine Mode: the Case of Martinique and Guadeloupe." *The Journal of Ethnic Studies*. 12.1 (Spring, 1984): 53-77.

An Annotated Listing of Bibliographies

Berrian, Brenda. *Bibliography of African Women Writers and Journalists*. Washington, D.C.: Three Continents Press, 1985. The most comprehensive bibliography on African women writers to date. An important resource organized according to genres with extensive appendices for easy cross-reference. Recognized by the compiler as already in need of updating because of additional entries generated by its publication. Builds on her "Bibliographies of Nine Female African Writers. *Research in African Literatures* 12.2 (Summer, 1981): 215-238.

Bell, Roseann P., Bettye J. Parker and Beverly Guy-Sheftall, and Parker. *Sturdy Black Bridges. Visions of Black Women in Literature*. New York: Anchor Press/Doubleday, 1979: 379-417. This important first anthology of black women in literature organized into critical material, interviews and creative writing includes selected bibliographies of African, African-American and Caribbean women.

House, Amelia. "Black South African Women Writers in English: A Preliminary Checklist." Evanston, Illinois: Program on Women, Northwestern University, 1980. Provides the first listing of South African women writers, includes some biographical descriptions of each writer and an interview with Fatima Dike, South African playwright and a discussion on Women Writers by South African writer, Boitumelo.

Hull, D. M. "African Women In Development: An Untapped Resource." A Selected Bibliography. (Moorland-Spingarn Research Center, Howard University, 1983.) Currently being updated by the compiler, the librarian responsible for this field at Moorland. It contains about 200 entries on women in the social and economic life in Africa. Dr. Hull is also editor-in-chief of *A Current Bibliography on African Affairs* which has subject headings for literature and for women.

Hull, Gloria T., Patricia Bell Scott and Barbara Smith, eds. All the Women are White, All the Blacks are Men. *But Some of Us Are Brave*. Black Women's Studies. New York: The Feminist Press, 1982. This important collection contains a section on Bibliographies and Bibliographic Essays which contains some occasional listings on African women. Martha Brown's "A Listing of Non-Print Materials on Black Women" (pages 307-327) has a section on African women in films.

Morgan, Robin, Ed. *Sisterhood is Global. The International Women's Movement Anthology*. New York: Anchor Press/Doubleday, 1984. Contains a selected bibliography on women organized according to countries along with a general bibliography. Entries are taken from a variety of sources including newsletters, journals, magazines and books, government publications. Material is largely socio-political.

Rushing, Andrea Benton. "An Annotated Bibliography of Black Women in Black Literature." *CLA Journal* 25:2 (1981): 234-262. Contains entries on women in African, Caribbean, Latin-American and African-American literature. A nice selection of works with informative notes. A revised and updated version of the earlier "An Annotated Bibliography of Images of Black Women in Black Literature." *CLA Journal* 21:3 (1977-78): 435-442.

Scheub, Harold. *African Oral Narratives, Proverbs, Riddles, Poetry and Song*. Boston: G. K. Hall, 1977. An extensive listing of various forms of African oral literature. An important tool for anyone doing research in this field.

Steady, Filomina. "Select Bibliography on the Black Women Cross-Culturally." *The Black Woman Crossculturally*. Ed. Filomina Chioma Steady. Cambridge,

Mass. Schenckman Publishing Co., Inc., 1981: 615-635. Entries are organized according to Africa, the United States, the Caribbean and South America following the organizational pattern of the collection along with an additional section "Some Useful Bibliographies." The anthology itself contains sociological, historical, anthropological, economic, political and literary approaches to the study of the black woman internationally. Steady's introductory essay also contains a separate bibliography.

Zell, Hans, Carol Bundy and Virginia Coulon. *A New Readers Guide to African Literature*. New York: Africana Publishing Corp./London: Heinemann, 1983. An updated and more comprehensive version of the 1971 Zell and Silver *Readers Guide* by the same publisher.

Editors

Carole Boyce Davies is Assistant Professor of English and African and Afro-American Studies at the State University of New York at Binghamton and Director of Undergraduate Studies there. She received degrees from the University of Maryland, Howard University and the University of Ibadan, Nigeria. Her research and teaching interests include oral and written literature of the African peoples, Black women writers, feminist aesthetics and the criticism of African literatures, and children's literature. She has authored several essays on women in African literatures including a chapter "African Women Writers" for an authoritative volume on African literature in the Twentieth Century. She is currently working on a book on Caribbean women writers.

Anne Adams Graves is Assistant Professor in the Africana Studies and Research Center at Cornell University. She pursued her studies in European and Caribbean languages at Fisk University; the Free University of Berlin, West Germany; the University of Michigan; and Kent State University. Previous teaching positions have been at Morehouse College, Kent State University, and Université Marien Ngouabi in Brazzaville, Congo. She is co-editor, with E.W. Crosby and L. Davis, of a two-volume Black Studies introductory anthology, *The African Experience in Community Development* (1981) and has prepared a translation from French of a collection of short stories, *Tribaliques*, by Congolese author Henri Lopès, scheduled for publication by Editions Naaman. In addition, she has presented several papers from her research and teaching areas in African women's literature, Congolese national literature, and Black literature among German audiences.

Contributors

Naana Banyiwa-Horne is completing a Ph.D. in African literature at the University of Wisconsin, Madison. Born in Ghana, her Masters Thesis was on African women writers.

Brenda F. Berrian is Associate Professor of Black Studies (Humanities) at the University of Pittsburgh. She received her B.S. and M.A. from Hampton Institute and the doctorate from the University of Paris III. Prof. Berrian is the author of two monographs, and has published book reviews, bibliographies and articles in African literature. Her *Bibliography of African Women Writers and Journalists* (Washington, D.C.: Three Continents Press, 1985) is an important resource on the subject. She is co-editor of the forthcoming *Critical Perspectives on African Women Writers*.

Abena P. A. Busia is Assistant Professor of English at Rutgers, The State University, New Brunswick, N.J. She was born in Accra, Ghana and has worked as a research associate and visiting lecturer at Yale University. She is also a poet whose poems have been included in *Summer Fires: New Poetry From Africa* (Heinemann, 1983). She will publish *Africa in Anglo-American Fiction 1880-1980; An Annotated Bibliography* (New York, Garland Publications, 1985) and an essay "Manipulating Africa: The Bucaneer as 'Liberator' in Contemporary Fiction" in *The Black Presence in British Fiction* ed. by David Dabydeen (Manchester University Press, 1985).

Irene Assiba d'Almeida recently completed a Ph.D. on African critical theory in the Department of Comparative Literature, Emory University in Atlanta. A native of the Republic of Benin, she received an M.A. degree in English from the University of Ibadan, Nigeria and has taught at the University of Calabar, Nigeria and at the University of Kentucky, Lexington. She is the author of several articles in African literature and has a monograph on the prostitution theme in African literature. She maintains an on-going interest in the problems of translation and has translated Achebe's *Arrow of God* into French (Presence Africaine, 1978).

Elaine Savory Fido has taught African literature since 1975 at the University of the West Indies, Cave Hill, Barbados. She taught at the University of Ghana 1970-72 and was visiting lecturer at the University of Ibadan from 1982-83. Interested in women's writing in the continent, in the African-Caribbean and in African-America, she is an avid researcher in these areas. She has published articles on various aspects of African and Caribbean literature, particularly drama and women's writing or writing about women by men. She is authoring a novel and a book on women in the theatre in the Caribbean and Africa.

Mildred Hill-Lubin is Associate Professor, Department of English with a joint appointment in the Center for African Studies, at the University of Florida, Gainesville, where she has served as Dean of Graduate Studies. One of the editors of *Toward Defining the African Aesthetic* (Three Continents Press, 1982), she has also published articles on parallels in African and African-American literature, the Ghanaian author, Ama Ata Aidoo and the image of the Black grandmother, in *Southern Folklore Quarterly, CLA Journal, Presence Africaine, Okike,* and *Sojourner* and in Readings for the Florida Endowment for the Humanities. She has maintained a consistent stream of writing and research on women in African literature and on the oral tradition as it interacts with the written tradition and is readying a book-length manuscript on the Black grandmother for publication.

Tobe Levin is a lecturer with the European Division of the University of Maryland. She is active in the women's movement in Germany, contributing occasional articles and reports on third world women's struggles and Afro-American women's literature to the West German feminist magazine EMMA. She is a contributing editor to *Women's Studies Quarterly*. She is a member of feminist organizations Amnesty for Women and Terre des Femmes. Her degrees were received from Ithaca College, New York University in Paris, Cornell University with a dissertation on Feminist Ideology and Aesthetics in Neo-feminist German Fiction. She has participated in several conferences and workshops with African feminists.

Beverly B. Mack is Project Assistant for the Center for Women in Development of the South East Consortium for International Development. She also teaches African history at Georgetown University. Her M.A. and Ph.D. degrees, both from the University of Wisconsin, Madison, are in African Literature. Her dissertation on Hausa women's oral poetry is based on field research conducted in Kano, Nigeria, in 1979-80. Subsequent research conducted in the same area focuses on the changing socio-economic roles of Hausa Muslim women. She has published several articles on Hausa women's poetry and edited a volume of Hausa women's poetry published in Hausa by a northern Nigerian press in 1983.

Edris Makward is a well-known scholar/teacher of African literature. He has been professor of African Languages and Literature at the University of Wisconsin, Madison, since 1967. He has also taught at the University of Ibadan and more recently at the University of Calabar, Nigeria. He is the author of *Contemporary African Literature* and of numerous articles on African literature. He has been past president of the African Studies Association (1977-1978).

Rafika Merini was born in Fez, Morocco. She attended the University of Sanaa in Yeman, and the University of Utah (where she earned a B.A. in 1978 and an M.A. in 1981). She recently transferred to the State University of New York at Binghamton to complete her Ph.D. in Romance languages with an emphasis on Moroccan literature. Her masters thesis was done at the University of Washington on Driss Chraibi's *Succession Ouverte* a section of which is her contribution to this collection.

Charles Nama has an article on Ayi Kewi Armah forthcoming in *World Literature Written in English* and is currently translating *Le Deboussole* by Abdoul Doukoure, into English. His areas of interest are critical theory, translation and comparative literatures of the African world. He recently completed a Ph.D. in Comparative Litearture on Aesthetics and Ideology in African and Afro-American Fiction from the State University of New York, Binghamton, where he served as visiting lecturer in Afro-American and African Studies (1984-5). He recently returned to teach and do research in his native Cameroon.

Chimalum Nwankwo is a lecturer in the English and Dramatic Arts departments at the University of Nigeria, Nsukka. He received his Ph.D. from the University of Texas, Austin. His poetry and critical essays appear in journals such as *Obsidian, Umoja, Greenfield Review, Okike, Kunappipi, Ufahamu*, etc.

Esther Y. Smith is the French Language Coordinator with the Cameroon Project of the University of Florida, Gainesville, where she also serves as a professor of French language and literature. She has previously worked on a number of international/university projects and served as a language coordinator for the Peace Corps Training Center, Virgin Islands. She has published many articles and book reviews of African literature in major journals.

Karen Smyley-Wallace is Associate Professor of French and francophone African and Caribbean literature at Howard University. She received the M.A. Degree from the Middlebury Graduate School of French in Paris and the Ph.D. from the City University of New York. Her doctoral dissertation was entitled: "The African Woman: Interpretations of Novelists Aboulaye Sadji and Ousmane Sembene." Her current research and publications focus upon Black francophone female novelists. She has presented a number of papers and chaired panels on women in African literatures at national conferences.

Marie Linton Umeh is a lecturer in the Department of English Language and Literature, Anambra State College of Education, Awka, Nigeria. She has consistently maintained a research and publication reputation in the field of women in African literature. She completed her dissertation on Buchi Emecheta which she is revising and extending for publication. She has been an instructor of Third World Literature at the State University of New York, Brockport, in Oneonta. Her article, "The African Heroine" appeared in *Sturdy Black Bridges* ed. by Bell, Parker and Guy-Sheftall (New York, Anchor Books, 1979) and is one of the first major essays published on the subject.